Ancient Christian Texts

Greek Commentaries on Revelation

Commentary on the Apocalypse
Oecumenius

Commentary on the Apocalypse
Andrew of Caesarea

TRANSLATED WITH AN
INTRODUCTION AND NOTES BY

William C. Weinrich

EDITED BY

Thomas C. Oden

SERIES EDITORS

Thomas C. Oden and Gerald L. Bray

IVP Academic
An imprint of InterVarsity Press
Downers Grove, Illinois

InterVarsity Press
P.O. Box 1400, Downers Grove, IL 60515-1426
World Wide Web: www.ivpress.com
E-mail: email@ivpress.com

InterVarsity Press® is the book-publishing division of InterVarsity Christian Fellowship/USA®, a movement of students and faculty active on campus at hundreds of universities, colleges and schools of nursing in the United States of America, and a member movement of the International Fellowship of Evangelical Students. For information about local and regional activities, write Public Relations Dept., InterVarsity Christian Fellowship/USA, 6400 Schroeder Rd., P.O. Box 7895, Madison, WI 53707-7895, or visit the IVCF website at <www.intervarsity.org>.

The LS Graeca® II font used to print this work is available from Linguist's Software, Inc., P.O. Box 580, Edmonds, WA 98020-0580 USA tel (425) 775-1130 www.linguistsoftware.com.

Design: Cindy Kiple
Images: Saints Peter and Paul by Carlo Crivelli at Accademia, Venice/Art Resource, NY
Early Christian monogrammatic cross from Monastero, at Kunsthistorisches Museum, Vienna, Austria. Erich Lessing/Art Resource, NY

ISBN 978-0-8308-2908-8

Printed in the United States of America ∞

InterVarsity Press is committed to protecting the environment and to the responsible use of natural resources. As a member of Green Press Initiative we use recycled paper whenever possible. To learn more about the Green Press Initiative, visit <www.greenpressinitiative.org>.

Library of Congress Cataloging-in-Publication Data

Greek commentaries on Revelation/Oecumenius, Andrew of Caesarea;
translated by William C. Weinrich; edited by Thomas C. Oden.
p. cm.—(Ancient Christian texts)
Includes bibliographical references and indexes.
ISBN 978-0-8308-2908-8 (hardcover: alk. paper)
1. Bible N.T. Revelation—Commentaries. I. Weinrich, William C.
commentarius in Apocalypsin. English. IV. Andrw, Archbishop of
Caesarea. Hermeneia eis ten Apokalypsin. English.
BS2825.53.G74 2010
228'.077—dc22

2010040597

P 24 23 22 21 20 19 18 17 16 15 14 13 12 11 10 9 8 7 6 5 4 3 2
Y 30 29 28 27 26 25 24 23

CONTENTS

OECUMENIUS
Commentary on the Apocalypse

ANDREW OF CAESAREA
Commentary on the Apocalypse

GENERAL INTRODUCTION

The Ancient Christian Texts series (hereafter ACT) presents the full text of ancient Christian commentaries on Scripture that have remained so unnoticed that they have not yet been translated into English.

The patristic period (A.D. 95-750) is the time of the fathers of the church, when the exegesis of Scripture texts was in its primitive formation. This period spans from Clement of Rome to John of Damascus, embracing seven centuries of biblical interpretation, from the end of the New Testament to the mid-eighth century, including the Venerable Bede.

This series extends but does not reduplicate texts of the Ancient Christian Commentary on Scripture (ACCS). It presents full-length translations of texts that appear only as brief extracts in the ACCS. The ACCS began years ago authorizing full-length translations of key patristic texts on Scripture in order to provide fresh sources of valuable commentary that previously was not available in English. It is from these translations that the ACT Series has emerged.

A multiyear project such as this requires a well-defined objective. The task is straightforward: *to introduce full-length translations of key texts of early Christian teaching, homilies and commentaries on a particular book of Scripture.* These are seminal documents that have decisively shaped the entire subsequent history of biblical exegesis, but in our time have been largely ignored.

To carry out this mission the Ancient Christian Texts series has four aspirations:

1. To show the approach of one of the early Christian writers in dealing with the problems of understanding, reading and conveying the meaning of a particular book of Scripture.

2. To make more fully available the whole argument of the ancient Christian interpreter of Scripture to all who wish to think with the early church about a particular canonical text.

3. To broaden the base of biblical studies, Christian teaching and preaching to include classical Christian exegesis.

4. To stimulate Christian historical, biblical, theological and pastoral scholarship toward deeper inquiry into early classic practitioners of scriptural interpretation.

For Whom Is This Series Designed?

We have selected and translated these texts primarily for general and nonprofessional use by an audience of persons who study the Bible regularly.

In varied cultural settings around the world, contemporary readers are asking how they might grasp the meaning of sacred texts under the instruction of the great minds of the ancient church. They often study books of the Bible verse by verse, book by book, in groups and workshops, sometimes with a modern commentary in hand. But many who study the Bible intensively hunger to have available to them as well the thoughts of some reliable classic Christian commentator on this same text. This series will give the modern commentators a classical text for comparison and amplification. Readers will judge for themselves as to how valuable or complementary are their insights and guidance.

The classic texts we are translating were originally written for anyone (lay or clergy, believers and seekers) who would wish to reflect and meditate with the great minds of the early church. They sought to illuminate the plain sense, theological wisdom, and moral and spiritual meaning of an individual book of Scripture. They were not written for an academic audience, but for a community of faith shaped by the sacred text.

Yet in serving this general audience, the editors remain determined not to neglect the rigorous requirements and needs of academic readers who until recently have had few full translations available to them in the history of exegesis. So this series is designed also to serve public libraries, universities, academic classes, homiletic preparation and historical interests worldwide in Christian scholarship and interpretation.

Hence our expected audience is not limited to the highly technical and specialized scholarly field of patristic studies, with its strong bent toward detailed word studies and explorations of cultural contexts. Though all of our editors and translators are patristic and linguistic scholars, they also are scholars who search for the meanings and implications of the texts. The audience is not primarily the university scholar concentrating on the study of the history of the transmission of the text or those with highly focused interests in textual morphology or historical-critical issues. If we succeed in serving our wider readers practically and well, we hope to serve as well college and seminary courses in Bible, church history, historical theology, hermeneutics and homiletics. These texts have not until now been available to these classes.

Readiness for Classic Spiritual Formation

Today global Christians are being steadily drawn toward these biblical and patristic sources for daily meditation and spiritual formation. They are on the outlook for primary classic sources of spiritual formation and biblical interpretation, presented in accessible form and grounded in reliable scholarship.

These crucial texts have had an extended epoch of sustained influence on Scripture interpretation, but virtually no influence in the modern period. They also deserve a hearing among modern readers and scholars. There is a growing awareness of the speculative excesses and spiritual and homiletic limitations of much post-Enlightenment criticism. Meanwhile the motifs, methods and approaches of ancient exegetes have remained unfamiliar not only to historians but to otherwise highly literate biblical scholars, trained exhaustively in the methods of historical and scientific criticism.

It is ironic that our times, which claim to be so fully furnished with historical insight and research methods, have neglected these texts more than scholars in previous centuries who could read them in their original languages.

This series provides indisputable evidence of the modern neglect of classic Christian exegesis: it remains a fact that extensive and once authoritative classic commentaries on Scripture still remain untranslated into any modern language. Even in China such a high level of neglect has not befallen classic Buddhist, Taoist and Confucian commentaries.

Ecumenical Scholarship

This series, like its two companion series, the ACCS and Ancient Christian Doctrine (ACD), are expressions of unceasing ecumenical efforts that have enjoyed the wide cooperation of distinguished scholars of many differing academic communities. Under this classic textual umbrella, it has brought together in common spirit Christians who have long distanced themselves from each other by competing church memories. But all of these traditions have an equal right to appeal to the early history of Christian exegesis. All of these traditions can, without a sacrifice of principle or intellect, come together to study texts common to them all. This is its ecumenical significance.

This series of translations is respectful of a distinctively theological reading of Scripture that cannot be reduced to historical, philosophical, scientific, or sociological insights or methods alone. It takes seriously the venerable tradition of ecumenical reflection concerning the premises of revelation, providence, apostolicity, canon and consensuality. A high respect is here granted, despite modern assumptions, to uniquely Christian theological forms of reasoning, such as classical consensual christological and triune reasoning, as distinguishing premises of classic Christian textual interpretation. These cannot be acquired by empirical methods alone. This approach does not pit theology against critical theory; instead, it incorporates critical historical methods and brings them into coordinate accountability within its larger purpose of listening to Scripture.

The internationally diverse character of our editors and translators corresponds with the global range of our audience, which bridges many major communions of Christianity. We have sought to bring together a distinguished international network of Protestant, Catholic and Orthodox scholars, editors, and translators of the highest quality and reputation to accomplish this design.

But why just now at this historical moment is this need for patristic wisdom felt particularly by so many readers of Scripture? Part of the reason is that these readers have been long deprived of significant contact with many of these vital sources of classic Christian exegesis.

The Ancient Commentary Tradition

This series focuses on texts that comment on Scripture and teach its meaning. We define a commentary in its plain-sense definition as a series of illustrative or explanatory notes on any work of enduring significance. The word *commentary* is an Anglicized form of the Latin *commentarius* (or "annotation" or "memorandum" on a subject or text or series of events). In its theological meaning it is a work that explains, analyzes or expounds a biblical book or portion of Scripture. Tertullian, Origen, John Chrysostom, Jerome, Augustine and Clement of Alexandria all revealed their familiarity with both the secular and religious commentators available to them as they unpacked the meanings of the sacred text at hand.

The commentary in ancient times typically began with a general introduction covering such questions as authorship, date, purpose and audience. It commented as needed on grammatical or lexical problems in the text and provided explanations of difficulties in the text. It typically moved verse by verse through a Scripture text, seeking to make its meaning clear and its import understood.

The general western literary genre of commentary has been definitively shaped by the history of early Christian commentaries on Scripture. It is from Origen, Hilary, the *Opus imperfectum in Matthaeum*, John Chrysostom and Cyril of Alexandria that we learn what a commentary is—far more so than in the case of classic medical, philosophical or poetic commentaries. It leaves too much unsaid simply to assume that the Christian biblical commentary took a previously extant literary genre and reshaped it for Christian texts. Rather it is more accurate to say that *the Western literary genre of the commentary (and especially the biblical commentary) has patristic commentaries as its decisive pattern and prototype.*

It is only in the last two centuries, since the development of modern historicist methods of criticism, that modern writers have sought more strictly to delimit the definition of a commentary so as to include only certain limited interests focusing largely on historical-critical method, philological and grammatical observations, literary analysis, and sociopolitical or economic circumstances impinging on the text. While respecting all these approaches, the ACT editors do not hesitate to use the classic word *commentary* to define more broadly the genre of this series. These are commentaries in their classic sense.

The ACT editors freely take the assumption that the Christian canon is to be respected as the church's sacred text. The reading and preaching of Scripture are vital to religious life. The central hope of this endeavor is that it might contribute in some small way to the revitalization of religious faith and community through a renewed discovery of the earliest readings of the church's Scriptures.

An Appeal to Allow the Text to Speak for Itself

This prompts two appeals:

1. For those who begin by assuming as normative for a commentary only the norms considered typical for modern expressions of what a commentary is, we ask: Please allow the ancient commentators to define *commentarius* according to their own lights. Those who assume the preemptive authority and truthfulness of modern critical methods alone will always tend to view the classic Christian exegetes as dated, quaint, premodern, hence inadequate, and in some instances comic or even mean-spirited, prejudiced, unjust and oppressive. So in the interest of hermeneutical fairness, it is recommended that the modern reader not impose on ancient Christian exegetes modern assumptions about valid readings of Scripture. The ancient Christian writers constantly challenge these unspoken, hidden and indeed often camouflaged assumptions that have become commonplace in our time.

We leave it to others to discuss the merits of ancient versus modern methods of exegesis. But even this cannot be done honestly without a serious examination of the texts of ancient exegesis. Ancient commentaries may be disqualified as commentaries by modern standards. But they remain commentaries by the standards of those who anteceded and formed the basis of the modern commentary.

The attempt to read a Scripture text while ruling out all theological and moral assumptions—as well as ecclesial, sacramental and dogmatic assumptions that have prevailed generally in the community of faith out of which it emerged—is a very thin enterprise indeed. Those who tendentiously may read a single page of patristic exegesis, gasp and toss it away because it does not conform adequately to the canons of modern exegesis and historicist commentary are surely not exhibiting a valid model for critical inquiry today.

2. In ancient Christian exegesis, chains of biblical references were often very important in thinking about the text in relation to the whole testimony of sacred Scripture, by the analogy of faith, comparing text with text, on the premise that *scripturam ex scriptura explicandam esse*. When ancient exegesis weaves many Scriptures together, it does not limit its focus to a single text as much modern exegesis prefers, but constantly relates it to other texts, by analogy, intensively using typological reasoning, as did the rabbinic tradition.

Since the principle prevails in ancient Christian exegesis that each text is illumined by other texts and by the whole narrative of the history of revelation, we find in patristic comments on a given text many other subtexts interwoven in order to illumine that text. In these ways the models of exegesis often do not correspond with modern commentary assumptions, which tend to resist or rule out chains of scriptural reference. We implore the reader not to force the assumptions of twenty-first-century hermeneutics on the ancient Christian writers, who themselves knew nothing of what we now call hermeneutics.

The Complementarity of Research Methods in this Series

The Ancient Christian Texts series will employ several interrelated methods of research, which the editors and translators seek to bring together in a working integration. Principal among these methods are the following:

1. The editors, translators and annotators will bring to bear the best resources of *textual criticism* in preparation for their volumes. This series is not intended to produce a new critical edition of the original-language text. The best Urtext in the original language will be used. Significant variants in the earliest manuscript sources of the text may be commented on as needed in the annotations. But it will be assumed that the editors and translators will be familiar with the textual ambiguities of a particular text and be able to state their conclusions about significant differences among scholars. Since we are working with ancient texts that have, in some cases, problematic or ambiguous passages, we are obliged to employ all methods of historical, philological and textual inquiry appropriate to the study of ancient texts. To that end, we will appeal to the most reliable text-critical scholarship of both biblical and patristic studies. We will assume that our editors and translators have reviewed the international literature of textual critics regarding their text so as to provide the reader with a translation of the most authoritative and reliable form of the ancient text. We will leave it to the volume editors and translators, under the supervision of the general editors, to make these assessments. This will include the challenge of considering which variants within the biblical text itself might impinge on the patristic text, and which forms or stemma of the biblical text the patristic writer was employing. The annotator will supply explanatory footnotes where these textual challenges may raise potential confusions for the reader.

2. Our editors and translators will seek to understand the *historical context* (including socioeconomic, political and psychological aspects as needed) of the text. These understandings are often vital to right discernment of the writer's intention. Yet we do not see our primary mission as that of discussing in detail these contexts. They are to be factored into the translation and commented on as needed in the annotations, but are not to become the primary focus of this series. Our central interest is less in the social location of the text or the philological history of particular words than in authorial intent and accurate translation. Assuming a proper social-historical contextualization of the text, the main focus of this series will be on a dispassionate and fair translation and analysis of the text itself.

3. The main task is to set forth the meaning of the biblical text itself as understood by the patristic writer. The intention of our volume editors and translators is to help the

reader see clearly into the meanings which patristic commentators have discovered in the biblical text. *Exegesis* in its classic sense implies an effort to explain, interpret and comment on a text, its meaning, its sources and its connections with other texts. It implies a close reading of the text, utilizing whatever linguistic, historical, literary or theological resources are available to explain the text. It is contrasted with *eisegesis,* which implies that interpreters have imposed their own personal opinions or assumptions on the text. The patristic writers actively practiced intratextual exegesis, which seeks to define and identify the exact wording of the text, its grammatical structure and the interconnectedness of its parts. They also practiced extratextual exegesis, seeking to discern the geographical, historical or cultural context in which the text was written. Our editors and annotators will also be attentive as needed to the ways in which the ancient Christian writer described his own interpreting process or hermeneutic assumptions.

4. The underlying philosophy of translation that we employ in this series, like that of the Ancient Christian Commentary on Scripture, is termed *dynamic equivalency.* We wish to avoid the pitfalls of either too loose a paraphrase or too rigid a literal translation. We seek language that is literary but not purely literal. Whenever possible we have opted for the metaphors and terms that are normally in use in everyday English-speaking culture. Our purpose is to allow the ancient Christian writers to speak for themselves to ordinary readers in the present generation. We want to make it easier for the Bible reader to gain ready access to the deepest reflection of the ancient Christian community of faith on a particular book of Scripture. We seek a thought-for-thought translation rather than a formal equivalence or word-for-word style. This requires the words to be first translated accurately and then rendered in understandable idiom. We seek to present the same thoughts, feelings, connotations and effects of the original text in everyday English language. We have used vocabulary and language structures commonly used by the average person. We do not leave the quality of translation only to the primary translator, but pass it through several levels of editorial review before confirming it.

The Function of the ACT Introductions, Annotations and Translations

In writing the introduction for a particular volume of the ACT series, the translator or volume editor will discuss, where possible, the opinion of the writer regarding authorship of the text, the importance of the biblical book for other patristic interpreters, the availability or paucity of patristic comment, any salient points of debate between the Fathers, and any special challenges involved in translating and editing the particular volume. The introduction affords the opportunity to frame the entire commentary in a manner that will help the general reader understand the nature and significance of patristic comment on the biblical texts under consideration and to help readers find their critical bearings so as to read and use the commentary in an informed way.

The footnotes will assist the reader with obscurities and potential confusions. In the annotations the volume editors have identified Scripture allusions and historical references embedded within the texts. Their purpose is to help the reader move easily from passage to passage without losing a sense of the whole.

The ACT general editors seek to be circumspect and meticulous in commissioning volume editors and translators. We strive for a high level of consistency and literary quality throughout the course of this series. We have sought out as volume editors and translators those patristic and biblical scholars who are thoroughly familiar with their original language sources, who are informed historically, and who are sympathetic to the needs of ordinary nonprofessional readers who may not have professional language skills.

Thomas C. Oden and Gerald L. Bray, Series Editors

ABBREVIATIONS

Series

ACCS	Ancient Christian Commentary on Scripture. 29 vols., Downers Grove, Ill.: InterVarsity Press, 1998-2010.
ACW	Ancient Christian Writers: The Works of the Fathers in Translation. Mahweh, N.J.: Paulist Press, 1946-.
ANF	A. Roberts and J. Donaldson, eds. Ante-Nicene Fathers. 10 vols. Buffalo, N.Y.: Christian Literature, 1885-1896. Reprint, Grand Rapids, Mich.: Eerdmans, 1951-1956; Reprint, Peabody, Mass.: Hendrickson, 1994.
FC	Fathers of the Church: A New Translation. Washington, D.C.: Catholic University of America Press, 1947-.
GCS	Die griechischen christlichen Schriftsteller der ersten Jahrhunderte. Berlin: Akademie-Verlag, 1897-.
LCL	Loeb Classical Library
MTS	Josef Schmid, *Studien zur Geschichte des Griechischen Apokalypse-Textes*, 1. Teil: *Der Apokalypse-Kommentar des Andreas von Kaisareia*. Münchener Theologische Studien, I, Historishe Abteilung. Munich: Karl Zink Verlag, 1955.
NPNF	P. Schaff et al., eds. A Select Library of the Nicene and Post-Nicene Fathers of the Christian Church. 2 series (14 vols. each). Buffalo, N.Y.: Christian Literature, 1887-1894. Reprint, Grand Rapids, Mich.: Eerdmans, 1952-1956; Reprint, Peabody, Mass.: Hendrickson, 1994.
PG	J.-P. Migne, ed. Patrologiae cursus completus. Series Graeca. 166 vols. Paris: Migne, 1857-1886.
SC	H. de Lubac, J. Daniélou et al., eds. Sources Chrétiennes. Paris: Editions du Cerf, 1941-.
TEG	Traditio Exegetica Graeca. Louvain: Peeters, 1991-.

Journals

VC	*Vigiliae christianae*

Classical, Early Christian and Patristic Writers

Athanasius

C. Ar.	*Orationes contra Arianos* (*Orations Against the Arians*)
Vit. Ant.	*Vita Antonii* (*Life of Anthony*)

Augustine

Tract. Ev. Jo. *In Evangelium Johannis tractatus* (*Tractates on the Gospel of John*)

Basil of Caesarea

Hom. in divites *Homilia in divites* (*Homily on Those Who Are Rich*)

Clement of Alexandria

Strom. *Stromata* (*Miscellanies*)

Epiphanius

Pan. *Panarion (adversus haereses)* (*Refutation of All Heresies*)

Eusebius

Chron. *Chronicon* (*Chronicle*)

Hier. *Contra Hieroclem* (*Against Hierocles*)

Hist. eccl. *Historia ecclesiastica* (*Ecclesiastical History*)

Evagrius Scholasticus

Hist. eccl. *Historia ecclesiasticus (Ecclesiastical History)*

Gregory of Nazianzus

Or. *Orationes* (*Orations*)

Hermas

Sim. *Shepherd* of Hermas *Similitudes*

Hesiod

Theog. *Theogonia* (*Theogony*)

Hippolytus

Antichr. *De antichristo* (*On Christ and the Antichrist*)

Comm. Dan. *Commentarium in Danielum* (*Commentary on Daniel*)

Homer

Il. *Iliad*

Irenaeus

Haer. *Adversus haereses* (*Against Heresies*)

Josephus

Ant. *Jewish Antiquities*

J.W. *Jewish War*

Methodius

Res. *De resurrectione* (*On the Resurrection*)

Symp. *Symposium*

Origen

Princ. *De principiis* (*On First Principles*)

Philo

Mut.	*De mutatione nominum (On the Change of Names)*
Somn.	*De somniis (On Dreams)*

Plato

Resp.	*Respublica (Republic)*

Theodoret

Hist. eccl.	*Historia ecclesiastica (Ecclesiastical History)*

General

LXX	Septuagint
NT	New Testament
c.	circa (about, approximately)

TRANSLATOR'S INTRODUCTION

The present volume publishes English translations of two early Greek commentaries on the Revelation of Saint John, that of Oecumenius and that of Andrew of Caesarea. Along with the commentary of Arethas of Caesarea (c. 900), who was very largely dependent on Andrew, these commentaries provide the only significant commentary on Revelation in the Greek tradition. The commentary of Oecumenius was the first full commentary on Revelation in the Greek language. The commentary of Andrew of Caesarea became the standard commentary on Revelation in the later Byzantine tradition. After Arethas no significant commentary on Revelation has been written by an Eastern commentator.

Presenting the commentaries of Oecumenius and Andrew together in one volume is of especial value for those interested in ancient commentary on Revelation.[1] It is evident that Andrew had read the commentary of Oecumenius, for he often reports on the opinions of Oecumenius, although never by name, and offers his own contrary interpretations. Therefore, not only are these two commentaries the first and most important commentaries from the Greek tradition but also together they present, as it were, an early dialogue on the meaning and significance of Revelation for the faith and life of the church. Publishing both in one volume allows the reader easy access to this conversation and gives an illustration of the breadth of interpretation of this mystical book even while providing demonstration of the unity of faith that Oecumenius and Andrew shared.

Oecumenius

Questions concerning the identity, date and provenance and literary output of Oecumenius continue to elicit various conclusions. In 1532 Donatus Veronensis published under the name of Oecumenius commentaries on the book of Acts, the seven Catholic Epistles and the letters of Paul.[2] Although some scholia from the commentary on the Pauline epistles may be authentic to Oecumenius, the remainder of these commentaries have

[1]After the publication of the volume on Revelation in the Ancient Christian Commentary on Scripture and during the preparation of this volume, an English translation of Oecumenius's commentary by John N. Suggit appeared in The Fathers of the Church series (FC 112; Washington, D.C.: Catholic University of America Press, 2006).

[2]For the textual history of Oecumenius see especially Franz Diekamp, "Mittheilungen über den neuaufgefundenen Commentar des Oekumenius zur Apokalypse," *Sitzungsberichte der Königlichen Preussischen Akademie der Wissenschaft* 43 (1901): 1046-56; John C. Lamoreaux, "The Provenance of Ecumenius' Commentary on the Apocalypse," *VC* 52 (1998): 89-93.

been demonstrated to be falsely ascribed to him.[3] A commentary consisting of scholia on Revelation was published by J. A. Cramer in 1844 and attributed to Oecumenius,[4] but this collection of comments has since been demonstrated to be only an abbreviation of the commentary of Andrew of Caesarea.

In 1901 Franz Diekamp discovered the authentic commentary of Oecumenius on Revelation in a twelfth-century manuscript from Messina (Messina S. Salvatore 99).[5] A critical text of Oecumenius's commentary on Revelation, however, did not appear until 1928, when H. C. Hoskier published his critical edition.[6] This edition has since been superseded by the more thorough and reliable work of Marc De Groote, and the translation of this volume is based on the critical edition of De Groote.[7]

Date and Identity of Oecumenius

His evaluation of the Messina manuscript convinced Diekamp that the commentary of Oecumenius must be dated very early in the 600s. He noted that in commenting on Revelation 1:1-2 ("what must soon take place"), Oecumenius says that many of the prophecies in Revelation have not yet taken place, although "a considerable span of time has passed, indeed more than 500 years."[8] Later, commenting on Revelation 1:9, Oecumenius follows Eusebius and dates the writing of Revelation to the time of the emperor Domitian (A.D. 81-96).[9] Five hundred years from the end of the first century would demand a writing of Oecumenius's commentary at the very end of the sixth century. Diekamp argued that three considerations made a much later date impossible. First, a seventh-century Syriac manuscript contained a citation from the eleventh book of Oecumenius's commentary. Second, toward the end of the commentary Oecumenius affirms that after the incarnation Christ is "one person, one hypostasis, and one energy."[10] However, Diekamp reasons, this remark is so void of polemical force that it must have been made before the beginning of the monoenergistic controversy. Finally, Diekamp considered Oecumenius's comments on Revelation 9:5 so open to Origen's teaching on universal restoration that he could not have written too long after the condemnation of Origen at the Fifth Ecumenical Council in 553.[11] Diekamp concluded that Oecumenius was a Monophysite Christian in the tradition of Severus of Antioch who

[3]The Greek text of Donatus, along with the Latin translation of J. Henten (1537), may be found, still under the name of Oecumenius, in Migne (PG 118; 119).

[4]J. A. Cramer, *Catenae graecorum partum in Novum Testamentum*, 8 vols. (Oxford, 1844), 8: 497-582.

[5]For a description of this find, see Diekamp, "Mittheilungen," 1047-49. A complete survey of manuscripts is provided by Marc De Groote, *Oecumenii Commentarius in Apocalypsin*, Traditio Exegetica Graeca 8 (Louvain: Peeters, 1999), 9-21 (hereafter TEG 8).

[6]H. C. Hoskier, *The Complete Commentary of Oecumenius on the Apocalypse* (Ann Arbor: University of Michigan Press, 1928).

[7]See note 5.

[8]TEG 8:67-68.

[9]TEG 8:74-75.

[10]TEG 8:287.

[11]TEG 8:148.

wrote his commentary "around 600, although not much later."[12]

However, the Syriac manuscript to which Diekamp had referred itself offers significant cause to doubt such a late dating of Oecumenius and his commentary. In their examination of the Syriac text, Anton Spitaler and Josef Schmid concluded that Oecumenius was a layperson of distinct Monophysite sympathies who enjoyed a close relationship with Severus of Antioch and who wrote his commentary in "the first half, at the latest in the middle of the sixth century."[13] The passage concerning Oecumenius lies within a catena of quotations from twenty-five different authors, and as a whole the catena evinces a definite Monophysite conviction.[14] The heading introducing the section on Oecumenius is interesting and important: "From Oecumenius, a careful man who is very orthodox, as the letters of Patriarch Mar Severus written to him show, from the sixth discourse which he composed on the Revelation of the Evangelist John."[15] From this Spitaler and Schmid argued that the Oecumenius of the commentary was also a correspondent of Severus of Antioch, and since Severus died in 538, Oecumenius must have written his commentary around that date. Letters of Severus to a certain Oecumenius refer to him as a count (Latin: *comes*) and even give greetings to his wife. This suggests that Oecumenius was a married layperson of high civil rank in the imperial administration and might even have enjoyed direct access to the emperor.[16] Concerning Oecumenius's mention of the five hundred years, Spitaler and Schmid argue that Oecumenius may be calculating in terms of Christian time, that is, from the time of Jesus.[17]

The opinion that the author of the commentary on Revelation and the correspondent of Severus were one and the same person, however, is not universal. In a detailed article, Adele Monaci Castagno argued against the position of Spitaler-Schmid, affirming that the reference by Oecumenius to the five hundred years is most naturally understood to be reckoned from the time of the writing of Revelation. Therefore, a time of writing c. 600 is to be conceded.[18] Castagno further disputes the identification of Oecumenius the commentator and Oecumenius the correspondent of Severus. While the correspondent of

[12]Diekamp, "Mittheilungen," 1052-53.

[13]Anton Spitaler-Josef Schmid, "Zur Klärung des Ökumeniusproblems," *Oriens Christianus* 3.9 (1934): 208-18.

[14]In addition to Oecumenius the list includes Basil of Caesarea, Gregory of Nazianzus, Gregory of Nyssa, Ephraim, Hesychius of Jerusalem, John Chrysostom, Clement of Rome, Cyril of Jerusalem, Cyril of Alexandria, Dionysius of Alexandria, Pseudo-Dionysius, Ignatius of Antioch, Irenaeus, Hippolytus, Julius of Rome, Methodius, Peter of Alexandria, Philoxenus of Mabbug, Severus of Antioch, Theodotus of Ancyra, Epiphanius of Salamis, John Philoponus, Theodore of Mopsuestia and Theodoret. Severus is the most quoted of these authors. When Theodore of Mopsuestia is cited, he is called "Theodore the heretic," a sure indication of Monophysite antipathy and perhaps a reflection of Theodore's condemnation at the Fifth Ecumenical Council.

[15]Spitaler-Schmid, "Klärung," 209-10. The quotation from Oecumenius's commentary is from the eleventh, not the sixth, discourse.

[16]At least this often is suggested by the title of *comes*. In some manuscripts Oecumenius receives the titles of "philosophos" and "rhetor," further indicating that he was a person of intellectual and civic ability.

[17]Spitaler-Schmid, "Klärung," 213, 216.

[18]Adele Monaci Castagno, "Il problema della datazione dei Commenti all' *Apocalisse* di Ecumenio e di Andrea di Cesarea," *Atti della Accademia delle Scienze di Torino: II. Classe di Scienze, Morali, Storiche e Filologiche* 114 (1980): 223-46; here, 229-32.

Severus is clearly a Monophysite compatriot of Severus, the distinct Monophysite themes of Severus cannot be found in the commentary. Rather, Castagno claims, the christological claims of Oecumenius reflect the general trend in the East during the sixth century to reconcile Chalcedonian and Monophysite positions and to assimilate christological terminology toward that of Cyril of Alexandria. This trend culminated in the *Sententia adversus tria Capitula* of the Fifth Ecumenical Council (553) and the council's dogmatic canons.[19] Indeed, according to Castagno many of the christological formulas found in the commentary are parallel to the dogmatic formula of the council of 553.[20] The statements of Oecumenius in the commentary concerning the person of Christ are best interpreted as coming after the Fifth Council, and if that is so, then the Monophysite correspondent of Severus is not the Oecumenius of the commentary. Finally, Castagno believes that Oecumenius reflects the Fifth Council's condemnation of Origen's doctrine of the "restoration of all things" when in his comments on Revelation 9:5 Oecumenius writes that he agrees "with the dogma of the church (τῷ δόγματι τῆς ἐκκλησίας) that the punishments in the coming age are eternal."[21]

The entire question of the date and identity of Oecumenius has more recently been reviewed by John C. Lamoreaux,[22] who presents a vigorous argument for the identity of Oecumenius the commentator and Oecumenius the correspondent of Severus. Lamoreaux emphasizes the importance of the Syriac fragment, which explicitly asserts that the author of the commentary was a Monophysite who was also the recipient of letters from Severus of Antioch. A serious weakness in the argument of Castagno is that the evidence of this seventh-century Syriac fragment is not considered.[23] Moreover, Lamoreaux claims, Castagno has not considered significant evidence concerning the christological terminology of Oecumenius. While he does not contest Castagno's claim that some of Oecumenius's christological statements are not distinctively Monophysite and that others are similar to those of the Fifth Council, Lamoreaux faults Castagno for not examining the scholia on the Pauline epistles, which may well be from Oecumenius.[24] Lamoreaux cites four scholia that he believes "most clearly" reveal that Oecumenius was a true Monophysite.[25] All four of these scholia in some manner speak of "one nature" (μία φύσις) bringing Lamoreaux to conclude that "the Monophysitism of Ecumenius' scholia

[19]Castagno, "Il problema," 233-36. The Three Chapters refers to various writings of three prominent theologians associated with the Antiochene school, namely, Theodore of Mopsuestia, Theodoret and Ibas of Edessa. An English translation of the *Sententia* is given in NPNF 2 14:306-11. In contrast, Cyril of Alexandria is called "Cyril of blessed memory" (NPNF 2 14:308).

[20]See especially Castagno, "Il problema," 235 n. 55, where canons 5, 7 and 8 of the Fifth Council are cited (NPNF 2 14:312-14).

[21]Castagno, "Il problema," 236-38; TEG 8:148.

[22]Lamoreaux, "Provenance," 88-108.

[23]Ibid., 95-96: "The witness of this compiler should not be passed over lightly."

[24]These scholia may be found in Karl Staab, *Pauluskommentare aus der griechischen Kirche*, 2d ed. (Münster: Aschendorff, 1984), 423-69. Staab presents these scholia under the name of Oecumenius of Trikka. This is, however, a misnomer, for Oecumenius of Trikka was a tenth-century bishop. Older scholarship often confused our Oecumenius with this later figure.

[25]Lamoreaux, "Provenance," 96-98. The four scholia are on Eph 1:17; 4:13; Col 2:9; Heb 1:4 (Staab, *Pauluskommentare*, 448, 449-50, 454-55, 462).

is beyond doubt, for it is hard to imagine a Chalcedonian, either before or after the Fifth Council, expressing such views."[26] As for the christological formula of the commentary, Oecumenius "seldom rises above the level of Christological banality." Yet the commentary does show a strong opposition to the views of Apollinarius,[27] and some phrases reflect the usage of Severus. Concerning the latter he mentions Severus's emphasis on "one energy" against the *Tome* of Leo,[28] that the expressions "from two natures" or "from divinity and humanity" are Severian and that the phrase "peculiarity in natural quality" was of first importance for Severus. As corroboration Lamoreaux points out that nowhere does Oecumenius affirm the Council of Chalcedon or Leo's *Tome*. This and other evidence leads Lamoreaux to date the commentary of Oecumenius between 508 and 518.[29]

What is one to make of these various arguments and the evidence that supports them? The evidence clearly does not go in one direction. However, the following seem to me to be reasonable conclusions from the evidence:

1. Oecumenius was a layperson of high imperial rank (*comes*); he was married and was respected as a person of intellectual capacity ("philosophos," "rhetor," "scholasticus").[30]

2. The Oecumenius who commented on Revelation and the Oecumenius who was a correspondent of Severus of Antioch are the same person. One must agree with Lamoreaux that the evidence of the Syriac fragment, which explicitly identifies them, is strong. The argument of Castagno is materially weakened by not taking that important evidence into account, and until that evidence should be rendered doubtful the death of Severus in 538 remains the certain *terminus ante quem* of the commentary. The statement of Oecumenius that the prophecies of Revelation have not all been fulfilled although "a considerable span of time has passed, indeed more than 500 years" remains troublesome. The solution of Spitaler-Schmid that the reckoning is from the time of Christ is not persuasive. Lamoreaux helpfully points out Oecumenius's own discussion of the passage (Rev 1:1-2). Oecumenius quotes Psalm 90:4 to say that the word *soon* does not refer to any period of time but to the power and eternality of God.[31] The five hundred years may therefore refer not to the time since the writing of Revelation but "rather to the length of the delay separating Christ's first and second coming."[32] It is not an ideal solution, but

[26]Lamoreaux, "Provenance," 98.

[27]It is an exaggeration when Lamoreaux writes that "the single issue about which [Oecumenius] feels strongly is the condemnation of Apollinarianism" ("Provenance," 98). To be sure, Oecumenius states his opposition to Apollinarian denial of the rational soul in Christ, but since the fourth century explicit affirmation of the rational soul became commonplace, often appearing in Cyril of Alexandria.

[28]Monophysite opposition to the *Tome* of Leo often centered on Leo's claim that "each form [= nature] performs its own acts in cooperation with the other" (*agit utraque forma cum alterius communione quod proprium est*). To the Monophysite this seemed to suggest that the source of Christ's human actions and the source of his divine actions were distinct, thus dividing Christ into two persons. Therefore, the Monophysite emphasis on "one energy."

[29]Lamoreaux, "Provenance," 101.

[30]Such information comes primarily from the letters of Severus. See ibid., 100-101.

[31]TEG 8:68.

[32]Lamoreaux, "Provenance," 103-4.

Oecumenius does seem to introduce some imprecision into his discussion that erodes confidence in using this reckoning for establishing the date of the commentary and of Oecumenius himself.

3. Oecumenius represented a Chalcedonian christology with a distinct Cyrillian emphasis. There is, however, no reason to insist that the statements of Oecumenius are best interpreted as written after the Fifth Council, as Castagno argues. To be sure, parallels exist, but these are perfectly harmonious with the christological climate during the end of the fifth and the beginning half of the sixth century. No formulation proffered by the canons of the Fifth Council are without parallel in the writings of Cyril, and it is clear that the canons of the Fifth Council that Castagno adduces are intended to harmonize Cyril and the *Definitio Fidei* of the Council of Chalcedon. Further, had Oecumenius written after the Fifth Council, one might expect some indication of the anathemas against the Three Chapters. No hint of that momentous condemnation, however, exists in the text of Oecumenius. The christological formulas of Oecumenius can easily be accommodated to the first decades of the sixth century. The dating that Lamoreaux suggests, between 508 and 518, seems reasonable.

At the same time, Lamoreaux has perhaps overemphasized the Monophysite character of Oecumenius. Were Oecumenius the strict Monophysite that Lamoreaux describes him to be, one might expect some hint of the Twelve Anathemas of Cyril against Nestorius. No hint of these anathemas exists in the text of Oecumenius. Indeed, some suggestion that the Council of Chalcedon was not legitimate might be expected of an avid follower of Severus of Antioch. However, the christological claims of Oecumenius remain fully within the Chalcedonian consensus, indicated by the fact that Oecumenius routinely condemns Nestorius and Eutyches together, as did Chalcedon. Furthermore, it is not evident that the scholia on the Pauline epistles are so certainly from Oecumenius, as Lamoreaux suggests.[33] Be that as it may, the use of the language of "one nature" (μία φύσις) in the scholia does not appear in the text of the commentary. If the use of this terminology was so usual for Oecumenius, why then does it never occur in the christological passages of the commentary? Rather, Oecumenius remains true to the basic Chalcedonian terminology and christological construct. For example, in his first christological statement Oecumenius writes that the Immanuel is united "from two natures, from divinity and humanity, the [natures] subsisting perfectly according to their own integrity."[34] Here the two natures that are united in the one Immanuel are said to "subsist perfectly" (τελείως ἐχουσῶν). This phrase reflects the Chalcedonian insistence on the integrity of the natures *after* the incarnation. In fact, the τελείως of Oecumenius may reflect the statements of the *Definitio* of Chalcedon that "the same is perfect (τέλειον) in divinity

[33]See ibid., 96 n. 35, for a brief defense of identifying the commentator of the epistles and the commentator of the Revelation.

[34]TEG 8:67: ἐκ δύο φύσεων νοῆται συνημμένος ὁ Ἐμμανουήλ, θεότητος τε καὶ ἀνθρωπότητος, τελείως ἐχουσῶν κατὰ τὸν οἰκεῖον λόγον. Similar language occurs at TEG 8:287.

and perfect (τέλειον) in humanity."[35] In the ACCS volume on Revelation, I claimed that Oecumenius was not opposed to the Council of Chalcedon but that he "interpreted it in a manner genial to the Monophysite interests of Severus of Antioch."[36] I remain convinced of the accuracy of that description.

The Theology of Oecumenius

In view of the preceding discussion, one need only briefly describe the Christology of Oecumenius. There is no sufficient reason to suppose that he was not a supporter of the Council of Chalcedon. Repeatedly, Oecumenius condemns Nestorius and Eutyches by name or by their false doctrines.[37] These were the two heretics condemned also by Chalcedon. However, Oecumenius represents the general tendency of the late fifth and early sixth century to interpret that council in terms of Cyril of Alexandria. That is, while the distinction of natures after the union is affirmed, there is a decided interest to emphasize the reality and indivisibility of the one Christ.[38] This is evidently clear in the christological statement that Oecumenius makes toward the end of his commentary. There he states that the Immanuel possesses divinity and humanity "perfectly" and then in a manner similar to the *Definitio Fidei* of Chalcedon says that the divinity and humanity are united "unconfusedly, unchangeably, immutably, really."[39] It is interesting to note that while Oecumenius uses the first two adverbs of the *Definitio* of Chalcedon that were directed against the Eutychian doctrine of mixture, he does not use the two adverbs that were directed against Nestorius, namely, "indivisibly" (ἀδιαρέτως) and "inseparably" (ἀχωρίστως). Rather, Oecumenius uses the additional adverbs of "immutably" (ἀναλλοιώτως) and "really" (ἀφαντασιάστως) that can only be directed against Eutyches.[10] All four adverbs of Oecumenius are directed against Eutyches! This suggests that Oecumenius, although clearly Cyrillian, is quite sensitive to the charge that the unitive christology of Cyril issued into a phantom and docetic reality. At the same time, however, and in the same context Oecumenius makes his strongest assertion of the unity of Christ. He says that "after the inexpressible union there is one person, one hypostasis, and one energy."[41] Here Oecumenius affirms Chalcedon's important equation of πρόσωπον and

[35]I have translated the phrase θεότητος τε καὶ ἀνθρωπότητος (n. 34) "from divinity and humanity" as interpreting the previous "two natures." However, the phrase could just as well interpret "the Immanuel" and be translated "of divinity and humanity." In this case distinction after the union would again be expressed.

[36]William Weinrich, ed., *Revelation*, Ancient Christian Commentary on Scripture, New Testament 12 (Downers Grove, Ill.: InterVarsity Press, 2005), xxviii.

[37]TEG 8:67, 70, 97, 171, 278, 287.

[38]This is clear, for example, for the common use made by Oecumenius of the Cyrillian formula that the Word is hypostatically united to the flesh (σαρκὶ καθ' ὑπόστασιν ἑνωθῆναι). See TEG 8:99, 278.

[39]TEG 8:287: ἀσυγχύτως, ἀτρέπτως, ἀναλλοιώτως, ἀφαντασιάστως.

[40]See, for example, TEG 8:97, where Oecumenius parallels φανασία and δόκησις, explicitly associating these errors with Eutychianism and, indeed, Manichaeanism.

[41]TEG 8:287: ἓν πρόσωπον καὶ μίαν ὑποστασιν καὶ μίαν ἐνέργειαν.

ὑπόστασις[42] but adds the idea that there was one operative energy in Christ.

This christological posture of reaffirming the doctrinal content of the *Definitio Fidei* of Chalcedon while strongly affirming that the operative subject in Christ was one and singular is typical of that party in the imperial East who were attempting to unite the Chalcedonian and Monophysite parties. One can discern the interests and even the terminology of Oecumenius in the failed attempt of Emperor Zeno and Patriarch Acacius to unify these opposing christological parties. In 482 Zeno issued his famous *Henotikon* ("Plan of Union") in which it was confessed that the Only-begotten Son of God, himself God, was truly incarnated; that he was of the same substance with the Father and of the same substance with us; and that this one who was made flesh of the Holy Spirit and of Mary the mother of God was "one and not two." "For we affirm that both the miracles and the sufferings which he willingly endured in the flesh are those of one. We altogether reject those who divide (διαιροῦντας) or confuse (συγχέοντας) or introduce a phantom (φαντασίαν)."[43] The *Henotikon* even reflects the beginnings of the theopaschite question of whether one of the Trinity was incarnated and suffered, as does Oecumenius.[44]

The letters of Severus to Oecumenius call him a *comes*, suggesting that Oecumenius is a friend and confident of the imperial court. It may well be that Oecumenius was serving the imperial attempt to bring christological compromise to the Chalcedonian and Monophysite parties of the East.

Oecumenius also gives evidence of the debates concerning eschatology contemporary to himself. This is especially evident in two contexts. Oecumenius notes that "certain of the fathers" had deduced from Revelation 9:5-6 the idea of restoration which taught that after a certain period of punishment sinners, having been purified, were no longer punished. He is aware, however, that "the majority of other fathers and the received Scriptures" teach that the final punishment of sinners will be everlasting. Oecumenius expresses his agreement with "the teaching of the church" that the future punishments are eternal, and he quotes in support of that teaching Jesus' words in Matthew 25:46 and the words of Isaiah 66:24. Yet, and as I shall note below, Oecumenius takes every opportunity to emphasize the beneficence and kindness of God. And perhaps it is because of this emphasis that Oecumenius is clearly not fully comfortable with the idea of a harsh, eternal punishment. He takes "a sort of middle path" and interprets the passage to say that while sinners will be severely punished for the mystical period of five months, afterwards they will be punished less severely.[45]

[42]This identification intended to exclude any Nestorian distinction of persons and emphasize the ontological reality of the one person of Christ.

[43]The Greek text of the *Henotikon* is given by Evagrius Scholasticus *Hist. eccl.* 3.14 (PG 86:2620-25).

[44]*Henotikon*: "For the Trinity remained a Trinity, even though one of the Trinity, the divine Word, became incarnate"; Oecumenius: "One of the holy Trinity has become incarnate and with his flesh the Son fills the holy Trinity and even now in heaven is not without his flesh" (TEG 8:278).

[45]TEG 8:148.

This may, as Diekamp suggests, reveal a "hidden preference" for Origenistic ideas.[46] However, the reference to "certain of the fathers" makes this less than certain.

The second passage is Oecumenius's discussion of Revelation 20:13–21:2 concerning the sea giving up its dead. Oecumenius refuses any spiritualizing of the doctrine of the resurrection of the dead. He gives an extended discussion of the reconstitution of the four elements that concern the body and concludes that "when each element has given back whatever was mixed with it of the human being, the resurrection is accomplished."[47]

The conviction of Oecumenius that God is essentially good, merciful and beneficent tempers throughout his interpretation of the judgment scenes in Revelation.[48] Unlike the devil, who "with hatchet and hammer" smashes the doors of those who do not receive him, God is eager to improve the works of humankind and bring repentance to those who have sinned. "Behold," God says, "I stand at the door and knock. If anyone hears my voice and opens the door, I will come in to him and dine with him and he with me." Oecumenius comments, "Here the Lord reveals his own humble and peaceful nature."[49] Because God is by nature merciful, Oecumenius understands divine punishments within time primarily as pedagogy. A good example of this is his interpretation of the appearance of God as jasper and carnelian (Rev 4:3). While jasper symbolizes the life-giving nature of God, carnelian represents the fearsomeness of God. At times the severity of God must also be depicted because the pure goodness of God may give sinners a false sense of security and give cause to them for further sin. Therefore, "with good reason does God desire his severity depicted along with his goodness and beneficence." Oecumenius observes, however, that the jasper is the jewel first mentioned, while the carnelian is mentioned second. Why is this? "For [God's] nature is in itself good and beneficent and gentle. And he wishes to be our Father rather than our Lord. But, if it is proper to speak in this way, we force him to become fearsome and punishing. And therefore, often he abandons that which is according to his nature, namely, gentleness, and assumes that which is contrary to his nature, namely, severity."[50]

Oecumenius gives a similar interpretation to Revelation 8:12-13, which speaks of a third of the earth, sea and heavenly bodies enduring calamity. These scenes, according to Oecumenius, depict events of the end time, but they depict only partial calamity (one-third) to evidence the final demonstration of God's goodness. By the partial dissolution

[46]Diekamp, "Mittheilungen," 1053: "eine versteckte Vorliebe." Diekamp, who dates the commentary toward the end of the sixth century, claims that this positive attitude toward Origen is unique after the condemnation of Origen at the Fifth Ecumenical Council. Castagno believes that the phrase "the teaching of the church" suggests an official position and thinks that the Edict of Justinian in 543 may be in view ("Il problema," 236-38). It seems to me that Oecumenius's semi-positive attitude toward the purgative function of punishment suggests an earlier date before the formal condemnation of Origen, especially that of the Fifth Council in 553.

[47]TEG 8:262-64.

[48]Suggit correctly also gives notice to this aspect of Oecumenius's theology (*Oecumenius*, FC 112:8).

[49]TEG 8:103 on Rev 3:20.

[50]TEG 8:105-6.

of the elements God intends to persuade sinners to repentance, for he "is opening a door for repentance and is calling people to a change of heart through fear of that which is coming to pass."[51]

The Interpretation of Revelation: Method, Structure and Content

In the introduction to his translation of Oecumenius, John Suggit has a section comparing Oecumenius with Origen. He claims that Oecumenius was "much indebted to Origen" and that, like Origen, Oecumenius was "much more interested in the spiritual or intellectual meaning of the text than in its literal meaning."[52] It seems to me, however, that drawing this connection is ill-advised. While there may be some few terminological similarities, such as the use of νοητός, Oecumenius never adopts the specific view of Origen that the sensual reality is but a symbolic image of higher, spiritual realities. The hermeneutics of Origen moves the reader from the realities of the senses or the historical to the realm of ideas and a purely noetic reality. As far as I can tell, Oecumenius never does this. In his discussion of Revelation 8:8-9, Oecumenius interprets the mountain burning with fire that is thrown into the sea. Although, he says, this may be interpreted in a literal (πρὸς τὸ γράμμα) and perceptible (τὸ αἰσθητόν) manner, "according to analogy and rhetorical custom (κατά τε ἀναγωγὴν καὶ τοὺς τῆς τροπῆς), the 'sea' may be regarded as the present life because of its turbulence and many distractions." Oecumenius continues, "And one might interpret the 'fish' and the 'boats' to be those persons who are made filthy by salty and bitter sins and who are dissipated by anxiety over useless regrets for what they did in life."[53] In the following section on Revelation 8:10-11, Oecumenius interprets the waters that became wormwood as figuratively (τροπικῶς) referring to people, and he derives this figure from the biblical speech of the Psalms.[54] Oecumenius then concludes: "Although these words are spoken figuratively (ἐν τροπολογίᾳ), it is not impossible that these things and other things like them will literally happen at that time."[55] In his discussion of Revelation 9:13-19, Oecumenius similarly interprets the river Euphrates "figuratively (τροπολογίαν), as is customary in visions." Here the river Euphrates refers to the vision of God, for "that which is divine is figuratively (ἀλληγορεῖται) called a 'river'" by Isaiah."[56] We see in these examples a variety of terms that seem to be synonymous. But in every case these terms indicate nothing other than symbolic speech, usually

[51]TEG 8:144-45.

[52]Suggit, *Oecumenius*, FC 112:9-13, here, 9. Also: "Following the example of Origen, Oecumenius is particularly concerned to discover the spiritual meaning of the text" (13). Suggit refers also to Lamoreaux, who speaks of "the commentary's place in the history of polemic against Origen" ("Provenance," 88). Lamoreaux, however, is referring to Oecumenius's eschatological discussions and claims that "one could read the text primarily as an attempt to provide an eschatological vision orthodox enough to replace that of Origen and his followers." In my opinion, that too is a vast exaggeration.

[53]TEG 8:143.

[54]TEG 8:143. He refers to Ps 93:4 (92:4 LXX).

[55]TEG 8:144.

[56]TEG 8:152.

of the spiritual reality of earthly and historical life, or in one case of the vision of God. Seldom does Oecumenius move allegorically from earthly reality to the purely spiritual, which is characteristic of Origenism.

Oecumenius understands Revelation to be an unveiling of the spiritual meaning of human history. For this he uses the term "mystery" (μυστήριον), and Revelation is full of mystery because the Evangelist John was "holier than all preachers and more spiritual than every other spiritual person." Oecumenius gives us his programmatic understanding of Revelation at the beginning of his commentary:

One might even rightly consider this present work of his to be especially mystical (μυστικωτάτην), inasmuch as it contains subtle and delicately intricate mysteries. For it does not discourse for us concerning present matters only, but rather also concerning matters which have happened in the past and matters which are going to happen in the future. In fact, the special characteristic of this entire prophecy is that it distinguishes and speaks of these three periods of time.[57]

We can see quite clearly that Oecumenius interprets Revelation to be a spiritual interpretation of "three periods of time." As it happens Oecumenius emphasizes events of the past, most especially those concerning the incarnation of the Word, and those of the future, that is, the events immediately preceding the end of the world. It is important to note, however, that the incarnation of the eternal Word made possible this revelation of the meaning of history. For this reason and at the beginning of the commentary proper Oecumenius makes his first significant christological statement. While John in other writing uses words proper to the Word's divinity, "in the present writing he rather uses words proper to his humanity, so that it should not appear that he acquired his understanding from that which is more divine rather than from human realities as well." It is the "pattern of pure theology," says Oecumenius, that just as one must believe that God the Word was eternally begotten from the Father, so one must believe that "in the last days for us and our salvation he became man."[58] The coming of Christ is the key for understanding the past, the present and the future.

Oecumenius makes no attempt to interpret Revelation in a sequential manner. Indeed, he explicitly notes that a vision does not demand a temporal sequence, so that which is first is sometimes narrated last and that which is last is sometimes narrated first.[59] Although he gives no explanation for this, Oecumenius divides his commentary into twelve discourses (λόγοι). His manner of commentary is to provide a more or less lengthy section of biblical text and follow it by repeating phrases and clauses with the appropriate commentary and interpretation. Depending on the text his comments can be quite short or can extend to lengthy expositions on various dogmatic and apologetic questions.

[57]TEG 8:64.
[58]TEG 8:66-67.
[59]TEG 8:214.

However, the basic structure of the commentary is determined by the interpretation that Oecumenius gives to the opening of the seven seals. Virtually unique to him,[60] Oecumenius interprets the opening of the seven seals as a revelation of the various works of the incarnate Son of God: "The gradual opening of the seals reveals the gradual recovery of our free and open relationship with God, which the Only-Begotten, having become incarnate, acquired for us when by his own righteousness he set aright our offenses. It is then to be noted that the loosing of each seal reveals a certain work done by the Lord for our salvation and effected by him against our spiritual enemies."[61] The seven seals represent the following events in the life of Christ: (1) the physical birth of the Lord, (2) the temptation of the Lord and his victory over the tempter, (3) his salvific teaching and the benefits of his miracles, (4) the lashes that Christ received, (5) the chains and beatings to which the Lord was subjected, (6) the cross and death of the Lord and the resurrection and ascension that follow after and (7) the second coming of the Lord and the giving of blessings as rewards.

The first six of these seals govern Oecumenius's exposition through Revelation 7.[62] Beginning at Revelation 8:1-2, however, with the opening of the seventh seal visions of the future become dominant. Since the seventh seal reveals the second coming and the granting of eternal rewards, Oecumenius's interpretation of the following sections has to do with the signs and events associated with the second coming of Christ and the consummation of the world with its final punishments and its final bliss. Thus, the blowing of the seven trumpets by the angels signals various events at the end, some concerning the blessed and some concerning the sinners.

Within these sections, however, as Oecumenius says by way of digression and by sharp U-turns, the narrative from time to time refers to events of the past, again to the time of the earthly life of Christ. Despite the fact that Oecumenius interprets the beast that wars against the two witnesses as the antichrist,[63] he interprets the woman of Revelation 12 to be the Virgin Mary and the child to be Christ. The vision, says Oecumenius, "intends to describe more completely to us the circumstances concerning the antichrist, whom we mentioned briefly in previous discussion." Since the incarnation of the Christ provided a pretext for Satan to raise up the antichrist, "the vision gives a certain order and sequence to the material that it is going to discuss and begins the discussion from the fleshly conception of the Lord by portraying for us the mother of God."[64] This conviction, then, de-

[60]A similar interpretation of the seven seals is given by Apringius of Beja.

[61]TEG 8:120.

[62]Since Oecumenius interprets the events within the first six seals to refer to the time of Christ, he understands the 144,000 from the twelve tribes to be the Jews of the first century and their fate at the hands of the Romans. However, the numberless throng (Rev 7:9-17) is the Gentiles who later would come to the faith, and therefore "the vision shows them as caught up beforehand and as having already obtained the blessedness which awaits them" (TEG 8:135). Here a vision of the future intrudes within visions of the past.

[63]Rev 11:7-10.

[64]TEG 8:170.

termines the interpretation that Oecumenius gives to the details of the woman: enclothed with the sun means she was pregnant with the Sun of righteousness, the twelve stars are the twelve apostles, her crying out in anguish refers to the natural shyness of a virgin, the desire of the dragon to devour the child refers to the plot of Herod to kill the baby Jesus, the flight of the woman into the wilderness refers to the flight into Egypt, and so on.

Oecumenius adopts the same procedure later in the commentary concerning the thousand-year reign. According to Oecumenius, at the end of Revelation 19 the narrative had begun to speak of the final judgment of the devil. However, the Evangelist wishes to preserve the coherence of the narrative and so speaks first of the suffering of the devil at the time of the incarnation. Unique to Oecumenius, the thousand years are interpreted to be the time of Christ's earthly life, and given this conviction the details of Revelation 20 are interpreted accordingly. Therefore, for example, the binding of the devil refers to his weakness in view of the miracles of Christ, the marks of deity. The loosing of the devil refers to "the time between the incarnation of the Lord and the consummation of the present age."[65]

Clearly the incarnation of the eternal Word plays an important hermeneutical role in the commentary of Oecumenius. The seven seals, the vision of the woman and the thousand years all refer to the incarnation and life of Christ. This explains too why significant christological statements occur in the commentary and especially at the beginning and at the end. The heresies of Nestorius and Eutyches destroy the true incarnation, which is the key to understanding the purposes of God and the destiny of the human race.

Finally, some mention must be made concerning Oecumenius's opinion of the authority of Revelation. He clearly believes that Revelation is an inspired and canonical text of the church. Indeed, Oecumenius begins his text by quoting 2 Timothy 3:16, "All Scripture is inspired by God and profitable." Furthermore, the authority of Revelation has received significant affirmation from the church's tradition. Oecumenius mentions six "authoritative fathers" who have received and confirmed the Revelation: Athanasius, Basil of Caesarea, Gregory of Nazianzus, Methodius, Cyril of Alexandria and Hippolytus.[66] Although he never again adduces Athanasius, Basil, Methodius or Hippolytus, he does quote a significant number of church fathers and other witnesses, including Josephus, Eusebius of Caesarea, Justin Martyr, Irenaeus, Clement of Alexandria, Evagrius and Gregory of Nyssa. Yet Oecumenius never mentions any previous work on Revelation; perhaps there was no commentary available to him. His own commentary evinces a remarkable vigor and creativity, and some of his interpretations are unique to himself. In this regard I mention again his interpretation of the thousand years as representing the time of the life of Christ, and I add his unique interpretation of the four living creatures (Rev 4:6-8). According to Oecumenius, the four living creatures symbolize the four fundamental elements from which

[65]TEG 8:250.
[66]TEG 8:65.

every creature is made: the lion is symbol of fire, the ox is symbol of the earth, the man is symbol of the air, and the eagle is symbol of water. This interpretation enables Oecumenius to affirm the providential care of God over the world in the face of certain Jews who believe that because of the sin of Adam God no longer cares for the world but only for the realm of the angels.[67] According to Oecumenius, these Jews believed that God desired to dwell only among the holy orders in heaven. We see the christological impulse that seems to drive the commentary of Oecumenius in his resistance to this false opinion.

Andrew of Caesarea

The commentary of Andrew of Caesarea is very different in form and content from that of Oecumenius. Andrew gives every indication that he is governed by traditional and accepted opinions, and very little of his commentary could be called original. He stands well within the churchly consensus on questions concerning Christology and eschatology that occupied the sixth century. Although he quotes with some frequency from established authorities such as Justin Martyr, Irenaeus, Methodius, Eusebius of Caesarea, Gregory of Nazianzus, Epiphanius of Salamis and Cyril of Alexandria, as well as from Papias and Pseudo-Dionysius, he never refers to any earlier commentary. However, Andrew evidently knew and had read the commentary of Oecumenius, for often he mentions or summarizes the views of Oecumenius, usually to disagree and to offer his own comments.

It might be argued that historically the commentary of Andrew is the most important of the Greek commentaries. Although that of Oecumenius is the first Greek commentary on Revelation, that of Andrew became the standard commentary on Revelation in the Byzantine tradition. Moreover, the text of Revelation presented in the commentary of Andrew became the standard text form in the Byzantine textual tradition and was followed by most of the so-called Majority Text.[68] Finally, Andrew of Caesarea seems to have been the first to divide Revelation according to a conceived pattern. He divides Revelation into twenty-four books (βίβλοι) corresponding to the twenty-four elders. Each book is further divided into three chapters (κεφάλαια) corresponding to the threefold nature of a person, body, soul and spirit.[69] There are, therefore, seventy-two chapters in all. The interpretative comments of Andrew are quite often rather short and rarely reach theological depth. However, from time to time, when he believes it is required, Andrew will offer a more extended discussion.

This translation is based on the critical text of Josef Schmid.[70]

[67]TEG 8:109-10.

[68]The text of Andrew and of those manuscripts that follow him are indicated in Nestle-Aland's Greek text by the *siglum* $\mathfrak{M}^A$.

[69]Josef Schmid, *Studien zur Geschichte des griechischen Apokalypse-Textes*, 1. Teil: *Der Apokalypse-Kommentar des Andreas von Kaisareia* (Münchener Theologische Studien, I, Historische Abteilung (Munich: Karl Zink Verlag, 1955), 10 (hereafter referred to as MTS).

[70]See the preceding note.

Date and Identity of Andrew of Caesarea

Very little is known with certainty of Andrew and of the circumstances of his commentary. In 1897 Franz Diekamp could write that the commentary of Andrew was the oldest Greek commentary on Revelation and perhaps even the oldest continuous commentary on Revelation in the church's history. Scholarly opinion on date showed considerable doubt, some scholars dating Andrew as early as the fifth century. Diekamp believed that some passages in the commentary reflected recent experience during the Hunnish invasions and dated the commentary c. 515.[71]

This dating had to be reassessed when in 1901 Diekamp discovered the Messina manuscript of Oecumenius's commentary and it was clear that Andrew had used Oecumenius and must, therefore, be dated later. Andrew certainly wrote his commentary before 637, when the city of Jerusalem fell to the armies of Islam. In his comments on Revelation 16:19, Andrew interprets the "great city" to be Jerusalem and the three parts into which it was split to be the division between Christians, Jews and Samaritans. He then comments, "For at the present time the Jews and Samaritans hide their real intentions out of fear of our pious rulers, and they seem to be associated with us, not daring to separate themselves with their own people."[72] There is no hint of the Arabs at "the present time," and the reference to "our pious rulers" makes it clear that the Christian Byzantine emperors were still in power.[73] A similar observation makes it unlikely that Andrew wrote his commentary during the years 614 to 627, for during that time Jerusalem was in the hands of the Persians. Had Andrew written between 627 and 637, both Diekamp and Castagno argue, Andrew would have most probably mentioned more explicitly the recent Persian occupation.[74] Concerning the *terminus a quo* of Andrew's commentary, it seems unlikely that it could have been before c. 563. The episcopal list of the bishops of Caesarea in Cappadocia is clear between 510 and 563, and only c. 563 could Andrew have become bishop of that metropolitan city.[75] It may be that Diekamp is correct that a closer dating than c. 563 to 614 is not possible. However, Castagno believes that the commentary of Andrew on Revelation 9:17-19, Revelation 16:8-9 and Revelation 20:7-8 well suits the invasions and plunderings of the Persians c. 610.[76] It would appear, therefore, that the commentary of Andrew on Revelation may be dated to the

[71]Franz Diekamp, "Das Zeitalter des Erzbischofs Andreas von Cäsarea," *Historisches Jahrbuch* 18 (1897): 1-36, here, 1-3, 27-28. In my introduction to *Revelation* (ACCS NT 12), I inadvertently allowed this dating of Diekamp to stand without further comment (xxviii). Clearly the correct dating places Andrew virtually one century later.

[72]MTS 1:178.

[73]Diekamp, "Mittheilungen," 30; Castagno, "Il problema," 240-41. Diekamp believes that Andrew is alluding to the effects of various imperial laws against the Jews and Samaritans that occasioned many to be baptized and assume the name of Christian although never abandoning their original faith in the heart.

[74]Franz Diekamp, "Andreas von Caesarea," *Analecta Patristica: Text und Abhandlungen zur griechischen Patristik* (Orientalia Christiana Analecta, 117; Rome: Pontifical Institutum Orientalium Studiorum, 1938), 162; Castagno, "Il problema," 241.

[75]Diekamp, "Mittheilungen," 3-8; "Andreas von Caesarea," 162. According to Diekamp, the bishops are Soterichus (510–537); Theodorus Askidas (537–c. 563); Theokritus (c. 563–?). There is some doubt concerning the transition date between Askidas and Theokritus. In his earlier article Diekamp gives the dating of Askidas as 537–558.

[76]Castagno, "Il problema," 239-42; also Diekamp, "Mittheilungen," 25. Caesarea itself fell to the Persians in 612.

first years of the seventh century, one century after that of Oecumenius.

How extensive the literary output of Andrew was is unknown. The commentary, however, was not his only work. Diekamp reports that a catalogue of the patriarchal library in Constantinople, published in Strassburg in 1578, attributes an interpretation of the book of Daniel to Andrew.[77] More important is the work *Therapeutike* in which Andrew apparently in question-and-answer form gives his understanding to various questions, especially concerning eschatology.[78]

The Theology of Andrew of Caesarea

Unlike Oecumenius, who reveals a distinct Cyrillian Christology and makes at times significant christological claims, Andrew of Caesarea gives only incidental christological comments and these without the slightest polemical tint. Andrew never mentions heresies by name, although it is clear that he is an avid adherent to the Nicene doctrine of the full deity of the Son and to the two natures doctrine of Chalcedon. Christ is true God "who rules all things, who is without beginning and similarly without end, who is and who was before and who is without limit, since he is eternal with the Father."[79] As King of kings and Lord of lords Christ is the ruler of kings, "for he is equal in strength to the Father and of one essence with him."[80] The phrase "who is, who was and who is to come" refers to the "tri-hypostatic deity" (τῆς τρισυποστάτου θεότητος) of Father, Son and Holy Spirit.[81] Other christological statements are equally traditional and without polemical focus. Among other possibilities Andrew interprets the bronze feet of the one like a son of man as referring to the two natures of Christ. "Since the bronze refers to the human nature and the incense refers to the divine nature, through these is indicated the sweet odor of the faith and the unconfusedness of the unity."[82] In a similar interpretation Andrew states that the bronze feet of the Son of God symbolize "the undivided and unmixed unity of the divinity and humanity."[83] If the commentary is any guide, Andrew was fully unengaged in the christological debates of the post-Chalcedonian era.

However, it is evident that Andrew was interested in eschatological questions that were agitating the sixth century. The excessive spiritualizing of Origen and his followers had led the Byzantine church to a condemnation of various opinions of Origen. In 543 the emperor Justinian issued an edict against Origen containing nine anathemas. The

[77]Diekamp, "Andreas von Caesarea," 162: *explication in visiones Danielis prophetae*. This work is otherwise unknown.

[78]Diekamp, "Andreas von Caesarea," 162-72. Diekamp provides the Greek text of the only fragments of this text that exist.

[79]MTS 1:17-18 on Rev 1:8.

[80]MTS 1:14 on Rev 1:5. Andrew uses the term (ὁμοούσιος) of the Nicene Creed.

[81]MTS 1:13 on Rev 1:4.

[82]MTS 1:21 on Rev 1:15. Andrew uses the term τὸ ἀσύγχυτον, perhaps reflecting the *Definitio Fidei* of Chalcedon that the two natures of Christ were united "unconfusedly."

[83]MTS 1:32 on Rev 2:18. The Greek of Andrew is τὴν ἄτμητον καὶ ἀσύγχυτον ἕνωσιν θεότητός τε καὶ ἀνθρωπότητος. If he has Chalcedon in mind, he is inexact in the use of terms. For the indivisibility of the two natures Chalcedon uses ἀδιαιρέτως and ἀχωρίστως.

fifth anathema says that "if anyone says or thinks that, at the resurrection, human bodies will rise spherical in form and unlike our present form, let him be anathema."[84] This condemnation was reiterated at the Fifth Ecumenical Council in 553 in its anathemas against Origen. That council stated in its tenth anathema that "if anyone shall say that after the resurrection the body of the Lord was ethereal, having the form of a sphere, and that such shall be the bodies of all after the resurrection, let him be anathema."[85] Andrew stands totally in consensus with the church's orthodoxy on this question. The question about the body's resurrection shape finds no clear echo in the commentary. However, the issue is directly addressed in the *Therapeutike*. In answer to a question after the shape of the resurrection body, Andrew replies that "when the holy apostle says there will be a transformation from corruption to incorruption,[86] he does not mean that the body will change into a spherical body, as some who have been deceived think, as though such a shape were superior to all others."[87]

Andrew's opposition to speculative spiritualizing in eschatological questions is evident also in his opinion on whether in the resurrection the body will retain all of its members, especially those that will have no further use, such as those for eating and for procreation. Origen had denied that such members would belong to the resurrection body, and he had been followed in this opinion by others.[88] In his *Therapeutike* Andrew rejects this opinion and asserts that after the resurrection the body will continue to possess all of its members. There is full continuity between the body given to Adam and Eve and those that will rise, for "nothing made by the creator is despicable (αἰσχρόν) and ugly (ἄκοσμον)."[89]

Eschatology dominates the commentary of Andrew. This was unavoidable given Andrew's conviction that Revelation has to do primarily with future events. Some discussions within the commentary reflect the Origenistic controversies. In his commentary on Revelation 16:10-11, one of his longer discussions, Andrew raises the issue of eternal torment. There are those who think that "the goodness of God and his foreknowledge and his power serve as a hindrance to eternal punishment." However, says Andrew, these persons should also consider the divine justice that always "apportions to each according to that which is deserved." Those who sin have done so by way of their free will and intention. These are the sources of human sin, and therefore, although God "is most prepared toward mercy and goodness," the verdict of eternal torment is just "because of the

[84]For the Greek see Diekamp, "Andreas von Caesarea," 171 (NPNF 2 14:320).

[85]NPNF 2 14:319.

[86]1 Cor 15:42, 53.

[87]For the Greek, see Diekamp, "Andreas von Caesarea," 166, discussion on 170-71. Given the clear interest of Andrew in such questions and his orthodoxy, it is interesting to note that Andrew neither mentions nor hints at the existence of the Fifth Ecumenical Council.

[88]Among those holding this view Diekamp mentions Clement of Alexandria, Basil of Caesarea, Gregory of Nyssa and Theodoret ("Andreas von Caesarea," 171).

[89]For the Greek, see Diekamp, "Andreas von Caesarea," 166-67.

evil which [sinners] freely did."[90] This argument goes directly counter to the doctrine of restoration, which claimed that eventually all rational souls will be purified and come to know the Word and participate in him. Nor does Andrew share the opinion of Oecumenius that after a certain span of time the torments of eternity will become less severe.[91]

Andrew is in the tradition of those who emphasize the continuity between the first creation and the consummation of the world. In commenting on Revelation 20:11 and Revelation 21:1, Andrew strongly rejects any suggestion that the material world will be annihilated, and for support of his position he refers to Irenaeus, Antipater of Bosra and Methodius. Rather, argues Andrew, the creation will also be transformed with us "into the freedom of the glory of the children of God,"[92] being made new into that which is more brilliant. "The creation, which was made for our sake, receives with us a change for the better, not going into nonexistence, just as we do not go into nonexistence after our death."[93] Here Andrew rejects two views of Origen, that the material world will be annihilated and only a spiritual existence will remain[94] and that the end will be like the beginning with the rational souls returning to a primordial bliss.[95] Finally, Andrew holds the position that on death souls do not go to the place of their final destination but rather to an intermediate place that is fitting to the life they lived and is an intimation of their final destiny. In his comments on Revelation 6:11, Andrew writes that the martyrs under the altar "see in the spirit" that for which they hope and "rightly rejoice, resting in the bosom of Abraham."[96] This view is reinforced in Andrew's *Therapeutike*. There, in direct dependence on Epiphanius, Andrew answers the question "where are the souls after they leave the body" by saying that they are in rooms worthy of that which they did in life (ἐν ταμιείοις ἀξίοις τῶν βεβιωμένων ἑκάστῃ).[97]

The Interpretation of Revelation: Method, Structure and Content

In the prologue to the commentary Andrew indicates his understanding of holy Scripture and the manner in which it is to be interpreted.[98] The Spirit inspires the text "in a tripartite manner corresponding to the tripartite nature of man."

---

[90]MTS 1:170-72.

[91]MTS 1:96-97.

[92]Rom 8:20-21.

[93]MTS 1:227-29, 232-33.

[94]Compare the eleventh anathema of the Fifth Council: "If anyone shall say that the future judgment signifies the destruction of the body and that the end of the story will be an immaterial nature, and that thereafter there will no longer be any matter, but only spirit (νοῦς), let him be anathema" (NPNF 2 14:319).

[95]Compare the fifteenth anathema of the Fifth Council: "If anyone shall say that the life of the spirits (νοῶν) shall be like to the life which was in the beginning while as yet the spirits had not come down or fallen, so that the end and the beginning shall be alike, and that the end shall be the true measure of the beginning, let him be anathema" (NPNF 2 14:319).

[96]MTS 1:67.

[97]For the Greek, see Diekamp, "Andreas von Caesarea," 165-66; for discussion, 169-70. Diekamp notes that Andrew is not alone in this view and mentions *Enoch* 22; *4 Esdras* 7:32, 82, 95; Irenaeus, Gregory of Nazianzus, Gregory of Nyssa, Hilary and Ambrose. Interestingly, in 1252 an unknown Latin accused Andrew of heresy for this view (169).

[98]MTS 1:8-10.

As it were, the body of Scripture is the letter and the story according to its literal meaning (τὸ γράμμα καὶ ἡ κατ' αἴσθησιν ἱστορία). As if it were the soul, the tropological meaning leads the reader from that which is of the sense to that which is intellectual (ἐξ αἰσθητῶν ἐπὶ τὰ νοητά). And as is the spirit, the anagogical and spiritual meaning (ἡ ἀναγωγὴ καὶ θεωρία) reveals that which is coming and the higher things.[99]

Despite the threefold nature of the divine speech, Andrew is not a follower of Origen in his interpretations. Unlike Origen, who moves from the senses to the realm of ideas, Andrew's hermeneutics remain within the economical structure of biblical thought. The spiritual meaning of the text does not lead the soul upward to higher realities. Rather, the spiritual meaning leads forward by revealing "that which is to come and the higher things." These "higher things" are themselves not a Christianized Platonic realm but the realities of the kingdom of God that are the future and eternal lot of the redeemed. Andrew admits that the "spiritual" meaning "is found with abundance" in Revelation, for it contains visions of future things. To be sure, the threefold nature of the text is proper to different persons depending on their spiritual aptitude.[100] Those such as the Theologian who are fully submitted to the Spirit are especially suited for receiving visions of the future bliss when all the redeemed will be of that "blessed lot."

Unlike Oecumenius, who at strategic points believes the visions of Revelation reveal past events, Andrew is very hesitant to see past events in the visions of the prophecy.[101] Revelation has to do with present and especially future events and realities. The perspective is clear already in Andrew's comments on Revelation 1:1-2 concerning the words "all things which are and that which must happen after them." Andrew explains, "These words are indicative of both present and future time."[102]

This governing perspective on Revelation is especially noticeable in three contexts that also contrast nicely with the procedure of Oecumenius. The first concerns the opening of the seven seals. According to Oecumenius, the seven seals symbolized events in the life of Christ, that is, events of the past. Andrew, however, explicitly rejects this interpretation and adopts the understanding of Methodius:

> Some have interpreted the loosing of the present seal and all those which follow thereafter to refer to the incarnate economy of God the Word. . . . But we have read Methodius and note how he spoke concerning this text: It is not necessary to think

[99]MTS 1:8.

[100]The literal is "proper to those who are taught of the Law"; the tropological is "proper to those who live in grace"; the spiritual is "proper to that blessed lot in whom the Spirit rules since all fleshly thoughts as well as movements are submitted to him" (MTS 1:8-9).

[101]Andrew allows that a past event might well be reflected in certain passages; however, very rarely is a past event regarded as the only referent. The sequence of the passage also refers to present or to future events. The events surrounding the pale horse happened before when Christians were persecuted under Maximinus. However, they reflect also contemporary occurrences (Rev 6:8; MTS 1:65). On Revelation 7:1 Andrew notes the view of Oecumenius that the passage refers to the suffering of the Jews under the Romans long ago. "However, how much more will these occur at the coming of the antichrist, and not only partially in the land of the Jews, but over the whole world" (MTS 1:73; also on Rev 6:12-13 [MTS 1:68-69]).

[102]MTS 1:12.

"that Christ is the one who has been born; for the mystery of the incarnation of the Word was fulfilled long before the Apocalypse, whereas John speaks of things which are present or future."[103]

He then interprets the seven seals as having to do with events beginning from the preaching of the apostles to the "dissolution of the earthly city" (Rev 8:1). Similarly, the four living creatures and the four horses (Rev 6:2, 4, 5, 8) refer to present and future realities.[104]

The second context is the vision of the woman, the dragon and the child (Rev 12:1-18). Oecumenius had interpreted this vision to refer to the Virgin Mary and the dangers surrounding the birth of Jesus. Again, Andrew explicitly rejects this interpretation and appeals to the authority of Methodius: "However, the great Methodius understands [the woman] to be the holy Church, believing that what is narrated concerning her is unsuited of the divine birth since the Lord had been born already a long time previously."[105] And a little later he quotes Methodius: "It is not necessary to think that it is Christ himself who is the one born. For long before the Apocalypse, the mystery of the incarnation of the Word was fulfilled. But John speaks concerning things present and things to come."[106] From this perspective Andrew adopts the various interpretations of Methodius: the birth of the child refers to the church bringing forth children of God through baptism; the "male" child refers to desires of the people of the church which are not effeminate; the wilderness to which the woman flees is that citizenship that is "devoid of every desire." Typical of Andrew's perspective are his concluding words: "To be sure, this occurs always, but it will especially be so at the coming of the antichrist."[107] The future reference is always close to Andrew's mind.

Finally, I mention Andrew's interpretation of the thousand years of Revelation 20. Oecumenius thought the millennial period to be the period of Christ's earthly life during which the devil was "bound" by the demonstrations of Christ's deity. Andrew too believes that the devil was bound by the cross of Christ. However, this binding of the devil is a present and future reality, for we see the effects of his being bound in "the disappearance of idol-worship, the destruction of pagan temples, the abandonment of the defilement of altars and the knowledge of the will of God throughout the world." The number one thousand itself is symbolic either of "many" or of "complete," and so it refers either to the time of the preaching of the church or represents the time from the incarnation of the Lord until the arrival of the antichrist during which time we are released from the life learned from the law and are called to the "perfect man," to the measure of the maturity of the fullness of Christ.[108]

[103]Methodius *Symp.* 8.7 (ACW 27:112).
[104]The white horse is the preaching of the apostles; the red horse is the suffering of the martyrs; the black horse is the sorrow of those who have fallen from faith; the pale horse is the death and destruction of persecution.
[105]MTS 1:121.
[106]MTS 1:122, quoting Methodius *Symp.* 8.5-8 (ACW 27:110-13).
[107]MTS 1:133.
[108]See Eph 4:13.

Why was Andrew so insistent on interpreting Revelation in terms of the present and the future? The answer lies in his understanding of the purpose for which the revelations were given to John. God wishes for all humankind to be saved and to come to the knowledge of the truth. For that reason God revealed to John that which is and that which is to come to entice and to persuade all persons to repentance and conversion. Andrew makes this point at the beginning of his commentary. *In persona Iohannis* Andrew says that the revelations were given that John "might testify and proclaim for the conversion of those who hear those things which are and lie hidden to humankind and those things which will come in the future."[109] Andrew comes to the same point at the end of the commentary. On the plea "Come, Lord Jesus," Andrew writes that "this present book is holy and inspired by God and leads those who read it to their blessed end and inheritance."[110] Finally, it is to be noted that throughout the commentary Andrew at times concludes his words with a prayer of exhortation and doxology. Revelation is for the strengthening of Christian conviction, perseverance and hope. At the end of his epilogue Andrew quotes 1 Timothy 2:4, that God "wishes that all be saved and come to the knowledge of the truth" However, Andrew adds, "each person partakes of [the divine] light according to the measure of the purity of their spiritual eyes. May he who is all-merciful, Christ our God, who suffered for us in the flesh, deem us worthy to receive this grace pure and undefiled. To him we owe all praise, honor and worship, together with the Father and the life-giving Spirit, forever and ever. Amen."[111]

The purpose of Revelation is to assist the readers to receive God's grace "pure and undefiled." Andrew wrote his commentary as a bishop and in the same cause.

As we have noted, Oecumenius divides the text of Revelation into twelve discourses, while Andrew of Caesarea divides the text into twenty-four books and seventy-two chapters. They were, of course, unaware of the chapter and verse textual divisions that are common in modern Bibles. For the reader's convenience I have added chapter and verse references to both commentary texts.

[109]MTS 1:12 on Rev 1:1-2.
[110]MTS 1:263 on Rev 22:20-21.
[111]MTS 1:267.

OECUMENIUS
Commentary on the Apocalypse

First Discourse

"All Scripture is inspired by God and profitable," as a holy saying says somewhere.[1] For all those who have preached to us the word of salvation—whether they were prophets, apostles or evangelists—were made wise by the Spirit. At least this is true of the divine John, who was holier than all preachers and more spiritual than every other spiritual person, since he "lay upon the breast" of the Lord[2] and because of his intimacy drew to himself a more abundant grace of the Spirit. And for this reason he was called a "son of thunder,"[3] since he filled the earth under heaven with the sound of his divine teachings. One might even rightly consider this present work of his to be especially mystical, inasmuch as it contains subtle and delicately intricate mysteries. For it does not discourse for us concerning present matters only, but rather also concerning matters that have happened in the past and matters that are going to happen in the future. In fact, the special characteristic of this entire prophecy is that it distinguishes and speaks of these three periods of time. For even those outside the faith adduce their own seers who had knowledge of "all things that were, and that were to be, and that had been before,"[4] coming thereby, as I think, to an understanding of our own prophets.[5] For those who delivered oracles among them never possessed the knowledge of all things, since the demons at work in them never required the one who was attempting to interpret spiritual and divine things to be spiritual and wise. Indeed, as the holy apostle says, "It is for the spiritual to judge spiritual things."[6] But I am as far from the work of the Spirit as I am from the divine and most high Wisdom. For this reason, this undertaking that I have assumed is rather more reckless than safe. For according to the opinion of Solomon and the Truth, "Wisdom will not enter a deceitful soul or dwell in a body enslaved to sin."[7] And so I endeavor to do this as a certain exercise, investigating in it what is uninvestigated.

It is known that some have been tempted to say that this writing is spurious[8] and is not to be associated with the other writings of John. However, I am among those who say that it contains what is profitable to the soul and has nothing that is ungodly and unworthy of the author. I, therefore, attest to its authenticity along with those authoritative fathers who have received and confirmed this text. Among these are the great Athanasius in his *Treatise on the Canonical Books of the Old and New Testaments*,[9] the holy Basil in his short investigation *On the Son*,[10] Gregory the Theologian in his oration *In the Presence of the Bishops*,[11]

First Discourse [1]2 Tim 3:16. [2]Jn 13:25. [3]Mk 3:17. [4]Homer *Il.* 1.70 (LCL 170:19; cf. Hesiod *Theog.* line 38). [5]Perhaps Oecumenius held to the early Christian view that pagan writers and thinkers knew and had read the Old Testament prophets. [6]2 Cor 2:13. [7]Wis 1:4. [8]See Eusebius *Hist. eccl.* 3.25.4. [9]See Athanasius *Letter* 39 (PG 26:1437; NPNF 2 4:552). [10]Perhaps Basil of Caesarea *Against Eunomius* I 2.14 (PG 29:600) or Pseudo-Basil (= Didymus the Blind?) *Against Eunomius* 4.2 (PG 29:677). [11]See Gregory of Nazianzus *Or. Bas.* 42 (PG 36:457-492; NPNF 2 7:385-95).

the most wise Methodius in his book *On the Resurrection*[12] and Cyril, who was great in word and deed, in the sixth book of his treatise *In Spirit and in Truth*.[13] To these we might also add the holy Hippolytus in his *Commentary on Daniel*.[14] Certainly there would have been no mention [of the Apocalypse] among the Fathers, who were so careful lest there were anything in it that was spurious or objectionable. And others of the saints would not dare to commend the writing unless they were aware of the common respect it had received by those who think rightly. If "a threefold cord is not quickly broken," as the Preacher says,[15] a sixfold cord could hardly be broken.[16] What, therefore, does the holy disciple of Christ, who even boasts of the divine love,[17] say to us through the Apocalypse? One must finally go to the divine words themselves, calling on earlier authorities[18] for assistance.

[1:1-2] ***The revelation of Jesus Christ, which God gave to him to show to his servants what must soon take place; and he made it known by sending it through his angel to his servant John, who bore witness to the word of God and to the testimony of Jesus Christ, even to all that he saw.***

It is good to note at the beginning that although in all of his writings the holy John is fond of using words of our Savior, Jesus Christ, which are proper to his deity, in the present writing he rather uses words proper to his humanity, so that it should not appear that he acquired his understanding from that which is more divine rather than from human realities as well. For it is the pattern of pure theology that just as one must believe that God the Word was begotten from God the Father before all ages and before all intervals of time, he being coeternal and consubstantial with the Father and the Spirit, and that [with the Father and the Spirit] he rules the ages and all creation, both the intellectual and the perceptible, as the most wise Paul says in his letter to the Colossians: "For in him all things were created, in heaven and on earth, visible and invisible, whether thrones or dominions or principalities or authorities—all things were created through him and for him; and he is the head of the body, indeed of the church, who is the first fruit, the firstborn of the dead, that in everything he might be preeminent,"[19] so also one must believe that in the last days for us and our salvation he became man, not by any loss of divinity but by the assumption of human flesh together with a rational soul, so that he who is Immanuel may be recognized as united from two natures, from divinity and humanity, the natures subsisting perfectly according to their own integrity and the distinction that arises from their natural qualities and peculiarities, neither nature being mixed or changed by coming together into unity or being separated after the ineffable and real union.[20] Similarly, both Nestorius and Eutyches are abominable, for they hold to evil teachings that are contrary and opposed to this doctrine.

Therefore, so that the teaching of the Lord might be correct and specific to him, although John used the divine words of the Lord in other writings, as we said, here he used human words and thoughts. Nonetheless, in those writings he did not express divine things apart

[12]See Methodius *Res.* 2.28 (GCS 27:385) *passim.* [13]See Cyril of Alexandria *On the Adoration and Worship in Spirit and in Truth* 6 (PG 68:433). [14]See Hippolytus *Comm. Dan.* 3.9; 4.22, 23, 34, 49 (SC 14:142, 186, 188, 200, 216). [15]Eccl 4:12. [16]Referring to the six Fathers just mentioned. [17]Most likely a reference to John's status as the disciple "whom Jesus loved" (Jn 13:23). [18]Translating τὰς αὐτοῦ πρεσβείας to refer to earlier commentators such as the six Fathers he had earlier mentioned. [19]Col 1:16, 18. [20]Oecumenius is reflecting the language and theology of a moderate "Monophysite" position not uncommon in the East in the aftermath of the Council of Chalcedon (451) at which Nestorius and Eutyches were declared heretical. Telltale is his use of the phrase "from two natures" (ἐκ δύο φύσεων) rather than the Chalcedonian "in two natures" (ἐν δύο φύσεων).

from that which was human, nor here does he express human things apart from that which is divine. Rather, in his writings he used both the strong and the weak side by side.

Therefore, when it is said to him, "The Revelation of Jesus Christ, which God gave to him," it is as though he said, "This revelation is given from the Father to the Son and then from the Son to us," his servants. By calling the saints the servants of Christ, he safeguards what is proper to his deity. For to whom would people belong, unless to him who is the maker and creator of humankind? And who is the creator of humankind and of all creation? No one other than the only-begotten Word and Son of God! For, the present author says in the Gospel, "All things were made through him."[21] And why does he wish to add "what must soon take place," although those events that will take place have not yet occurred, even though a considerable span of time has passed, indeed more than five hundred years, since these words were spoken? Because to the eyes of the eternal and endless God all ages are regarded as nothing, for, as the prophet says, "A thousand years in your sight, O Lord, are as yesterday when it is past, or as a watch in the night."[22] For this reason, therefore, he added "soon," not to indicate a measure of time that must pass before the fulfillment of what must happen but to indicate the power and eternality of God. For to him who is, any passage of time, even should it be great and considerable, is something small when compared with that which is unending.

He says Jesus the Christ "showed" to me "what must take place." However, it was not Jesus himself who appeared and spoke to him. Rather, he says, it was "through his angel" that Christ led me into his mysteries. Take note of the honesty of this holy man who acknowledges that the revelation was given to him through an angel and not directly from the mouth of the Lord. I am the one, John says, who "bore witness to the word of God and to the testimony of Christ, whatsoever he saw." He used this manner of speaking also in the Gospel to maintain the trustworthiness of his teaching by referring to himself. He said, "This is he who is bears witness to these things and who has written these things, and we know that his testimony is true."[23] Also in this passage he says that he is a witness of the divine word that was revealed to him—he speaks of the word of present revelation and of the witness given from Christ—that is, he says, by way of a witness I am a witness and an author of these things.

[1:3] ***Blessed is he who reads and he who hears the words of this prophecy and those who keep what is written in it, for the time is near.***

He does not only say that those who read are blessed—for in that way many would be blessed, for there are many readers—but also those who hear and thereby become convinced by the exhortations in the book and afterward keep and observe what is spoken as divine precepts. "For," he says, "the time is near." Indeed, the time of blessedness is near to anyone who observes the commandments of God. It means either that, or it means that the time of escape from that which is predicted is "near." However, "near" has been interpreted in what was previously said.

[1:4] ***John to the seven churches that are in Asia: Grace to you and peace from God, who is and who was and who is coming.***

This is the same as saying, "Grace to you from the God of us all." For the Father calls himself "he who is," making known this name to the most wise Moses from the bush, saying, "I am who am."[24] And our holy Evangelist

[21]Jn 1:3. [22]Ps 90:4 (89:4 LXX). [23]Jn 21:24. [24]Ex 3:14.

uses "who was" to speak concerning the Son, saying, "In the beginning was the Word, and the Word was with God, and the Word was God."[25] Moreover, in the first of the Catholic Letters he writes, "What was from the beginning, what we have heard, what we have seen with our own eyes, what we have beheld and our hands have touched concerning the Word of life."[26] The phrase "who is coming" refers to the Holy Spirit, for not only did he come on the day of Pentecost as that is narrated in the Acts, but also he comes always to those souls worthy to receive him.

[1:4] ***And from the seven spirits that are before his throne.***

The seven spirits are seven angels. However, they are not to be regarded as of equal honor or coeternal with the holy Trinity, by no means, but as true assistants and faithful servants. For the prophet says to God, "All things are your servants,"[27] and among "all things" are included also the angels. And in another place he says concerning them, "Bless the Lord, all his hosts, his ministers that do his will."[28] And the apostle uses this manner of speaking in his first letter to Timothy: "I urge you before God and Jesus Christ and the elect angels."[29] And so when he says, "which are before his throne," he is giving added witness to their order as servants and ministers but in no way to any equality in honor.

[1:5] ***And from Jesus Christ, the witness, the faithful one, the firstborn of the dead and the ruler of the kings of the earth.***

Having previously written of the preincarnate Word of God and referring to him as "he who was," he now speaks concerning the incarnated Word, saying, "and from Jesus Christ." By speaking in this manner he does not divide Christ into two, but he testifies by the one statement and the other that he who is the Word of the Father is also he who has become flesh. He it is who is the "faithful witness," for, as the apostle says, "before Pontius Pilate [he] made the good confession."[30] And the good confession was that he is God and the Lord of all, even though he is become incarnated. To be sure, such a testimony is true, for he calls him "faithful" who is true and worthy of belief.

"The firstborn of the dead." Paul also ascribes this title to him, saying, "who is the first fruits, the firstborn of the dead."[31] They call him the "firstborn of the dead" since he initiated the general resurrection and "has renewed for us a new and living way" (namely, the resurrection of the dead) "through the veil, that is, through his flesh," as it is written.[32] For all of those who rose again from the dead before the coming of the Lord were again handed over to death, for that was not the true resurrection but merely a reprieve from the time of death. Therefore, none of those people is named the "firstborn from the dead," but the Lord is indeed called this, since he is become the source and cause of the true resurrection and, as it were, has become a certain first fruits of the resurrection of people, becoming such as they were and going forth as from a certain bridal chamber out of death to life. In his letter to the Romans the holy Paul was speaking only of the Lord when he wrote, "knowing that Christ being raised from the dead will never die again; death no longer has dominion over him; the death he died he died to sin, once for all, but the life he lives he lives to God."[33]

"The ruler of the kings of the earth." Daniel also spoke of this to Babylon: "until you know that the Most High rules the kingdom of heaven and gives it to whomever he thinks fit."[34] Therefore, Christ also governs all things

[25]Jn 1:1. [26]1 Jn 1:1. [27]Ps 119:91 (118:91 LXX). [28]Ps 103:21 (102:21 LXX). [29]1 Tim 5:21. [30]1 Tim 6:13. [31]Col 1:18. Oecumenius reads ἀπαρχή ("first fruits") instead of ἀρχή ("beginning"). [32]Heb 10:20. [33]Rom 6:9-10. [34]Dan 5:21.

in heaven. However, this present passage speaks of those on the earth, although later the text reveals that he rules also the ranks of the saints in heaven.

[1:5-6] ***To him who loved us and has washed[35] us from our sins by his blood and made for us a kingdom, priests to God and his prophets, to him be glory and power forever and ever. Amen.***

The arrangement of this saying moves backward from what is last to that which is first. It says, "to him who loved us be glory and power." For how did he not love us "who gave himself as a ransom" for the life of the world?[36] [And to him be glory] "who has washed us from our sins by his blood." For he took "the bond that stood against us with its demands and nailed it to the wood of his cross,"[37] paying in full for our sins with his own death and setting us free from transgressions by his blood and healing our disobedience by his submission to death, even the death of the cross.

"He made for us a kingdom." What benefit is there for us to become "priests to God and his prophets"? That people might be made worthy of these things he makes certain for us the coming kingdom and in the present time procures for us unspeakable glory. This is even greater and more marvelous and noteworthy than the divine gift of his washing away our sins by his own blood, that we who brought nothing for such a gift would be made priests of God and prophets.

[1:7] ***Behold, he is coming on the clouds of heaven, and every eye will see him, every one who pierced him, and all tribes of the earth will wail on account of him. Even so. Amen.***

The Lord said in the Gospel of Mark that he would come on the clouds of heaven, saying, "And the powers in heaven will be shaken, and then they will see the Son of man coming in clouds with great power and glory."[38] For I think that he will come again with a cloud, just as it is written of him in Acts that as he was going up into heaven on the day of his ascension, a "cloud took him out of their sight."[39] I think that the divine Scripture figuratively calls the holy angels "clouds" because of their lightness and sublimity and movement in the air, as though it were saying, "The Lord will come, being carried and attended by his holy angels." And the prophet speaks of him in this way: "And he rode on cherubs and he flew; he flew on the wings of the wind."[40]

And it says, "Every eye will see him, every one who pierced him." At his second and glorious coming, Christ will not come as though he were hiding in a corner. Nor will he come secretly as he did in his previous coming, when he visited the world in the flesh. The prophet showed that this coming would be hidden when he said, "He will come down as rain on a fleece and as raindrops that fall on the earth."[41] He will rather come openly and visibly, so that he will be seen by every eye, even by those who are especially sinful and impious. And of these, those who maltreated or pierced him must be regarded as a class of their own.

"And all tribes of the earth will wail on account of him," namely, those peoples who have remained in unbelief and have not come to bend their neck to his saving yoke. The words "on account of him" indicate that this grief will be at his appearance and coming. Then, to show that this will without question occur, it adds, "Even so, Amen," as though to say, "These things will happen precisely and indisputably." For just as among the Greeks the word "even so" gives an assent to that which is to happen, so also the word "amen" among the Hebrews.

[35]The text of Oecumenius reads λούσαντι ("wash"), not λύσαντι ("loose"). [36]See 1 Tim 2:6. [37]See Col 2:14. [38]Mk 13:25-26. [39]Acts 1:9. [40]Ps 18:10 (17:10 LXX). [41]Ps 72:6 (71:6 LXX).

[1:8] ***"I am the Alpha and the Omega," says the Lord God, who is and who was and who is to come, the Almighty, and the Lord of creation.***

"Alpha" indicates the beginning; "omega" indicates the end. Therefore, he is saying, "I am the first and the last," showing through "first" that God is without beginning and showing through "last" that God is without end. Since nothing exists among people that is without beginning or without end, he uses the terms "first" and "last," which are common among us, rather than "without beginning" and "without end." God also speaks of this through Isaiah, saying, "I, God, the first, and to that which is yet to come, I am."[42] He calls God "Almighty" and "Lord of the creation," not only of that which is sensible but also of that which is intellectual.

[1:9] ***I, John, your brother and a fellow participant in the tribulations and kingdom and patient endurance.***

He wrote to the faithful who for the sake of the word and the proclamation of Christ were suffering much at the hands of those who persecute the pious. For this reason, he calls himself a "participant in Jesus," not only of the sufferings and endurance but also of the kingdom of God, which the sufferings here on behalf of the word benefit.

[1:9] ***I was on the island called Patmos on account of the word of God and the testimony of Jesus.***

"For the sake of Jesus," it says, for this is what "in Jesus" means. And "on account of his word and testimony" to which I gave witness by proclaiming his gospel, I was exiled on Patmos. In his *Chronikon Kanon* Eusebius reports that he suffered under Domitian the emperor.[43]

Then, he says, while still on the island . . .

[1:10] ***I was in the spirit on the Lord's Day.***

When he says, "I was in the spirit," it indicates that the vision that he saw was not a material one that he perceived with fleshly ears and eyes but rather with prophetic ears and eyes. Isaiah also spoke of such spiritual auditions: "In the morning he has given him to know; in the morning he has given me an ear to hear; and the teaching of the Lord opens my ears."[44]

[1:10-11] ***And I heard a loud voice like a trumpet, saying to me: "John, write what you see in a book and send it to the seven churches—to Ephesus and to Smyrna and to Pergamum and to Thyatira and to Sardis and to Philadelphia and to Laodicea."***

There are many churches in Asia. However, he is commanded to write to those that were taught by him and had already received the faith of Christ. For why would anyone exhort those who were unbelievers and had departed from the word of salvation?

[1:12-16] ***And I turned to see the voice that was speaking with me, and turning, I saw seven golden lampstands, and in the midst of the seven lampstands, one like a son of man, clothed with a long robe and girded around the breasts with a golden girdle. His head and his hair were like white wool, like snow; and his eyes were like a flame of fire; and his feet were like burnished bronze refined in a furnace, and his voice was as the sound of many waters; and he had in his right hand seven stars; and from his mouth issued a sharp, two-edged sword; and his face was as the sun shining in full strength.***

As he will explain a little later, the seven

[42]Is 41:4 (LXX). [43]Eusebius *Chron.* (PG 19:552). [44]Is 50:4-5.

lampstands are the seven churches to which he is commanded to write. He calls them lampstands since they carry in themselves the "illumination of the glory of Christ."[45] He did not call them lamps but lampstands, for a lampstand itself does not possess the capacity to shine, but it bears that which is capable of illumination. Likewise, Christ mentally illuminates his churches. For just as the holy apostle exhorts those who have received the faith, "be as lights in the world, holding fast the word of life"[46]—for indeed the lamp does not in itself possess light, but it is receptive of that light that comes to it—so also here the Evangelist saw the churches as lampstands and not as lights. For it is said concerning Christ, "You shine forth marvelously from the everlasting mountains,"[47] probably meaning to the angelic powers; and again he says to the Father, "Send out your light and your truth";[48] and again, "the light of your countenance, O Lord."[49] And so, those who partake of the divine light are described on the one hand as lights and on the other hand as lampstands. He says that the lampstands are golden on account of the value and excellence of those made worthy to receive the divine light.

"In the midst of the seven lampstands," he says, "there was one like a Son of man." If the Lord himself promised that he would indwell and accompany the souls of those who received him, is it not to be expected that he would be seen in the midst of the lampstands? He calls him "Son of man" who for our sakes "humbled himself to the form of a servant,"[50] namely, Christ, who became "fruit of the womb," as the holy psalmist says,[51] that is, of the womb of the unwedded and ever-virgin Mary. For since Mary was a human being and our sister, it is appropriate that God the Word, conceived virginally according to the flesh, is also called "Son of man." And he has spoken with precision, for he did not say "Son of man" but "like a Son of man," since Christ is also God and Lord of all, the Immanuel. The vision therefore reveals his complex nature, delineating his form according to his activities and powers. At first it clothes him with a priestly form, since the long robe and the girdle present a priestly image. In the person of God the Father it was said to him, "You are a priest forever after the order of Melchizedek,"[52] and the apostle calls Christ "the high priest and apostle of our confession,"[53] since as one who functions as a priest, he offers our confession of faith to himself and as well as to the Father and to the Spirit. He is also clothed in a golden girdle, since priests customarily wear a girdle made from embroidered cloth.

And it was necessary to make clear the distinction between the servants and the master and between the Law that was in shadow and the reality that is in the New Testament. "His head," it says, "and his hairs were like white wool, like snow," for the mystery of Christ was new at its appearance, although to be sure it is eternal according to good pleasure.[54] The holy apostle has written concerning this: "the mystery which was hidden from the ages and generations, which has now been revealed to his saints, to those whom he willed."[55] Therefore, the whiteness of his head, which is compared with wool and with snow, represents the antiquity of the mystery, such as relates to the good pleasure of God. "And his eyes," it says, "were as a flame of fire." The flame indicates either his radiance, since Christ is indeed a light and calls himself this, saying, "I am the light and the truth,"[56] or it represents his fearsomeness and the threats he makes against the seven

[45]2 Cor 4:4. [46]Phil 2:15-16. [47]See Ps 76:4 (75:4 LXX). [48]Ps 43:3 (42:3 LXX). [49]Ps 44:3 (43:3 LXX). [50]Phil 2:7-8. [51]Ps 127:3 (126:3 LXX). [52]Heb 5:6. [53]Heb 3:1. [54]"Good pleasure" (εὐδοκία) expressed the will of God for humankind in the incarnation of the Son. The Son was made man "according to the good pleasure" of the Father (Irenaeus *Haer.* 1.9.3; Athanasius *C. Ar.* 2.11). This "good pleasure," however, also characterized the eternal relation of the Father toward the Son (Athanasius *C. Ar.* 3.64-65 [NPNF 2 4:428-30]). [55]Col 1:26-27. [56]Jn 8:12; 14:6.

churches to which the visions of the revelations are being sent, since they are not perfectly following his laws.

"His feet," he says, "are like burnished bronze." They say that the bronze mined in the mountains of Lebanon, although pure naturally, becomes even more pure when the moderate amount of impurity in it is refined in a furnace. This image symbolizes the permanence and immovability, along with the brightness and eminence, of the faith in Christ that is firmly established. For Christ is called a "rock" by the apostle,[57] and by Isaiah he is called a "precious stone" in the foundations of Zion.[58] Or, by "burnished bronze" he means that incense that has the appearance of bronze and that the students of physicians are wont to call "strong."[59] When this is being burned it is sweet-smelling, and the burning furnace is an indication of that which is being burned, which is the foundation of the evangelical proclamation—for the feet are the foundation of the rest of the body—and this foundation is Christ.[60] For indeed, he is sweet-smelling and by a spiritual fragrance enchants that which is in heaven and on the earth. Paul also calls Christ a "foundation," writing in his first letter to the Corinthians, "like a skilled master builder I laid a foundation, and another man is building on it; let each man take care how he builds upon it, for no other foundation can anyone lay than that which is laid, which is Jesus Christ."[61] And the bride in the Canticles bears witness that Christ is fragrant when, having sampled his fragrance, she says, "the smell of your ointment is beyond all aromas," and says again, "your name is oil poured out."[62] Moreover, the Lord presents himself as sweet-smelling in the words that he speaks to the bride: "I am a flower of the field, a lily of the valleys."[63] What then? Did not also Paul, who became sweet-smelling from his communion with Christ, say, "for we are the aroma of Christ"[64] and again "and to him who reveals to us the fragrance of the knowledge of him"?[65]

"His voice," it says, "was as the sound of many waters." This is an appropriate way of speaking. For how would his voice reach into all the earth and the proclamation concerning him into the corners of the world[66] unless it were audible, and not merely by virtue of the perceptible voice but also by the power of the proclamation? "And he has," he says, "seven stars in his right hand." He interprets these stars a little later saying that they are the angels of the seven churches. Of these angels Gregory spoke in the presence of the bishops: "To the presiding angels, for I believe, as John teaches in Revelation, that each church has its own guardian."[67] I think that he calls the holy angels stars because of the abundant brightness of Christ that they have in themselves. They are in his right hand, for they were found worthy of this most exalted status before God and, as it were, they rest on the hand of God.

"From his mouth issued a sharp, two-edged sword." The holy David said to the Lord, "Gird your sword on your thigh, O mighty One."[68] He had not yet at that time given to us the evangelical precepts, the transgression of which was destruction. Therefore, the place where the sword was put suggests a delay of punishment, for it was not prepared for slaughter.[69] But now the sword comes forth from the mouth, the image showing that those who are disobedient to the evangelical commandments will bring on their souls the threat of being cut into two by the sword, which the Lord indeed mentions in the Gospels.[70] The apostle also reveals this when he says, "For the word of

[57]1 Cor 10:4. [58]Is 28:16. [59]The Greek is ἄρρενα, which indicates that which is masculine. [60]That the feet are like burnished bronze, which here is interpreted as incense, allows Oecumenius to combine the images of sweet-smelling incense and foundation and refer both to Christ. [61]1 Cor 3:10-11. [62]Song 1:3. [63]Song 2:1. [64]2 Cor 2:15. [65]2 Cor 2:14. [66]See Ps 19:4 (18:5 LXX); Rom 10:18. [67]Gregory of Nazianzus *Or.* 42.9 (NPNF 2 7:389). Gregory presented this oration to the assembled bishops at the Council of Constantinople (381). [68]Ps 45:3 (44:3 LXX). [69]A sword in its sheath is not ready to kill. [70]See Mt 24:51.

God is living and active and is sharper than a two-edged sword."[71] He is clearly indicating that he is making a threat against the disobedient. And so, while the sword is said by John to be sharp, it is said by Paul to be very sharp.

"His face," he says, "was like the sun shining in full strength." Well does he say "like the sun," for according to the prophet Malachi the Lord is the "sun of righteousness."[72] However, lest you think that the brightness of the face of Christ, who enlightens every person coming into the world,[73] is that of a luminous body and enlightens by way of the senses, he adds "in full strength." It is as though he said, "The light of Christ is intellectual and is effectual by power, illuminating the eyes of the soul, not those of the body."

[1:17-19] ***When I saw him, I fell at his feet as though dead. But he laid his right hand on me, saying, "I am the first and the last, and the living one, and I was dead, and behold I am alive forevermore, and I have the keys of death and hades. Therefore, write what you see, what is and what is to take place hereafter."***

When the holy prophets receive a vision, it is common that they are astounded and display human weakness since divine realities excel those of mortals and surpass them by incomparable differences. We see this reaction in Joshua, the son of Nun, when he saw the commander of the army of the Lord,[74] and in Daniel, when in the visions given to him he saw the "man of desires."[75] And so the Evangelist, who was astounded at the sight, writes, "I fell at his feet as though dead." But "he laid his right hand on me, saying, 'Fear not.' " The holy John would not have been strong enough to survive his astonishment had the saving right hand of the Son of God not touched him, which by mere touch had accomplished so many wonderful things. And he said to me, "I am the first and the last," which is as though he had said, "I am he who for the salvation of you all sojourned among you in the flesh at the end of times, even though I am the First and the Firstborn of all creation. How is it possible that anything evil transpire from my appearance? For if I who am living and am the wellspring of life became dead for you, and trampled death underfoot and lived again, how is it possible that you who are living become dead on account of me and my appearance? And if 'I have the keys of death and of hades,' so that I make dead and make alive those whom I wish, and that I will bring down to hades and bring up again, as it is written concerning me, and that, as the prophet says, 'the ways of escape from death' are mine,[76] I would not have sent my own worshipers and disciples to an untimely death." Therefore, since John was not to die, he says, "Write what you have seen, both those things that are and those things that are going to be." The words "that are" indicate both past and contemporary events; the phrase "that are going to be" indicates events that are yet in the future. For of the events revealed to the saint, some had already occurred, which, although they had already happened, yet had not gone into nothingness, and, therefore, he speaks also of them as "things that are." But the things that were and that were in the future, the book shows as it goes along.

[1:20] ***"The mystery of the seven stars that you saw in my right hand, and the seven golden lampstands, the seven stars are the angels of the churches and the seven lampstands are the seven churches."***

Since he made the significance of the stars and lampstands clear to him, it remained to speak to each of the churches as was necessary. Therefore, that he might bring accusation to that church that was walking utterly outside

[71]Heb 4:12. [72]Mal 4:2. [73]Jn 1:9. [74]Josh 5:3-15. [75]Dan 9:23; 10:11, 19. [76]See Ps 68:20-22 (67:20-22 LXX).

the divine purpose and praise the uprightness of those churches who to some extent were preserving the law of the gospel even as he corrected those who were stumbling in other matters, Christ, who desires that all be saved and who wills that all become heirs and partakers of his benefits, reveals to the holy Evangelist that word and teaching that he is commanded to send as the appropriate medicine to each of the churches. To him be glory forever and ever. Amen.

Second Discourse

The first task of my discourses and interpretations is completed. Now another purpose must gain our attention, namely, to show what exhortation is given to the churches. Therefore, he is commanded to write first to the church at Ephesus, since it is preeminent in all of Asia. He writes in the following manner:

[2:1-7] ***"To the angel of the church in Ephesus write: The words of him who holds the seven stars in his right hand, who walks in the midst of the seven golden lampstands. I know your works and your toil and your patient endurance, and that you cannot bear evil men but have tested those who call themselves apostles but are not, and you have found them false. You have patient endurance and have borne up for my name's sake and have not grown weary. But I have this against you, that you have left your first love. Remember, therefore, from where you have fallen and repent and do the works you did at first in righteousness. If you do not, I will come to you and move your lampstand from its place, should you not repent. But you have this good thing, that you hate the works of the Nicolaitans, which I also hate. He who has an ear, let him hear what the Spirit says to the churches. To him who hears, I will give him to eat from the tree of life, which is in the paradise of my God."***

He speaks periphrastically of the church in Ephesus as an "angel of the church in Ephesus." For the guardian angel of the church had not committed sin, so that it required the admonition to repent. He is rather most holy and for this reason exists at the right hand of the Lord, giving as proof of this the purity of his nature and flashes as of light. Moreover, what need would there be for him who is conversing with the Evangelist to say, "write to him [the angel]," since the holy angel was present and was listening to the conversation (being on the right hand of the one speaking)? And, finally, the saint himself interprets the vision seen by him and says, "He who has ears, let him hear what the Spirit is saying to the churches." He did not say "to the angels of the churches" but "to the churches." And so also in the remaining interpretations you will find the words "write the following to the angel of the church," not that he is speaking about the angel but about the church.

Now, what is he commanded to write to the church in Ephesus? He says, "The words of him who holds the seven stars in his right hand, who walks in the midst of the seven golden lampstands." This is as though he had said, "The words of him who honors, governs and upholds the holy angels in heaven"—these are the seven stars—"and humankind on the earth"—these are the seven lampstands, as I said above. He said also through the prophet that he walks in the midst of those who worship him: "I will dwell among them and walk in their midst."[1]

He says, "I know your works and your toil and your patient endurance." That is, "none of the good deeds you have done has escaped me who 'has formed your hearts individually and understands all your deeds.' "[2] Then he says, "You are not able to bear evil men," for you have acquired the habit of hating evil, and "you have tested those who call themselves

Second Discourse [1]Lev 26:12. [2]Ps 33:15 (32:15 LXX).

apostles but are not, and you have found them to be false." Those in Ephesus fulfilled the divine command that they should not believe every spirit but test the spirits to see whether they are from God.[3] Therefore, they tested those who preached the gospel among them, and through this testing they found some to be false apostles who were proclaiming counterfeit doctrines. He speaks of those who were disciples of Cerinthus, who were contemporary with the Evangelist and were proclaiming profane teachings.[4]

He says, "You have patient endurance and have borne up for my name's sake, and you have not grown weary." This is most properly said, for it is said elsewhere, "Bear one another's burdens, and so fulfill the law of God."[5] "But I have this against you," he says, "that you have abandoned the love you had at first. Remember then from where you have fallen, repent and do in righteousness the works you did at first." He means, just as your good works have not escaped my notice, so I am also aware that you have ceased your love toward those in need. Return, therefore, to your previous charity, which was taught by me but which you have to some extent forsaken. "If you do not return," he says, "to the place from which you have fallen, I will come to you and remove your lampstand from its place, if you do not repent." By the words "I will come to you," he does not suggest any movement that involves a change of position, since God fills all things. Rather, he indicates, as it were, a change from his longsuffering to punishment. He speaks of the removal of the lampstands, that is, of the churches as his own abandonment of them, which, when it comes against the sinners, brings them into every kind of distress and trouble, so that they might even say, "My eye is troubled with anger"[6] and "my heart is troubled within me."[7]

He says, "Yet this good thing you have, you hate the works of the Nicolaitans, which I also hate." He has mentioned their transgression in between mention of their two accomplishments. In this way he tempers his censure in the middle by words of praise that come at the beginning and at the end, and so no one is overcome by too great a grief. This Nicolaus, of whom the passage speaks, was a blasphemous and disgusting heresiarch, and so those in Ephesus who avoided those who were deceived by him and were advocates of his evil works found praise from Christ.[8] After this warning, the Evangelist adds his own words: "He who has an ear," that is, who is obedient by obeying the divine precepts, "let him hear what the Spirit says to the churches." He says "the Spirit," either because the visions of revelation are effected by the Spirit, or he calls Christ "spirit," in that he is and is known to be God, just as he does not fail to be called "Son of man" in that he is and is known to be man. For the Godhead is said to be all together spirit, as the Lord himself says in speaking to the Samaritan woman: "God is spirit, and it is necessary that those who worship him worship in spirit and in truth."[9] What, then, does the Spirit say? "To him who conquers, I will grant to eat of the tree of life, which is in the paradise of my God." The saying is figurative. By "tree of life" he means the blessed and everlasting life that the saints shall enjoy in the kingdom of God, which here he calls "paradise." Of this kingdom, he says, those are worthy who here are victors over present temptations and avengers of the enemy. And that the Lord said "of my God" ought to scandalize no one. For expressions of humility are proper to his economy in the flesh. For indeed, even in the Gospel he said, "I go to my Father and your

[3]1 Jn 4:1. [4]Cerinthus was an early Gnostic teacher in Asia Minor who claimed that the spiritual Christ descended on the man Jesus at his baptism and left him before the passion. For an early description of Cerinthus, see Irenaeus *Haer.* 1.26.1 (ANF 1:351-52). [5]Gal 6:2. [6]Ps 31:9 (30:9 LXX). [7]Ps 55:4 (54:4 LXX); 143:4 (142:4 LXX). [8]For the Nicolaitans, see below on Rev 2:12-17, 20-25. [9]Jn 4:24.

Father, to my God and your God."[10] These are the messages that were sent to the church at Ephesus.

[2:8-11] ***"And to the angel of the church in Smyrna write: The words of the first and the last, who was dead and came to life. I know your tribulation and your poverty [but you are rich] and the blasphemy of those who say that they are Jews and are not, but are a synagogue of Satan. Do not fear what you are about to suffer. Behold, the devil is about to throw some of you into prison, that you may be tested, and for ten days you will have temptation. Be faithful to death, and I will give you the crown of life. He who has an ear, let him hear what the Spirit says to the churches. He who conquers shall not be hurt by the second death."***

The Lord calls himself "first" because of the essence of his deity but calls himself "last" because of the incarnation and the economy of the flesh. "Who was dead," he says, "and came to life." He who came into the trial of death, he says, by death put death to death. "I know your tribulation and your poverty"—indeed, you do not speak, as do the wicked Jews, who say, "Why have we fasted, and you did not notice it? Why have we humbled ourselves, and you paid no heed?"[11] But "you are rich," he says, since you have Christ as a wealthy patron, although indeed for us he became poor, "taking the form of a slave,"[12] "and the blasphemy" of those falsely called Jews. *Judah* means "confession," and *Israel* means "those who spiritually see God." Therefore, those who are true Jews and the spiritual Israel would be those who confess Christ. "For he is not a Jew who is one outwardly, nor is the circumcision that is outwardly and physical" pleasing to God, as Paul says: "Rather, he is a Jew who is one inwardly, and circumcision is a matter of the heart," not of the flesh.[13] For that reason, those who have remained Jews in unbelief are a blasphemous synagogue, under the leadership of Satan.

"Do not fear what you are about to suffer. Behold, the devil is about to throw some of you into prison, that you may be tested, and for ten days you will have temptation." Indeed, through the inspiration of the devil people wreak evil on the pious. However, God acquiesces in this, so that through trials he might make them more approved. But be of good courage, he says, for your tribulation will be of short duration and quickly over. "Be faithful to death, and I will give you a crown of life." This is a true saying, for it is also said, "He who endures to the end will be saved."[14] To be sure, this is not so of the cowardly and of those who show weakness in battles. "He who has an ear, let him hear what the Spirit says to the churches. He who conquers will not be hurt by the second death." This is a very apt statement. For while all, the just and the sinner alike, are subject to the first death, which is the separation of the soul from the body, so that the divine judgment might be enforced, "You are earth and to earth you will return,"[15] those who have overcome temptations should not be harmed by the second death, which is the result of sin and which the Lord specified when he said, "Let the dead bury their own dead."[16]

[2:12-17] ***"And to the angel of the church in Pergamum write: The words of him who has the sharp two-edged sword. I know where you dwell, where Satan's throne is; you hold fast my name and you did not deny my faith even in the days of Antipas, my faithful witness, who was killed among you, where Satan dwells. But I have a few things against you. You have there some who hold the teaching of Balaam, who taught Balak to put a stumbling block before the sons of Israel, that they might eat food sacrificed to idols and practice fornication. So you also have some who hold the teaching of***

[10]Jn 20:17. [11]Is 58:3. [12]Phil 2:7. [13]Rom 2:28-29. [14]Mt 10:22. [15]Gen 3:19. [16]Mt 8:22.

the Nicolaitans. Repent. If not, I will come to you soon and war against them with the sword of my mouth. He who has an ear, let him hear what the Spirit says to the churches. To him who conquers, I will give a white stone, and on the stone a new name that no one knows except him who receives it."[17]

He says, "Write to the church at Pergamum: I, who bear a sword in my mouth, say to you, that I shall avenge those who transgress my commandments." For the sword in the mouth indicates the imminent danger of those who disobey the divine decrees. "You dwell," he says, "near the throne of Satan." For the whole of Asia is full of idols, and that is especially so of Pergamum. "But," he says, "although you reside in such a place, yet you have kept my faith inviolate and have not succumbed to any pressure of the many toward evil. Rather, you speak against them even on their idolatrous feast days, even as did 'my faithful witness' who spoke out boldly in my name. Since this came to the attention of persons plotting against you, you came near to death for my sake; yet you preserved your integrity." However, since blame touches even the most holy, and "we all make many mistakes," as the Scriptures say,[18] he says, "I have a complaint even against persons such as yourselves. You have there some who hold the teaching of Balaam, who taught Balak to put a stumbling block before the sons of Israel, that they might eat food sacrificed to idols and practice fornication. So you also have some who hold the teaching of the Nicolaitans."[19] That "he taught Balak" shows that he became as a teacher to him. To be sure, the story of Balaam and Balak is clearly set down and reported in Numbers, a book written by the most wise Moses.[20] Josephus narrates that on the advice of Balaam, the Midianites were sent against Israel to entice them to fornication and apostasy from God.[21] And so he says, you have persons from the Nicolaitans who do such things, but you do not remove them from you. Then he says, "Repent. If not, I will come to you soon and war against them with the sword of my mouth." Oh, the depth of the richness and wisdom and goodness of God! For he did not say, I will come to you and "war against you," but I will "war against them," that is to say, against the Nicolaitans. For he spared those in Pergamum who were faithful and pious. "He who has an ear, let him hear what the Spirit says to the churches. To him who conquers, I will give the mysterious hidden manna." He speaks periphrastically, intending to say, I will give to him the fullness of the spiritual gifts of the future age. "And I will give to him a white stone," that is, a stone indicating victory and bright with glory, "and on the stone a new name that no one knows except him who receives it." For it is said, "What eye has not seen, nor ear heard, nor has come into the heart of man, that has God prepared for those who love him."[22]

[2:18-29] ***"And to the angel of the church at Thyatira write: The words of the Son of God, who has eyes like a flame of fire, and whose feet are like burnished bronze. I know your works, your love and faith and service and your patient endurance, and that your latter works exceed the first. But I have this against you, that you tolerate the woman Jezebel, who calls herself a prophetess and is teaching and beguil-***

[17]The reference to "hidden manna" is absent here, although Oecumenius knows of it and refers to it in his discussion below. [18]Jas 3:2. [19]Irenaeus claims that the Nicolaitans were the followers of Nicolaus, one of the Seven appointed by the apostles in Jerusalem (*Haer.* 1.26.3; Acts 6:5). This would assume that Nicolaus fell into heresy. Clement of Alexandria claims that Nicolaus promoted an ascetic way of life by saying, "One must misuse the flesh." His followers, however, forced the meaning of this saying to imply that one might engage in promiscuous behavior (*Strom.* 2.4-5). The Venerable Bede agrees with Clement and adds the information that the Nicolaitans held to pagan ideas about the beginning of the world (*Explanatio apocalypsis.* 2.12-17). Oecumenius makes no mention of Nicolaus himself. [20]Num 22:1–24:25. [21]Josephus *Ant.* 4.126-40. [22]1 Cor 2:9.

ing my servants to practice fornication and to eat food sacrificed to idols. I gave her time to repent, but she refuses to repent of her fornication. Behold, I will throw her on a sickbed, and those who commit adultery with her I will throw into the great tribulation, unless they repent of her works; and I will kill her children with death. And all the churches shall know that I am he who searches mind and heart, and I will give to each of you according to your works. But to the rest of you in Thyatira, who do not hold to this teaching, who do not know the deep things of Satan, as they say, I will not lay on you any further burden; only hold fast what you have, until I come. He who conquers and who keeps my works until the end, I will give him power over the nations, and he shall rule them with a rod of iron, as when earthen pots are broken in pieces, even as I myself have received from my Father; and I will give him the morning star. He who has an ear, let him hear what the Spirit says to the churches."

He who is speaking with the Evangelist further clarifies his title. He says, "The words of the Son of God, who has eyes like flames of fire." These words indicate the terrifying threat that he directs against sinners. "Whose feet are as burnished bronze." This suggests either the steadfast immutability of faith in him or the spiritual fragrance of the evangelical teachings, as we suggested above.[23] "I know," he says, "your works and your love and your faith and your service." This is as though he said, "I praise you for your total devotion." He says "I know," rather than "I praise," since he had said to Moses, "I know you beyond all men,"[24] and "the Lord knows the path of the righteous."[25] By "service" he means the succor that one gives to those in need. "Your latter works are more than the first." This shows that as they progressed, they improved in their obedience to the commandments. To show that God alone possesses perfect sinlessness, he says, "I have this against you." And what do I have against you? "That you tolerate the woman Jezebel, who calls herself a prophetess," and you do not throw her out. For in the person of Jezebel, the wife of Ahab, he sees a paradigm for the wickedness of that woman who lived at that time. And she, he says, "who calls herself a prophetess, teaches and deceives" many to commit fornication and to eat food sacrificed to idols. He refers either to physical fornication or to that apostasy from God of which it is said, "And they committed fornication in their works,"[26] and again, "They committed adultery with wood."[27] But the Lord does not wish the death of a sinner but rather her conversion and life, and so he says that he gave to her an opportunity for repentance. But if she does not wish to repent, he says, I will do such and such to her and to those who commit adultery with her, so that all might know that it is I who am God—for it is the prerogative of God to search minds and hearts. For it is said, "It is God who searches the heart and mind."[28] But, indeed, to those who have nothing in common with that adulterous woman, that is, those who are more simple and do not know the deceitful crafts of the evil one—for this is what you say—on you I will place no greater burden, for your simplicity suffices. Only hold fast the teaching that has been handed over to you until my second coming. To him who conquers the evil one "I will give," he says, "power over the nations, and he shall rule them with a rod of iron, as when earthen pots are broken in pieces, even as I myself have received from my Father." In the Gospels this was spoken to those who had managed well the money and the talents that had been entrusted to them—"you will be over ten cities," and to another, "you will be over five cities"[29]—and even to Daniel it was said,

[23]See the comment on Rev 1:15. [24]Ex 33:12, 17 (LXX). [25]Ps 1:6. [26]Ps 106:39 (105:39 LXX). [27]Jer 3:9. [28]Ps 7:9; cf. Jer 17:10. [29]Lk 19:17, 19.

"the kingdom will be given to the saints" of God.[30] These passages make it clear that a certain rule and authority will be granted to the saints as a kind of compensation for those times of lack and want. Therefore, he says, he will govern them with a harsh authority, and, to be sure, those who are disobedient he will crush as though they were clay pots. "And I will give him," he says, "the morning star." He speaks of the Assyrian, namely, of Satan, of whom the prophet speaks, saying, "How has the Day Star, he who rises in the morning, fallen from heaven!"[31] And even now the Lord calls him the "Morning Star." And so, he says, I will make Satan to be subject to my servants. The apostle also made a similar statement: "God will trample Satan quickly under your feet."[32] And in another place it says, "You will tread on the asp and the basilisk, and you will trample on the lion and the dragon."[33]

[3:1-6] ***"And to the angel of the church in Sardis write: The words of him who has the seven spirits of God and the seven stars. I know your works; you have the name of being alive, but you are dead. Be watchful and strengthen what remains and is on the point of death, for I have not found your works perfect in the sight of my God. Remember then how you received and heard; keep that and repent. If you are not watchful, I will come like a thief, and you will not know at what hour I come on you. Yet you have a few names in Sardis who have not soiled their garments; and they walk with me in white, for they are worthy. He who conquers shall be clothed in white garments, and I will not blot his name out of the book of life; and I will confess his name before my Father and before his angels. He who has an ear, let him hear what the Spirit says to the churches."***

I have discussed above[34] the seven stars that he here calls the "spirits of God." But now we must listen to what he says concerning those who live in Sardis. "I know your works," he says, that you possess a name as though you were living a virtuous life according to the will of God, but "you are dead" in sins. For in the holy Scriptures, it is customary that those snared in sins are called dead, as, for example, in this passage from the most wise Paul concerning those who have passed from unbelief to faith in Christ: "And you, although dead in trespasses, he made alive together with Christ."[35] Likewise, the *Shepherd* says that those who go down into the water of baptism are "dead," but those who come up are "living."[36] But, he says, wake up from your slumber of sin and "strengthen what remains and is on the point of death." There still remain among you works and practices that are weak but that have not totally disappeared. Preserve those things that are still alive, even though they are already tending toward death. When he says "strengthen," it is as though he said "make stable and strong that which is loose and in danger of falling into disuse." For, he says, there are no works among you that are done in earnestness; rather, some have died away, and others are increasingly moribund. Remember, therefore, "how you received" the faith and "how you heard" the word concerning the faith, and maintain in life those works that are still alive, and for those that have already died away, "repent." "If you are not watchful," that is, if you are as one waking from the sleep of a lazy stupor, "I will come" to you as one ready to punish, and when you least expect it. The holy apostle spoke similarly concerning others: "When people say, 'There is peace and security,' then sudden destruction will come on them as travail comes on a woman with child."[37] "You have a few names in Sardis,"

[30]Dan 7:27. [31]Is 14:12. [32]Rom 16:20. [33]Ps 91:13 (90:13 LXX). [34]See the comment on Rev 1:16. [35]Eph 2:5. Oecumenius has "you," not "we." [36]Hermas *Sim*. 9.16.4 (ANF 2:49; GCS 48:90). [37]1 Thess 5:3.

he says, "who have not soiled their garments; and they walk with me in white, for they are worthy," and being in the meantime entreated by them, he says, I delay my coming and am longsuffering toward you.

By the garments that have not been soiled he means the bodies of the saints, just as the patriarch Jacob said: "He will wash his robe in wine."[38] And Isaiah said much the same thing: "Why are your garments red as if from a trodden winepress? as one full of trodden grape?"[39] And so the white garment signifies the purity of the body. "He who conquers" the passions, he says, will wear white robes in the age to come, for indeed he has promised in the Gospels that the saints will shine as the sun and the moon.[40] The pure, he says, will be inscribed in the book of those who are living that blessed and eternal life. And the Lord made mention of this inscription in the Gospels when he spoke to his disciples and said, "Do not rejoice that the demons are subject to you; but rejoice that your names are written in heaven."[41]

"And I will confess your name before my Father and his angels." He will confess them as his faithful servants and as house slaves who are well-disposed toward their master, for indeed also in the Gospels he says that whosoever should confess "me before men, him will I also confess before my Father who is in heaven."[42] And that he speaks of the Father and his angels does not suggest that the holy angels are not also his own. For at times he speaks of the angels as the Father's, and at other times he speaks of them as his. For he says in Matthew, then the Son of man "will send out his angels with a loud trumpet sound, and they will gather his elect from the four winds, from one end of heaven to the other."[43]

[3:7-13] ***"And to the angel of the church in Philadelphia write: The words of the holy one, the true one, who has the key of David, who opens and no one shuts and shuts and no one opens. I know your works. Behold, I have set before you an open door—no one is able to shut it—I know that you have but little power, and yet you have kept my word and have not denied my name. Behold, I will make those of the synagogue of Satan who say that they are Jews and are not, but lie—behold, I will make them come and bow down before your feet, and they will know that I have loved you. For you have kept the word of my endurance, and I will keep you from the hour of trial that is coming on the whole world to try those who dwell on the earth. I am coming soon. Hold fast what you have, so that no one may seize your crown. He who conquers, I will make him a pillar in the temple of my God; never shall he go out of it, and I will write on him the name of my God and the name of the city of my God, the new Jerusalem that comes down from my God out of heaven and the new name. He who has an ear, let him hear what the Spirit says to the churches."***

To those in Philadelphia, he says, "Write: the words of the holy one, the true one." The holy One is the Son of God. And the seraphim also bear witness to this when they ascribe the threefold holiness to the one lordship,[44] since he possesses nothing earthly or sinful, and even though the Word became flesh, "he did not sin, nor was any guile found in his mouth," as the prophet Isaiah says.[45] He is said to be "true," for he is, and he truly is what he is said to be. He is said to be God, and this title is not false, for he is truly God, Immanuel, even though the accursed Nestorius does not agree to this.[46] He became man, not because he ceased to be God, but he is truly man, even though Eutyches, hated by God, is displeased

[38]Gen 49:11. [39]Is 63:2-3. [40]See Mt 13:43. [41]Lk 10:20. [42]Mt 10:32. [43]Mt 24:31. [44]Oecumenius is referring to the "holy, holy, holy" of Is 6:3; Rev 4:8. [45]Is 53:9. [46]Condemned at Ephesus in 431, Nestorius was accused of denying the personal identity of the eternal Son of God and of the man born of Mary. The man Jesus was not "hypostatically" one with the Son of God.

with this claim.[47] What he is, he is truly, and there is nothing concerning him that is by way of mere ascription, as the Nestorians say, nor is there anything that is mere appearance and fantasy, as the Eutychians would have it, and also that accursed and despicable race of Manichaeans.[48]

"He who has the key of David." He calls authority a "key." Whoever is entrusted with the key of a house is entrusted with the authority to open and to close it. And this is made quite clear in the Gospels in the promises made to Peter. For Jesus said, "I will give you the keys of the kingdom of heaven," and then immediately he continues, "and whatever you bind on earth shall be bound in heaven, and whatever you loose on earth shall be loosed in heaven."[49] Since the key signifies authority, when he says "he who has the key of David," it is clear that just as David ruled the physical Israel, so in addition to the physical Israel, I also rule the spiritual Israel. However, to be sure, the distinction of authority differs by an incomparable superiority. For what equality does humankind have with God? And this is the good news that the holy angel, Gabriel, proclaimed to the Virgin concerning the Lord: "And the Lord God will give to him the throne of David, his father, and he will rule over the house of Jacob forever; and of his kingdom there will be no end."[50] Therefore, since Christ possessed a likeness to the kingdom of David, it is appropriate that he says "he who has the key of David." Then, remaining with the image of the key, he adds, "who opens and no one shuts, and shuts and no one opens." For "it is God who justifies. Who is to condemn?"[51] Likewise it is God who condemns. Who can justify? For "to open" and "to close" simply mean "to justify" and "to condemn." "I know your works," he says, for they are pious, and "I have given" to you the "open door" of blessings. And he repeats what he had said: "Who opens and no one shuts." And so, no one will close that open door that I have given.

I know, he says, "that you have but little power, and yet you have kept my word and have not denied my name." Philadelphia was a small city and therefore possessed but little power. Nonetheless, by keeping the faith of Christ, it rose above its own strength, as one undaunted to live among those who trouble the faithful. Then, as a reward for their genuine sincerity toward him, he promises that many on the Jewish registry will come to her and accept the faith in Christ. For this is what it means for them to worship at her feet, namely, in the last days to choose to be enrolled in the church, that is, to be a part of the church. And the prophet also joyfully spoke of this: "I have chosen to be thrown aside in the house of my God rather than to dwell in the tents of sinners."[52] Since, therefore, you have in patient suffering preserved my faith, also I "will keep you from the hour of the evil trial." He is speaking of the persecution that occurred against the Christians under the emperor Domitian. As Eusebius reports in his *Ecclesiastical History* and in his *Chronikon Canon*, Domitian was the second persecutor of the Christians after Nero, and it was under this emperor that the holy Evangelist was condemned to live on the tiny and barren island of Patmos.[53]

And, he says, "I am coming soon" in order to help you and lay claim to you. "Hold fast what you have, so that no one may take your crown." And what is it that you are to hold fast? Clearly one's genuine love for the Lord, in which, should you contend to the end, you

[47]Condemned at Chalcedon in 451, Eutyches was accused of denying that after the incarnation the body of Christ was "of the same substance" with ours and that Christ after the incarnation possessed "two natures." [48]The Manichaeans represented a Persian dualism very influential during the fourth and fifth centuries that denied the reality of Christ's humanity. His humanity, they said, existed only in appearance. [49]Mt 16:19. [50]Lk 1:32-33. [51]Rom 8:33-34. [52]Ps 84:10 (83:10 LXX). [53]Eusebius *Hist. eccl.* 3.17–18.1: "Nero's successor in his enmity and hostility toward God"; *Chron.* II (PG 19:551).

will obtain the crown of life. For the victors' prizes go only to those who remain to the end. And I will make him who conquers temptations to rejoice always in the vision of God, for this is what it means to become a pillar of the divine temple. For certainly the pillar would not leave for no reason the place in which it is established.

"And I will write on him the name of my God, and the name of the city of my God, namely, of the heavenly Jerusalem, and the new name." Through these names he reveals the joy of God, the dwelling in the midst of good things and the blessedness that they will have in the coming age. The "new name" has never been heard anywhere, which the saints, who reign with Christ and who are called "friends" and "brethren" and "servants" will obtain. But the new name transcends even these designations. For these names are written in holy Scripture and have been heard by the human ear. But the new name has been unnamed in every place. And that he says "of my God" suggests that he does not deem himself unworthy of the limitations of his condescension or of the humility of his human nature. For if he disdained these things, who would have compelled him to be personally united to the flesh[54] and so to fashion our salvation? To him be glory forever and ever. Amen.

Third Discourse

I have recounted in the second discourse what he prophesied to the six cities, namely, to Ephesus and to Smyrna, to Pergamum and to Thyatira, and to Sardis and Philadelphia. Now I must add what was written also to this city.

[3:14-22] ***"And to the angel of the church in Laodicea write: The words of the Amen, the faithful and true witness, the beginning of the creation of God. I know your works; you are neither cold nor hot. Would that you were cold or hot. So, because you are lukewarm, and neither hot nor cold, I will spew you out of my mouth. You say, I am rich and I have prospered, and I need nothing; but you do not know that you are wretched, pitiable, blind, naked and poor. Therefore, I counsel you to buy from me gold refined by fire, that you may be rich, and new white garments to clothe you and to keep the shame of your nakedness from being seen, and salve to anoint your eyes, that you might see. Those whom I would love, I reprove and chasten; be zealous, therefore, and repent. Behold, I stand at the door and knock; if anyone hears my voice and opens the door, I will come in to him and eat with him and he with me. He who conquers, I will grant him to sit on my throne, as I myself conquered and sat down with my Father on his throne. He who has an ear, let him hear what the Spirit says to the churches."***

"The words of the Amen." This is equivalent to the phrase "the words of the true One," which we discussed above.[1] "Amen" means "yes," and in him there is a yes, but there is no no in anything that is said concerning him. Also the phrase "the faithful witness" was discussed above,[2] and it would be verbose to speak of this a second time.

"The beginning of the creation of God," he says. Most likely, that Arian gang of Christ fighters would adduce this passage as though through these words the Son was rendered a creature. But let us not accept these impious words of theirs. Rather, it must be considered whether in any other Scripture such a view is advanced, so that someone might make a judgment by comparing like with like. Writing to the Colossians, the wise apostle spoke of the Son: "Who is the first fruit, the firstborn of all creation."[3] He did not say "first-created."

[54]Σαρκὶ καθ' ὑπόστασιν ἑνωθῆναι. This phraseology indicates that Oecumenius followed Cyril of Alexandria in his Christology.
Third Discourse [1]See the comments on Rev 3:7. [2]See the comments on Rev 1:5. [3]Col 1:15.

And so also the prophet says, "From the womb before the morning star, I begot you,"[4] not "I created you." And so also Solomon said: "Before all the hills, he begets me."[5] In his treatise *Concerning the Son*, among other holy sentiments Gregory interpreted the passage "The Lord created me as the beginning of his ways"[6] to refer to the body of the Lord with its rational soul, but the language "he begets" to the divinity.[7] Since all these witnesses claim as dogmatic truth the "generation" of the only Word and Son but not his "creation," what then do these words, "the beginning of the creation of God," mean? Nothing other than that he who possesses the beginning in all things is the "ruler" of the creation of God. For since the Father made all things through the Son, rightfully does he who is the creator and maker of all things and who brought all things from nonbeing into being rule those things made by him.

"I know your works," he says, "you are neither cold nor hot." One who is fervent in the Spirit is hot, for the holy apostle speaks of those who are "fervent in the Spirit."[8] Likewise, one who lacks the power and indwelling of the Holy Spirit is cold. But you, he says, "are lukewarm." He calls that person lukewarm who in baptism received the communion of the Holy Spirit but has quenched that grace through sloth and attention to temporal matters. And so, this divine directive: "Do not quench the Spirit."[9] "It were better were you cold or hot, but you are lukewarm." Would that you were either hot, aglow by the work of the Spirit, or totally cold, unbaptized and utterly void of the Spirit's grace, but not lukewarm! For the person whose mind has the fire of the Spirit comes to maturity, since the senses have been trained to distinguish that which is good from that which is evil, and that person is spiritual. And that person who has never received the grace of the Spirit yet may hope at some time to receive it and so is not counted among the hopeless. But that person who is lukewarm is moribund and moving toward death and risks losing both baptism and the previous zeal. "I will spew you out of my mouth," he says. Of necessity he uses the metaphor of lukewarm water. For as those knowledgeable in medicine say, a large amount of lukewarm water induces vomiting in the one who drinks it. And so, to those having difficulty in vomiting, they give lukewarm water to swallow and in this way cause vomiting to occur. He speaks as though to say, I am going to ban you from the family of my household.

And what is the reason for this situation? You place your hope, he says, in the uncertainty of riches and choke the gift of God as though it were among thorns. For you did not listen to him who said, "Should wealth increase, do not set your heart on it."[10] He calls "riches" anything that is earthly and temporary. You do not know that "you are poor and naked" of those spiritual realities that endure. "I counsel you," therefore, "to buy gold refined in fire, that you may be rich." The prophet teaches what that gold is which is refined by the fire of the Spirit when he says, "The words of the Lord are pure words, silver refined by fire, proven in an earthen furnace and purified seven times."[11] In this way he spoke of the proclamation of the gospel. And therefore he gives this advice: seek "from me" that which is able to make you wise and cause you to live near to God. For one who possesses this will be aglow in virtue and will be cleansed in soul and body. This is the meaning of the new, white garments.

And buy from me "salve to anoint your eyes, that you might see." Jeremiah spoke reproachfully to some who were blind concerning the spiritual light of the Lord and said, "Behold,

[4]Ps 110:3 (109:3 LXX). [5]Prov 8:25. [6]Prov 8:22. [7]Gregory of Nazianzus *Or.* 30.2 (NPNF 2 7:310). [8]Rom 12:11. [9]1 Thess 5:19. [10]Ps 62:10 (61:11 LXX). [11]Ps 12:6 (11:6 LXX).

neither your eyes nor your heart is whole."[12] And so he advises that they undertake the cure of repentance for such blindness, just as the barren fig tree received improvement through the application of manure and inexpensive treatments.

"Those whom I love," he says, "I reprove and chastise." Oh, the superabundant greatness of the love of Christ! He promises to love those who are such as the passage describes. Therefore, when he reproves and chastises, he is eager to improve their works and bring repentance to those who have sinned. "Behold," he says, "I stand at the door and knock. If anyone hears my voice and opens the door, I will come in to him and dine with him and he with me." Here the Lord reveals his own humble and peaceful nature. The devil "with hatchet and hammer" smashes the doors of those who do not receive him, as the prophet said,[13] but the Lord even now in the Song of Songs says to the bride, "Open to me, my sister, my bride."[14] And should someone open to him, he will come in, but if not, he will go away. That supper that is with the Lord signifies the reception of the holy mysteries.[15]

To one who conquers the enemy, he says, "I will grant him to sit on my throne," that is, he shall reign with me. The wise Paul also says, "If we suffer [with him], we will also reign with him."[16] As I myself conquered, he says, and reign with my Father. The Lord speaks this way also in the Gospels: "Be of good cheer, I have overcome the world."[17]

[4:1-3] ***After this I looked, and lo, an open door in heaven! And the first voice, which I heard speaking to me like a trumpet said, "Come up here, and I will show you what must take place after this." At once I was in the Spirit, and lo, a throne stood in heaven, and on the throne one seated who appeared like an emerald.***[18]

Obviously there is not in heaven a real door that is closed and opened from time to time. But it appeared that way to the Evangelist, so that he might see realities that are truly transcendent. For whenever there is a door open, of necessity one is able to see what is inside. And I heard a voice, he says, that had the sound of a trumpet, and it said to me, "Come up here," so that you might see events that are yet to occur. And I ascended "in the Spirit"—for the ascent was neither bodily nor sensible—and I saw, he says, a throne, and there was on it God, who is spirit,[19] having the appearance of jasper and carnelian. God is not like these things—of course not!—nor is he who is invisible, incorporeal and without form like in any way to the body of any perceptible being. Even the seraphim hide their faces with their wings when they are shown his invisible nature. Similarly, when God was speaking with Moses, he said, "No one will look on my face and live."[20] And even the Evangelist himself, as though contradicting what he says here, says, "No one has ever seen God."[21] Therefore, since God is similar to nothing in appearance, the vision of him in the revelation is depicted on the basis of his activities.

The jasper is a green precious stone, something like an emerald and similar to the rust of a shield, from which it receives its name.[22] The carnelian is another precious jewel and is fiery bright and blood red. And so the jasper symbolizes the life-bearing and life-providing nature of God, since all food

[12]Jer 22:17. [13]Ps 74:6 (73:6 LXX). [14]Song 5:2. [15]The "mysteries" refer to the Lord's Supper. [16]See Rom 8:17. [17]Jn 16:33. [18]De Groote gives the variant readings and reads "emerald" (TEG 8:104). Below Oecumenius will say that God appeared as "jasper and carnelian." [19]De Groote reads τὸν θεὸν καὶ Πνεῦμα (TEG 8:104). Some manuscripts add a definite article before "Spirit," indicating clearly the Holy Spirit. De Groote's capitalization of πνεῦμα suggests his agreement with that meaning. However, it seems doubtful that Oecumenius would depart so evidently from the biblical text. I have translated in view of Jn 4:24. [20]Ex 33:20. [21]Jn 1:18. [22]Epiphanius *On the Twelve Gems* 6 (PG 43:334-35).

of humankind and of four-footed animals and of birds and of creeping creatures has its beginning and likewise its effective cause in vegetation. For the prophet says, "Who makes the grass to grow for the cattle and plants for the service of men, to bring forth bread from the earth. And wine gladdens the heart of man, to make his face cheerful with oil."[23] And again at the creation of the world, God said, "Let the earth bring forth vegetation, bearing seed according to its kind."[24] And so, while the jasper depicts such things, the carnelian depicts the fearsomeness of God,[25] for the holy Moses said our "God is a devouring fire."[26] And the prophet spoke to God and said, "You are terrible! Who can stand before your face,"[27] and the wise apostle wrote in agreement, "It is a fearful thing to fall into the hands of the living God."[28] Since the pure goodness of God is incompatible with those who love to sin and who are scornful, not moving them to repentance but giving them a sense of security for further transgression, with good reason does God desire his severity depicted along with his goodness and beneficence. Paul also is aware that at times severity and not gentleness alone is required for those who are learning, for he writes to the Corinthians, "What do you wish? Shall I come to you with a rod, or with love in the spirit of gentleness?"[29] Finally, in a preface one of our saints said, "Gehenna does not frighten you, and the kingdom does not persuade you; we speak together with a heart of stone."[30] And so he knows as well that fearsomeness and unexpected severity are useful to those who are under instruction.

However, the carnelian is not the first jewel mentioned to describe God. Rather, the jasper is the first. For God's nature is in itself good and beneficent and gentle. And he wishes to be our Father rather than our Lord. But, if it is proper to speak in this way, we force him to become fearsome and punishing. And therefore, often he abandons that which is according to his nature, namely, gentleness, and assumes that which is contrary to his nature, namely, severity.

"And around his throne," he says, "there was a rainbow that looked like an emerald." The natural rainbow, which the holy Scriptures call the "bow" of God,[31] occurs from the reflection of the sun's light, which when taken into the thickness of clouds is intercepted and produces multiple and various colors. But this spiritual rainbow that encircles the divine throne is of one color, for it was like an emerald, and this reveals the multitude of holy ministering spirits that surrounds God. And for this reason it is called a rainbow, even though it is of one color, in order that from the multiple colors of the rainbow we might recognize the many distinct orders of the holy angels. And yet, all are bound together into one color since all alike imitate their Lord according to his good works, and therefore the emerald color testifies to their sustaining work, even as the jasper did for God. Nor should anyone who reads this object and say, "Why is it that the holy ranks of incorporeal angels around God are compared with the more valuable jewel of the emerald, while God is compared with the jasper and the carnelian, which are jewels of lesser worth?" The present passage is not concerned with the value of that which is seen but with the symbolic meanings of the colors. For should anyone in a way unsuitable to the passage seek merely after value, there would be nothing to which God might be compared. Nor should anyone object that the Lord is compared with a stone. For Isaiah spoke about the Lord, saying, "Behold, I am laying in Zion a cornerstone,"[32] and the prophet said concerning him, "The stone that the builders

[23]Ps 104:14-15 (103:14-15 LXX). [24]Gen 1:12. [25]Epiphanius *On the Twelve Gems* 1 (PG 43:323). [26]Deut 4:24. [27]Ps 76:7 (75:7 LXX). [28]Heb 10:31. [29]1 Cor 4:21. [30]See Basil of Caesarea *Hom. in divites* 6 (PG 31:297). [31]Gen 9:13. [32]Is 28:16.

rejected."[33] [In an analogous manner] the evil ranks of the demons are allegorically called "mountains," as David himself writes: "Though the mountains are removed into the heart of the sea, and the mountains have been troubled by his strength."[34] In comparison with mountains nothing may be found more preeminent in greatness.[35]

[4:4-6] ***Round the throne were twenty-four thrones, and seated on the twenty-four thrones were twenty-four elders, clad in white garments, with golden crowns on their heads. From the throne are sent flashes of lightning, and voices and peals of thunder, and before the throne burn seven lamps of fire, which are the seven spirits of God; and before the throne there is a sea of glass, like crystal.***

God alone, who knows every mystery, and that person to whom he might reveal it, know the identity of the twenty-four elders who are seated on the thrones. In my own opinion there were Abel and Enoch and Noah, Abraham and Isaac and Jacob, Melchizedek and Job, Moses and Aaron, Joshua the son of Nun and Samuel, David, Elijah and Elisha, the twelve minor prophets who are accounted as one,[36] Isaiah and Jeremiah, Ezekiel and Daniel, Zechariah and John, James the son of Joseph, and Stephen, the two martyrs of the New Testament. One might have mentioned Peter and Paul and James, the brother of John whom Herod killed with the sword, and the rest of the choir of the holy apostles, had not the Lord promised them that not at the present time but at the regeneration they would sit on twelve thrones, these clearly being different thrones from the ones mentioned above. For according to the Gospel of Matthew, the Lord spoke to them in the following words: "Truly I say to you, in the regeneration when the Son of God shall sit on his glorious throne, you who have followed me will also sit on twelve thrones, judging the twelve tribes of Israel."[37]

The white garments are demonstration of the purity of their lives, and the crowns signify the victory they have achieved over their sufferings and their spiritual enemies. The flashes of lightning and the peals of thunder that come from the throne signify once more the fearsomeness of God. For the divine beauty does not possess its happiness in some kind of dissipation or delight in pleasure but in that fear that comes with a deep awe. And the prophet knew this when he said, "Serve the Lord with fear, and rejoice in him with trembling."[38]

"And before the throne," it says, "there were burning seven lamps of fire, which are the seven spirits of God." In his sixth *Stromata*, Clement claimed that among the angels there are seven archangels, perhaps being led to that opinion from this passage.[39] He says that these seven spirits are similar to lamps of fire, for somewhere it says concerning angels, "he who makes the winds to be his angels, and flames of fire his servants."[40] Through such words the holy Scriptures signify those of whom the present passage is speaking.

"And before the throne," he says, "there is a sea of glass, like crystal." The vision of the sea indicates the multitude; the glass and crystal indicate the purity and utter cleanliness of the holy spirits who are around God, who are as a sea in multitude. For Daniel says, "A thousand thousands stood before him, and ten thousand times ten thousand served him."[41] And, although they are so many, they are all pure, similar to glass and crystal.

[4:6-8] ***And around the throne are four living creatures, full of eyes in front and behind; the***

[33]Ps 118:22 (117:22 LXX). [34]Ps 46:2-3 (45:2-3 LXX). [35]The argument seems to be that one ought not object to comparing God with a stone, when the demons, who are less powerful than God, are compared with mountains than which nothing is greater. [36]The twelve prophets were gathered together into one book. [37]Mt 19:28. [38]Ps 2:11. [39]Clement of Alexandria *Strom.* 6.16.143 (GCS 15:504). [40]Ps 104:4 (103:4 LXX). [41]Dan 7:10.

first living creature is like a lion, the second living creature is like an ox, the third living creature has the face of a man, and the fourth living creature is like a flying eagle. And the four living creatures, each of them with six wings, are full of eyes all round and within, and they never rest by night or by day, saying: "Holy, holy, holy, is the Lord God, the Almighty, who is and was and is to come!"

This passage does not imply that these living creatures are the same ones that the prophet Ezekiel was thought worthy to behold.[42] For each of those creatures had four faces and eight wings, and they drew chariots that were called Gelgel,[43] even though they did have many eyes, as these also have. However, in this passage, each creature has but one face, although they are different, and six wings. Moreover, Ezekiel was told that those creatures were cherubim, but these, as I believe, are the seraphim that were revealed to holy Isaiah, although Isaiah did not say what faces they had, only that they hid their faces with their wings. Nor did he say whether they had many eyes, only that they had six wings.[44]

But what did these creatures shown to the Evangelist signify? That would be good to explain. There was among some Jews a certain falsehood, that God exercised providential care among the holy orders in heaven and desired to dwell among them only, while he removed himself from those on the earth on account of Adam's sin and did not care about their well-being. And for that reason, they spoke in Isaiah the following: "Why have we fasted, and you did not know it? Why have we humbled ourselves, and you did not pay attention?"[45] And some such falsehood among them is suggested by this statement from the Scriptures: "Lord, your mercy is in the heavens, and your truth is unto the clouds."[46] It is as though the providence of God did not extend to the earth, regarding that as unworthy on account of sin. And therefore, the vision given to the Evangelist reveals that the providence of God pervades all things, sustaining those who dwell in heaven but also extending to those who dwell on the earth.

And this providence is what the four living creatures who are around the throne of God symbolize. For every sensible and earthly creature is a compound of the four fundamental elements—fire, earth, air and water—and each of the living creatures symbolizes one of these: the lion is a symbol of fire, because of its vigorous ferocity; the ox is a symbol of the earth, because it is a beast that works the earth; the man is a symbol of the air, since he is heavenly and sublime on account of the subtlety of his mind; the eagle is a symbol of water, since the origin of birds is from water.[47] And these creatures are seen to encircle the throne of God, indicating through the four creatures that what is on the earth is worthy of attention and providential care.

They possess many eyes to show that they have a universal oversight over the creatures of God. "And they do not rest by day or by night." This does not mean that they lead some sort of painful and distressful existence, never resting from hardship or necessary tasks. Rather, they never cease from glorifying God and luxuriating in their song to him. That they say "holy" seven times indicates that they do this often and without ceasing, for the holy Scriptures customarily use the number seven to mean "many." The following may serve as examples: "The barren has borne seven children, but she who has many children is grown weak";[48] "seven eyes of the Lord that range throughout the whole earth";[49] "the righteous person is saved seven times from necessity."[50]

He says, "Who was, and is, and is to come."

[42]See Ezek 1:4-28; 10:1-11:24. [43]Ezek 10:13. [44]See Is 6:2. [45]Is 58:3. [46]Ps 36:5 (35:5 LXX). [47]See Gen 1:20. [48]1 Kings 2:5 (= 1 Sam 2:5). [49]Zech 4:10. [50]See Prov 24:16.

These words indicate the holy and awesome Trinity, as we noted before.[51] But there is nothing wrong with saying this also now, for the holy apostle said, "To write the same things is not irksome to me, and for those who read it, it is safe."[52] Moses names the Father "he who is," for God said to him, "I am he who is."[53] And the Evangelist himself wrote of the Son as "he who was," saying, "In the beginning was the Word, and the Word was with God, and the Word was God."[54] And "he who is to come" speaks of the Holy Spirit, for he always visits those who are worthy to receive him.

[4:9-11] ***And whenever the living creatures give glory and honor and thanks to him who is seated on the throne, who lives forever and ever, the twenty-four elders fall down before him who is seated on the throne and worship him who lives forever and ever; they cast their crowns before the throne, saying: "Worthy are you, the Lord, our God, to receive glory and honor and power, for you did create all things, and by your will they existed and were created."***

The text says that along with the living creatures the elders give glory to God. This is indicated by their throwing their crowns before God. The crown is a symbol of victory and of rule, and so when they cast them before the throne of God, they ascribe to God, who is over all, that kingdom that is real and true and the victory over all enemies, and they say, "To you, O Lord, glory is due from every creature, for you did bring all things from nonexistence into existence, and by your will did you establish what formerly did not exist."

[5:1-7] ***And I saw in the right hand of him who was seated on the throne a scroll written on the inside and the outside, sealed with seven seals; and I saw a strong angel proclaiming with a loud voice, "Who is worthy to open the scroll [and to break its seals?" And no one in heaven or on earth or under the earth was able to open the scroll]***[55] ***or to look into it, and many wept, for no one was found worthy to open the scroll or to look into it. Then one of the elders said to me, "Weep not; lo, the Lion of the tribe of Judah, the Root of David, has conquered, so that he can open the seven seals of the scroll. And I looked, and between the throne and the four living creatures and among the elders, there was a Lamb standing, as though it had been slain, with seven horns and seven eyes, which are the seven spirits of God sent into all the earth; and he went and took the scroll from the right hand of him who is seated on the throne.***

The holy Scriptures depict for us a certain book in which all of humankind is registered, perhaps calling God's memory of us a book, except that the prophet calls it a "scroll,"[56] saying, "Your eyes saw my unformed substance, and in your scroll shall they all be written."[57] And the most wise Moses, making propitiation for sinful Israel, weeps and cries out to God, "But now, if you will forgive their sin, forgive, but if not, blot me out of your book that you have written."[58] The holy Evangelist saw this book written "within and without." That written "within" may be those from Israel who are registered as pious through the guidance of the Law, while that written "on the back"[59] would be those from the Gentiles who by a worse fate had been idolaters before they believed in Christ.

The scroll was in the right hand of God. This is, as I certainly think, the ways of the saints[60] who walked uprightly in the old

[51]See the comments on Rev 1:4. [52]Phil 3:1. [53]Ex 3:14. [54]Jn 1:1. [55]In the critical text of De Groote the words in brackets are left out, indicating a lacuna in the manuscript. Other manuscripts include them, and the discussion of Oecumenius demonstrates that he read them in his text. [56]Oecumenius is making a distinction between ὁ βίβλος ("book") and τὸ βιβλίον ("scroll"). τὸ βιβλίον is used in Ps 138:16 LXX. [57]Ps 139:16 (138:16 LXX). [58]Ex 32:32. [59]Oecumenius writes here ὄπισθεν ("on the back") instead of ἔξωθεν ("on the outside"). [60]Translating αἱ ὁδοὶ τῶν ἁγίων ("the ways of the saints").

covenant. The scroll was rolled up and was sealed with seven seals. As a perfect number, the seven seals show how exceedingly securely the scroll is closed and sealed up. Why would he wish the scroll to be rolled up? Because except for a very few, no one was worthy of the vision of God. For how could that which was rolled up because of Adam's transgression be seen and contemplated? The majority were sinners and were a sufficient reason for the book being rolled up—for they were unspeakably numerous—rather than the few who were pleasing to God being sufficient to open the scroll. Even all the freedom toward God of those inscribed in the scroll was altogether shut up, since indeed "they have all gone astray, they are together become good for nothing," as the prophet says.[61] For even though there was a small number of persons in the Old Testament who walked uprightly, yet being humans, they were not sufficiently worthy to restore that intimate freedom [toward God] that was lost because of sin. The prophet understood this and therefore addressed God, saying, "In the morning you shall hear the voice of my supplication; in the morning I will stand in your presence and you will look on me."[62] He is speaking here of the spiritual morning, namely, of the appearance of the Christ, the Sun of righteousness, which has dispelled the gloom of ignorance, since by this coming only will humankind acquire intimacy [which was lost], that is, when Christ has destroyed sin, which separates us from God as though it were a wall and when he hears those who pray to him and accounts them worthy of the vision of God. To be sure, before Christ's visitation to humankind "every mouth was stopped and the whole world was accountable to God," as the Scripture says.[63] Therefore, as I said, that the scroll is rolled up and sealed indicates the secrecy and hiddenness of that which is written within it.

"And I saw a strong angel proclaiming, 'Who is worthy to open the scroll and to loose its seals?' " Someone might reply to him and say, "No one whomsoever, O most holy angel, except he only who is God become man and who has taken away sin and has torn up the bond of debt against us[64] and by his own obedience has healed our disobedience." "And no one," he says, "in heaven or on earth or under the earth was able to open the scroll." No angel could set things right for us, as Isaiah says: "No ambassador or messenger, but he himself saved them, because he loved them."[65] Nor could any living person or even any person from the dead assist us, as it is written somewhere: "A brother is not ransomed, nor shall a man ransom himself."[66] But why, he says, do I say to open the scroll when there is no one strong enough to look into it? How could anyone whose eyes are dim by the mist of sin[67] look into the scroll before the throne of God, where it had been placed? And because of the unworthiness of all, I began to lament. However, one of the elders consoled me by pointing out him who had opened the seals. He said to me, "Behold, the Lion of the tribe of Judah, the Root of David, has conquered, so that he can open the scroll and its seven seals." He who has conquered our conqueror, the devil, he says, that is the one who has opened the scroll and its seals. And who was this "Lion from the tribe of Judah"? Obviously the Christ, concerning whom the patriarch Jacob spoke: "He lay down and couched as a lion and as a lion's whelp. Who will arouse him?"[68] The holy apostle also is witness that the Lord was from Judah according to the flesh: "It is evident that our Lord Jesus Christ was descended from Judah."[69] Someone might wonder why he was not called "a rod from the root of Jesse" or "flower coming out of the root," as Isaiah said,[70] but

[61]Ps 14:3 (13:3 LXX). [62]See Ps 5:3. [63]Rom 3:19. [64]See Col 2:14. [65]Is 63:9 (LXX). [66]Ps 49:7 (48:7 LXX). [67]The Greek suggests the film over the eyes of one dying. [68]Gen 49:9. [69]Heb 7:14. [70]See Is 11:1.

rather the "root of David." He says this to show that although according to his humanity he was a rod coming forth from the root of Jesse and David, according to his deity he was the root not only of David but also of every visible and invisible creature, since he was the source of them all, as I said above.[71]

And I looked, he says, and between all those on either side of the throne of God "there was a Lamb standing, as though it had been slain, with seven horns and seven eyes, which are the seven spirits of God sent out into all the earth. And he went and took" the scroll "from the right hand of the one seated on the throne." He has called the Lord a "lamb" because of his innocence and because he provides for us. For just as every year the lamb provides by giving of its wool, so also the Lord "opens his hand and satisfies the desire of every living thing."[72] And so, through Isaiah, prophecy also speaks of him in this way: "As a lamb that is led to the slaughter, and like a sheep that before its shearer is dumb";[73] and also through Jeremiah: "I was like an innocent lamb led to the slaughter, and I did not know."[74] But the lamb [in the vision] had not been slain, but it was "as though it had been slain." For Christ returned to life, having trampled death and having despoiled hades of all the souls held by it. And so the death of Christ was not a death that held him fast; it was a death cut short by the resurrection. And since even after the resurrection the Lord carried about the trophies of death—the imprint of the nails, his life-giving body made red by his blood, as Isaiah says in front of the holy angels, "Why is your apparel red and your garments as if from a trodden winepress? I am full of trodden grape"[75]—for this reason he was seen in the vision "as though slain." The seven horns witness to his great power, since the number seven, being perfect, indicates a great amount, as I noted above.[76] And certainly the horns are symbolic of power, as the prophet says, "And all the horns of the sinners I will break, and the horn of the righteous one will be exalted,"[77] and as Habakkuk says, "His horns are in his hands."[78] And to be sure, Isaiah has interpreted for us the "seven eyes, which are the seven spirits of God sent out into all the earth," saying, "And there will rest on him the spirit of wisdom and understanding, the spirit of counsel and strength, the spirit of knowledge and piety. The spirit of the fear of God will fill him."[79] These spirits, that is, these spiritual gifts, were sent from God to every person. However, as those who had worked a little in their distribution to all, none had received rest in Christ. And this event was greater than any word or thought.[80] For the spiritual gifts that he sent from above as God, these he himself received from below as man, since he was man and also God. To him honor is forever and ever. Amen.

Fourth Discourse

Therefore, according to the previous vision no one in heaven or on the earth or under the earth was deemed worthy to open the scroll or to look within it. Christ alone, the Son of God, who for us became as we are while remaining what he was, took the scroll.

[5:8-12] ***And when he had taken the scroll, the four living creatures and the twenty-four elders fell down before the Lamb, each having a harp, and golden bowls full of incense, which are the prayers of the saints; and they sang a new song, saying: "Worthy are you to take the scroll and to open its seals, for you were slain and by your blood did ransom us for God from every tribe and tongue and people and nation, and have made them kings and priests for our God,***

[71]See the comments on Rev 1:8. [72]Ps 145:16 (144:16 LXX). [73]Is 53:7. [74]Jer 11:19. [75]Is 63:2-3 (LXX). [76]See the comments on Rev 4:8; 5:1. [77]Ps 75:10 (74:10 LXX). [78]Hab 3:4 (LXX). [79]Is 11:2-3 (LXX). [80]The idea appears to be that while the spiritual gifts had been given to many, this was a partial endowment. In Christ the spiritual gifts were possessed, however, in a full and complete manner.

and they shall reign on earth." And I looked, and I heard around the throne and the living creatures and the elders a voice of many angels, numbering myriad of myriads, saying with a loud voice: "Worthy is the Lamb who was slain, to receive power and wisdom and wealth and might and honor and glory and blessing."

Knowing beforehand the salvation that he was going to accomplish for humankind and the punishment that he would give to the unclean demons, all worshiped the Lord who took the scroll. That the elders have harps reveals the euphonious harmony of their doxology to God, as it is written: "Sing praises to our God, sing praises."[1] The incense depicts the offering from all the Gentiles. For in the person of God, Malachi says to disobedient Israel, "I do not accept an offering from your hands. For from the rising of the sun to its setting my name is praised among the nations, and in every place incense is offered in my name, and a pure offering."[2] Through these words Malachi foretold the faith and worship of the Gentiles.

"And they sang a new song." The song was new because it was sung to God who had become flesh, for this song had formerly never been offered, until the incarnation. And what was the song? "You are worthy," it says, you who were slain for us and who by your blood did acquire an inheritance from the many nations under heaven, to effect this salvation for humankind. And with very good reason he said "from every tribe and tongue and people and nation." For while he did not gain all nations—for many have died in unbelief—yet he acquired from every nation those worthy of salvation. And the prophet said something similar: "Arise, O God, judge the earth; for you will inherit [some] from among all the nations,"[3] not to be sure, "all the nations."[4]

And he made "them kings and priests for our God, and they shall reign on earth." In addition to the faithful servants of Christ who are kings and leaders of the churches, perhaps you will also be able to understand the kings in this passage to be those who have ruled their passions and have not been ruled by them and the priests to be those who have offered their own bodies as a "living sacrifice, holy and pleasing to God," as the Scripture says.[5] However, not only the elders but also the incorporeal powers of the angels sing this triumphal hymn to Christ. And Daniel had already foretold the number of the angels mentioned in this passage.[6] The hymn of the angels bring forth a sevenfold honor to Christ, showing by the number seven that it is proper to crown Christ with thousands of songs of praise.

[5:13-14] ***And I heard every creature in heaven and on earth and in the sea, and all therein, saying, "To him who sits on the throne and to the Lamb be blessing and honor and glory and might forever and ever!" And the four living creatures said, "Amen!" and the elders fell down and worshiped.***

This passage shows the doxology that all creation, both in heaven and on earth, harmoniously renders to God the Father and to the Word who was made flesh and became man, the Holy Spirit manifestly also being worshiped together with them.

[6:1-4] ***And when I saw that the Lamb opened one of the seven seals, I heard the four living creatures say,[7] as with a voice of thunder, "Come!" And I saw, and behold, a white horse, and its rider had a bow; and a crown was given to him, and he went out conquering and to conquer. When he opened the second seal, I heard the second living creature say, "Come!"***

Fourth Discourse [1]Ps 47:6 (46:6 LXX). [2]Mal 1:10-11. [3]Ps 82:8 (81:8 LXX). [4]The LXX reads ἐν πᾶσι τοῖς ἔθνεσιν, not πάντα τὰ ἔθνη. Oecumenius takes the former to indicate some "within" all nations. [5]Rom 12:1. [6]Dan 7:10. [7]Oecumenius reads ἐκ τῶν τεσσάρων ζῴων λεγόντων, the plural suggesting that all four living creatures were speaking. In Rev 6:3, 5, 7 Oecumenius uses the singular.

And out came another horse, a red one; its rider was permitted to take peace from the earth, so that they might slay one another; and he was given a great sword.

The closing and sealing of the scroll signifies the fearful alienation[8] of those inscribed in it and the closing of their mouths from making any defense or plea before God, according to what was mentioned previously.[9] Therefore, the gradual opening of the seals reveals the gradual recovery of our free and open relationship with God,[10] which the Only-begotten, having become incarnate, acquired for us when by his own righteousness he set right our offenses.

It is then to be noted that the loosing of each seal reveals a certain work done by the Lord for our salvation and effected by him against our spiritual enemies. For the intention of the Lord on our behalf is the destruction of their domination of us. Let no one reading this marvel that before the incarnation of the Only-begotten is mentioned, the Lamb is nevertheless seen in the revelation as though he were slain—for through the vision his works and deeds are shown to the holy Evangelist before his sojourn among us.[11] For it is common that future events foreseen by the prophets receive a foretelling of them. Thus, for example, a man wrestled with Jacob,[12] who was a type of Christ; Isaiah saw the prophetess conceiving in her womb and giving birth to a son, whose name was "Despoil quickly; Plunder speedily";[13] and Daniel saw the preincarnate divine Word as a son of man approaching the Ancient of Days.[14]

Therefore, the first good work of Christ our Savior toward our race, which loosed the first seal of the scroll, was the physical birth of the Lord. For his birth initiated our restoration from that exile that was occasioned by Adam's sin, and it began the recovery of that closeness of God with us that we had lost and the change of our fearful alienation into a confident freedom. For his birth sanctified our birth, so that we might no longer be conceived in transgressions or be born in the sins of our mothers but that we might have a sanctified birth, Christ having blessed human birth through his own birth. The holy apostle witnesses to this goodness toward humankind when he writes, "Since your children are unclean, but now they are holy."[15]

When the first seal was loosed, I saw, he says, someone on a white horse who was commanded to come from those holy, spiritual living creatures, and he had a bow, and there "a crown was given to him, and he went out conquering and to conquer." The white horse is a symbol of the gospel, since through it good deeds will be done to humanity. The crown is an image of strength and victory. And the white horse went out to bring the crown to Christ, who had begun to conquer the devil, who had placed our race under bondage. "He went out," he says, "conquering and to conquer." Christ was he who was conquering that he might conquer utterly and totally, and he brought the crown as a symbol of victory to him.

This is the first seal. The second good work of Christ toward us is the temptation of the Lord and his victory over the tempter. This loosed the second seal of the scroll and granted to us the loosing of our shame and the restoration of the vision of God. And this occurred not only that Christ might know victory but also that the interloper, beaten down, might no longer "bite the heel of the horseman"[16] or trip us up in our spiritual walk, but rather that he might fall down, and be sent away like a slave

[8]Translating ἀπαρρησίαστος ("deprived of boldness and freedom"). [9]See the comments on Rev 5:1. [10]Translating τῆς πρὸς θεὸν παρρησίας καὶ οἰκειότητος. [11]In the opinion of Oecumenius, the opening of the first seal (Rev 6:1) represents the incarnation. However, the seer had already seen the Lamb as though slain (Rev 5:6). [12]Gen 32:24. [13]Is 8:3 (LXX). [14]Dan 7:13. [15]1 Cor 7:14. [16]Gen 49:17 (LXX).

and hear from humans whom he had defeated, "Begone, Satan!"[17]—although God was in this man! And so, he who boasted that he would put his throne on the clouds and make himself like the Most High, as Isaiah dramatically depicted it,[18] departs with shame and now for the first time learns of his own weakness.

And when this happened, "a red horse came out," urged on by one of the living creatures, and authority was given to the rider "to take peace from the earth, that they might kill one another, and a great sword was given to him." The red horse is a figure of blood, and so a sword is given to the rider on the horse so that he might attack and cut to pieces that consensus of evil that exists among those who dwell on the earth—for among them there is an agreement to idolatry. "That they might kill one another," that is, that they might slay each other's eagerness toward increased evil. For the Lord did not come "to bring peace to the earth but a sword" and to set "a son against his father and a bride against her mother-in-law"[19] and the young and pious against the old and accused.

[6:5-8] *And when he opened the third seal, I heard the third living creature say, "Come!" And I saw, and behold, a black horse, and its rider had a balance in his hand; and I heard a voice in the midst of the four living creatures saying, "A quart of wheat for a denarius, and three quarts of barley for a denarius, but do not harm the oil and wine." And when he opened the fourth seal, I heard the fourth living creature say, "Come!" And I saw, and behold, a pale horse, and its rider's name was "Death," and Hades shall follow him; and they were given power over a fourth of the earth, to kill with the sword and with famine and with death and by wild beasts of the earth.*

The third mercy of Christ toward us opened the third seal and restored us, who had been condemned, to God the Father. This is his salvific teaching and the benefits of his miracles, for these contributed to the dissolution of the devil. For through these we know who is truly God by nature, so that we may "no longer be children, tossed about by every wind of doctrine"[20] or honor that which our hands have made, but that we might exchange the corrupting demons for the glory of God. As yeast draws flour, the divine teaching of the Lord drew to itself those being taught according to the discourses of the Lord and those who were benefiting from the miracles that healed souls rather than bodies.

And when this occurred, a black horse came out, and "its rider had a balance in his hand." The black horse is indicative of shame and sorrow, for the destruction of the devil had received increased intensity by the divine teaching, and therefore he laments his dissolution, which was lasting for such a long time. The balance, by contrast, is a figure of equality and righteousness, for "he who judges in righteousness sat on his throne and rebuked the nations of demons, and the impious one who led them was destroyed."[21] The balance is, therefore, a symbol of the righteous judgment of the Lord on our behalf, so that we may speak boldly to him, "You have executed my cause and my right,"[22] so that we nations might "know that we are men"[23] and may not be pulled about like beasts with bit and bridle or allowed to be led astray by destructive tyrants.

"And I heard a voice in the midst of the four living creatures saying, 'A quart of wheat for a denarius, and three quarts of barley for a denarius, but do not harm the oil and wine.'" The word of teaching is figuratively called seed in the holy Scriptures. In Matthew it is written, "A sower went out to sow," and his most devoted servants say to their master, "Sir,

[17]Mt 4:10. [18]Is 14:13-14. [19]Mt 10:34-35. [20]Eph 4:14. [21]Ps 9:4-5 (LXX). Oecumenius added the words "of demons" and "who led them," thus allowing Ps 9 to speak directly to the context of Rev 6:5. [22]Ps 9:4. [23]Ps 9:20.

did you not sow good seed in the field? Then why are there weeds?"[24] From the seed comes the wheat, that is, the preaching of the gospel, which as a food fit for mature persons trains the minds to distinguish between good and evil. And what is the barley? It is the teaching according to the law of Moses, for barley is less expensive than wheat and when ripe is food fit for cattle, and so it represents that which nourished the children of Israel. Therefore, God speaks from the midst of the four living creatures: "A quart of wheat for a denarius and three quarts of barley for a denarius," symbolizing through this that there would be a famine and a scarcity of evangelical teaching among the people at that time, a famine of both the teaching that comes from the Lord and that from the Law, as is written: "I will give to them not a famine of bread or a thirst for water, but a famine of the hearing of the word of the Lord."[25] And if for the most part it is necessary that those who despise all teaching and conversion must suffer so and so, he says, "Do not harm the oil and the wine." Leave them alone, and do not bring any destruction on them. There is still mercy from me for them, God says, since there is hope for them to be gladdened spiritually by the divine preaching of my Only-begotten. This is the wine that spiritually gladdens the hearts of people. Surely he who was exiled for the former disobedience would harm that mercy from God that is intended for them and that spiritual gladness that is founded on faith.[26]

But why do I speak only of the spiritual gladness? For the teachings of the Lord also possessed a perceptible grace, and the prophet is a witness of this, saying to the Lord, "Grace is poured out on your lips."[27] And another witness is Josephus, a Jewish man who, constrained by the truth, wrote the following concerning Jesus in the eighteenth book of his *Antiquities*:

At this time there was a man, Jesus, a wise man, if one indeed might call him a man. For he accomplished remarkable works and was the teacher of those who accept the truth with pleasure. He attracted many from the Jews as well as many from the Greeks. He was the Christ. When Pilate, upon the accusation of the chief men among us, condemned him to the cross, those who had loved him from the first continued to be attached to him. On the third day he appeared to them as one who had come back to life, for the holy prophets had foretold of this and of many other wonders concerning him. And to this day the tribe of those called "Christians" after him have not disappeared.[28]

The loosing of the fourth seal and of the remaining seals is the beginning of the loosing of sin that was brought about by the transgression of Adam. For the loosing of this seal reveals our friendship with God. For if, as Isaiah says, "our iniquities have made us separated from God,"[29] the removal of sins brings us close to God. And what is this loosing of the seal? It is the lashes that Christ received and through which we have been freed. For since we were condemned by the pleasure of taste, we have been healed through the opposites. Lashes are the opposite of pleasure, for they give a painful sensation. For Christ has paid in full for us all things through which we were brought down into the corruption of death. And he paid the debt in full through opposites—disobedience through obedience, pleasure through a painful submission, and the hands that lay hold of the forbidden tree through those hands that were valiantly stretched out on the cross.

When this happened, at the summons of

[24]Mt 13:3, 27. [25]Amos 8:11. [26]Had God not commanded that the oil and wine not be harmed, the devil would have worked harder to ensure that those who despise the word of God would not receive the mercy of conversion. [27]Ps 45:2 (44:2 LXX). [28]Josephus *Ant.* 18.63-64. [29]Is 59:2.

the fourth holy creature a pale horse came out, and "its rider's name was Death, and Hades followed him. And there was given to them authority over a fourth of the earth." The pale horse is symbolic of wrath, for pale is the color of gall and is so named by physicians. Death and Hades were sent to wage spiritual warfare against the wicked demons and to exact vengeance for the destruction of humankind. But since, according to the logic of the vision, the salvific passion of Christ through which he paid for all our sins had not yet happened, the complete destruction of the demons had not yet been effected, but at that time only a fourth part. And this destruction he figuratively calls a slaughter and a famine brought on those who long ago worshiped them, and "death," revealing the end of their tyranny through death, and "destruction" by the beasts of the earth. For he calls the passions of arrogance and vainglory among the demons "beasts of the earth," which, as they are cast out of their dominion over people, consume and devour them, since they are earthly and as it were revel in the muddied passions of the earth, although they had received incorporeal natures.

[6:9-11] ***When he opened the fifth seal, I saw under the altar the souls of those who had been slain for the word of God and for the church that they had; they cried out with a loud voice, saying, "O Sovereign, both holy and true, how long before you will judge and avenge our blood on those who dwell on the earth?" Then they were each given a white robe and told to rest a little longer, until their fellow servants and their brethren should be completed, who were to be killed as they themselves had been.***

The fifth work of salvation that the Lord gave to the human race and that loosed the fifth seal of the Lord and offered to us freedom from sin and friendship with God was the chains and beatings to which the Lord was subjected before he was brought to Pilate and those he suffered from Pilate because of his timidity. Isaiah spoke of these beatings, when the Lord was asked by the divine angels, "What are these wounds between your hands?" and he said, "The wounds I received in my beloved house."[30] For these wounds have healed our wounds that we suffered when we were going down from Jerusalem to Jericho and fell among thieves who beat and wounded us and left us half dead, as the story in Luke says.[31] But he loosed our chains, namely, the bonds of sin that were holding us tightly. For the prophet says, "The cords of sinners ensnare me."[32] Therefore, while he was working evil, the devil was ignorant concerning him, and through his drunken violence against the Lord thrust a sword into himself and fell from that rule that he had wickedly established.

When the fifth seal was opened, the saints who had given witness in the old covenant remained silent. They could recall nothing like this treatment ever having happened to them, and they had not yet seen any such thing done against Christ. For although within the lawless Sanhedrin of the high priests he had been spit on, slapped and beaten, this had occurred in secrecy and only on the testimony of servants and of others summoned to the trial. But when they saw the Lord bound and whipped publicly by Pilate before the crowd of the Jews, they altogether rose up, and regarding that which was happening against their Master as intolerable, remembered also what had happened to them.

For, he says, "I saw under the altar the souls of those who had been slain for the word of God and for the church that they had." I saw, he says, the souls of the martyrs that had the most exalted place, for they were under the heavenly altar. Then he remarks about these martyrs, namely, that they had been slain for

[30]The citation is from Zech 13:6. [31]Lk 10:30. [32]Ps 119:61 (118:61 LXX).

the holy word of the old covenant and for the church or synagogue that they had. For the martyrs die not only for themselves, but also they effect a common benefit. Their courage becomes an exhortation to others, and by the blood of the saints the knowledge of God is built up.

"And they cried out with a loud voice, saying, 'O Sovereign, both holy and true, how long before you will judge and avenge our blood on those who dwell on the earth?' " They were not making petition against human persons but against the demons who like to dwell in earthly things. For it is not according to the love of the saints to rise up against their own kind but against those who lead people to their own destruction. And having said these things, they first receive white robes. This image signifies that they have been cleansed by their own blood and have put off every filth.

Then they hear that they ought "rest a little longer, until their fellow servants and their brothers should be completed, who were to be killed as they themselves had been." For it would not be just were those who were similar to them in courage be deprived of their martyr crowns because the demons who were struggling against them had been destroyed prematurely.

[6:12-17] ***And I saw when he opened the sixth seal, and there was a great earthquake; and the sun became black as sackcloth, and the full moon became blood, and the stars of the sky fell to the earth as the fig tree sheds its fruit when shaken by a great wind; the heaven vanished like a scroll that is rolled up, and every mountain and island was removed from its place. And the kings of the earth and the great men and the generals and the rich and the strong, and every servant and freeman hid themselves in the caves and among the rocks of the mountains. And they said to the mountains and rocks, "Fall on us and hide us from the face of him who is seated on the throne and from the wrath of the Lamb, for the great day of their wrath has come, and who can stand before it?"***

The loosing of the sixth seal effected the completion of our salvation. It dissolved death and brought back life. It dethroned the conqueror of humanity and was openly triumphant in accordance with that which is written: "The Only-begotten ascended on high and led captivity captive and received gifts among people."[33] And what is this loosing of the sixth seal? It is the cross and death of the Lord. The resurrection and the ascension follow after these, and for these every spiritual and physical creature has prayed, for they "renew for us a new and living way,"[34] that is, the way back from death to life through the curtain of his flesh. And he accomplished this good work not only for the living but also for those who have gone before. For the Lord "went and preached to the disobedient in hades," as the divine apostle Peter says,[35] and he saved those there who believe, as Cyril thought.[36]

When these things had happened, "there was a great earthquake; and the sun became black as sackcloth, and the full moon became blood, and the stars of the heaven fell to the earth as the fig tree sheds its fruit when shaken by a great wind." The vision clearly depicts for us the signs that occurred at the time of the crucifixion: the earthquake and the turmoil of the earth, the darkness of the sun and the transformation of the full moon into blood. And with complete accuracy did he add the word *full* to the moon. For the moon was fully visible, not merely partially visible on the day of the crucifixion, and so

[33]Ps 68:18 (67:18 LXX); Eph 4:8. Oecumenius added "Only-begotten" to ensure the reference to Christ. [34]Heb 10:20. [35]1 Pet 3:19-20. [36]Cyril of Alexandria *Fragments on the Catholic Epistles* (1 Pet 3:19-20; PG 74:1013).

greeted the passion in its fullness. For it is customary for such events to occur during the illuminated period of the lunar phases. Indeed, the prophet Joel foretold that these things were to happen: "The sun shall turn to darkness, and the moon to blood, before the great and manifest day of the Lord comes."[37] The stars falling from heaven was perhaps a physical occurrence, but if not, the passage indicates that all lights from heaven ceased and everything became darkened.

"And the heaven vanished like a scroll that is rolled up." By the word *heaven* he speaks of the heavenly powers of the angels, who were themselves also thoroughly terrified, not being able to tolerate the abuse directed against their Master, and who were flitting to and fro as a scroll that was unrolled and shaking.

"And every mountain and island was removed from its place." By mountains and islands he means the ranks of the arrogant demons, as it is written of them: "The mountains shake in the heart of the sea."[38] Moreover, by islands he speaks of those who in the vain foolishness of their minds think themselves superior and exalted in the fickle and bitter circumstances of the present life.

"And the kings of the earth and the great men and the generals and the rich and the strong and every servant and freeman hid themselves in the caves and among the rocks of the mountains. And they said to the mountains and rocks, 'Fall on us and hide us from the face of him who sits on the throne and from the wrath of the Lamb, for the great day which is of their wrath has come, and who can stand?' " By kings and great men and generals and rich and strong he refers to those sinful demons who tyrannize those on the earth through deceit and guile, and he calls servants and freemen those among the demons who are of inferior and superior status. That they seek to hide themselves in the caves and among the rocks of the mountains and nevertheless also say "fall on us and hide us" is spoken figuratively, indicating that they are fugitives who are attempting to escape from the punishment of Christ that is coming on them. For were there not a certain invisible punishment and retribution coming on them, what would be the meaning of that spoken by the prophet Isaiah in the person of Christ: "I have trodden the winepress utterly alone, and from the peoples there was none with me, and I have trod them in my anger and trampled them in my wrath, and I have poured out their blood on the earth,"[39] and what would be the meaning of that spoken by the demons, hated of God, according to Matthew: "What do you have to do with us, O Son of God? Have you come to torment us?"[40]

Someone might think that these things reported in the revelation were not only concerning the sufferings of the demons but also of those lawless Jews who nailed the Lord to the cross and who, accosted by the war with the Romans, became fugitives in the mountains and the caves and the crevices of the earth and from every direction were hemmed in by difficulty and strife.

[7:1-8] ***After this I saw four angels standing at the four corners of the earth, so that no wind might blow on the earth or on the sea or against any tree. And I saw another angel ascend from the rising of the sun, with the seal of the living God, and he called out with a loud voice to the four angels who had been given the power to harm the earth and the sea and the trees, saying, ". . . or the sea or the trees, until we have sealed the servants of our God on their foreheads. And I heard the number of the sealed, one hundred and forty-four thousand from every tribe of the sons of Israel," and he adds that there were "twelve thousand" sealed from every tribe.***

[37]Joel 2:31. [38]Ps 46:3 (45:3 LXX). [39]Is 63:3. [40]Mt 8:29.

What happened to the Jews during the war against the Romans is clearly shown to the Evangelist. These things occurred to them because of the crucifixion and their blasphemy against the Lord. For the four angels who held the four corners of the land of the Jews[41] were keeping guard lest any of the Jews who were deserving of death should escape. And so they either brought on the Jews a fear of flight or dissensions or an untimely devotion to the land or to their wives and relatives, and it is these things that are figuratively signified by the four corners of Judea being guarded. And that the four winds are restrained so that they blow neither on the land nor on the sea nor against any tree indicates that no respite was found by them in the war or any consolation from their woes, neither for those who fought on the land nor for those who fought at sea—for, according to Josephus, there were many sea battles—nor for those whose concern is with farming. For these evils wholly overpowered everyone, since the cities were destroyed by fire and the land was devastated and wasted. And Josephus accurately relates all of these events in his account of the siege of Jerusalem.[42]

"And I saw an angel ascend from the rising of the sun, with the seal of the living God, and he called out with a loud voice to the four angels who had been given the power to harm the earth and the sea, saying, 'You are to harm nothing,' he says, 'until the servants of our God have been sealed.' " That the divine angel appears from the rising of the sun and not from its setting that brings on the evening is symbolic of the gospel and the promise of its blessings. For the prophet foresaw in the spirit that seal that now prevails when he said, "The light of your face, O Lord, was sealed on us."[43] Meanwhile he rightly commands that nothing be harmed until those from the Jews who are worthy of being saved should be sealed, so that none of the righteous should suffer any of these calamities along with the sinners. And the sealed, it says, was 144,000. For those from the Jews who believed in Christ were numerous and greater than this number, and they were accounted worthy to be saved from the common destruction, as those testified who spoke to Paul when he was in Jerusalem: "Do you see, brother, how many thousands there are of the Jews who have believed?"[44] However, it was likely that not only the faithful escaped but also those who were deceived and in ignorance assisted in the crucifixion of the Lord, about whom he said, "Father, forgive them, for they know not what they do"[45]—although in his thirteenth book against Julian, Cyril says that this petition of the Lord is not in the Gospels but is rather said by us.[46] And perhaps not only these escaped, but also those who were not present at that time or were not living in Jerusalem and so were not complicit in the impious plot of the accursed high priests concerning the crucifixion, and those who were perhaps present but were not involved in that murderous defilement. Indeed, Christ blessed everything under heaven, in contrast to what the irreligious council of transgressors had wanted. It is likely that all of these were later sealed in the faith of Christ; otherwise the angel would not have called them the servants of God. And when these had been rescued, either by flight or by desertion to the Romans, those wicked ones who remained were destroyed in a terrible manner, "having become a spectacle to the world, to angels and to men,"[47] in a way quite different from what Paul had said of the blessed apostles. And of these things, Josephus is again witness, counting those who were

[41]Translating τὰς τέσσαρας γωνίας τῆς 'Ιουδαίων γῆς. Oecumenius adds "of the Jews" interpreting "the earth" to be "the land of the Jews." [42]Josephus *J. W.* 5–6. [43]Ps 4:6. By the seal Oecumenius most likely means the Holy Spirit given in baptism as the seal. See *On the Incarnation and Against the Arians* 15, where this psalm is quoted along with allusion to Ex 34:30 and a quotation from Eph 1:13-14, where the seal is explicitly said to the "promised Holy Spirit" (PG 26:1009). [44]Acts 21:20. [45]Lk 23:34. [46]Cyril of Alexandria *Contra Julianum* 13. Cyril represents a considerable textual tradition that does not include these words of Jesus. [47]1 Cor 4:9.

killed by famine as more than ten thousand.[48]

That an equal number from each tribe is said to have been sealed and to have believed indicates the equality of their zeal and the unanimity of their faith, although there would have been more from one tribe and less from other tribes of those who were saved and believed on Christ, who although dishonored by the Jews, is worshiped by us and by every supernatural creature now and always and forever more. Amen.

Fifth Discourse

The previous discourse explained what was revealed to the holy Evangelist concerning those from the nation of Israel[1] who were sealed and therefore were saved[2] and who afterward also had come to faith. But, lest something be lacking in what was revealed to him, the vision also shows to him the countless thousands of Gentiles who later embraced the faith and being with the Lord stand before the throne of God. However, since the prophetic vision has not yet depicted the second coming of the Lord when the saints "are caught up in the clouds to meet" the Savior, as the holy apostle says,[3] the vision shows them as caught up beforehand and as having already obtained the blessedness that awaits them. For what is more blessed than to be found worthy of being with Christ and to behold the divine throne? But see what he says:

[7:9-17] ***After this I looked, and behold, a great multitude that no one could number, from every nation, tribes and peoples and tongues, standing before the throne and before the Lamb, clothed in white robes, with palm branches in their hands. And they cried out with a loud voice, saying, "Salvation belongs to our God who sits on the throne." And the holy ones of the elders stood round the throne and the elders and the four living creatures, and they fell on their faces before the throne and worshiped our God forever and ever. Amen. Then one of the elders addressed me, saying, "Who are these, clothed in white robes, and from where have they come?" I said to him, "Sir, you know." And he said to me, "These are they who have come out of the great tribulation and have enlarged[4] their robes and made them white in the blood of the Lamb. Therefore are they before the throne of God, and serve him day and night within his temple; and he who sits on the throne will dwell with them. They shall hunger no more, neither thirst anymore; the sun shall not strike them, or any scorching heat. For the Lamb in the midst of the throne will be their shepherd, and he will guide them to springs of living water; and God will wipe away every tear from their eyes."***

As I said above, he sees the countless thousands from the Gentiles who, having received the faith of Christ and having attained the blessed portion, have been allotted a place in the glorious choir and stand before the Lord and the throne of his Father. They are clothed in white robes as a sign of the purity of their life, and the palm branches are symbolic of victory and reveal that they rejoice in the victory of Christ against every spiritual and physical foe. And they cry out, "Salvation belongs to our God and to the Lamb," confessing that salvation is with them, since, having been sealed as servants of God, they were rescued from the universal destruction of the world. And when they rendered their thanksgiving, all the heavenly hosts, together with the elders, respond with "Amen," adding their approval to that which had been said. Then the holy angels add their praise to God, giving him honor with

[48]Josephus *J.W.* 5.567-69; 6.420-25. **Fifth Discourse** [1]Translating ἐξ αἵματος Ἰσραήλ ("from the blood of Israel"). This refers to physical Israel, which is determined by natural blood relationship. [2]That is, saved from the Romans. [3]1 Thess 4:17. [4]Reading ἐπλάτυναν rather than ἔπλυναν.

a sevenfold praise, which, as was earlier noted,[5] signifies the never-ending praise of the angels, for the number seven suggests perfection.

One of the elders asked the Evangelist who those were who were from the nations and were clothed in white robes. He asked this not because he did not know but rather to urge the Evangelist to know about them more fully. And so he says, "These are they who have come out of the great tribulation." For the righteous endured not a small struggle but indeed an exceedingly great struggle during the rule of the antichrist.

It says, "And they have washed their robes and made them white in the blood of the Lamb." To be sure, one might think that robes dipped in blood would be red, not white. And so, how is it that they have become white? Because, according to the opinion of all-wise Paul,[6] baptism is accomplished into the death of the Lord and wipes one clean from every filth of sin, so that those baptized in him[7] are made white and clean. However, the reception of the life-giving blood of Christ[8] also gives the same grace, for the Lord said concerning his blood that it was poured out "for many" and "for the sake of many" and "for the forgiveness of sins."[9] Therefore, these serve God forever, and God dwells among them. Indeed, one of the saints said that this dwelling of God is the never-ending remembrance of God that remains in the souls of the saints.[10] Rightly, then, does God dwell with those who "serve him day and night."

"They shall hunger no more, nor shall they thirst anymore." For while formerly those from the Gentiles came through every trial, now they will be satisfied with countless blessings. "Nor," it says, "will the sun strike them." The sun is used figuratively by some writers of holy Scripture to refer to temptations. For example, the prophet said, "The sun will not strike you by day, or the moon by night,"[11] or the Evangelist, who wrote that the shining sun scorched that seed that sprouted on the stony soil, interpreting the sun to be temptations.[12] And so also in this present passage it says that temptation would no longer harm them. For they were counted worthy to have Christ as their shepherd and to be refreshed at living waters. "And God will wipe away every tear from their eyes." For the reward of those who lived in this manner and who fought diligently against that which is unprofitable is neither tears nor weeping nor the gnashing of teeth but every good and supernatural blessing.

[8:1-2] *And when he opened the seventh seal, there was silence in heaven for about half an hour. And I saw the seven angels who were standing before God, and seven trumpets were given to them.*

Perhaps someone who has been very attentive might see these words and say to me, "What are you doing? Have you utterly forgotten what was said at the beginning of this revelation? For it said, 'And the first voice that I heard speaking to me like a trumpet, said, "Come up here, and I will show you what must take place after this."'[13] But you have become the interpreter for us, not of future events but of that which has already occurred. You have discussed the birth of the Lord, his temptation, his teachings and miracles, his beatings and chains and floggings from Pilate, the cross and his death, his resurrection, and his ascension, or rather his return, to heaven." To such a person I would respond, "O friend, you have certainly heard also of that which is yet to happen whenever we explain the righteous from the Gentiles who are with Israel near the throne of God and are with Christ. But you will now hear also of the loosing of the seventh

[5]See the comment on Rev 5:12. [6]See Rom 6:3. [7]Ἐν αὐτῷ, which could also be translated "in it," that is, "in the death of the Lord." [8]That is, in the Eucharist. [9]Mt 26:28. [10]The saint to whom Oecumenius refers is unknown. [11]Ps 121:6 (120:6 lxx). [12]Mk 4:5-6.

seal. For the oracle that said to the Evangelist, 'Come up here, and I will show you what must take place after this,' did not repudiate what he had seen of events that have happened, but along with them he showed also future things. Listen therefore! The loosing of the seventh seal effected for us the most perfect and complete glory. No longer is there as before the loosing of sin and our turning to God and God's turning to us. Rather, there is now the most unspeakable blessings: to be called 'sons of God,' to be inheritors of God, to be coheirs with Christ, to be brothers and friends and children of Christ, also to rule with him and to be glorified with him, and those blessings that 'eye has not seen nor has ear heard nor has come into the heart of man.'"[14]

And what is the loosing of the seventh seal? It is the second coming of the Lord and the giving of blessings as rewards. For although some are handed over to the punishment of sinners, nonetheless it is the aim of Christ and the intention of the incarnation that everyone become an heir of his kingdom. Therefore, when the seventh seal was loosed, "there was," it says, "silence for about half an hour," since the king of creation was coming and every angelic and supernatural power, astounded at the exceeding greatness of the glory of him who was coming, for that reason became silent.

Then, it says, seven trumpets were given to the seven angels, so that they might sound the signal that the king was arriving. But by these very trumpets the angels will also awaken those who are dead. For the apostle, who is wise in divine things, wrote in his first letter to the Thessalonians that "the Lord himself will descend at a command, at the call of an archangel, and with the sound of the trumpet of God."[15] And again, "The trumpet will sound, and the dead will be raised incorruptible."[16]

[8:3-6] ***And an angel came and stood at the altar with a golden censer; and he was given much incense to mingle with the prayers of all the saints on the golden altar before the throne; and the smoke of the incense rose with the prayers of the saints from the hand of the angel before God. Then the angel took the censer and filled it with fire from the altar and threw it on the earth; and there were voices, peals of thunder, flashes of lightning and an earthquake. And the seven angels who had the seven trumpets made ready to blow them.***

He calls the altar a censer because it receives incense. When Christ appears, the prayers of the saints, which are by nature fragrant but made even more fragrant by the cooperation of the holy angels, are brought to him by those angels that govern us as though they were his spoils and the first offerings of homage given to him. And for this reason it is said that "much incense was given to him." It is clear that the governance of people was given to the angels from God that they might make our prayers acceptable to him. Receiving [the prayers of the saints], they give fragrance to the prayers of the saints.

"And the smoke of the incense rose with the prayers of the saints from the hand of the angel." You see that the prayers of the saints are made more fragrant by the angel and rendered worthy to be offered before God. Then, it says, the holy angel took and filled the altar with divine fire and "threw it on the earth, and there were voices and peals of thunder and flashes of lightning and an earthquake." Similarly, an angel threw some of this heavenly fire on Mount Sinai, and there was thunder and voices and trumpets and lightning, and the mountain was covered in smoke, since God had come and was present. Therefore, just as at that time thunder and fearsome wonders preceded him, so also now such wonders occur before the glorious advent of the Lord. Then also the angels blew

[13]Rev 4:1. [14]1 Cor 2:9. [15]1 Thess 4:16. [16]1 Cor 15:52.

their trumpets to announce the coming of God, for indeed also then trumpets heralded great events.

[8:7] ***The first angel blew his trumpet, and there followed hail and fire, mixed with blood, and it was cast on the earth, and a third of the earth was burned up.***

Since the righteous have been accounted worthy of this blessed portion—as it was told to me at the conclusion of the breaking of the sixth seal—and so are to be caught up "in the clouds of the air" prior to the coming of the Lord, that they might greet the coming Lord,[17] according to the witness of the apostle that was given to me at that time, the vision now finally discusses the fate of the rest of humankind and the punishment of the sinners. When the coming destruction occurs, there will necessarily be various kinds of death and various rewards for the wicked. The greater part of these will be consumed by fire, for in his first letter to the Corinthians the holy apostle wrote that that day will be revealed in fire.[18] For if there are "many rooms" for rest, as the Lord says,[19] there are also different places for torment. And these trumpets that bring death to those on the earth are the same that also raise the dead afterwards.

Why does it say that when the first angel blew his trumpet, hail and fire consumed a third of those on the earth? Were someone to think that this will happen literally, he would not be interpreting this passage incorrectly. But if we understand the passage figuratively, we will also not be saying anything wrong, for the passage speaks of fire when it refers to the distress and profound grief of the sinners who see the saints "caught up in the clouds to meet the Lord," while they themselves remain dishonorable on the earth and are regarded as worthless. The passage refers figuratively to sinners as trees and grass that are on fire because of their folly and the insensitivity of their souls, which are hard as dry wood and are suitable for burning.

[8:8-9] ***And the second angel, it says, blew his trumpet, and something like a great mountain, burning with fire, was thrown into the sea; and a third of the sea became blood, and a third of the living creatures in the sea died, and a third of the ships were destroyed.***

The holy apostle writes to the Romans that "the creation was subjected to futility, not of its own will but by the will of him who subjected it in hope; because the creation itself will be set free from its bondage to decay and obtain the glorious liberty of the children of God."[20] And when will it be set free? When there will be "new heavens and a new earth according to his promises," as Peter proclaims to us in his second letter.[21] And since the earth changes that it might be freed from corruption and made new, it is necessary that also the sea suffer this same fate, for the sea is on the earth. And how would it also be purified unless by means of purifying fire? And so fire is thrown into it and changes it into blood and kills one third of those in it. This may be interpreted in a literal and perceptible way. However, according to analogy and rhetorical custom, the sea may be regarded as the present life because of its turbulence and many distractions. And one might interpret the fish and the boats to be those persons who are made filthy by salty and bitter sins and who are dissipated by anxiety over useless regrets for what they did in life.

[8:10-11] ***And the third angel blew his trumpet, and a great star fell from heaven, blazing like a torch, and it fell on a third of the rivers and on the fountains of waters, and the name***

[17]1 Thess 4:17. [18]1 Cor 3:13. [19]Jn 14:2. [20]Rom 8:20-21. [21]2 Pet 3:13.

of the star is Wormwood. And a third of the waters became wormwood, and many people died of the water, because it was made bitter.

Naomi, who lived long ago, was called Bitter because of the many troubles she had with her children and with other circumstances of her life.[22] Bitterness is, therefore, a sign of the extraordinary plagues that we sinners might suffer at that time should we become embittered at the glory of the saints, namely, that although such good things have been prepared for humankind, we ourselves exchanged the things of the present for those that are to come. I think the falling star refers to a certain wrath of God that makes the waters bitter. He speaks figuratively of people as waters, according to that spoken by the prophet, "From the voice of many waters, wonderful are the waves of the sea,"[23] and again, "The floods have lifted up, O Lord, the floods have lifted up their voice, the floods lift up their roaring."[24] Although these words are spoken figuratively, it is not impossible that these things and other things like them will literally happen at that time.

[8:12-13] ***The fourth angel blew his trumpet, and a third of the sun was struck, and a third of the moon and a third of the stars, so that a third of the stars was darkened; a third of the day was kept from shining, and likewise a third of the night. Then I looked, and I heard an eagle crying with a loud voice, as it flew in mid-heaven, "Woe, woe, woe to those who dwell on the earth, at the remaining blasts of the trumpet that the three other angels are about to blow."***

We have been taught by Joel the prophet that "the sun shall be turned to darkness, and the moon to blood, before the great and glorious day of the Lord comes,"[25] namely, that all of these events will occur on that day. And in his second letter, Peter said, "The day of the Lord will come as a thief, on which the heavens will pass away with a loud noise, and the elements will be dissolved with fire."[26] And the Lord also says in the hundred and ninth section of Matthew, "Immediately after the tribulation of those days the sun will be darkened, and the moon will not give its light, and the stars will fall from heaven."[27] And now we are taught in this revelation that these things will occur at the consummation of the present age. And why is it said that only a third of what is on earth and in the sea and the rivers and only a third of the heavenly bodies endure these calamities that are mentioned here? This is certainly a clear proof of the goodness of God toward humankind that he calls to repentance the people [overtaken by the afflictions] of that time by the partial dissolution of the elements, rather than their total destruction. On those who do not repent he finally brings a complete destruction. And the prophet says something similar: "He made a path for his anger; he did not spare them from death."[28] For since the wrath of God is incrementally made clear and advances and progresses as though on a road, God is opening a door for repentance and is calling people to a change of heart through fear of that which is coming to pass. But when no change came from them, "he did not spare their souls from death."

We recognize in the eagle flying in mid-heaven a certain divine angel who looks with sorrow on the sufferings of those on the earth and is sympathetic with humankind in their plight.

[9:1-4] ***And the fifth angel blew his trumpet, and I saw a star fallen from heaven to earth, and he was given the key of the shaft of the bottomless pit; and from the shaft rose smoke like the smoke of a great furnace, and the sun and the air were darkened with the smoke.***

[22]Ruth 1:20. [23]Ps 93:4 (92:4 LXX). [24]Ps 93:3 (92:3 LXX). [25]Joel 2:31. [26]2 Pet 3:10. [27]Mt 24:29. [28]Ps 78:50 (77:50 LXX).

Then came locusts on the earth, and they were given power like the power of scorpions of the earth; they were told not to harm the grass of the earth or any green growth or any tree, but only those of humankind who have not the seal of God on their foreheads.

Until now the vision has explained to us how and by what manner of plagues the things on the earth and in heaven and humankind with them shall be brought to completion or will be changed. But now, since the consummation has already occurred and the resurrection has been effected, the vision indicates the punishment of sinners. "I saw a star fallen from heaven to the earth," calling an angel of God a star because it descends to the earth with brightness. For the judgment of sinners will be on the earth, which was called the "valley of Jehoshaphat" by one of the holy prophets.[29] "And he was given," it says, "the key of the shaft of the bottomless pit." He calls Gehenna "the shaft of the bottomless pit." And "smoke rose from the shaft," as though a significant fire was evidently burning in the shaft. So the smoke indicates not only fire but also darkness. For the words of the prophet, "the voice of the Lord divides the flame of fire,"[30] is interpreted by the saints in this way, that the light-giving fire of Gehenna will be divided, so that only the burning heat of the fire along with the darkness remain in it.

"And the sun and the air were darkened with the smoke of the shaft." This does not suggest that these elements were themselves darkened but that those cast into the shaft were filled with darkness because of their punishment and could not any longer see the air and the sun. One of the holy prophets said, "The sun will be darkened at midday,"[31] referring by this to the misfortunes of the Jews, even though the sun had not been darkened. But those who were suffering in this tribulation were not able to see the sun, because the magnitude of their misfortunes could cause dizziness.

"And from the smoke," it says, "came forth locusts on the earth." I think that he calls locusts those worms of which Isaiah spoke: "Their worm will not die, and their fire will not be quenched,"[32] perhaps calling a worm that gnawing of the soul and the unceasing, creeping pain that it suffers.

And, it says, "and they were given power like the power of scorpions on the earth; they were told not to harm the grass of the earth or any green growth or any tree, except human persons only, and of these only those persons who have not the seal of God on their foreheads," since by a transformation the earth had become new. Somewhere it says concerning this, "You will send forth your spirit, and they will be created, and you will renew the face of the earth."[33] It was not yet good that anything that adorns the earth to be stricken, neither a tree nor any plant, except only those persons who "have not the seal of God on their foreheads." For those persons who were perfectly holy and pure had received that place mentioned above, being always with Christ and gazing on the throne of God. However, those persons who are less holy but yet are baptized and bear the sign of Christ on their foreheads and who have not been altogether rejected or have deeply soiled themselves and their baptism by wicked behavior, such persons are, so to speak, halfway between virtue and evil, and these remain on the earth, although without punishment. Were this not the case, why would the Lord say to those who had acted wisely with the pounds entrusted to them, "You shall have authority over ten cities," while to others he said, "over five cities,"[34] since they were to rule over a lesser number? And certainly those ruled by them were without punishment. For who would choose to govern those who were

[29]Joel 3:2, 12. [30]Ps 29:7 (28:7 LXX). [31]Amos 8:9. [32]Is 66:24. [33]Ps 104:3 (103:3 LXX). [34]Lk 19:17, 19.

being punished and constantly gnashing their teeth and mourning their fate inconsolably—I do not speak of the saints or of others like them but merely of persons who nevertheless sympathize—[who would choose to govern such persons] except he who also would agree to endure a fate similar to the incurable circumstances of those being tormented? In any case, a third part of humankind is handed over to torment, since they are sinners and impious and have never received the faith of Christ. And there it is said that those persons suffer calamities who have not been sealed with the seal of God.

[9:5-6] ***And they were not allowed to kill them, it says, but to torture them for five months, and their torture was like the torture of a scorpion, when it stings a person. And in those days people will seek death and will not find it; they will long to die, and death will fly from them.***

Was it not the case that certain Fathers deduced the idea of restoration from this passage, saying that sinners are punished until now but afterward no longer, since they had been purified through punishment?[35] But what is to be done when the majority of the other Fathers and the received Scriptures claim that the torments of those suffering at that time will be everlasting? What should one say, and how should one decide between these options? One must combine these two opinions. I say this as a kind of exercise and not as an outright assertion. For I agree with the teaching of the church that affirms that the punishments in the future age will be everlasting, for this is also what the Lord asserted according to the Gospel of Matthew: "And they will go away into eternal punishment."[36] And Isaiah also said, "Their worm shall not die, and their fire shall not be quenched."[37] But by way of an exercise this must be said, taking a sort of middle path between the two opinions, that until a certain time, which this revelation says is five months, using a certain mystical number, the sinners will be punished with a great severity as though a scorpion were biting them. But after this, they will be punished less severely—for we will not be altogether without punishment—yet to such an extent that they seek death but do not attain it. For what purpose would there be for those to seek death who were not being punished at all? "But death flees from them," it says. For they will endure forever along with their punishment.

[9:7-12] ***In appearance the locusts were like horses arrayed for battle; on their heads were what looked like crowns of gold; their faces were like human faces, and their hair was like women's hair, and their teeth like lions' teeth; they had scales like iron breastplates, and the noise of their wings was like the noise of many chariots with horses rushing into battle. They have tails like scorpions, and stings, and their power of hurting people for five months lies in their tails. They have as king over them the angel of the bottomless pit; his name in Hebrew is Abaddon, and in Greek he is called Apollyon. The first woe has passed; behold, two woes are still to come.***

After this the blessed Evangelist describes for us the character of the worms in a way that is both precise and fearsome. And one might marvel at the accuracy of all that is said concerning them. For he does not say, "they had the teeth of lions and the tails of scorpions and the faces of people," but using in each instance the word *like* he describes them by means of a certain similitude and clarifying analogy, but not literally. Through these images, therefore,

[35]Oecumenius has in mind the Origenists who believed that at the end, all things would be purified and restored. This opinion was condemned at the Council of Constantinople II (Fifth Ecumenical Council) in 553. [36]Mt 25:46. [37]Is 66:24.

he either reveals their fearsome and terrifying nature or sketches what in fact they look like.

"And they have," it says, "over them as king the angel of the bottomless pit, and his name in Hebrew is Abaddon, and in Greek he is called Apollyon." The name suggests either the substance of the details of the vision and what is appropriate to it, or at least it shows that there are not only "ministering spirits sent forth to serve, for the sake of those who are to obtain salvation," as the apostle says,[38] but there are also spirits sent forth for the punishment of those worthy of punishment. Such a spirit was that spirit who in one night destroyed 185,000 Assyrians,[39] and such were those who burned by fire the five cities of the Sodomites.[40] "The first woe has passed," it says, "behold, two woes are still to come." A woe is a cry of those who are in distress that indicates what afflictions they are presently suffering or will suffer in the future. It says that one woe has been mentioned and that two more will be narrated.

[9:13-19] ***And the sixth angel blew his trumpet, and I heard a great voice from the horns of the golden altar before God, saying to the sixth angel who had the trumpet, "Release the four angels who are bound at the great river Euphrates." So the four angels were released, who had been held ready for the hour, the day, the month and the year, to kill a third of humankind. The number of the troops of cavalry was ten thousand times ten thousand; I heard their number. And this was how I saw the horses in my vision: the riders wore breastplates the color of fire and of hyacinth and of sulfur, and the heads of the horses were like lions' heads, and fire and smoke and sulfur issued from their mouths. By these three plagues a third of humankind was killed, by the fire and smoke and sulfur issuing from their mouths. For the power of the horses is in their mouths and in their tails; their tails are like serpents, with heads, and by means of them they wound.***

When the angel blew his trumpet, it says, "I heard a voice from the horns of the altar." By the "horns of the altar" he refers to those preeminent among the angels and who are superior to all the others. He says that the altar is golden, for in mentioning that element that is of great value among us, he describes the altar as precious and holy and wondrous. And since we understand the horns of the altar to refer to the leaders of the angels, it follows that we interpret the altar itself to refer to all the ministering spirits on account of the spiritual sacrifice they bring to God.

But what is that voice heard from the horns of the altar? It says, "Release the four angels bound at the great river Euphrates." The divine Scriptures sometimes represents to us the apostate angel—by which I mean Satan and those who fell along with him—as having been bound in darkness by eternal chains. At other times it represents him as having been condemned to the depths of the sea. In his second letter, Peter says, "For if God did not spare the angels when they sinned but cast them into Tartarus and to the pits of gloom, to be held for judgment,"[41] and in his letter Jude says, "The angels that did not keep their own rule but left their proper dwelling, he kept in gloom by eternal chains for the judgment of the great day."[42] Also in the book of Job it says that the apostate was cast into the sea, in many ways speaking figuratively of the form, size and bitterness of his abode, saying also that "the angels of God make sport of him."[43] And concerning him Isaiah also spoke, saying that the sword of God will come down "on the dragon, the fleeing serpent, the dragon, the twisting snake, and will slay on that day the dragon that is in the sea."[44] And having mentioned everything in creation, the prophet

[38]Heb 1:14. [39]2 Kings 19:35; Is 37:36. [40]Gen 19:1-29; 2 Pet 2:6. [41]2 Pet 2:4. [42]Jude 6. [43]Job 41:25 LXX. [44]Is 27:1.

speaks concerning him and adds this about the creatures in the sea: "The dragon itself, which you did make to play in the sea."[45] And in agreement with these passages, the blessed prophet Ezekiel also says concerning the Egyptian, "You are like a lion among the nations, and you are like a dragon in the sea, and you have burst forth in your rivers."[46]

But there is no tradition among us that these angels are bound at the river Euphrates or will ever be loosed, or that people will be punished through them. For when Jude says that they are bound "by eternal chains," he excludes the idea that they will ever be released. And when Isaiah says that the dragon that is in the sea will be killed on the day of judgment, he does not say that he will kill others but that he will be killed. When, moreover, in the Gospels the Lord sends the sinners "into the fire prepared for the devil and his angels,"[47] he is not saying that he would use them as his instruments of vengeance and retribution. Rather, he means that they would be subjected to punishment. How, therefore, should someone understand the present claim that they are bound "at the river Euphrates" and that they will be released and that they will punish sinners? I think that he is speaking figuratively, as is customary in visions. I think he means to say that the angels are bound to the vision of God, which gladdens the soul. For that which is divine is figuratively called a river by Isaiah, "Behold, I will turn toward them as a river of peace and the wealth of nations as an overflowing stream,"[48] and by the prophet, "The streams of the river make glad the city of God."[49] And in section twenty-two of the Gospel of John, the Lord says of the Holy Spirit, "He who believes in me, as the Scripture says, rivers of living water will flow from his belly."[50] It says that he loosed these angels from the vision of God and sent them for the punishment of the wicked, for these have been set apart for the coming day. What kind of angels are these four? Perhaps they are those mentioned in the Scripture—Michael, Gabriel, Uriel and Raphael. When the trumpet is blown, they went out with an army of cavalry of a great, indeterminate size. This indicates the invincible power of the angels of God, whom he compares with a very large cavalry.

"I saw the riders on the horses, and they wore breastplates the color of fire and of hyacinth and of sulfur." The fire is symbolic of wrath and punishment. The hyacinth reveals that these who are sent are of heaven, for the sky is similar to hyacinth.[51] The color of sulfur indicates that they are pleasing to God, since they are delightful to God—for to delight is to please.[52] And who would please God more than the holy angels? Then the vision changes imagery and exalts the power of the holy angels, comparing them with lions and with fire, smoke and brimstone and snakes. In all of these analogies their fearsomeness and irresistibility is signified.

[9:20-21] ***The rest of humankind, who were not killed by these plagues, did not repent of the works of their hands or cease to worship the demons and idols of gold and silver and bronze and stone and wood, which cannot either see or hear or walk; nor did they repent of their murders or their sorceries or their thefts.***

As though plucking on a spiritual lyre, the prophet had described for us the fate of those being punished in hades, saying to God, "In death there is no one who remembers you;

[45]Ps 104:26 (103:26 LXX). [46]Ezek 32:2. [47]Mt 25:41. [48]Is 66:12. [49]Ps 46:4 (45:5 LXX). [50]Jn 7:38. [51]The hyacinth is blue in color. [52]There is a clear wordplay here. Θειώδης means both "yellow like sulfur" and "godlike." Since these angels are godlike, they are pleasing to God. θεοάδης is here translated "delightful to God." De Groote believes that the Greek is based on the verb ἁδεῖν(= ἁνδάνω), "to please, gratify, delight" (TEG 8:153). Hence the translation "to delight is to please." It is possible that Oecumenius wishes also to play on the verb ᾄδειν, "to sing." In that case, θεοάδης would suggest one who "sings to God." The angels sing to God and so are pleasing to him.

in hades who will confess you?"[53] He thus indicates that they are deprived of both joy with God and repentance. Since they did not remember God, they were deprived of spiritual joy—for somewhere else he says, "I remembered God and was made glad"[54]—and since they did not confess, they were deprived of repentance. Confession is the declaration of faults out of sorrow and a conversion that comes from contrition in the soul. Indeed, God has set before us two kinds of life, the present one and the future one. In the present one we are to live according to prudent judgment and authority, while in the future life there are rewards for how one has lived. The present life is not one of judgment, unless someone should perhaps be beneficially reminded and urged toward repentance. Nor is the future one of works and habits, so that we may be changed from a life filled with accusations into something better. This being the case, how is it then that this verse says of those being punished there, "and the rest of humankind, who were not killed by these plagues, did not repent of the works of their hands"? He did not say this of those who did not repent in the life there but of those who are still living and have not repented from their various evil deeds either out of obedience or from the sight of that which will occur then. And by this present plague they will not die the spiritual death—calling punishment "death"—since they endure forever with the wicked, unless they will be punished in another, harsher manner, which he wisely kept secret in his explanation. May all of us remain free from such things by the grace and goodness of our Lord, Jesus Christ, with whom be glory to the Father with the Holy Spirit forever. Amen.

Sixth Discourse

In this discourse the blessed John continues his explanation concerning what occurred when the sixth angel blew his trumpet. I did not give an interpretation of all of these under one discourse, because the fifth discourse was becoming too long. What else does he write concerning these events?

[10:1-4] ***Then I saw a mighty angel coming down from heaven, wrapped in a cloud, with a rainbow over his head, and his face was like the sun, and his legs like pillars of fire. And he had a little scroll open in his hand. And he set his right foot on the sea and his left foot on the land, and he called out with a loud voice, like a lion roaring. And when he called out, the seven thunders sounded their voices. And when the seven thunders had sounded, I was about to write, but I heard a voice from heaven saying, "Seal up what the seven thunders have said, and do not write it down."***

He says, "I saw an angel descending from heaven." The angel comes with various forms of punishment against those who were still alive, and even though they had heard or seen the torments of the sinners, they had nonetheless not repented but had remained in their wickedness. His appearance and equipment were as follows. He was wrapped in a cloud. The cloud signifies the formlessness and invisibility of the holy angels, for the cloud is a symbol of invisibility, as the prophet clearly indicates when he speaks of the invisibility of God, saying, "A cloud and deep darkness were around him."[1] "And a rainbow was over his head." This is as though he had said, "The primary and distinctive feature of the good angels is brightness," for they are angels of light.

"And his face was as the sun," it says. This is a demonstration of his unmixed brightness. While the rainbow gives of a created brightness and is indicative of that brightness that comes through virtues—for that reason, the brightness of the rainbow is not uniform but is varied, signifying all the virtues of the

[53]Ps 6:5 (6:6 LXX). [54]Ps 76:4 (LXX). **Sixth Discourse** [1]Ps 97:2 (96:2 LXX).

angels—the sun is symbolic of their natural brilliance. Therefore, he was wrapped in a rainbow—for the virtues of the angels are around us—but his face resembled the sun, for in us there is every natural excellence. "And his feet were like pillars of fire." Fire symbolizes that punishment that he brought against the impious.

"And he had in his hand," it says, "a little scroll opened." Daniel recalled such scrolls when he said, "The tribunal sat before him, and books were opened."[2] It was the little scroll in which were written both the names and the transgressions of the severely wicked who are going to be punished. And therefore he used the diminutive "little scroll," since there is a book or a scroll—both are mentioned in holy Scripture—in which the names of all people are written, as I said above.[3] But here he speaks of a little scroll in which the names of the exceedingly wicked are written. For those who worship idols and are marked by murders and sorceries and are enfeebled in other ways that he mentions would not be sufficient in number to fill an entire book.

"And he set his right foot on the sea and his left foot on the land." On the one hand, this is an indication of the multitude of the saints, but on the other hand this indicates that he was carrying the instruments of punishment for those who transgressed on the land and on the sea, in that they were drowned in it, and who had otherwise done evil. "And he called out with a great voice, like a lion roaring." That the holy angel roars like a lion is symbolic of his wrath against the impious. "And when he called out," it says, "the seven thunders sounded their voices." He calls the seven ministering spirits seven thunders. They were mentioned earlier.[4] Here he mentions them by way of the definite article, "the seven thunders," referring to those seven spirits who bear the offering. What does it mean that the seven spirits cry out? It means that these also concur fully with the punishments against the sinners and bring forth a hymn of thanksgiving to God, that all that he has done is just. And they cried out together revealing the forms of the punishments.

"I was about to write" what was said by the seven spirits, it says, but "I heard a voice from heaven, saying, 'Seal up what the seven thunders have said, and do not write it down.' " The command to seal up in effect means "hold it in the memory imprinted on your mind." To be sure, the reason for prohibiting the writing down of what was said is known to God alone. Perhaps the punishments would be thought too light and unworthy of the goodness of the one who punishes, and so they would become contemptible to people. What do the holy Gregory and Evagrius, who are great in knowledge, say of these things? Gregory says, "The retribution that comes to those who followed Adam is benevolence, for it is in mercy, I am persuaded, that God inflicts punishment,"[5] and in another place, "There is neither mercy without judgment, nor judgment without mercy." And Evagrius says, "Let the more sublime word concerning judgment be kept hidden from the young and the worldly. For they do not understand the suffering of the rational soul that is condemned to ignorance."[6]

[10:5-7] ***And the angel whom I saw standing on the sea and land lifted up his right hand to heaven and swore by him who lives forever and ever, who created heaven and what is in it, the earth and what is in it, and the sea and what is in it, that there should be no more delay, but that in the days of the seventh angel, when he should blow his trumpet [the mystery of God,***

[2]Dan 7:10. [3]See the comments of Oecumenius on Rev 5:1. Oecumenius distinguishes between βίβλος ("book"), βιβλίον ("scroll") and βιβλιάριον ("little scroll"). Those who are especially heinous sinners are not of sufficient number to require a full book or scroll. [4]In his comments on Rev 9:11. [5]Gregory of Nazianzus *Or.* 38.12 (NPNF 2 7:348); 45.8 (NPNF 2 7:425). [6]Evagrius Ponticus *Gnosticus* 36.

as he announced to his servants the prophets, should be fulfilled].

This is said in the manner of an ellipsis. For it says, "When the seventh angel was about to blow his trumpet," all the various and different punishments against the impious will be fulfilled. He does not say that this will now occur when he blows his trumpet in this vision, since the other woes have not yet occurred. Rather, this will happen when he blows his trumpet at the appointed time. And when this has happened, "the mystery of God as he proclaimed it to his servants, the prophets" will receive its completion. For the prophets prophesied until the judgment and the recompense of the good and the wicked, but after that they prophesied no longer. Therefore, when the seventh angel blows his trumpet at that time, every mystery and every prophecy will receive its fulfillment.

[10:8-11] ***And the voice that I heard from heaven spoke to me again, saying, "Go, take the scroll that is open in the hand of the angel who is standing on the sea and on the land." And I went to the angel and told him, "Give me the scroll." And he said to me, "Take it and eat; it will be bitter to your stomach but sweet as honey in your mouth." And I took the little scroll from the hand of the angel and ate it; it was sweet as honey in my mouth, but when I had eaten it my stomach was made bitter. And he said to me, "It is necessary that you prophesy again about many peoples and nations and tongues and kings."***

"And the voice that I heard from heaven," it says, "I heard it again speaking to me." What did it say? "Take the scroll from the angel." When I took it, it says, I ate it, and "it was sweet in my mouth," but after the eating, it was bitter to my stomach. Then the blessed Evangelist saw and heard the torments against the wicked that he might learn by experience, and not only by report, how bitter and abominable are the transgressions of people that are brought to God. He was taught this through this vision—for as a holy and chaste man, he did not know this from his own experience—and through the vision he came to know that the wrath of God against the wicked is just. For the scroll contained the names and also the sins of the most grievous transgressors, as I noted before.[7] He is therefore commanded to eat it, and as though by taste and a sort of spiritual experience of the bitterness of sin that comes through his vision, he found that what had been sweet to the mouth was, when eaten, bitter to the stomach afterward. For such it is with every sin. It is sweet in the doing but bitter in its consequences. And this becomes a sort of agent for punishment, since it makes bitter with regret those who have made use of it. This was also the case with the tree in paradise that was forbidden by God and that all interpret figuratively in reference to sin. For it produced the knowledge of good and of evil, of good in the tasting and of evil after the experience.

And he said to me, "It is necessary that you prophesy again about many peoples and nations and tongues and kings." This is as though he had said, "Although you have seen the consummation of the age and the wrath against the wicked in this vision, do not think that the day of fulfillment has in fact come. There remains much time yet for you to prophesy to many nations and to kings." And so it is that up to the present time the blessed Evangelist prophesies through his Gospel and his Catholic Epistles and this Revelation. For all things have been spoken and prophesied to him by the Spirit.

[11:1-2] ***And I was given a measuring rod like***

[7]See his comments on Rev 10:2.

a staff, and I was told, "Rise and measure the temple of God and the altar and those who worship there, but do not measure the court outside the temple; leave that out, for it is given over to the nations, and they will trample over the holy city for forty-two months."

The blessed John had earlier seen a vision of the multitude of saints who are with Christ and who behold the throne of God. Among these there were many more Gentiles than there were those from Israel.[8] The present vision now reveals something else to John. It reveals how many were pleasing to God at the time of the Old Testament and how many at the time of the New Testament. And note how cleverly this is sketched out for him. He is given a measuring stick that he might measure "the temple of God and the altar" in the temple (clearly the one in Jerusalem) "and those worshiping in it." And he measured. Those who pleased God during the time of the Old Testament were easily measured because there were so few of them. "But do not measure the court outside the temple; leave that out, for it is given over to the nations." When he had measured the temple and the altar and those sacrificing within, he heard that it was necessary to place the court on the outside and to widen it but definitely not to measure it, since it was greater than any measure. The court, it says, is given over to the nations, and it is adjacent to and lies outside the temple. Likewise, the New Testament follows immediately on the Old, for it fulfills spiritually and in reality that which has but shadow in it. And realities of a different kind arise next to the Old Testament, as Jeremiah says, "Behold, the days are coming, says the Lord, and I will make a new covenant with the house of Israel and the house of Judah, not like the covenant that I made with their fathers when I took them by the hand to bring them out of the land of Egypt."[9] For this reason he calls the New Testament the "court of the temple." And so the vision indicates in a mystical manner that he who in the New Testament is named "Christ" and "Beginning" was Lord of the Old Testament. Paul also expressed this idea, for he says concerning Israel, "for they drank from the spiritual rock that followed them, and the rock was Christ."[10] Moreover, the vision calls the New Testament the court of the Old Testament. For the court is the beginning and entrance to God, but it is not the temple. Therefore, he did not measure the court by which both the New Testament and those in it are signified. For both the New Testament and those justified in it are beyond comprehension, these because of their unspeakable magnitude and the New Testament because of its subtlety and the sublimity of its teachings. For, it says, "it was given over to the nations." The blessings of the New Testament were given also to Israel, but since the Gentiles in it are greater in number than those who were pleasing from Israel, it indicates the whole from the greater part, saying that the court was given to the nations.

"And they will trample on the holy city for forty-two months." It speaks of the city, not of the temple, calling the church a city, about which it says, "Glorious things are spoken of you, O city of God, the heavenly Jerusalem, the mother of the firstborn who are enrolled in heaven."[11] And what does it mean that the measuring will be for forty-two months? It indicates that there is little time remaining on the earth for the citizenship given in the New Testament and that afterward the end will come. For the number forty, the sum of four tens, is not complete, nor is the number two. By these numbers the verse shows that the duration of the New Testament does not last long in the present life, and so the Scripture

[8]See his comments on Rev 7:9. [9]Jer 31:31-32. [10]1 Cor 10:4. [11]A conflation of Ps 87:3, 5 (86:3, 5 LXX); Gal 4:26; Heb 12:22-23.

calls the time of the New Testament the "last" hour or the "eleventh" hour,[12] at which time the Only-begotten became man. But he will endure forever in the coming life. That the nations are said to trample the holy city, that is, the church, means that they dwell in it.

[11:3-6] ***And I will grant my two witnesses power to prophesy for two thousand two hundred and sixty days, clothed in sackcloth. These are the two lampstands that stand before the God of the earth. And if anyone would harm them, fire pours from their mouth and consumes their foes; if anyone would harm them, thus he will be killed. They have power to shut the sky, that no rain may fall during the days of their prophesying, and they have power over the waters to turn them into blood, and to smite the earth with every plague, as often as they wish.***

Since the vision outlined for the Evangelist the entire economy of the Lord's incarnation—the birth, the temptation, his teachings, the beatings, also the cross and resurrection, the second coming and the reward of both the holy and the sinners—it had left unmentioned any information about the forerunners of his second coming. Now, as though by a sharp U-turn, the vision teaches him about them. When Malachi said, "Behold, I will send you Elijah the Tishbite before the great and terrible day of the Lord comes, who will turn the heart of a father to the son and the heart of a man to his neighbor, lest I come to trample the land utterly,"[13] the holy Scripture with great clarity foretold that Elijah the Tishbite will come. And in Matthew, the Lord spoke of the Baptist: "And if you are willing to accept it, this is Elijah who is to come."[14] Concerning other forerunners we have heard nothing with clarity except that Genesis said concerning Enoch that "having pleased God, he was taken,"[15] and the wise apostle said concerning him, "By faith Enoch was taken up so that he should not see death; and he was not found, because God had taken him."[16] An old, traditional saying is prevalent in the church, that with Elijah the Tishbite also Enoch will come as a forerunner of the second coming of Christ and at the coming of the antichrist.[17]

This passage says that they come and proclaim beforehand that the signs performed by the antichrist are deceptive and that it is not necessary to believe the sinful one. Using either a certain figurative number or a literal description of what will be, the vision now reports of these forerunners that they will prophesy so many days. They will prophesy "clothed in sackcloth," for they will lament over the disobedience of those who live at that time. "These," it says, "are the two olive trees and the two lampstands that stand before the Lord of the earth." The holy prophet Zechariah saw a lampstand holding seven lamps and two olive branches. But these two branches were placed in two holes of the lampstand as though to say, "What are the two olive branches who are near the two golden holes?"[18] And he heard the response of the angel, "These are the sons of oil who stand by the Lord of all the earth."[19] And so, is he not still speaking of them here? Using the definite article, "these are the two olive branches and the two lampstands," he shows how the symbol is to be regarded, although there he called them "two holes" and here "two lamps." The saints are fully aware that the two olive branches have been interpreted to be the two peoples, namely, those from the Jews and those from the nations. However, it is also

[12]"Last" (Jn 6:39, 40, 44, 54; Acts 2:17; 2 Tim 3:1), although the phrase is "last day," not "last hour." For "eleventh" see Mt 20:9. [13]Mal 4:4-5 (3:23-23 LXX). [14]Mt 11:14. [15]Gen 5:24. [16]Heb 11:5. [17]From the second century onward it was common opinion that Enoch would accompany Elijah as forerunners of Christ at the end of time. See Tertullian *On the Soul* 50; Hippolytus *Antich.* 43; perhaps already Irenaeus *Haer.* 5.5.1. [18]Zech 4:12. "Holes" translates οἱ μυξωτῆρες, a rare word meaning "nostrils," and hence the holes that hold the wicks of a lamp. [19]Zech 4:14. In the LXX, "sons of oil" is literally "sons of fatness." The phrase means that they are anointed.

possible that the present passage is speaking of two prophets. The fire that comes out of their mouths keeps those away who wish to do them harm, and "they have power to shut the sky that no rain may fall during the days of their prophesying." Such is the power of these most persuasive individuals. For if one of them, Elijah the Tishbite, had such power even before he fulfilled his service to Christ,[20] how would he have less power as the precursor of Christ? "And they had power," it says, "over the waters to turn them into blood, and to smite the earth with every plague as often as they wish." For since "the coming of the antichrist will be by the activity of Satan with all power and with deceitful signs and wonders," as Paul says in his second letter to the Thessalonians, [21] these signs will attract to agreement and faith. And for this reason these two prophets who speak of him as a deceiver and a cheat will also make use of various signs, so that they might attract those who hear to faith.

[11:7-10] ***And when they finished their testimony, the beast that ascends from the bottomless pit will make war on them and conquer them and kill them; and he will put their dead bodies in the street of the great city that is spiritually called Sodom and Egypt, where also their Lord was crucified. And people from the peoples and tongues and tribes and nations will look at their dead bodies and will not allow them to be buried, and those who dwell on the earth will rejoice over them and make merry and exchange presents, because these two prophets had been a torment to those living on the earth.***

"And when," it says, "they finished their testimony." The witnesses will testify that the one who is present is not the Christ but a certain rogue, a deceiver and a destroyer. He will in no way come as the Son of God in whom one must believe as Savior and as God and who came for the benefit of humankind both in his appearance long ago and in his present appearing.

It speaks of "the beast that ascends from the bottomless pit." He calls the antichrist a beast because of his savagery, his inhumanity and his thirst for blood. He calls the life of people a bottomless pit, for it is bitter and distasteful on account of sins and unstable because it is buffeted about by evil spirits. For the sinful one will not arise out of any other substance but out of our own human nature, for he will be a man "whose coming is in the activity of Satan," as was just now said. This beast, it says, will kill the two witnesses and will cast their dead bodies unburied in the streets of Jerusalem. For in it he will rule as king of the Jews whom he will deceive, and he will come to those who assist and trust him in every thing. As the Lord said in the Gospel of John: "I have come in my Father's name, and you do not receive me; if another comes in his own name, him you will receive."[22] He calls Jerusalem Sodom, not in a literal sense but in a spiritual sense on account of the licentiousness and ill repute it possessed at that time. And he calls it also Egypt because it had enslaved and abused the servants of Christ, just as the actual Egypt did to Israel. And it was there "where also their Lord," that is, the Lord of the two witnesses, "was crucified." Seeing the destruction of the witnesses, those from every nation who have been deceived by the antichrist will rejoice over them, as though their own king had conquered. That they exchange gifts is another indication of their glee and delight.

"Because these two prophets," it says, "had been a torment to those living on the earth." The prophets will not torment them with any physical torment, but they will torment them spiritually by mocking and reproving them for their sins and by making their deceit utterly clear.

[20]See 1 Kings 17:1; 18:1, 41-45; Lk 4:25. [21]2 Thess 2:9. [22]Jn 5:43.

[11:11-14] ***But after the three and a half days a breath of life from God entered them, and they stood up on their feet, and a great fear fell on those who saw them. And they heard a loud voice from heaven saying to them, "Come up here!" And they went up to heaven on a cloud, and their enemies saw them. And at that hour there was a great earthquake, and a tenth of the city fell; seven thousand were killed in the earthquake, and the rest were terrified and gave glory to the God of heaven. The second woe has passed; behold, the third woe is soon to come.***

Since all these things are clearly occurring and will happen visibly at that time, it would be unhelpful to dwell on that which has already received consensus.

[11:15-19] ***And the seventh angel blew his trumpet, and there were loud voices in heaven, saying, "The kingdom of the world has become the kingdom of our Lord and of his Christ, and he shall reign forever and ever." And the twenty-four elders who sit on their thrones before God fell on their faces and worshiped God, saying, "We give thanks to you, Lord God, the Almighty, who is and who was, that you have taken your great power and begun to reign. The nations raged, but your wrath came, and the time for the nations to be judged, for rewarding your servants, the prophets and saints, and those who fear your name, both small and great, and for the destroying the destroyers of the earth." And the temple of God in heaven was opened, and the ark of the covenant was seen within his temple; and there were flashes of lightning, voices, and thunder, an earthquake and heavy hail.***

By way of digression the vision related the attacks on the two witnesses or prophets and discussed everything about them. The vision now returns to the previous narrative from which it departed. It has spoken of the future reward of the saints and that those from the nations were more numerous than those from Israel, and those who pleased God in the New Testament more numerous than those who pleased him in the Old Testament.

And, it says, when the seventh angel blew his trumpet "there were voices in heaven saying, 'The kingdom of the world has become the kingdom of God and of his Christ.'" To be sure, God always is king and has never begun or indeed shall ever cease to rule the heaven and the earth and that which is visible and invisible in them, for he is without beginning and without ending Master and Lord of all things. However, since also people take the title of king on earth and after a manner God has these reigning with him, when the earthly kingdom of people is dissolved at the consummation of the present age, God alone will rule. And for this reason it says that "the kingdom of the world has become the kingdom of God and of his Christ," because those people who rule on the earth and the tyrannical demons have been destroyed and brought to an end.

When the voice was heard, "the elders worshiped God," bringing their own thanksgiving and saying, "We give you thanks, O Lord God, the Almighty, who is and who was." The phrases "who is" and "who was" are fitting to be used of the holy Trinity, although usually "who is" is used of the Father and "who was" of the Son.[23] For "to be" is true of the Father and of the Son and of the Holy Spirit, and we speak rightly when we say "was" of the Father and Son and Holy Spirit. Therefore, the thanksgiving of the elders is ascribed to the holy Trinity. "For," it says, "you have taken your great power" and your rule that you gave to them from those on the earth, and you now alone rule. And since the earthly kingdom is

[23]See the comments of Oecumenius on Rev 1:4; 4:6-8.

destroyed, naturally "the nations raged," for they had been deprived of their dominion—by "nations" he speaks of the ranks of the demons and those of unfaithful people. "But your wrath has come," it says, "and the lot of the nations to be judged and to give the reward to your servants the prophets and the saints." Although, it says, you exercised great longsuffering toward them in the past, they made no use of your kindness, and now, that is, in the day of judgment, you have brought your wrath against them, that is to say, that the fate that has been determined for the nations has come and is present. And what is this? This, namely, that they are judged and that recompense is given to the saints who had suffered evil from them, and that they who had corrupted the earth by polluting it with their sins be destroyed by the recompense of punishment.

"And the temple of God in heaven was opened," it says, "and the ark of his covenant was seen in his temple." When this had been said, those good things that had been hidden, and in addition to these certain new mysteries, were seen by the saints. For this is the significance of the ark of the covenant being opened. And Paul shows that the good things of the coming age are hidden from people at the present time by saying, "What no eye has seen, nor ear heard, nor the heart of man conceived, that God has prepared for those who love him."[24] And that there will be certain mysteries and another knowledge that is now unknown, the Lord shows when he said, "I shall not drink again of this fruit of the vine until that day when I drink it new with you in my Father's kingdom."[25] While the saints have been thought worthy of these things, for the sinners "there were flashes of lightning, voices, and thunder, earthquakes and heavy hail." This is the third woe. From that which is familiar to us, the passage depicts those punishments and terrors from God that come on the wicked.

[12:1-2] ***And a great sign appeared in heaven, a woman clothed with the sun, with the moon under her feet, and on her head a crown of twelve stars; she was with child, and she cried out in her pangs of birth, in anguish for delivery.***

The vision intends to describe more completely to us the circumstances concerning the antichrist, whom we mentioned briefly in previous discussion. However, since the incarnation of the Lord, which made the world his possession and subjected it, provided a pretext for Satan to raise up the antichrist and to choose him as his instrument—for the antichrist will be raised to cause the world again to fall from Christ and to persuade it to desert to Satan—and since moreover his fleshly conception and birth was the beginning of the incarnation of the Lord,[26] the vision gives a certain order and sequence to the material that it is going to discuss and begins the discussion from the fleshly conception of the Lord by portraying for us the mother of God.[27] What does he say? "And a sign appeared in heaven, a woman clothed with the sun, and the moon was under her feet." As I said, it is speaking about the mother of our Savior. And the vision appropriately depicts her as in heaven and not on the earth, for she is pure in soul and body, equal to an angel and a citizen of heaven. She possesses God who rests in heaven—"for heaven is my throne," it says[28]—yet she is flesh, although she has nothing in common with the earth, nor is there any evil in her. Rather, she is fully exalted, wholly worthy of heaven, even though she possesses our own human nature and substance. For the Virgin is consubstantial with us. Let the impious teaching of Eutyches, which makes

[24]1 Cor 2:9. [25]Mt 26:29. [26]Ἐνανθρώπησις, or "incarnation," often refers, especially in the Greek tradition, not merely to the assumption of the flesh but to the entire work of Christ for humankind. [27]Θεοτόκος, a term for Mary used by the councils of Ephesus (431) and Chalcedon (451) to claim that Mary was the mother not only of a man but of the divine Son who assumed flesh and was born from her. [28]Is 66:1; Acts 7:49.

the fanciful claim that the Virgin is of another substance than we,[29] be excluded from the belief of the holy courts together with his other opinions.

And what does it mean that she was clothed with the sun and the moon was under her feet? The holy prophet Habakkuk prophesied concerning the Lord, saying, "The sun was lifted up, and the moon stood still its course for light,"[30] calling Christ our Savior, or at least the proclamation of the gospel, the "sun of righteousness."[31] When he was exalted and increased, the moon—that is, the law of Moses—"stood still" and no longer received any addition. For after the appearance of Christ, it no longer received proselytes from the nations as before but underwent diminution and cessation. You will, therefore, observe this with me, that also the holy Virgin is covered by the spiritual sun. For this is what the prophet calls the Lord when concerning Israel he says, "Fire fell on them, and they did not see the sun."[32] But the moon—that is, the worship according to the Law and the way of life according to the Law—being subdued and become much less than itself, is under her feet, for it has been conquered by the brightness of the gospel. And rightly does he call the things of the Law by the word *moon*, for they have been given light by the sun, that is, Christ, just as the physical moon is given its light by the physical sun. The point would have been better made had it said not that the woman was clothed with the sun but that the woman enclothed the sun, which was enclosed in her womb. However, that the vision might show that the Lord, even as he was being carried in the womb, was the shelter of his own mother and of the whole creation, it says that he was enclothing the woman. Indeed, the holy angel said something similar to the holy Virgin: "The Spirit of the Lord will come on you, and the power of the Most High will overshadow you."[33] For to overshadow is to protect, and to enclothe is the same according to power.

"And on her head," it says, "a crown of twelve stars." For the Virgin is crowned with the twelve apostles who proclaim Christ, while she is also proclaimed with him. "And she was with child," it says, "and she cried out in her pangs of birth, in anguish for delivery." Clearly Isaiah speaks concerning her: "Before she was in labor she gave birth; before the pain of her labor she fled and gave birth to a son."[34] Also in his thirteenth homily on the Song concerning the Lord, Gregory says, "whose pregnancy remains without union, and the childbirth without defilement, and the labor free of pain."[35] If according to such a prophet and to such a teacher of the church the Virgin escaped the pain of childbirth, how is it that here it says "she cried out in her pangs of birth, in anguish for delivery"? What is said is not contradictory. By no means! For there would be nothing contradictory said by the same Spirit who was speaking through both. Rather, you will understand the present phrase "she cried out and was in anguish" in this way. Until the holy angel said to Joseph that that which was borne in her womb was of the Holy Spirit, she was faint of heart, as is natural for a virgin, and she blushed before her betrothed and thought that perhaps from the secrecy of the marriage he might think that she was in labor. And so, according to the rules of figurative language, he calls this faintheartedness and sorrow a "crying out" and "anguish." Nor is this unusual. For even to the blessed Moses, when he was spiritually conversing with God and losing heart—for he saw Israel in the desert surrounded by the sea and the enemy—God said, "Why are you crying to me?"[36] So also here, the vision calls the troubled disposition

[29]The Council of Chalcedon (451) condemned Eutyches for claiming that the unity of Christ was by way of a "mixture," which seemed to deny that the flesh of Christ, taken from the Virgin Mary, was of the same substance (ὁμοούσιος) as is our flesh. [30]Hab 3:11. [31]The phrase comes from Mal 4:2, not from Habakkuk. [32]Ps 57:9 (LXX). [33]Lk 1:35. [34]Is 66:7 (LXX). [35]Gregory of Nyssa *Homilies on the Song of Songs* 13 (PG 44:1053). [36]Ex 14:15.

of the Virgin in her mind and heart a crying out. But may you, who by your unspeakable birth did bring to an end the faintheartedness of your undefiled servant, your mother according to the flesh, but my mistress, the holy mother of God, also forgive my sins. For it is proper to give you glory forever. Amen.

Seventh Discourse

Having completed in part the vision concerning our common mistress, the holy, ever-virgin Mary, the mother of God, he presents to us another vision.

[12:3-6] ***And another sign appeared in heaven; behold, a great red dragon, with seven heads and ten horns, and seven diadems on his heads. His tail swept down a third of the stars of heaven and cast them to the earth. And the dragon stood before the woman who was about to bear a child, that he might devour her child when she brought it forth; she brought forth a male child, one who is to rule all the nations with a rod of iron, but her child was caught up to God and to his throne, and the woman fled into the wilderness, where she has a place prepared by God, that there they might nourish her for one thousand two hundred and sixty days.***

I indicated at the beginning of the preceding vision that it intended to explain more fully the events concerning the antichrist, starting with the conception and birth of the Lord. This would be the occasion for the common foe and enemy of all to cause the rise of that destroyer, so that he might enslave once more those whom the Lord had gathered to himself. Now the vision intends to depict more fully the events concerning the antichrist, starting with an event even prior to that mentioned earlier (I refer here to the birth of the Lord). It speaks now of the casting of Satan down from heaven. Although he will speak more plainly of this in the following vision, explaining that he had even plotted against the Lord, with this beginning he lays down as it were a foundation, so that he might build on it with further discussion of the antichrist and his works. And so, this being said by way of introduction, we must now move on to a consideration of the words of this passage.

"And another sign appeared in heaven." As though rebuking Satan, that author of evil, who although a heavenly being became base because of his pride,[1] the passage shows him first in heaven, so that the apostate might know from what heights to what depths he has fallen. "Behold, a great red dragon," it says. He calls Satan a dragon because of his deceitful ways. Isaiah also speaks of him in this way, saying, "against the dragon, that twisting serpent."[2] He is said to be red because of his thirst for blood and his angry nature. He had "seven heads and ten horns, and seven diadems on his heads." The prophet also knew that he had many heads, and therefore he says to God, "You have crushed the heads of the dragon; you did give him as food to the people of Ethiopia."[3] It refers to him as having many heads, since, as we have often noted, seven signifies many, for he exercises many dominions and performs many crafty plots against people by which he enslaves them. The diadem too is a symbol of tyranny, and the ten horns signify his very great power, for the number ten is perfect and the horn is a symbol of power. For it is said, "My horn will be exalted like that of a unicorn."[4] And one may learn that he is powerful by reading the book of Job.

"And by his tail he swept down a third of the stars of heaven and cast them to the earth." Along with himself, the dragon cast down a very great number of angels. For he had persuaded them along with himself to apostatize from God and so made those who were heavenly to become earthly and those who were

Seventh Discourse [1]See Is 14:12-15; Lk 10:18. [2]Is 27:1. [3]Ps 73:14 (LXX). [4]Ps 92:10 (91:11 LXX).

bright as stars to become dark. "By his tail" is as to say "by his rear parts and his hindermost transgressions," for at first devising rebellion and apostasy, he thoroughly reviewed this in the arrogance of his mind and so achieved also the corruption of the others.

"And the dragon stood before the woman who was about to bear a child, that he might devour her child when she brought it forth." He is speaking of events in the Lord's life. Since he who was to destroy Satan's dominion was going to be born, Satan watched with close attention, so that when the Virgin gave birth, he might kill the child. And so, too, he took no chances but incited Herod, a lascivious man with a harem of women, to destroy the male and manly child. For Isaiah proclaims to us, "Before the child knows how to cry 'father' or 'mother,' he will take the power of Damascus and the spoils of Samaria before the king of Assyria."[5] Reveal to us more clearly, O John, who this is who was born, this male child! He says, "who is to rule all the nations with a rod of iron." O inspired one, you have declared clearly to us that he is our Savior and Lord, Jesus, the Christ. For his own Father promised him, "Ask of me, and I will give to you the nations as your inheritance and the ends of the earth as your possession. You will shepherd them with a rod of iron, and you will dash them like a potter's vessel."[6]

"But her child was caught up to God and to his throne." The poisonous dragon lay in wait and incited Herod to kill the children in Bethlehem, thinking that certainly among them he would locate the Lord.[7] But by the providence of the Father the child escaped the plot. For Joseph heard a warning from heaven and took the child and his mother and fled into Egypt, since Herod was seeking the life of the child. "And the woman fled into the wilderness, where she has a place prepared by God, that there they might nourish her for one thousand two hundred and sixty days." And so, was the child saved from the plot of the dragon but the woman given over to destruction? Indeed not. But she too was saved by the flight into Egypt, which is a desert, and there was free from the plot of Herod. And there she was hid away and was nourished for one thousand two hundred and sixty days, which equals three and a half years, more or less. Thus, for some such length of time the mother of God remained in Egypt, until the death of Herod, after which another message from an angel brought them to Judea.

[12:7-9] *And there was war in heaven, Michael and his angels fighting against the dragon; and the dragon and his angels fought, but they were defeated, and there was no longer any place for him in heaven. And the great dragon was thrown down, that ancient serpent, who is called the devil and Satan, who deceives the whole world; he was thrown down to the earth, and his angels were thrown down with him.*

As though by way of an ongoing progression, the vision that is to explain to us the events concerning the antichrist refers to a beginning earlier than the beginning just described. This earlier beginning, which was partly discussed above, is the first beginning of the events concerning him, namely, the fall of Satan from heaven. The Lord also spoke of this: "I saw Satan fall like lightning from heaven."[8] Why, then, does it say, "And there was war in heaven"? The holy Scripture says that Satan exalted himself against God, that is, he lifted up a stiff and insolent neck to him and devised an apostasy. Although God, who is by nature good and forbearing, was patient with him, the holy angels did not tolerate the arrogance of their master and banished him from their ranks. This passage speaks of this event. Michael, who was himself one of the great leaders

[5]Is 8:4. [6]Ps 2:8-9. [7]See Mt 2:1-18. [8]Lk 10:18.

of the angels, made war against Satan and his followers, and Satan did not prevail in this war against him. "And there was no longer any place" either for refuge or, indeed, for dwelling "in heaven, and he was thrown down to the earth." Either the dragon experienced this in a physical way, or, having been deprived of his heavenly and angelic position, he was cast down to an earthly mind. Then, as though avenging himself on God because of his fall and since he could not harm God, he harms the servants of God and deceives people and tempts them to apostatize from God. In this way he thinks that he is harming the Master himself.

[12:10-12] ***And I heard a loud voice in heaven, saying, "Now the salvation and the power and the kingdom of our God and the authority of his Christ have come, for the accuser of our brethren has been thrown down, who accuses them day and night before our God. And they have conquered him by the blood of the Lamb and by the word of their testimony, for they loved not their lives even to death. Rejoice then, O heaven and you that dwell therein! But woe to the earth and sea, for the devil has come down to you in great wrath, because he knows that his time is short!"***

The holy angels hint at the joy they received at the banishment of Satan by singing a triumphal hymn to God, saying, "Now have the salvation and the kingdom come and the power of God and the authority of his Christ appeared," since he is all-powerful. For by the assistance of Christ's authority, it says, we have conquered the enemy, and "the accuser of our brethren, who accuses them day and night before God," has departed from us. O, the moderation of the holy angels! How much like their own Master they are! They call people their brothers. But why should this seem so marvelous, when even our common Master did not think it improper to call them by this name, saying, "I will proclaim your name to my brothers, in the midst of the congregation I will praise you"?[9] But why does it say that Satan has departed? Because he has been deprived of his rank and there is no longer any place for him to stand before God and accuse people. But these gained their revenge in equal measure, for they defeated him who seemed so unconquerable when he had even dared to rise up against God. And they conquered by the efficacious and beneficial and precious blood of Christ and the word of witness about him, which they regarded as more precious than their own lives.

And when these events occurred, it says, "Rejoice, all you angels of God, for you have been delivered from the bitter association with Satan." But "woe to the earth and to the sea, for the devil has come down to you in great wrath, for he knows that his time is short." Someone might ask, "If by his coming down Satan was intending to do evil on the earth and sea, why was he allowed to come down?" Because, for those who are sober and have hope in God, this by no means occurred for their harm but rather for their benefit. It trained them, as though by a gymnastics instructor, so that by these trials they might be made more approved and hardened to be like iron. But this does harm the slothful and the weak, who, since the one urging them on is himself without foundation, would quickly become evil out of themselves and exchange the passions for what they are by nature. When they say "woe to the earth and to the sea," they are not saying "woe to those who live on the earth and sail on the sea." Rather, as it is written,[10] they call those earth and dust who are earthly in thought and, moreover, fickle, without direction and unstable in mind. Against such as these, our common enemy makes war and enslaves the weak who are willing to submit

[9]Heb 2:12. [10]See Gen 18:27.

to his tyranny. "Knowing," it says, "that his time is short." The time from the downfall of Satan until his judgment and recompense, when he will be thrown aside into unending ages, is short. For this reason, when Pharaoh had inquired concerning his age, Jacob the patriarch, although he was 130 years old, said to Pharaoh, "Few and evil have been the days of the years of my life."[11]

[12:13-17] ***And when the dragon saw that he had been thrown down to the earth, he pursued the woman who had borne the male child. But the woman was given the two wings of the great eagle that she might fly from the serpent into the wilderness, to her place where she is to be nourished for a time, and times, and half a time. The serpent poured water like a river out of his mouth after the woman, to sweep her away with the flood. But the earth came to the help of the woman, and the earth opened its mouth and swallowed the river that the dragon had poured from his mouth. Then the dragon was angry with the woman and went off to make war on the rest of her offspring, on those who keep the commandments of God and have the testimony of Jesus.***

The present passage contains a repetition of what has already been said. For he did not say that when the dragon saw that he had been cast down to the earth, he immediately pursued the woman. Rather, he said that when the dragon saw himself in these bad circumstances and that he had fallen from his angelic rank, he became exceedingly bitter against humankind and persecuted the woman who had given birth to the Savior of humankind, in order that he might kill her. "He pursued the woman," for he knew that her child was too great to be captured, and he envied people their salvation from the Lord, for he could not tolerate such a change that while he had been expelled from heaven, people would ascend from earth to heaven through virtue.

"But the woman," it says, "was given the two wings of the great eagle, that she might fly from the serpent into the wilderness, to her place where she is to be nourished for a time, and times, and half a time." And so the woman did not come into the control of Satan but fled into the desert. This is Egypt, as I said above.[12] And therefore, while the prophet sought "wings like a dove" so that he might fly away and take rest in the desert,[13] the all-holy Virgin was given even more powerful wings, namely, those of the great eagle. By the phrase "wings of an eagle," he refers to the visitation of the holy angel who urged Joseph to take the boy and his mother and flee into Egypt. By means of this visitation, as though by means of the wings of an eagle, they arrived in Egypt. And since the dragon failed in this plot, which he had devised through Herod, he developed another one against the Virgin, namely, the death of her son. Consequently, the remaining portion of the narrative relates the cross and death of the Lord.

"And the serpent poured water like a river out of his mouth after the woman, to sweep her away with the flood." The holy Scripture figuratively speaks of temptation as a river. For example, Jonah said, "You have cast me into the deep, into the heart of the sea, and the rivers encircled me,"[14] and the Lord spoke similarly: "The rain fell, and the rivers came, and the winds blew, but they did not blow that house down, because it was built upon the rock."[15] And so here the trial of the Lord's passion is called a river, and it says that through this the dragon intended to drown the Virgin. And truly, since they [the rivers] did bring her to this [the cross] and to very great grief, the dragon was able to fulfill his intention. For why did Simeon say to her, "And a sword will pierce through your own soul also, that the

[11]Gen 47:9. [12]See his comments on Rev 12:6. [13]Ps 55:7-8 (54:7-8 LXX). [14]Jonah 2:4. [15]See Mt 7:25.

thoughts of many hearts might be revealed"?[16]

"But the earth came to the help of the woman, and the earth opened its mouth and swallowed the river that the dragon had poured out of its mouth" on the woman. That the earth swallowed the river signifies that it received the trial in itself, that is, it received the Lord, who had suffered death. But the help that the earth rendered was not simply in this. Rather, its help was in this, that it gave the Lord back again. For on the third day he came to life again, having trampled on death, since it was not strong enough to hold him who was the author of life, as the blessed Peter says.[17] And that the whole narrative might be told, one must know the ending to the words "the earth came to the help of the woman." Consequently, as though responding to a question after the manner of this aid, it says, "it swallowed the river," that is, it received in itself the Lord, who had been betrayed, and gave him back again, and in this way the earth rendered its assistance. And since the dragon had failed also in his second plot [to kill the male child], what further is there for him to do? He has persecuted those called sons and brothers of the Lord, that is, the faithful—for it says that these are the offspring of the woman, since the faithful are the sons and brothers of the Lord, as it is written, "I will proclaim your name to my brothers,"[18] and again, "Behold, I and the children God has given to me."[19] Therefore, they are relatives of his mother. And the dragon made war with them, persecuting them and plotting against them and killing them through the tyrants and powers of the earth, since they were giving witness that the one born from the Virgin was God.

[13:1-4] ***And I stood by the sand of the sea. And I saw a beast rising out of the sea, with ten horns and seven heads, with ten diadems on its horns and blasphemous names on its head.[20] And the beast that I saw was like a leopard, its feet were like a bear's, and its mouth was like a lion's mouth. And to it the dragon gave his power and his throne and great authority. One of its heads seemed to have a mortal wound, but its mortal wound was healed, and the whole earth followed the beast with wonder, and they worshiped the dragon, for he had given his authority to the beast.***

In the previous vision the holy Evangelist saw "a sign in heaven, and behold," it says, "a red dragon."[21] But now he says that he saw "a beast rising out of the sea, like a leopard." Moreover, in the following vision he sees "another beast that rises out of the earth," and it had "two horns like a lamb." Therefore, we have three beasts altogether: the first is in heaven, the second is from the sea, and the third is from the earth.[22] Who the first and the third beast are is clear to everyone. The first is the dragon who was the author of evil, namely, Satan, who became apostate and exalted himself against God Almighty. The third is the antichrist. But this second beast who now appears to us in the vision, who is he? I think that he comes after the apostate dragon, that is, Satan who was the leader of the other demons—for many fell with Satan and were cast down to earth—and from this it is clear that the holy Scripture says that this leader of all the demons is condemned to the sea and to Tartarus, as I indicated above.[23] And perhaps it speaks of him in this figurative way because of the disorder and turmoil in which he exists, recognizing also from where he has fallen and into what condition he has

[16]Lk 2:35. [17]Acts 3:15. [18]Heb 2:12. [19]Is 8:18. [20]The text of Oecumenius has the singular here, which guides the interpretation below. [21]Rev 12:3. [22]Oecumenius distinguishes three beasts: the dragon in heaven, who is Satan (Rev 12:3); the beast from the sea, who is the devil (Rev 13:1); and the beast from the earth, who is the antichrist (Rev 13:11). As De Groote notes, Oecumenius is not completely consistent in his comments (TEG 8:184). See the comments of Oecumenius on Rev 13:11-13; 16:12-16; 20:8-10. [23]See his comments on Rev 9:14; for the Scripture: Is 14:15; 27:1; 2 Pet 2:4; Jude 6.

come, and that "he is kept for the judgment of the great day," as it is written.[24] But were it otherwise and he was literally in the sea and in Tartarus, how is it that in the previous vision he is described as plotting many things against the Lord and his mother? Nonetheless, according to the literal meaning of the narrative—and this is not to be denied—he is assigned to Tartarus and the deep.

But this second beast that now appears to us is introduced in the book of Job, conversing with God and seeking Job and bringing on him many trials and even saying that he is come "walking to and fro on the earth under heaven."[25] But it is not only the book of Job that speaks of him, but the Lord too makes mention of him when in the Gospel of John he says to the Jews, "You are of your father the devil, and your will is to do your father's desires. He was a murderer from the beginning and has nothing to do with the truth, because there is no truth in him. When he lies, he speaks according to his own nature, for he is a liar and his father."[26] He calls the apostate dragon the "father of the devil," namely, of this one who is present in this vision. For Satan is father as their leader and the author of the apostasy, even as the holy Abraham was called "father of nations," since he was progenitor of the faith before them, as it was said to him, "I have made you the father of many nations."[27] Since, in my opinion, these matters have been adequately explained, let us return to the passage at hand.

"I saw a beast rising out of the sea, with ten horns and seven heads, with ten diadems on his horns." He saw him coming out of the sea. For him it is an ascent, since he is elevated from the troubled, unstable life of people who have elected him to be their master. The ten horns testify to his powerful lordship, even as the seven heads suggest his various cunning deceits and tricks. For the numbers ten and seven are perfect numbers. The diadems on his horns reveal that he has become a powerful force against humankind, since through deception we have willingly given ourselves over to him. "And blasphemous names were on his head." Rightly does it say "on his head," for he rages against himself and his own head, even insulting God. And stripping from God that worship that is proper to him, he grants it to himself. "And the beast that I saw was like a leopard," because, I think, of his ability to turn sharply and quickly to form devious plans. "And its feet were like a bear's," it says, since they are sturdy and steadfast, that he might "walk to and fro on the earth under heaven,"[28] plotting against humankind. "And its mouth was like a lion's," for "our adversary, the devil, prowls around like a lion, seeking someone to devour," as it is written.[29] "And to it the dragon gave his power." Without question the power of the apostate dragon inhabits these deceptions and wiles, for he has become for the devil both the instigator and the teacher of them.

And I saw "one of its heads as though it were mortally wounded, but its mortal wound was healed." The inspired Evangelist himself would know the meaning of this. But, as it seems to me, the meaning is something like this. The death-bearing wound that the devil received on one of its heads was because of the reverent worship of Israel. But this was healed through their subsequent idolatry. "And the whole earth followed the beast with wonder." How would this not be the case, since even the pious people of Israel came to worship him? And this is indicated by Isaiah, who in the person of God speaks to Israel: "Because of you, my name is forever blasphemed among the nations."[30] But with the beast they worshiped also the dragon who is the instigator and cause of such deception and deleterious wiles.

[13:4-8] ***And they worshiped the beast, saying,***

[24]Jude 6. [25]See Job 1:7. [26]Jn 8:44. [27]Gen 17:5. [28]Job 1:7. [29]1 Pet 5:8. [30]Is 52:5.

"Who can fight against it?" And the beast was given a mouth uttering haughty and blasphemous words, and it was allowed to exercise authority for forty-two months; it opened its mouth to utter blasphemy against God, blaspheming his name and his dwelling, that is, those who dwell in heaven. And authority was given to it over every tribe, people, tongue and nation, and all who inhabit the world will worship it, everyone whose name is not written in the book of the life of heaven of him who was slain before the foundation of the world.

Those from Israel whom he conquered devise for him songs of praise, saying, "Who is like the beast, and who can fight against it?" And since all were vanquished and placed under his feet, "he was given a mouth uttering haughty and blasphemous words." By whom was it given? By those persons who had been deceived and had come to worship him. For such boasting comes from arrogance. And what is more haughty than saying, "I will ascend to heaven; I will set my throne above the stars of heaven"?[31] And a little further down: "I will make myself like the Most High."[32] Isaiah here is lampooning him, since such claims are blasphemies against God. "And it was allowed to exercise authority for forty-two months." I earlier noted that forty-two months indicates a short period of time,[33] for compared with the unending ages, all time is short, even if it should seem to be very long.

"And he opened his mouth to utter blasphemy against God, to blaspheme his name and his dwelling, that is, those who dwell in heaven." Such are the blasphemies against God spoken by the apostate. The "dwelling" of God is the holy angels, since God dwells among them. For if it is said concerning people, "I will dwell among them and I will walk among them,"[34] how should one speak of the heavenly powers among whom God dwells?

"And authority was given to him over every tribe, people, tongue and nation. And all who dwell on the earth will worship it." I said earlier that he received his authority from those persons who had willingly placed themselves under his destructive lordship. And so it correctly says that "all who dwell on the earth will worship it." For with the exception of faithful Israel, the rest of humankind worshiped idols, and since even Israel suffered from this, it finally says that every clan and tribe of people had come to worship the wicked one. "Everyone whose name is not written in the book of the life of heaven of him who was slain before the foundation of the world." With great care does the vision place limits on this. For although it says that all who dwell on the earth worshiped the apostate devil, there were a few persons from both the Gentiles and from Israel who kept themselves pure from his cult, such as Job and his four friends, and Melchizedek, and from Israel the holy prophets and they who gave a pious witness in the Old Testament. It means that all worshiped him except those who through their piety and the pure and perfect manner of their lives are inscribed in heaven and are protected by God. For this is the significance of the fact that the book is sealed. Therefore, according to Luke, the Lord speaks of this book when he says to his holy disciples: "Nevertheless, do not rejoice in this, that the spirits are subject to you; but rejoice that your names are written in heaven."[35]

[13:9-10] ***If anyone has an ear, let him hear, "If any [captures another], to captivity he goes; if any one slays with the sword, with the sword he must be slain." Here is a call for the endurance and faith of the saints.***

If anyone has a mind able to understand what is being said, it says, "let him hear" what is being spoken and let him know that whoever

[31]Is 14:13. [32]Is 14:14. [33]See the comments on Rev 11:2. [34]2 Cor 6:16. [35]Lk 10:20.

is ready to bring others into captivity will be captured by the beast and will desert willingly to him. For having no defense from God, he will be carried away into utter evil. And should anyone be prepared for murders, he will die a spiritual death by worshiping the devil. "Here is a call for the endurance and faith of the saints." In this manner is one free from the servitude of the evil one. May it be that we all be found free from such servitude by the grace of God, who has called us to his knowledge. To him be glory forever. Amen.

Eighth Discourse

After making many digressions and moving from beginnings to even earlier beginnings, he now comes to that which is the real subject of interest. That is, he now gives an explanation to us about the impious and vile antichrist. This figure is therefore now the center of attention. Let us see what it says of him.

[13:11-13] ***Then I saw another beast that rose out of the earth; it had two horns like a lamb, and it spoke like a dragon. It exercises all the authority of the first beast in its presence and makes the earth and those who dwell on it worship the first beast, whose mortal wound was healed. It works great signs, even making fire come down from heaven to earth in the sight of people.***

"Then I saw," he says, "another beast that rose out of the earth." [It rises from the earth] because the earth is the source of origin for all humankind, for the antichrist is a man "whose coming will be by the activity of the devil," as the all-wise Paul says.[1] "And it had two horns like a lamb, and it spoke like a dragon." Rightly does it say that it had two horns "like a lamb," not the horns of a lamb, and that it spoke "like a dragon," not that it was a dragon. For since the wicked one makes himself out to be the Christ but is not, the vision has given to him horns like a lamb. And since through every kind of unholy work he spreads what is similar to the devil but in fact is not the devil, it does not say that he is a dragon but that he speaks like a dragon. And since such is the case, the discourse has preserved for him an image also in the vision, and it gives to him a form, not that of a lamb but like a lamb, and not that of a dragon but like a dragon. For Christ is said to be a lamb, and the devil is said to be a dragon, but this one is neither one nor the other.

"It exercises all the authority of the first beast in its presence." This means that it is a successor to the authority of the devil and works to devise plans for everyone to worship him "whose mortal wound was healed." Since this was discussed in previous material, it is necessary now simply to give a brief summary. When it says that "it exercises all the authority of the first beast in its presence"—the vision mentioned the red dragon first of all, namely, whom it depicted in heaven—it is not that anyone should think that now the vision speaks of him as one who received the authority of that first beast. [The text says in effect], I do not speak of that beast who was first of all but of that beast who came after him [i.e., the red dragon] but is before the antichrist, the one whom the vision depicted coming out of the sea and like a leopard.[2] The mortal wound of this one was healed, as I noted above.[3] "It works great signs, even making fire come down from heaven to earth in the sight of people." The apostle testifies that the antichrist will perform signs and wonders by the activity of the devil, for after saying "whose coming will be by the activity of the devil," he continues, "with all power and with pretended signs and wonders."[4]

[13:14-18] ***And by the signs that it is allowed to work in the presence of the beast, it deceives***

Eighth Discourse [1]2 Thess 2:9. [2]See Rev 13:1-2. [3]See the comments on Rev 13:3. [4]2 Thess 2:9.

those who dwell on earth, bidding those who dwell on earth to make an image for the beast since[5] he was wounded by the sword and yet lived; and it was allowed to give breath to the image of the beast [so that the image of the beast should even speak, and to cause those who would not worship the image of the beast][6] to be slain. Also it causes all, both small and great, both rich and poor, both free and slave, to receive a mark,[7] the name of the beast or the number of its name. This calls for wisdom: let him who understands reckon the number of the beast, for it is a number of a man, and its number is six hundred and sixty-six.

"And he deceives," it says "those who dwell on earth by signs." He does signs, beguiling the eyes of those who look on, even as the magicians did in front of Pharaoh, for both they and this one are led by one and the same deceitful demon. And it rightly says that he does signs in the presence of the beast. For since he will set up an image for him, which he will compel all to worship, he will perform signs before it, and as though regarding the image as divine, claim that from it he has the power to do these things.

"And it was allowed to give breath to the image." They say that many statues both perspire and seem to speak by the activity of the devil.[8] And it says that the antichrist gives a mark and seal of his own name, without which no one will either buy or produce. "This calls for wisdom." Let anyone search for the name of the beast and through this search let him find it. For it says, I will speak of a reckoning that is strange and unusual, nor will I present a name that is secret and unclear, but I will give a calculation that is oft-used and known to people, which adds up to the number 666. While to be sure this number signifies also many other names, both proper names as well as titles, it signifies also these following. Among the proper names it can render Lampetis [Λαμπέτις] and Benedict [Βενέδικτος] and Titan [Τιτάν]. "Titan" is written with an iota, but it can also be written with a diphthong. For if Teitan [Τειτάν] is derived from *teisis* [τεῖσις "stretching"]—the verb is *teinō* [τείνω] and the future is *tenō* [τενῶ]—then it is correctly written with the diphthong, even as *phtheirō* [φθείρω] is from *phtherō* [φθερῶ] and *speirō* [σπείρω] is from *sperō* [σπερῶ]. Among the titles, the number can render "the Conqueror" [ὁ νικητής]—for perhaps he named himself this when he warred against the three horns or three kings and rooted them out. See what Daniel says about them in his eighth vision: "I considered his horns [i.e., those of the fourth beast] and behold, there came up among them another little horn, and three of the former horns were rooted out before it; and, behold, in this horn were eyes like the eyes of a man, and a mouth speaking haughty things."[9] And then there are also these titles, "the Unstable" [ὁ ἐπίσαλος], "Evil Guide" [κακὸς ὁδηγός], "Truly Harmful" [ἀληθὴς βλαβερός], "Ancient Slanderer" [πάλαι βάσκανος], "Unjust Lamb" [ἀμνὸς ἄδικος]. Perhaps he was called these names by those who opposed him. But this one will not be ashamed to be called these things; he will rather even rejoice in such appellations, since he is not ashamed even to call himself such things. Rebuking such wicked and vile choices, the wise apostle says, "Whose glory is in their shame."[10] Therefore, since many names have been found, anyone who wishes has the right to bestow a more suitable name on the accursed.

[14:1-5] ***Then I looked, and behold, the Lamb stood on Mount Zion, and with him a hundred and forty-four thousand who had the name of***

[5]The text of Oecumenius has the conjunction ὡς, not the pronoun ὅς. [6]The words in brackets appear in manuscripts P and B; the manuscript M has a lacuna at this point. [7]Manuscripts P and B add the words "on the right hand or the forehead, so that no one can buy or sell unless he has the mark, either." [8]See Eusebius *Hier.* 31 (PG 22:840-41). Hierocles was a governor of Bithynia who had written a treatise claiming that Apollonius of Tyana was superior to Jesus. [9]Dan 7:8. [10]Phil 3:19.

his Father written on their foreheads. And I heard a voice from heaven like the sound of many waters and like the sound of loud thunder; and the voice I heard was like the sound of harpers playing on their harps, and they sang a new song before the throne and before the four living creatures and before the elders. And no one could learn that song except the hundred and forty-four thousand who had been redeemed from the earth. These are they who have not defiled themselves with women, for they are virgins; these are they who follow the Lamb wherever he goes; these have been redeemed from humankind as a first fruit for God and for the Lamb, and in their mouth no lie was found, for they are spotless.

In the Gospels the Lord is depicted speaking to the lawless people of the Jews, "Behold, your house is desolate."[11] For after the insanity of the cross, they were no longer worthy of the divine visitation. How is it, then, that the Lord, as though through a change of mind, is shown by the vision "standing on Mount Zion"? For that their city and temple and entire populace was left wholly desolate, the Romans have clearly shown, having burned the temple and having torched the cities, having laid waste to the entire land and having enslaved the capital city itself. But that now the Lord is shown having come to Mount Zion represents the conversion of Israel by faith in the last days, when indeed the Lord will make them his own possession and bring them to himself. For this was proclaimed through Isaiah, saying, "The Redeemer will come from Zion and will remove ungodliness from Jacob, said the Lord."[12] And both the prophet and the apostle stand in agreement with Isaiah. For the one sings, "You will make them turn their back; among those who remain you will prepare their face,"[13] and the other writes, "When the full number of the Gentiles come in, then all Israel will be saved."[14]

"And with him," it says, "a hundred and forty-four thousand who had the name of his Father written on their foreheads." In a previous section he said that the 144,000 were those from Israel who had come to faith, 12,000 from each of the tribes.[15] Does he now also again refer to these? I do not think so. For he does not designate them here with a definite article—he did not say "the 144,000" but only "144,000"—let alone indicate that they had vigilantly practiced virginity. For virginity was in no way eagerly practiced in Israel, just as later the Gentiles were not interested in it. Therefore, we must regard those mentioned to be a mixture of persons from Israel and from the Gentiles, and the greater part from the Gentiles. And that they had the name of the Father and of his Son written on them shows that they were wreathed in a certain divine glory.

"And I heard," it says, "a voice like harpers singing a new song before the throne and before the living creatures and before the elders." That the sound was like that of harpists indicates the divine euphony and harmony of the song. For if "praise is not seemly in the mouth of a sinner," as it is written,[16] it is certainly seemly and fitting in the mouth of the righteous. "And no one," it says, "could learn this song except the one hundred forty-four thousand who had been redeemed from the earth." I think that no one is strong enough even to hear the mysteries of the new song except for those who are thought worthy to sing them. For knowledge is given to each according to the measure of his purity. For "there are many rooms," says the Lord, or rewards of good things, "with my Father."[17] Those are the "redeemed" who had been purchased by the blood of Christ. For the precious blood of Christ was poured out on behalf of all humankind. Yet for some it was without profit, namely, for

[11]Mt 23:38. [12]Is 59:20-21. [13]Ps 20:13 (LXX). [14]Rom 11:25-26. [15]Rev 7:4-8. [16]Sir 15:9. [17]Jn 14:2.

those who willingly robbed themselves of the salvation that came from it—indeed, through the prophet the Lord reproached these, saying, "What profit is there in my blood, when I go down into destruction?"[18] But for those who have been saved and made righteous, of whom these, about whom the passage now speaks, are the first fruit and the first offering, it was immensely profitable, more than anyone could say. "These are they," it says, "who have not defiled themselves with women, for they are virgins; these are they who follow the Lamb wherever he goes; these have been redeemed from humankind as a first fruit for God and for the Lamb, and in their mouth no lie was found, for they are spotless." The language of the vision relays how surpassingly excellent and beyond human nature are those who are in Christ.

[14:6-7] ***And I saw another angel flying in mid-heaven, with an eternal gospel to proclaim to those who dwell on earth, to every nation and tribe and tongue and people; and he said with a loud voice, "Fear God and give him glory, for the hour of his judgment has come; and worship him who made heaven and earth, the sea and the fountains of water."***

"Mid-heaven" signifies the exalted and sublime nature of the holy angel. He had "an eternal gospel." The saving teaching that one should fear the Lord is from eternity, since the "beginning of wisdom is the fear of God, and its end is love."[19] But, it says, the harsh beast who works spiritual death, the antichrist, is not to be feared, even though he may threaten and do the most amazing feats. For "the hour of his judgment has come," and he who is fearful to those who live on the earth will punish him in a way wholly unprecedented. Rather, we should "worship him who made" every creature rather than worship the wicked devil who is hated by God.

[14:8] ***And another angel, a second, followed, saying, "Fallen is Babylon the great, she who made all nations drink the wine of her impure passion."***

I think that by "Babylon" he is referring to the confusion and random trials of the present life—for "confusion" is the meaning of Babylon[20]—and to the manic stupefaction of those who worship idols. And the city is embellished with names, being called by them the "inspired" city.[21] And were you to consider this to be the physical Babylon, you would not fall far from the truth. By the "wine of the wrath of her fornication" he refers to the city's apostasy from God, as it is written: "You have destroyed everyone that goes whoring from you."[22] Such fornication entails a darkness for any process of thought, for who, possessing a sound mind, would choose to worship wood and stones and call forth the wrath of God? Therefore, concerning this wine it is said, "Their wine is the wrath of serpents and the incurable wrath of asps."[23] Babylon herself at first drank of this deadly wine, and then she compelled all the nations that she ruled to drink.

[14:9-12] ***And another angel, a third, followed them, saying with a loud voice, "If anyone worships the beast and its image and receives a mark on his forehead or on his hand, he also shall drink the wine of God's wrath, poured unmixed into the cup of his anger, and he shall be tormented with fire and sulfur in the presence of the holy angels and in the presence of the Lamb. And the smoke of their torment goes***

[18]Ps 30:9 (29:10 LXX). [19]See Prov 1:7; 1 Tim 1:5. [20]That the name *Babylon* was symbolic of the confusion of the present became a common understanding in the Christian exegetical tradition. It can be found already in the third century in Methodius *Symp.* 4.3. [21]The Greek word ἐνθουσιασμός means "possessed by a god," often expressed by ecstasy. [22]Ps 73:27 (72:27 LXX). [23]Deut 32:33.

up forever and ever; and they have no rest, day or night, these worshipers of the beast and its image, and whoever receives the mark of its name." Here is a call for the endurance of the saints, those who keep the commandments of God and the faith of Jesus.

The third angel forbids people to worship the beast and to receive its mark. For to worship any other as God rather than he who really and truly is God is most unholy. "And he also shall drink the wine of God's wrath poured unmixed into the cup of his anger." The holy David mentioned this cup and this wine when he said, "There is a cup in the hand of the Lord, full of unmixed wine; and he has turned it from side to side, but its dregs have not been wholly poured out; all the sinners of the earth shall drink."[24] He calls the wrath of God wine, not using this metaphor because of the gladness elicited by wine but because of the darkness and the derangement that oppresses those brought under the wrath of God. And, it says, it is "poured out unmixed," that is, utterly poured out. For the wrath of God is poured out along with his benevolence and goodness, wholly poured out. For there is not an equal measure of wrath and goodness, but the benevolence of God is many times greater. Indeed, were the righteous anger and the goodness of God in equal measure, no one would be able to withstand it. Aware of this, the prophet said, "If you, O Lord, should mark iniquities, Lord, who could stand?"[25] And the same writer indicated that goodness is much greater in the cup of God than is his righteous anger, when he said, "Merciful is the Lord, and righteous; yea, our God is merciful."[26] In this passage he placed God's righteousness in the middle, so that hemmed in by mercy on either side, his righteousness would not work its way without constraint. For it is characteristic of justice to meet each according to his merit.

Having mentioned wine, and by this referring to God's wrath, he continues the metaphor and calls the "cup" what is given from the hand of God to sinners. Perhaps someone might say, "How can you say that the mercy of God is many times greater in the judgment at that time, when the vision tells us that the torments of those who are punished are little short of everlasting? And why does it say, 'And the smoke of their torment goes up forever and ever, and they have no rest, day or night?' " To such a person one might respond, "What is suffered is indeed eternal, but it is not suffering according to merit. If someone is deserving of fire and darkness, why is he condemned only to the darkness? Such a one is tormented only in this, that he does not share in the good things of God, and he suffers only this, but he is not also tormented physically."

By the phrase "the smoke of their torment goes up" he refers to the heaving breath of the sinners that they exhale from below in their lamentations over their situation. "Here is a call for the endurance of the saints," it says. This will be manifested at this time of the antichrist and in this ordeal. For however great is the danger and the tribulation at that time, so great is the need for endurance. Then the passage continues as though in response to a question. And who are those, it says, whom you call holy and patient? "Those who keep the commandments of God and the faith of Jesus." For when the tribulations and death have come, such persons as these will regard all things as second in importance to faith and to the love of God.

[14:13] And I heard a voice from heaven saying to me, "Write this. Blessed are the dead who die in the Lord henceforth." And the Spirit says, "That they might rest from their labors, for their deeds follow them."

[24]Ps 75:8 (74:9 LXX). [25]Ps 130:3 (129:3 LXX). [26]Ps 116:5 (114:5 LXX).

He blesses those who did not choose to worship the image of the beast or to receive the mark on their foreheads and on their hands, and who for this reason were killed. Being crowned with the crown of martyrdom, these attain to the same lot with the martyrs.

[14:14-16] And I looked, and behold, a white cloud, and seated on the head*[27] *one like a son of man, with a golden crown on his head and a sharp sickle in his hand. And another angel came out of heaven, calling with a loud voice to him who sat on the head, "Put in your sickle and reap, for the hour to reap has come, for the harvest of the earth is fully ripe." And he who sat on the cloud swung his sickle.

He sees the Lord who was worthy to become the Son of man and who is riding on a cloud. This is either in reality a cloud, for the Gospel also speaks of this, whose witness I have referred to in an earlier discussion,[28] or the cloud is a certain angelic power, for it is written, "He mounted on cherubim and flew, he flew on the wings of the winds."[29] He calls the angels a cloud on account of their sublimity and their exalted nature and rank. Or rather, he calls the mother of God a cloud on whom he rode, honoring her who is his mother according to the flesh. For, indeed, Isaiah foresaw her in this manner, saying, "Behold, the Lord is seated on a swift cloud, and he will come to Egypt, and the idols of Egypt will tremble at his presence."[30] Interpreting this saying, Aquila says that the cloud is a "light material." "Material," as I think, because she was a human being and flesh, and "light" because of her purity and blamelessness and because not even one sin weighed her down, and in addition because of the excellence and heavenward character of her soul. You will consider the cloud in this manner. It is white because of the purity and radiance of those things that are here seen.

To be sure, the crown signifies the kingdom of our Lord, Jesus Christ. For Christ is king of things both unseen and seen. And the crown is gold to depict the glory of the kingdom by means of that which among us is of great value. That he has a sickle in his hand signifies that the consummation of the age rests in his power. And why does the angel say to him, "Put in your sickle and reap, for the hour to reap has come, for the harvest of the earth is fully ripe"? And he swung his sickle, it says, and the earth was reaped. A "plentiful harvest" is mentioned in the Gospels, while "the laborers are few."[31] However, in that passage the harvest signified the gathering of the faithful, while here it represents the consummation of humankind, so that, should there be any chaff or impurities in them that is worthy of fire, it might be given over to fire.

[14:17-20] And another angel came out of the temple in heaven, and he too had a sharp sickle. Then another angel came out from the altar, the angel who has power over fire, and he called with a loud voice to him who had the sharp sickle, saying, "Gather the clusters of the vine of the earth, for its grapes are ripe." So the angel swung his sickle on the earth and gathered the vintage of the earth, and threw it into the great wine press of the wrath of God; and the wine press was trodden outside the city, and blood flowed from the wine press, as high as a horse's bridle, for one thousand six hundred stadia.

The angel who has the sickle and comes out of the heavenly temple is in God's service, and the same will also be a servant of the coming consummation. Since he is heavenly and a minister of God, he is described as one who has come

[27]The text of Oecumenius reads ἐπὶ τῆς κεφαλῆς ("on the head"), not ἐπὶ τῆς νεφέλης ("on the cloud") both here and in the next sentence.
[28]See his comments on Rev 1:7, where Mk 13:25-26 is quoted. [29]Ps 18:10 (17:11 LXX). [30]Is 19:1. [31]Mt 9:37.

out of the temple in heaven. "And another angel who has power over fire," it says, "came out from the altar." I think that this angel has been appointed for the punishment of the ungodly. Therefore, he says, "Put in the sickle and gather the clusters of the vine of the earth." The harvest mentioned above[32] described the righteous and the sinners being brought to completion together. Their separation will be accomplished through "the winnowing fork of the Lord, by which he will clear his threshing floor and gather the wheat into the granary, but the chaff he will burn with unquenchable fire," according to the words of the Gospels.[33] However, this vintage of the clusters of grapes refers especially to the serious transgressors, for the vision depicts them lifelike as drunken and deranged. It is clear from the passage that their Lord did not regard them as worthy to be gathered in as were the first ones. Rather, a certain angel casts them immediately outside "into the wine press of the wrath of God," since they were thought worthy for neither a defense nor even an interrogation. They come straightway to judgment, just as sinners are presented in the Gospels, for whom exclusion and banishment become the means of punishment.[34] I think that the prophet spoke of these persons when he said, "The wicked will not stand in the judgment."[35]

And he has called the punishment a wine press, fittingly extending the metaphor of the grape clusters and the vintage. "And the wine press," it says, "was trodden outside the city." It would not be seemly were those punished to receive the rewards of their evil deeds in the heavenly Jerusalem allotted to the saints, or if the happiness of the saints was spoiled by any experience with those who are justly being punished. Moreover, there is a "great chasm" that separates the godly from the ungodly, as the patriarch Abraham said when he spoke to the rich man in the Gospels.[36] "And blood flowed from the wine press," it says. He speaks rightly of "blood," to show that he was speaking figuratively when he spoke of "clusters of grapes." For, to be sure, it is real persons who are being trampled on and cut up, so that their blood flowed "as high as a horse's bridle, for one thousand and six hundred stadia." In the holy Scriptures there is a common usage whereby God has certain horses with himself as the rider, these horses symbolizing an angelic power. For in the Song of Songs the heavenly bridegroom says to the bride, "I have compared you, my love, my love, to my horse in the chariot of Pharaoh,"[37] and Habakkuk the prophet sings to God, "You will mount on your horses, and your chariots are salvation."[38] The Apocalypse says that the bridles of these horses are soaked with the blood of sinners, not only of those close by but also of those standing far away. The passage is wholly figurative, intending to show the great amount of blood. For those who walk in the wide road are much more numerous than those who walk in the straight and narrow path,[39] so that they soak the bridles of the horses responsible for punishment, even though these are angels.

[15:1-4] ***And I saw another sign in heaven, great and wonderful, seven angels with seven plagues, which are the last, for with them the wrath of God is ended. And I saw what appeared to be a sea of glass mingled with fire, and those who had conquered the beast and its image and the number of its name, standing beside the sea of glass with harps of God. And they sing the song of Moses, the servant of God, and the song of the Lamb, saying, "Great and wonderful are your deeds, O Lord God the Almighty! Just and true are your ways, O King of nations! Who shall not fear and glorify your name, O Lord? For you alone are holy. For all***

[32]Rev 14:15. [33]Mt 3:12. [34]See, for example, Mt 19:23-24; Lk 6:24; 16:19-31. [35]Ps 1:5 (LXX). [36]Lk 16:19-31. [37]Song 1:9. [38]Hab 3:8. [39]Mt 7:13-14.

nations shall come and worship before you, for your judgments have been revealed."

"And I saw," it says, "seven angels with seven plagues." He speaks of seven to indicate the many plagues prepared for the sinners through which the wrath of God will reach its end. "And I saw," it says, "a sea of glass mingled with fire, and those who had conquered the beast and its image and the number of its name, standing beside the sea of glass with harps of God." Somewhere the most wise Paul says, "Should anyone build on this foundation with gold, silver, precious stones, wood, hay, straw, fire will test the quality of the work of each, for it will be revealed by fire."[40] Will then not only sinners, who bring loads of kindling wood through their sins, but also the righteous, who offer gold and precious materials, be tested by fire? He says as much when he here says that those who have in every way defeated the beast stand on the sea of glass mixed with fire. For the sea is glass because of the brightness and purity of the righteous on it. However, it is mixed with fire because it cleanses and purifies from all filth, for there is need of purification even for the righteous. "For we all make mistakes," as it is written,[41] and "Who is clean from filth, even if his life on the earth is but one day?"[42]

As we have frequently noted, the harps are a figure for the euphonious hymn to God sung by the saints. "And they sing," it says, "the song of Moses," clearly indicating that song that Moses sang when Pharaoh was drowned along with his entire army: "Let us sing to the Lord, for he has triumphed gloriously; the horse and the rider he has thrown into the sea. He has become for me a helper and protector for salvation."[43] This song of triumph is because of the punishment of the wicked and the victory over the devil and the son of lawlessness, the antichrist. "And the song of the Lamb," it says, referring to the agreement of Moses with the Lord and his just judgment against the wicked. And therefore, indeed, they marvel at the truth and righteousness of the Lord.

It says "the king of the nations." To be sure, Christ is the king of everyone; however, since it is said by Isaiah, "And there will be a root of Jesse, and he who arises to rule over the nations, on him shall the nations hope,"[44] the prophecy [of Revelation] says that he is "the king of the nations" and that all the nations will come and worship him, and in this way this passage fittingly foretells the call of the nations and the faith that they will have in the Lord.

[15:5–16:1] ***And after this I looked, and the temple of the tent of witness in heaven was opened, and out of the temple came seven angels with the seven plagues, robed in a pure bright stone,[45] and their breasts girded with golden girdles. And one of the four living creatures gave the seven angels seven golden bowls full of the wrath of God who lives forever and ever; and the temple was filled with smoke from the glory of God and from his power, and no one could enter the temple until the seven plagues of the seven angels were ended. Then I heard a loud voice from the temple, saying to the seven angels, "Go and pour out on the earth the seven bowls of the wrath of God."***

In the holy Scriptures it is customary to call the tent constructed in the desert by Bezalel, the architect of the things made at that time, the "tent of witness" because it was the tent of the testimonies and ordinances of God. There was in it the ark of the covenant, the mercy seat, the table, the altars either for incense or for fruit offerings, the lampstand and whatever else God commanded the holy Moses to provide, saying, "According to all that I show

[40]1 Cor 3:12-13. [41]Jas 3:2. [42]Job 14:4-5. [43]Ex 15:1-2. [44]Is 11:10. [45]The text of Oecumenius reads λίθον ("stone"), not λῖνον ("linen").

you on the mountain you shall make for me."[46] Therefore, in view of the image of the ancient tabernacle he has called also the supercelestial temple, whatever it might be, a tent of witness. From there, it says, "the seven angels came out." From where else could the ministers of God be seen coming out other than from the heavenly temple?

And they had in their hands, it says, seven plagues that they were going to release against the earth. For at the time of the consummation there will be many signs on the earth of which also Christ made mention in the Gospels when he was teaching about the end.[47] That the angels are clothed in a pure, bright stone is indicative of their rank, purity and brightness, and that they possess a nature wholly given to the good, since they have put on Christ. For the Lord is called a stone by the divine Scriptures. For example, Isaiah said, "Behold, I am laying for the foundations of Zion a costly and select stone,"[48] and the prophet said, "The stone that the builders rejected, he has become the head of the corner."[49] The all-wise Paul also exhorts us to put on this stone, saying, "Put on our stone, Jesus Christ, and make no provision for the flesh to gratify its desires."[50] And whoever is enclothed with this stone is free from every desire destructive of the soul.

Their girdles are symbolic of the fact that they are effective and well equipped for their task. For concerning them it is said, "Mighty in strength are those who do his word."[51] These seven angels take from one of the four living creatures, concerning whom we have said much, the wrath of God in seven golden bowls. And aptly did he say golden, for the wrath of God is worthy, bearing within itself that which is good and beneficial rather than that which is just, even though those who are tormented might experience distress. "And the temple was filled with smoke from the glory of God and from his power." The smoke is a sign of the divine anger, for it is written, "Smoke went up in his wrath."[52] Smoke indicates a fire, but the holy Isaiah also says that he saw smoke in that place: "And the lintel shook at the voice as the seraphim loudly uttered the 'holy, holy, holy,' and the house was filled with smoke."[53] He was revealing the wrath of God against the temple of Jerusalem: He speaks periphrastically when he says that the smoke was from the glory of God and from his power. It is as though he said, "It was filled with smoke from the wrath of God," for God is himself power and himself glory, and who can withstand his wrath? "And no one could enter the temple until the seven plagues of the seven angels were completed." For who will confront the wrath of God, or who will live when enveloped by it? For if no one has "stood in the counsel of the Lord," as it is written,[54] one could hardly be able to endure the wrath of God. And I heard, it says, someone issuing the command that they pour out the seven bowls of the divine wrath on the earth.

[16:2-7] ***And the first angel went and poured his bowl on the earth, and a foul and evil sore came on people who bore the mark of the beast and who worshiped its image. And the second angel poured out his bowl on the sea, and it became like the blood of a dead person, and every living soul died. And the third angel poured out his bowl into the rivers and the fountains of water, and they became blood. And I heard the angel of the waters say, "Righteous are you, who is and who was and the holy One, in these your judgments, for they have shed the blood of saints and prophets, and you have given them blood to drink, for it is their due." And I heard the altar say, "Yea, Lord, God Almighty, true***

[46]Ex 25:9. [47]See, for example, Mt 24:1-36. [48]Is 28:16. [49]Ps 118:22 (117:22 LXX). [50]Rom 13:14. Manuscripts P and B have the usual reading "put on the Lord, Jesus Christ." However, the reading "stone" is clearly the correct one in this context of Oecumenius's discussion. [51]Ps 103:20 (102:20 LXX). [52]Ps 17:9 (LXX). [53]Is 6:4. Oecumenius adds τὰ ἅγια to the text, referring to the threefold ἅγιος in Is 6:3. [54]Jer 23:18.

and just are your judgments!"

Someone might interpret these things in a twofold manner. Either these events will occur literally at the time of the consummation, or they are to be understood allegorically. When the Lord addressed his disciples about the many signs of the end, he spoke openly about the evil events that will happen at that time, saying, "And you will hear of wars and rumors of wars; and nation will rise against nation, and kingdom against kingdom, and there will be famines and plagues and earthquakes in various places. All of this is the beginning of the birth pangs."[55] And a little later he said, "For then there will be great tribulation, such as has not been from the beginning of the world until now, no, and never will be."[56] The events in the present passage that are said to occur when each bowl is poured out might best be interpreted according to what the Lord said. In this case, the sore that comes from the first bowl would symbolize the tribulations and distresses that vex the souls of people at that time because of the rumors of wars. The blood in the sea would suggest those who are killed in naval battles, while the blood in the rivers and streams would refer, most likely, to the deaths of those who were killed in battles on the land while they were encamped alongside such waters.

"And I heard," it says, "the angel of the waters saying." To be sure, God is all-powerful and provides for his creatures and is sufficient for the beneficial care of all things, and so he has no need for anyone to assist him in this task. For since his willing a work is for it at the same time to be effected, and since by the movement of his will all things were brought into being, how is it that he should be in need of a coworker and an assistant for his providential care? But since he is good, he wishes that also the holy angels be benefited through the succor that goes to those in need—for the one who aids another in need benefits not so much the other as he does himself, and there is none in the angelic ranks who is in want and in need of the aid of any other. And so God has ordained that the holy angels provide aid and succor to those on the earth who are in need of any good thing. For indeed, in earlier sections we noted that angels were placed as benefactors of the churches,[57] and the all-wise Daniel wrote that the leader of the angels, Michael, looked after the race of the Jews.[58] And now the revelation explains to us that an angel is set over the waters. For although the world is constituted from the four elements of air, fire, earth and water—although some think that the heavenly things are established from some fifth element that they say is ethereal and moves in a circle—only the three elements of fire, earth and air are richly abundant for the purpose of breathing and for other common necessities. Even if they say that air is altogether the element of fire, yet it is abundant and independent on the earth, hiding in its holes and rocks. Some draw fire even out of water kept in glass vessels when they stand over against the rising sun. And the earth is the common mother of all, and their tomb and a solid footing. Water alone is not present to everything in abundance, whether it is fresh water in wells, springs, cisterns or rivers, or that water of the air that moves in the sky in clouds and gives to us timely rain by the command of God and nourishes every living thing on the earth. Therefore, since water is not everywhere abundant, one of the holy angels is set over it, so that when sufficiently abundant for what is needed he might provide to those who are in need of it that water that often is sparse and lacking due to our vices, causing draught and famine and the sickness that follows them. Most certainly it is this angel who is placed by the providence of God over the waters whom, he says, "I heard saying, 'Righ-

[55]Mt 24:6-8. [56]Mt 24:21. [57]Rev 2:1, 8, 12, 18; 3:1, 7, 14. [58]See Dan 10:13, 21.

teous are you, who is and who was, the holy One.' " The phrase "who is" shows the endlessness of God, and "who was" that he is without beginning. The "holy One" refers to the fact that he is righteous in all things on behalf of all things. For it says, "You have judged these things" so that those who have spilled the blood of the saints might drink blood. And it is necessary that those who encamped and fought by streams and rivers drink the water polluted by the blood of the dying being carried away downstream.

Those who stand around the heavenly altar send up a thanksgiving in agreement with that of the angel, for when he says, "I heard the altar saying" something, it signifies thereby those who minister at the altar. May it be that, being delivered from all the sufferings described above, we send up to Christ a hymn of thanksgiving, to whom be glory forever. Amen.

Ninth Discourse

The three bowls poured out by the three angels effected the events already narrated. We must now consider what the fourth and fifth bowls cause to occur.

[16:8-11] ***The fourth angel, it says, poured his bowl on the sun, and it was allowed to scorch people with fire; people were scorched by the fierce heat, and they cursed the name of God who had power over these plagues, and they did not repent and give him glory. The fifth angel poured his bowl on the throne of the beast, and its kingdom was in darkness; people gnawed their tongues in anguish and cursed the God of heaven for their pains and sores, and did not repent of their deeds.***

It is not difficult to interpret this passage according to the figures of speech. That the sun scorches people could be the draught, affliction and distresses of those remaining in war. Although they are pressed by evils and find it needful to petition God, who is powerful, for help and release from those who are oppressing them with sorrows, yet they cursed God and did not repent. It is clear that the plagues are for this purpose, to bring those to acknowledge God through torments who did not acknowledge their Master through his beneficent works.

The bowl of the fifth angel was poured out, it says, "on the throne of the beast, and its kingdom was in darkness." The apostle wrote concerning the antichrist, "whom the Lord will slay with the breath of his mouth,"[1] and Isaiah said, "Let the ungodly be taken away, that he see not the glory of the Lord."[2] By "glory" Isaiah was referring to the coming of the Lord in glory. Therefore, when it says here that the bowl was poured out "on the throne of the beast," it shows that the impious tyranny of the antichrist will receive its end and that he will be mercifully taken away, while by the unexpected retribution of the accursed, darkness will seize all those who allowed themselves to become his subjects. For they will endure a darkness of their reason, becoming befuddled by what is happening. "And they gnawed their tongues in anguish," it says. This often happens in the most serious of afflictions when people are wont to cut off their tongues or some other part of the body with their teeth, thinking that this will bring the tribulation to naught. And it is necessary that these themselves repent, if for no other reason than because of the destruction of the antichrist whom they chose to be their king and god. But they continue to blaspheme the true God because of the destruction of the wicked one.

[16:12-16] ***The sixth angel poured out his bowl on the great river Euphrates, and its water was dried up, to prepare the way for the kings from the east. And I saw, issuing from the mouth of the dragon and from the mouth of***

Ninth Discourse [1]2 Thess 2:8. [2]Is 26:10.

the false prophet, three foul spirits like frogs; for they are demonic spirits, performing signs, who go abroad to the kings of the whole world, to assemble them for battle on the great day of God the Almighty. "Lo, I am coming like a thief! Blessed is he who is awake, keeping his garments that he may not go naked and be seen exposed!" And he assembled them at the place that is called in Hebrew Meggido.[3]

The sixth angel made the Euphrates River passable, perhaps by drying up some of its tributaries, so that the crossing of it would be easy for the many kings who by the work of the devil and the allowance of God were gathered together for war against each other. For, in the saying adduced a short time above, the Lord said that there would also be wars near the time of the consummation.[4]

"And I saw," it says, "issuing from the mouth of the dragon and from the mouth of the false prophet." He calls the devil, that originator of evil, a dragon. But by the title of "false prophet" he refers either to a certain other who prophesies through the operation of the devil or to the antichrist. However, should he be speaking completely of the antichrist whom above he introduced as one slain by the breath of the Lord and whom now he depicts as still alive—he pours out demons through his mouth—let not the reader be amazed. For that which is seen is a vision, and the Evangelist often shows that which comes first as last, and contrariwise that which is last as first. "And I saw," it says, "three spirits like frogs; for they are demonic spirits, performing signs, who go abroad to the kings." He calls the demons frogs because they rejoice at that life of people that is muddy and slimy. Moreover, they take pleasure in the life of sinners, which is moist and without constraint, rather than in the life of the righteous, which is steadfast and austere, being also very envious and joyful at the destruction of the living. One form of the wonders worked by the demons is that they gather the kings for war against each other at the time of the consummation. And he calls this day or that time great, for it is truly great and fearful and is so called also by Joel, who says, "before the great and glorious day of the Lord comes."[5]

"Lo, I am coming like a thief," says the Lord. He says "like a thief" because of the suddenness and unexpectedness of his second coming. "Blessed is he who is awake and keeps his garments that he may not go naked." He continues the image of the thief. Therefore, he said that it is necessary to preserve one's garments that they not be lost. By the term "garments" he refers either to the virtuous and decent life through which we become worthy of God's protection, or he refers to the body, that it be pure and holy. For he who does not keep his garments will be ashamed in front of the divine throne of the angels and of people, harried by the judgment at that time and left naked of divine succor.

The demons, it says, gathered the kings of the earth "at the place that is called in Hebrew Meggido." Meggido means "deep wound" or "being severely wounded" and is named this because of the mayhem and slaughter of those gathered there.

[16:17-21] ***The seventh angel poured his bowl into the air, and a loud voice came out of the temple, from the throne, saying, "It is done!" And there were flashes of lightning, voices, peals of thunder, and a great earthquake such as had never been since people were on the earth, so great was that earthquake. The great city was [split into three parts, and the cities of the nations fell, and the great city Babylon was]***[6] ***remembered by God, to give to her the***

[3]The text of Oecumenius reads Μαγεδδών not Ἀρμαγεδών. [4]See his comments on Rev 16:2-7, where Oecumenius quotes Mt 24:6-8. [5]Joel 2:31. [6]These words are contained only in manuscripts P and B. As the discussion below indicates, they were original to the text of Oecumenius.

cup of the wine of the wrath of my God. And every island fled away, and no mountains were to be found; and great hailstones, heavy as a hundred-weight, dropped on people from heaven, and they cursed God for the plague of the hail, for that plague was very severe.

He poured out the bowl in the air, and the voice said, "It is done!" What is done? To be sure, the commandment of God and his will. And when from the air the voice said, "It is done," there were flashes of lightning and voices, lightning from on high and voices from those on the earth who were alarmed by the lightning. "And peals of thunder and an earthquake." By "earthquake" he means either the turmoil of the earth, since this also is included in the signs of the end, or he means the transformation of the visible world, as it is said in Haggai, "Once again I will shake, not only the heaven but also the earth and the sea and the dry land; and I will shake all nations."[7] Therefore, he also indicated that there had never been such an earthquake.

"And the great city was split into three parts," it says, "and the cities of the nations fell." By the words "the great city" he speaks of Jerusalem, and it is clear that in this way he distinguishes it from the cities of the nations. For it is customary in the holy Scriptures to call the rest of humankind apart from Israel by the term "nations." And he speaks of it as great, as though it were famous. But all the cities fell. For when the earth is being transformed and is becoming new, how could it be that the cities in it would stand, having been defiled by the habitation of sinners?

"And God remembered great Babylon, to give to her the cup of the wine of the wrath of his anger." In a foregoing passage it says, "And a second angel followed, saying, 'Fallen, fallen, is Babylon the great.'"[8] But in this present passage, he intends for us to think of another Babylon, not that one, and he assigns to it another sense. I think that he is speaking of Rome and of those who will capture it at that time, as the narrative will teach further on. And, therefore, he says, "God remembered great Babylon," that is, God remembered its former sins, when they persecuted and killed the saints. "The cup of the wine of the wrath of God" has already been discussed,[9] so it is not necessary to repeat ourselves.

"And every island fled away," it says, "and no mountains were to be found." By "islands" he speaks of the Gentile churches, as the prophet says: "The Lord has reigned; let the earth be glad, and let the many islands rejoice."[10] He calls them islands because they lifted their heads and rose above their bitter and distasteful idolatry. Someone might also think otherwise and interpret the islands to refer to the impure orders of the demons, since they wallow in this briny and turbulent life. But that he refers to demons when he mentions the mountains, even the holy psalmist shows, singing, "The mountains melt like wax before the Lord, for he is coming."[11] Therefore, this passage transmits to us that the ranks of the demons at that time will be wiped out and obliterated. And, where might the wretched flee from God, in whose hand are the corners of the earth[12] and who measured the heaven with a span and the earth with his hand[13]—unless those who are struck by these events should attempt a futile flight and escape? When these things take place and there is a violent hailstorm, it will be necessary that people at that time turn to prayers and entreaties—for these signs against them might, in that case, cease—but they rather will curse God and therefore these evils against them will even intensify.

[17:1-5] ***And one of the seven angels who had***

[7]Hag 2:6-7. [8]Rev 14:8. [9]See the comments on Rev 14:9-12. [10]Ps 97:1 (96:1 LXX). [11]Ps 97:5, (96:5, LXX). [12]Ps 95:4 (94:4 LXX). [13]See Is 40:12.

the seven bowls came and said to me, "Come, I will show you the judgment of the great harlot who is seated on many waters, with whom the kings of the earth have committed fornication, and with the wine of her fornication the dwellers on earth have become drunk." And he carried me away in the Spirit into a wilderness, and I saw a woman sitting on a scarlet beast that was full of blasphemous names, and it had seven heads and ten horns. The woman was arrayed in purple and scarlet and was bedecked with gold and a precious stone and pearls, and she held in her hand a golden cup full of abominations and the impurities of the fornication of the earth; and on her forehead was written a name, a mystery, "Babylon the great, the mother of harlots and of the abominations of the earth."

Having completed its discourse about the consummation of the present age and what will happen at that time, the vision now reveals to the Evangelist what will befall Rome. He said to me, it says, "Come, I will show you the judgment of the harlot who is seated on many waters." By "judgment" he means that way of life and conduct in which God has judged her to exist and that she pursued. He calls Rome a harlot because she had fornicated, that is, apostatized from God. For this is called fornication by the divine Scriptures, as in the saying by the prophet to the God of all things, "You have destroyed every one who fornicates from you."[14] By "many waters" he refers to the nations that Rome rules and governs, as he says later on.[15] "With whom the kings of the earth have committed fornication," it says. These are those who ruled among them. For these kings of the earth are those who participated in her fornication and the madness of her idolatry. "Those who dwell on the earth have become drunk with the wine of her fornication," it says. For indeed also the rest of humankind, over whom she was ruling, apostatized from God along with her. Sometimes she compelled them to this, and sometimes she led the way.

"And he carried me away in the Spirit into a wilderness." The wilderness symbolizes her coming desolation. "And I saw," it says, "a woman sitting on a scarlet beast." The beast is the devil on whom she was resting and by whom she was being commanded, and it is scarlet because it has become red by the blood of the saints. And the beast was full of blasphemous names, for by attributing to himself that worship due to God, the devil sinned against God. "He had seven heads and ten horns," it says. The Evangelist will explain this later on, saying that the heads and the horns are kings who have ruled in the harlot and those who will rule.[16] "The woman was arrayed in purple and scarlet," purple because of her sovereignty and scarlet because she had shed the blood of many saints. She was "bedecked with gold and a precious stone and pearls." The passage appropriately describes her as a queen in royal garb. "She held in her hand a golden cup full of abominations." It was gold because of the rank of her sovereignty but yet full of idolatries and defilements by which she was nourished and by which she offered a libation to her own demons. "And the impurities of the fornication of the earth," it says. It ascribes to her the idolatries also of other nations, since she was the primary cause of their own evils and of the madness of their idolatry. And there was written on her forehead, as though inscribed on a public monument, as I might put it, that she was "Babylon, the mother of harlots." She is Babylon because of the terror and confusion in her and the persecutions of the saints—for the name Babylon means "confusion," as we have said[17]—and she is mother because of her fornication, that is, her apostasy from God. For how is she not mother and teacher who persecutes the gospel and those who preach it and

[14]Ps 73:27 (72:27 LXX). [15]Rev 17:15. [16]See Rev 17:9-12. [17]See the comments on Rev 14:8.

persuades the nations to remain loyal to the error traditional to their ancestors?

[17:6-9] ***And I saw the woman, drunk with the blood of the martyrs of Jesus. When I saw her I marveled greatly. But the angel said to me, "Why marvel? I will tell you the mystery of the woman, and of the beast with seven heads and ten horns that carries her. The beast that you saw was, and is not, and is to ascend from the bottomless pit and go to perdition; and the dwellers on earth whose names have not been written in the book of life from the foundation of the world, will marvel to behold the beast, because it is not and is to come. This calls for a mind with wisdom."***

Not only was the harlot sated on the blood of the saints; she was indeed drunk on it, for those who ruled in her had shed so much blood in different ways. "I will tell you," it says, "the mystery of the woman and of the beast." That is, he mystically reveals to you that which is written through the revelation as though it were in a picture. "The beast that you saw," it says, "was, and is not, and is to ascend from the bottomless pit." For the devil "was" before the foundation of the visible world, having been created by God for good works, even as were also the other holy angels. But he "is not" in respect to the events surrounding the consummation of the age that are shown to the Evangelist, in which he will go "into the fire prepared for him and his angels." For to exist among these is not to exist in any meaningful sense. Accordingly, since by his activity the antichrist will be manifested around the days of the end, it says that "he will ascend from the bottomless pit and go to perdition." For through the antichrist the devil will experience an ascent and a kind of increase, since the antichrist will deceive humankind and persuade them to worship the devil, as the many predictions above have indicated.[18] Or you might interpret the phrase "he was and is not" in this way. Writing to the Philippians, the apostle says, "to all the saints in Christ Jesus who are at Philippi,"[19] calling the saints those "who are" because they are in Christ and in the possession and memory of God. If, therefore, the saints are those "who are," the wicked devil "is not" now, although he "was" before he acted arrogantly against God and fell from his rank.

It is similar also with the ungodly. Although they appear to exist so far as their substance and essence are concerned, yet they do not exist in regard to the judgment and memory of God. And since this is the case, the book of Genesis gives no genealogy of those who descended from Cain, because they "were not" because of their ungodliness.[20] Rather, it speaks of "perdition" to which he is destined to go, namely, to the just punishment of Gehenna against him. For in Matthew the Lord says that those condemned in it are destroyed: "Rather fear him who can destroy both soul and body in Gehenna."[21]

And, it says, "the dwellers on earth will marvel." Not all dwellers, but those whose names are not in the Book of Life. And why will they marvel? Because the beast was and is not and will come and be destroyed. For those who trusted in him will be amazed at the great change that has come on him. For desiring to be ruler of the world and manifesting himself in this way, he not only will be stripped of his power but also will receive a fate corresponding to his depravity.

"This calls for a mind with wisdom," it says. This calls for a mind made wise and discerning, it says. Let it understand the riddle how "he was and is not and will ascend from the bottomless pit." For even though he is passing from being into nonbeing, his re-emergence from the bottomless pit seems to indicate the opposite, only it is not so if one understands

[18]See Rev 13:12-17. [19]Phil 1:1. [20]See Gen 5:1-6:1. However, see also Gen 4:17-22. [21]Mt 10:28.

according to the words here stated.

[17:9-14] ***The seven heads are seven mountains on which the woman is seated; they are also seven kings, five of whom have fallen, one is, the other has not yet come, and when he comes he must remain only a little while. And the beast that was and is not, it is an eighth but it belongs to the seven, and it goes to perdition. And the ten horns that you saw are ten kings who have not yet received royal power, but they will have[22] it as kings; they receive royal power for one hour, together with the beast. These are of one mind and give over their power and authority to the beast; they will make war on the Lamb, and the Lamb will conquer them, for he is Lord of lords and King of kings, and those with him are called and chosen and faithful."***

"The seven heads are seven mountains," it says, "on which the woman is seated." From this it is especially evident that the passage refers to Rome, for it and no other city is reported to be on seven hills. "And seven kings," it says, "five of whom have fallen, one is, the other has not yet come, and when he comes he must remain only a little while." It is appropriate that he recognizes kings in the heads, for the kings exercise the leadership[23] of Roman hegemony. However, why, when so many kings have ruled for Rome, did he mention only seven heads on the beast? He mentions these seven only, since they especially have represented the beast, that is, the devil and have caused it to raise its head against the Christians by initiating persecutions against the church. Of these the first was Nero, the second was Domitian, then Trajan, after him Severus, Decius, Valerian and Diocletian.[24] Of those who ruled Rome, these constantly persecuted the church, as Eusebius reports in his *Chronicle*.[25] The passage says that five of these seven have fallen by death—Nero, Domitian, Trajan, Severus, Decius—while one is, namely, Valerian. "The other has not yet come, and when he comes he must remain only a little while." He identifies this "other" as Diocletian after whom the government seated in Rome ceased and was transferred to the city named for pious Constantine when Constantine moved the seat of government there.

All these things were with great accuracy announced to the Evangelist, especially the information about Diocletian that "when he comes he must remain only a little while." By "remain" he means the persecution directed against the Christians. For although he reigned for twenty years, Diocletian instigated his persecution in the final two years and then forfeited his imperial power. "And the beast that was and is not, it is an eighth but it belongs to the seven and it goes to perdition." He has ranked the devil first and last as a persecutor and one of like mind with the seven. For how would this one not be ranked with the seven when he in fact had been their guiding power?

"And the ten horns that you saw," it says, "are ten kings who have not yet received royal power." The all-wise prophet, Daniel, remarked concerning these ten kings or horns that they would arise in the last times out of the Roman rule.[26] And the antichrist will rise up in the middle of them. And for this reason it says that "they have not yet received royal power, but they will have it as kings." It rightly says "as kings" because of the rapid demise and fleeting nature of their reign. Then it continues, "They receive it for one hour, together with the beast." Here it calls the antichrist

[22]The text of Oecumenius reads ἕξουσιν rather than ἐχουσία. [23]Translating τὸ κεφάλαιον. [24]Nero (54–68); Domitian (81–96); Trajan (98–117); Septimius Severus (193–211); Decius (249–251); Valerian (253–260); Diocletian (284–305). [25]Eusebius *Chron.* II, Olympia: for Nero (211; PG 19:543-44); for Domitian (218; PG 19:549-52); for Trajan (221, 223; PG 19:553-54); for Severus (245, 247; PG 19:567-68); for Decius (258; PG 19:573-74); for Valerian (259; PG 19:575-76); for Diocletian (270; PG 19:581-82). [26]See Dan 7:7-12. See Irenaeus *Haer.* 5.26.1 (ANF 1:554-55).

"beast" as it had also in earlier passages, saying, "I saw another beast coming up from the earth, and it had two horns like a lamb."[27] That they rule for one hour signifies either the short duration of their rule, or it is a figure of speech indicating by one hour one year.

"These are of one mind," it says, "and give over their power and authority to the beast." Although these future ten kings have no agreement among themselves, yet they are of one mind in this, that they give their power and authority to the beast, that is, to the antichrist. For they will be defeated by him, and he alone will finally rule over all things. Although they will be defeated against their will, it is said nonetheless that they have one mind, since the ten suffer the same experience of defeat and ruin. It is as though he had said, "The ten agreed and consented to be defeated by the antichrist."

"These will make war on the Lamb," it says. For before they are wholly destroyed by the antichrist, these kings, about whom the passage is speaking, will persecute the church. However, Christ will triumph, for he will hand these evil men over to the yet more evil antichrist for death. And Christ will triumph in another way also, since his servants struggle to death for their faith in him. For it says, "they are called and chosen and faithful," that is, the servants of Christ.

[17:15-18] ***And he said to me, "The waters that you saw, where the harlot is seated, are peoples and nations and multitudes and tongues. And the ten horns that you saw, they and the beast will hate the harlot; they will make her desolate and naked and devour her flesh and burn her up with fire, for God has put it into their hearts to carry out his purpose by being of one mind and giving over their royal power to the beast, until the words of God shall be fulfilled. And the woman that you saw is the great city that has dominion over the kings of the earth."***

It says that the waters on which the harlot sits are the peoples and nations, clearly those over which the city exercises its rule. But how will these kings lay waste to Rome, for we see that Revelation depicts it so? Perhaps it will be the object of warfare among the kings, as a queen who is both strong and populous and the recipient of tribute. Thus, in the war for the city, it will be necessary that it, lying open as the prize of victory, suffer terribly at the hands of all, being ravaged by fire and made desolate. "For God has put it into their hearts to carry out his purpose." Through God's allowance of these things, those who oppose her and desire to capture her follow along. And God causes them to be of one mind and to give their royal power to the beast, just as they agreed to be handed over to the antichrist as subjects, as I explained above.[28] "Until the words of God shall be fulfilled." They will become subject to the beast, it says, until the punishment of the antichrist overtakes him and all the words spoken by God through the prophets against him receive their fulfillment. And wishing to indicate even more clearly what will befall the city, the passage continues, "The woman is the great city that has dominion over all."

[18:1-3] ***After this I saw another angel coming down from heaven, having great authority; and the earth was made bright with his splendor. And he called out with a mighty voice, "Fallen, fallen is Babylon the great! It has become a dwelling place of demons, a haunt of every foul spirit, a haunt of every foul and hateful bird; for all nations have fallen[29] from the wrath of her fornication, and the kings of the earth have committed fornication with her,***

[27]Rev 13:11. [28]See his comments on Rev 17:9-14. [29]The text of Oecumenius reads πέπτωκε ("have fallen") rather than πέπωκαν ("have drunk").

and the merchants of the earth have grown rich with the wealth of her wantonness."

"And I saw," it says, "another angel having great authority." He says that this authority is of a bright luminary who illumines the earth "with his splendor." "Fallen is Babylon," it says. He openly announces the sentence of condemnation that God has rendered against her. He has decreed, it says, that she should suffer these things. "It has become a dwelling place of demons." For as those who hate humankind and are desirous of blood, these wicked demons search out places in which the blood of people killed in warfare or in some other manner has been shed, and as though rejoicing at what has happened, they make their abode in such places. Therefore, since most will be killed in the city, as I have said, she finally becomes the "dwelling place of demons and a haunt of every foul spirit," since the place safeguards the hedonistic lifestyle of the demons in her. "And a haunt of every foul bird and every unclean beast," it says. For such animals flee the abode of people and take possession of abandoned places, keeping them free from those who intend them harm and hunt wild animals. The prophet Isaiah also said something like this concerning Babylon: "And sirens will rest there, and demons will dance there, and satyrs will dwell there, and hedgehogs will make their nests in their houses."[30]

"For all the nations have drunk from the wrath of her fornication." By fornication he means their insatiable greed and their love of money, for such is the manner of harlots. For those in the city of which we speak have clung close to all nations, since they have placed them in subjection and commanded that they pay tribute. "And the kings," it says, namely, those who have become partners with her and companions in her love of money. "And the merchants" who have traded in her "have grown rich from her wantonness." That is, they have become rich from her arrogance and from her unconstrained, prodigal and slothful way of life, since they put out for sale in her every kind of merchandise.

[18:4-8] ***Then I heard another voice from heaven saying, "Come out of her, my people, lest you take part in their sins, lest you share in her plagues; for her sins are heaped high as heaven, and God has remembered her iniquities. Render to her as she herself has rendered, and repay her double for her deeds; mix a double draught for her in the cup she mixed. As she glorified herself and played the wanton, so give her a like measure of torment and mourning. For in her heart she says, 'A queen I sit, I am no widow, mourning I shall never see.' Therefore, her plagues will come in a single day, death and mourning and famine, and she shall be burned with fire; for mighty is the Lord who has judged her."***

When the angels of God took hold of the city of the Sodomites and on that occasion exacted punishment on its inhabitants and the surrounding cities—or rather, as it would seem to the saintly Cyril, when the Son of God and the Holy Spirit visited there, for "the Father judges no one," as it is written, "but has given all judgment to the Son,"[31] the life-giving Spirit clearly being with him according to nature and essence[32]—then the angels said to holy Lot, "Save your own life. Do not look back or remain in all the country round about; escape to the mountain, lest you be overtaken together with them."[33] This is what Revelation now is also teaching us. For although the servants of Christ are not in one large and populous city, namely, Rome, it says to them, "Come out of her, my people, lest you take part in their sins, lest you share in their plagues." For to partake of sins is also to partake of the plagues, since

[30]Is 13:21-22. [31]Jn 5:22. [32]Cyril of Alexandria *Adoration in Spirit and Truth* 1 (PG 68:169-76). [33]Gen 19:1-25, here, Gen 19:17.

the plagues come on account of sins.

"For her sins are heaped high as heaven," it says. This is as though he had said, "And they polluted the air all around with their sins." And so it says, although God is in every way longsuffering, he has now arisen to give to the city its due. Therefore, it says, "repay her double for her sins." It is true that through wise Moses God has commanded us, "You will not take vengeance twice at the same time."[34] How, therefore, does God repay double? The word *double* does not mean twofold or twice. Rather, since God is a lover of humankind and good and punishes to a much lesser degree than is deserved, he deems that he has given back double, and indeed not only double but even sevenfold, whenever he gives back only a part. And knowing this, the prophet said, "Repay to your neighbors sevenfold into their bosom the reproach with which they have reproached you, O Lord."[35] In this petition for the punishment of their enemies according to their deserts, they implore God to give back sevenfold.

Similar to these words, it says "give back to her," who was exalted and lived wantonly during this present life, giving no thought to the divine will. For Babylon said, I will never lose my rule—for by "widow" it means to be bereft of rule—nor will I see any evil. Therefore, on account of her arrogance utter evil will come on her all of a sudden. For, it says, God is mighty, and he will be hindered by no one from bringing on her judgment and torment. From this judgment may we all be free by the grace of him who has called us into his knowledge and into the hope of Christ, to whom be glory forever. Amen.

Tenth Discourse

Revelation continues its discussion concerning Rome, speaking at some length concerning the great and strange mutation that the city undergoes. What, then, does it say?

[18:9-19] ***And the kings of the earth, who committed fornication and were wanton with her, will weep and wail over her when they see the smoke of her burning; they will stand far off, in fear of her torment, and say, "Alas!, alas! The great city, Babylon, the might city! In one hour has thy judgment come." And the merchants of the earth weep and mourn for her, since no one buys their cargo any more, cargo of gold, silver, jewels and pearls, fine linen, purple, silk and scarlet, all kinds of scented wood, all articles of ivory, all articles of costly wood, bronze, iron and marble, cinnamon, incense, myrrh, frankincense, wine, oil, fine flour and wheat, cattle and sheep, horses both for chariots and people, and slaves. "The fruit for which your soul longed has gone from you, and all your dainties and splendor are lost to you, and they will never again find her!"[1] The merchants of these wares, who gained wealth from her, will stand far off, in fear of her torment, weeping and mourning and saying, "Alas! Alas! The great city that was clothed in fine linen, in purple and scarlet, and was bedecked with gold, with jewels, and with pearls! In one hour all this wealth has been laid waste." And all shipmasters and everyone who sails on the river,[2] sailors and all whose trade is on the sea, stood far off and cried out as they saw the pain[3] of her burning, saying, "What city was like the great city?" And they threw dust on their heads, as they wept and mourned, crying out, "Alas! Alas! The great city where all who had ships at sea grew rich by her wealth! In one hour she has been laid waste."***

How intricately and carefully he has constructed the lament against the city and the extent of the mourning! Although virtually

[34]Nah 1:9. [35]Ps 79:12 (78:12 LXX). **Tenth Discourse** [1]The text of Oecumenius reads αὐτήν ("her"), not αυτά ("them"). [2]The text of Oecumenius reads ποταμόν. [3]The text of Oecumenius reads πόνον ("pain"), not καμνόν ("smoke").

everything is clear, there is one thing that is somewhat difficult to interpret and that I will mention in passing and then move on to the remaining passages. It says, "and horses both for chariot and for people." The word *rheda*[4] is a Latin expression. When the Romans were in power, it was reasonable for the holy Evangelist to make use of a Latin term. But the Scriptures have put the term in a Greek form, for *radium* is a chariot among the Romans, and in this passage the word has been declined as a general plural. One would have to write *rhedioroum*[5] to correspond to the Latin plural [*radiorum*], and so he has given the word a Greek form by writing a Greek plural ending, saying *rhedōn*[6] so that he might say the same thing.

"And horses for chariots and for people," it says. This is as though to say, horses for chariots that are suitable for chariots, and for people, that is, riding horses trained for riders.

[18:20-24] ***"Rejoice over her, O heaven, O saints and apostles and prophets, for God has given judgment for you against her!" And an angel took up a great[7] stone like a great millstone and threw it into the sea, saying, "So shall Babylon the great be thrown down with violence and shall be found no more; and the sound of harpers and minstrels, of flute players and trumpeters, shall be heard in you no more; and a craftsman of any craft shall be found in you no more; and the sound of the millstone shall be heard in you no more; and the light of a lamp shall shine in you no more; and the voice of bridegroom and bride shall be heard in you no more; for the merchants were the great men of the earth, and all nations were deceived by your sorcery. And in her was found the blood of prophets and of saints, and of all who have been slain on earth."***

While the merchants and the kings of the earth and all with whom the city did commerce while she yet stood and was prosperous will weep bitterly for her, the heavens will rejoice, that is, the angels in heaven and the souls of the righteous. The souls will rejoice because the vindication from God has happened, while the angels will rejoice as those who are glad for the vindicated. Moreover, through the description of the behavior in the narrative, the suffering of the spiritual Babylon is highlighted. These things being clear, it is not necessary to discuss further what enjoys a consensus of opinion.

[19:1-5] ***After this I heard a loud voice of a great multitude in heaven, saying, "Hallelujah! Salvation and glory and power belong to our God, for his judgments are true and just; for he has judged the great harlot who corrupted the earth with her fornication, and he has avenged on her the blood of his servants." A second time they cried, "Hallelujah! The smoke from her goes up forever and ever." And the twenty-four elders and the four living creatures fell down and worshiped God who is seated on the throne, saying, "Amen. Hallelujah!" And from the throne came a voice, crying, "Praise our God, all you his servants, you who fear him, small and great."***

"I heard a voice from heaven as of a great multitude," it says. The ranks of the holy angels are beyond counting. As one of the Fathers has said, the ninety-nine sheep who were kept safe and did not go astray represent the angels, while the one sheep who went astray represents the entirety of humankind.[8] They said, "Hallelujah!" "Hallelujah" is a Hebrew expression that means "praise God" or "sing to God." Therefore, they are singing a hymn of

[4]ῥέδα. [5]ῥεδιορούμ. [6]ῥεδῶν. [7]In the text of Oecumenius the adjective ἰσχυρόν modifies the stone, not the angel. [8]See Mt 18:12-13. To whom Oecumenius refers is unknown. However, this interpretation can be found in Epiphanius *Homily 4, On the Ascension of Christ* (PG 43:481).

thanksgiving for the righteous judgment of the spiritual Babylon. And they cried out the same hymn a "second time," and yet later they spoke it again.[9] And so by this threefold offering of the hallelujah they give glory to the holy and much to be praised Trinity, for this [the Trinity] is God.

"The smoke from her goes up forever and ever." The doxology of the hallelujah interrupted the flow of the discourse, since clearly the sequence of the narrative is this: "And he has avenged on her the blood of his servants. And the smoke from her goes up forever and ever." He mentions "smoke" since the city of which he speaks is completely in flames. For smoke is an indication of fire.

The elders and the living creatures say "Amen," signifying their agreement with the doxology that was proffered by the holy angels. For when rendered from the Hebrew into the Greek, "Amen" means "let it be" [γένοιτο]. It says, "Praise our God, you small and you great." By "small" he refers to those who are greater in holiness; by "great" he refers to those who are outstanding in holiness.[10]

[19:6-9] ***Then I heard what seemed to be the voice of a great multitude and like the sound of many waters and like the sound of mighty thunderpeals, crying, "Hallelujah! For the Lord our God the Almighty reigns. Let us rejoice and exult and give him the glory, for the marriage of the Lamb has come, and his bride has made herself ready; and it was granted to her to be clothed with fine linen." This is the righteous deeds of the saints. And he said to me, "Write this. Blessed are those who are invited to the marriage supper of the Lamb." And he said to me, "These are the true words of God."***

According to the holy prophet Isaiah,[11] the seraphim said "holy" three times and so composed a threefold hymn to one lordship. In this manner they showed that there are three individual existences or, which is to speak in a similar way, three persons of whom to sing, while there is one essence of the Godhead. So also in this passage the holy angels, having spoken the hallelujah three times in the passages above and having rendered homage to each of the three holy hypostases, now sing the hallelujah to the holy Trinity, showing that the holy and much-sung Trinity is in one unique essence and Godhead.[12]

"For the Lord our God reigns," it says. As the only-begotten Son and Word of the Father and the maker of all things, our Lord, Jesus Christ, even before his saving incarnation, reigned over what is in heaven and on earth with the Father and the all-holy Spirit. But even after the incarnation he is similarly Lord and King of all things, for by his taking of flesh he was in no way made inferior in regard to his rule and dominion over all things. However, as the all-wise apostle says, we do not yet see all things subjected to him, but all things will be subjected to him in the coming age,[13] including those who now until then behave insolently toward him. Even death itself is to be subjected, for "the last enemy to be destroyed is death."[14] The holy angels, therefore, properly say "the Lord our God reigns." In this way they lift up a doxology regarding the future age, since then by the subjection of all things, Christ will have acquired a perfect sovereignty over all things. Some will experience this subjection by way of torment, while others will experience it by way of a direct knowledge that is not through a dim mirror or an enigma, as is the case now.[15]

[9]Hallelujah is spoken at Rev 19:1, 3, 4. [10]Apparently Oecumenius thinks the word "small" is unsuited to the hosts in heaven who are to give praise to God. And so he interprets "small" to mean "greater in holiness" and correspondingly "great" to refer to those "outstanding in holiness." [11]Is 6:3. [12]The threefold hallelujah of Rev 19:1, 3, 4 is to the three persons or hypostases. The singular hallelujah of Rev 19:6 is to the Trinity as one God. [13]See 1 Cor 15:27-28. [14]1 Cor 15:26. [15]1 Cor 13:12.

"For the marriage of the Lamb has come," it says, "and his bride has made herself ready." In the present age the marriage of the Lord with the church is still in the stage of courtship and is not yet a consummated marriage. The holy apostle indicates this when he writes his second letter to the Corinthians and says, "For I betrothed you as a pure bride to one husband to present you to Christ."[16] Therefore, the time of courtship remains. For "I betrothed" refers to courtship, and we receive the pledge of the Spirit as a sign of courtship. However, when the church becomes one spirit with Christ, as a husband becomes one body with his wife, then will the marriage be perfected. For indeed the wise apostle has spoken wisely concerning bodily marriage when he wrote, "The two shall become one flesh."[17] But then he continues, "This is a great mystery, and I am saying that it refers to Christ and the church."[18] For this reason the holy angels say, "The marriage of the Lamb has come," signifying that the marriage, which now is in the stage of courtship, will then be consummated. And the Gospel also clearly gives this understanding to us. For on one occasion it introduces the wedding festivities of a son, prepared by his father who is a king. Although many have been invited to the banquet, some partake of the feasting while others excuse themselves from the supper, and one person is excluded because he is not dressed in a wedding garment.[19] On another occasion the Gospel speaks of ten virgins, five of whom it says are wise and enter with the bridegroom into the blessed bridal chamber. The other virgins are locked outside since they did not fill up their lamps with sufficient oil.[20] It is not suitable to regard any of this as referring to the present time; it rather refers to that which is coming. Therefore, the marriage of the Lamb has come, and his bride, the church, is presented ready as to receive those ineffable gifts that come by her union with Christ.

She is clothed, it says, with fine linen, that is, with a robe made of virtues. It is linen because it is bright and of fine texture, bright from her incomprehensible manner of life, and fine because of her teachings and convictions concerning God.

"And the angel said to me, 'Write this: Blessed are those who are invited to the marriage supper of the Lamb,' " even if some will be forced to leave. For we know from the Gospels that many who are invited excused themselves from the spiritual banquet or even attended but were cast outside since they did not have the wedding garment, as I showed a short time ago. Indeed, as the holy apostle said, "Many are called, but few are chosen."[21]

[19:10] ***Then I fell down at his feet to worship him, but he said to me, "See that you do not do that! I am a fellow servant with you and your brethren who hold the testimony of Jesus. Worship God!" For the testimony of Jesus is the spirit of prophecy.***

The Greeks, though accursed and hated by God, heard of the teaching given in our prophecies that by the good will of God the holy angels protect the nations and the churches and every individual. That the angels govern the nations is indicated by the all-wise Daniel when he writes, "And I have come because of your words. The prince of the kingdom of Persia withstood me,"[22] and again, "But now I will return to fight against the prince of Persia, and I was going out, and the leader of the Greeks came,"[23] and again, "And there is no one that contends with me concerning this, except Michael your prince,"[24] and again, "And at that time Michael the great prince shall stand up, he who stands over the sons of your people."[25] That the angels govern the churches

[16]2 Cor 11:2. [17]Eph 5:31. [18]Eph 5:32. [19]Mt 22:2-14. [20]Mt 25:1-13. [21]Mt 22:14. [22]Dan 10:12-13. [23]Dan 10:20. [24]Dan 10:21. [25]Dan 12:1.

has been indicated by foregoing passages in the present revelation.[26] And among the saints, Gregory has written a similar opinion about the holy angels: "For I believe, as John teaches me in his Revelation, that each church has its guardian."[27] And that the angels watch over each individual is asserted by the prophet: "The angel of the Lord encamps around those who fear him, and he will deliver them."[28] And the apostle also writes concerning the holy angels, "Are they not all ministering spirits sent forth to serve, for the sake of those who are to obtain salvation?"[29]

Since the Greeks have heard that such things were being taught by us, they say to us, "Since you claim the same things as we do, O people, why do you find fault with the teaching that we advance concerning the gods that rule over the nations? For those whom you call angels we call gods, so that we differ only in the use of the names but not in the substance of the matter. But since you also call the order of angels 'gods,' there is no difference with us even in regard to the use of names."

To such persons one must say the following. "You accursed people. You worship the works of your own hands and until very recently have established for yourselves gods with whom you associated for every vile purpose. You have purloined most of our divine teachings and, adding these to your destructive teachings, you have made a grand mixture of them. But since you use your own mind as guide and not God, you have not been able to maintain the nobility of our teachings in every regard. Rather, although you followed him for a short while, somewhere at the beginning of things, you suffered shipwreck. There is, therefore, nothing in common between us and you, just as there is nothing in common between light and darkness or between Christ and Beliar, as it is written.[30] Assuming the gods, or rather the unclean demons, to be the rulers of the nations, you bring yourselves into league with them, ascribing reverence to them and wishing to worship them as gods. Moreover, these demons are regarded by you as divine, while no mention is made of that God who has ordered all things for the providential care of humankind, these rather governing the nations by their own counsel, as they themselves wish. Therefore, you have assigned to Ares[31] the most savage and bloodthirsty Scythians and Germans, who became such since they were ruled by that murderous plague of man, Ares. But you assigned the Greeks, because of their understanding, to Athena,[32] since from her they received understanding as their lot. And you assigned other peoples to other gods, each of the gods training the nations according to their own passions."

But let us also say something from what we might learn from the words under discussion. For when the Evangelist wished to worship the holy angel, although certainly not to worship him as God—for who is more aware than John who is God by nature and in truth and who are the angels, namely, that they are ministers and servants and creatures of God?—nonetheless, the angel is seen rejecting even this worship of an angel, since it was certainly worship. Rather, the angel says, "See that you do not do this! I am a fellow servant with you and your brethren who hold the testimony of Jesus." The exclamation "See!" is not simply the cry of someone who wishes only to hinder but of someone who wants to prevent something altogether. He calls himself a fellow servant with all of those who confess themselves to be servants of Christ and who testify that he is God incarnate. What, then, is to be done, O most holy angel, since you forbid yourself to be worshiped? "Worship God!" he says, "for the testimony of Jesus is the spirit of proph-

[26]See Rev 2:1, 8, 12, 18; 3:1, 7, 14. [27]Gregory of Nazianzus *Or.* 42.9 (NPNF 2 7: 389). [28]Ps 34:7 (33:8 LXX). [29]Heb 1:14. [30]See 2 Cor 6:14-15. [31]The Greek god of war. [32]The Greek goddess of wisdom, justice and war.

ecy." This is as though he had said, "Do you seek to worship me, since I announced to you ahead of time what was to take place? Whoever witnesses to the lordship and deity of Christ is filled with the prophetic grace, not I alone. Why therefore, he says, do you worship that grace which I have in equal measure with my fellow servants? Are the things which the Greeks think about the rulers of the nations really the same as what the Christians say about the holy angels?"

[19:11-16] ***Then I saw heaven opened, and behold, a white horse! He who sat on it is called Faithful and True, and in righteousness he judges and makes war. His eyes are[33] a flame of fire, and on his head are many diadems; and he has a name inscribed that no one knows but himself. He is clad in a robe sprinkled with[34] blood, and the name by which he is called is The Word of God. And the armies in heaven, arrayed in fine linen, white and pure, follow him on white horses. From his mouth issues a sharp sword with which to smite the nations, and he will rule them with a rod of iron; he will tread the wine press of God, of the wrath of God the Almighty. And on his robe and on his thigh he has a name inscribed, King of kings and Lord of lords.***

After the time of the fall of Babylon—it is clear what Babylon this is intended to be—the Evangelist now receives the revelation of the fall of the antichrist and of the arch-evil dragon. He sees moreover the punishment they will receive at the time of the end and their recompense, as well as the fall of those kings who at that time will oppose the servants of Christ. And see what it says. "I saw heaven opened, and behold, a white horse," and the rider is faithful and true and just. He sees the Lord as he is about to join the battle and fight for the saints and make war against his adversaries. For this reason the vision depicts him in the form of a general, giving him a horse and a sword and the leadership of armies. "And, behold, a white horse" on which the Lord was riding. By this the vision reveals that Christ depends on no others than those who are pure and are not tainted by any stain of sin. For this reason, the Lord also said of that "chosen instrument," namely, Paul, that he would "carry my name before the Gentiles and kings and the sons of Israel."[35] You see, therefore, that Christ depends on and rides on such persons as Paul.

"He who sat on it," that is, on the horse, "is called Faithful and True, and in righteousness he judges and makes war." He who is true is also faithful, as the apostle said concerning him, "He remains faithful, for he cannot deny himself,"[36] and so he is the Faithful and True. And about him two assertions are made that address the same matter. The prophet was witness that he judges righteously and that he makes war on behalf of his servants against their visible enemies: "O God, give your judgment to the king, and your righteousness to the king's son,"[37] that is, to Christ—for according to the flesh Christ was the son of Solomon, to whom [Christ] the psalmist was referring—and then it continues, "that he might judge your people with righteousness and your poor with judgment."[38] That he also makes war the psalmist shows when he speaks of him arming himself as a soldier: "Gird your sword on your thigh, O mighty one, in your comeliness and in your beauty, and bend your bow and prosper and reign."[39] Then he adds, "Your weapons are sharpened, O mighty one, the nations shall fall under you."[40]

"His eyes are a flame of fire." The fiery appearance of his eyes reveals his wrath against his enemies. "And on his head are many diadems," indeed, as many as there are ranks

[33]The text of Oecumenius does not have ὡς ("like"). [34]The text of Oecumenius has ἐρραμμένον ("sprinkled"), not βεβαμμένον ("dipped"). [35]Acts 9:15. [36]2 Tim 2:13. [37]Ps 72:1 (71:1 LXX). [38]Ps 72:2 (71:2 LXX). [39]Ps 45:3-4 (44:4-5 LXX). [40]Ps 45:5 (44:6 LXX).

in heaven and on the earth over which he rules. "He has," it says, "a name inscribed that no one knows but himself." In the seventh part of Exodus, God speaks to holy Moses: "I am the Lord. I appeared to Abraham, to Isaac and to Jacob, being their God, but I did not reveal to them my proper name,"[41] showing that it is too great to be heard by any person. And for this reason, the Lord also handed over to his apostles how those who had turned to the knowledge of God ought to be baptized, saying, "baptizing them in the name."[42] And when he said "name," he did not transmit the proper names—for he was not able to give utterance to their names. Rather, instead of the proper names, he transmitted names of relation and of designation. He spoke names of relation when he said, "in the name of the Father and of the Son," while he added a name of designation when he said "and in the Holy Spirit." Therefore, with great certainty, also in Revelation he ensures that the proper name of the Only-begotten remains unknown to everyone.

"He is clad," it says, "in a robe sprinkled with blood." Also in the vision the Lord carried the tokens of his passion, and he showed his all-holy body to be altogether smeared with his precious blood. "And the name by which he is called is The Word of God." Do you see how above the vision avoided the proper name but instead now gives a personal designation, saying, "The Word of God." "And the armies, arrayed in fine linen, white and pure, followed him on white horses." Christ is the commander-in-chief of the heavenly powers. The Lord in fact called himself that when bearing the name of Jesus, son of Nun, he said, "I, as commander of the army of the Lord have now come."[43] The horses that belong to the holy angels are also white, for the angels too rejoice over the pure deeds of humankind, since they are pure by nature and are free from every stain. This is symbolized by their raiment of fine linen, which is white and pure.

"And from his mouth," clearly the mouth of the commander, "issues a sharp sword." While in the passage cited just above the holy prophet located the sharp sword on the thigh of the Lord, the vision gives a more accurate depiction and places it in the mouth. In this way it is indicated that all things have their existence by the Word of God and that whoever in any way disobeys him will not remain unpunished. "So that with it he might smite the nations." Which nations? Those that are arrayed with the antichrist for war against the servants of Christ and have been gathered under him. "And he will rule them," it says, "with a rod of iron." Since he is intrinsically good and merciful, the Lord desired to rule these nations, of whom the passage speaks, with a staff of comfort, as would a shepherd and lead them to "green pastures and to nourish them by the waters of rest."[44] But since they did not wish this, they will be governed with a rod of iron, that is, with severity and death. For certainly punishment awaits those whom the Word does not reform. To indicate that the rod of iron is that of severity and punishment, the prophet suggests the rule of the Romans[45] about which Daniel spoke in saying, "Arise, devour much flesh,"[46] when he spoke to God, saying, "You

[41]Ex 6:2-3. The context of Revelation clearly indicates that this inscribed name is not revealed. Perhaps for this reason Oecumenius does not render the LXX text exactly. The LXX reads καὶ τὸ ὄνομα μου κύριος οὐκ ἐδήλωσα αὐτοῖς. This translates as follows: "But I did not reveal to them my name, [the] Lord." Here κύριος is the name that is now revealed to Moses. In the text of Oecumenius this passage reads: καὶ τὸ ὄνομα μου τὸ κύριον οὐκ ἐδήλωσα αὐτοῖς. Here κύριον is not a name but a modifier of ὄνομα, and together they indicate a proper or personal name. According to Revelation this name remains undisclosed and by Oecumenius is distinguished from the "names of relation" (σχετικά) and the names of designation (προσηγορικά) that are given in the baptismal formula. According to Oecumenius, when Jesus says to "baptize in the name," he does not continue with the "proper names" (τὰ κύρια) but rather continues with "names of relation" and a "name of designation." Hence, the "proper name" of the Only-begotten as well as those of the Father and the Holy Spirit remain unknown. [42]Mt 28:19. [43]Josh 5:14. [44]Ps 23:2 (22:2 LXX). [45]A traditional interpretation of the fourth beast spoken of in Dan 7:19. [46]Dan 7:5.

will rule them with a rod or iron and dash them in pieces as a potter's vessel."[47] However, when there existed a favorable time, God ruled them with the former rod, but at the last time, he will rule them with this latter rod. "He will tread the wine press of the fury of the wrath of God the Almighty." In the Gospels, the Lord says of his own Father, "The Father judges no one but has given all judgment to the Son."[48] Most appropriately, therefore, it says in Revelation that "he will tread the wine press of the fury of the wrath of God." For through the judgment and recompense of the wicked, he fulfills the will of his Father in that he fulfills the righteous anger of the Father.

"On his robe and on his thigh he has a name inscribed, King of kings and Lord of lords." The robe symbolizes the flesh of the Lord, which was endowed with a rational soul. The holy angels spoke of his flesh through Isaiah: "Why are your garments red and your apparel as if from a trodden wine press, utterly stained by trodden grapes?"[49] Moreover, the thigh indicates his birth in the flesh, for it is written in Genesis, "All the souls that came with Jacob into Egypt, who came out of his thighs."[50] Therefore, when the vision shows that on the robe and on the thigh it is written that the Immanuel is king of all, it shows that the Word, united personally[51] to the flesh and having undergone a fleshly birth from a virgin, was in no way established less a King and Lord of all things in heaven and on earth; nor was he diminished in rank by virtue of his incarnation. For even as such he was God and is and shall be God.

[19:17-21] ***Then I saw another angel standing in the sun, and with a loud voice he called to all the birds that fly in mid-heaven, "Gather for the great supper of God, to eat the flesh of kings, the flesh of captains, the flesh of mighty men, the flesh of horses and their riders, and the flesh of all people, both free and slave, both small and great." And I saw the beast and the kings of the earth with their armies gathered to make war against him who sits on the horse and against his army. And the beast was captured, and with it the false prophet who in its presence had worked the signs by which he deceived those who had received the mark of the beast and those who worshiped its image. These two were thrown alive into the lake of fire that burns with sulfur. And the rest were slain by the sword of him who sits on the horse, the sword that issues from his mouth; and all the birds were gorged with their flesh.***

I think that this holy angel, which is now mentioned, is a certain military herald of the divine army and that he commands all the holy angels in heaven, here called birds because they are sublime and fly in the air, to partake of the slaughter of the enemies. To be sure, even one angel was sufficient to destroy an entire army of the enemy, as that angel clearly demonstrated who destroyed 185,000 Assyrians in one night.[52] However, he orders all to partake so that all might share in the joy against God's enemies. For I think that also these say with the prophet, "Do I not hate them that hate you, O Lord? And have I not wasted away because of your enemies? I have hated them with a perfect hate, and they were counted among my enemies."[53] And since he commanded angels who were flying in mid-heaven, he too was standing in mid-heaven when he gave them orders. For the sun is established in the middle of the seven planets, with three above it and three below it. Either this is the meaning, or he was giving his commands in the light, that is as it were, in the Spirit and was speaking of the coming slaughter. For the Spirit is the

[47]Ps 2:9 (LXX). [48]Jn 5:22. [49]Is 63:2-3. [50]Gen 46:26. [51]Translating καθ' ὑπόστασιν, "according to hypostasis," a common phrase from the Alexandrian tradition of Cyril of Alexandria. [52]2 Kings 19:35. [53]Ps 139:21-22 (138:21-22 LXX).

spiritual light, as the prophet teaches when he was discoursing with God the Father, and said, "In your light shall we see light,"[54] that is, in the Spirit we shall see the Son.

"That you might," it says, "eat the flesh of kings." The delight over the death of one's enemies is called food for these angels. Similarly, the Lord also speaks of joy as food when he says to his disciples and apostles, "I have food to eat that you do not know."[55] In this way he calls food that delight that will come to those who believe. And they waged war against the Lord and his holy angels, that is, the devil and the antichrist—for it calls the latter the false prophet of that brutal devil—and the kings who are arrayed with them. However, they were defeated more quickly than a word is spoken. For what do the divine Scriptures say about them? Speaking of their sudden destruction, Isaiah says, "Let the ungodly be taken away, that he not see the glory of the Lord."[56] And the apostle says, "whom the Lord will slay with the breath of his mouth."[57] For what is shorter than to breathe or to blow on one's enemies?

"These two," it says, "were thrown alive into the lake of fire. And the rest were slain by the sword." O, what a superabundance of justice! God does not reckon those responsible for the war and those who were accomplices worthy of the same punishment. Rather, the two, namely, the devil and the antichrist, were condemned to the fire, in which they will live for eternity—for this is the meaning of their being thrown alive into the fire. The rest are killed by the sword. It is, certainly, much different to give swift justice with the sword than to condemn to fire.

Once he began to speak of the devil and what kind of punishment God was to give to him, the Evangelist preserves, as it were, the coherence of the narrative and speaks also of the suffering of the devil at the time of the incarnation of the Lord. Having adopted this line of thought, he now speaks more about the coming of the Lord in the flesh and says:

[20:1-3] ***Then I saw an angel coming down from heaven, holding in his hand the key of the bottomless pit and a great chain. And he seized the dragon, that ancient serpent, who is the devil and Satan, and bound him for a thousand years, and threw him into the pit, and shut it and sealed it over him, that he should deceive the nations no more, till the thousand years were ended. After that he must be loosed for a little while, that he might again deceive the nations.***

He continues in this way. Revelation certainly does not present to us the millennialism of the atheistic Greeks and the transmigration of souls and the Lethian water and I do not know what other idle talk and nonsense when it says that the devil will be bound for a thousand years and will again be loosed to deceive the nations.[58] Stay away from such destructive teachings, which are suitable to the silliness of the Greeks. What, however, does it say? The prophet says, "For a thousand years in your sight, O Lord, are as yesterday which is past, and as a watch in the night."[59] Therefore, a thousand years in the sight of God is regarded as one day. And in his second letter, the holy Peter says the same thing when he writes, "But do not ignore this one fact, beloved, that with the Lord one day is as a thousand years, and a thousand years as one day."[60] And this is so. Moreover, the holy Isaiah speaks of the entire incarnation of the Lord as a day, saying, "In the time of favor I have answered you, in a day of salvation I have helped you."[61] And, not only this, the psalmist calls this same day also a morning. For some-

[54]Ps 36:9 (35:10 LXX). [55]Jn 4:32. [56]Is 26:10. [57]2 Thess 2:8. [58]For the transmigration of souls, see Plato *Resp.* 614e-615a; 620a-621b. In Greek Lethe (λήθη) means "forgetfulness." In Greek mythology Lethe was one of several rivers in hades. When the dead drank of the waters of Lethe, they forgot their past lives. [59]Ps 90:4 (89:4 LXX). [60]2 Pet 3:8. [61]Is 49:8.

where it says, "This is the day that the Lord has made; let us rejoice and be glad in it,"[62] speaking of the joy of our salvation. And somewhere else the psalmist says, "In the morning you will hear my voice; in the morning I will wait on you and you will see me."[63] For our prayers have become worthy in the sight of God the Father and become acceptable through the mediation and reconciliation of the Lord. And moreover, it says concerning Jerusalem, "God will help her right early."[64] And so, the incarnation of the Lord was a day and a morning, since, as it were, the "sun of righteousness"—for Malachi speaks of him in this way[65]—shone on us, providing us with the "light of knowledge."[66] And Zechariah foretold of this divine light when he said, "Whereby the dayspring will visit us from on high, to give light to those who sit in darkness and in the shadow of death."[67] And in agreement with this, the prophet said, "God is the Lord, and he has shined on us; celebrate the feast with thick branches, even to the horns of the altar."[68]

Having made these introductory remarks, I must now proceed to the material in the text. Since it says that the day is reckoned by God "as a thousand years," and moreover since the sojourn of the Lord on the earth is called a day, it calls this day [of the Lord's sojourn] a "thousand years," since with God there was no distinction between one day and a thousand years. At this time, the time of the incarnation of the Lord, the devil was bound and was not able to resist the marks of the Savior's deity.[69] And, therefore, when they sensed that they were spiritually bound, the wicked demons cried out, "What have you to do with us, O Son of the living God? Have you come here to torment us before the time?"[70] And the Lord also made clear their bondage when he said, "Or how can one enter a strong man's house and plunder his goods, unless he first binds the strong man? Then indeed he may plunder his house."[71] Since, therefore, as it was indicated, we understand the incarnation of the Lord and his sojourn upon earth to be called "one day" and a "thousand years" without distinction in the holy Scriptures, such a number is used figuratively. Note, therefore, what Revelation says. "I saw another angel coming down from heaven holding the key of the bottomless pit and a chain." And it says, when he seized the devil, "he bound him and threw him into the bottomless pit." That which is effected spiritually by the Lord against the devil is shown to the Evangelist as though on a painted tablet. For since John was a human being and could not see spiritual realities, that which occurred is depicted for him in material terms. And therefore an angel is said to hold a chain and to bind the devil and to throw him in the bottomless pit. The book of Job also narrates the plan of the devil and the agreement that he has with God in material terms. On the one hand it presents the devil as one who requests that God surrender Job to him while at the same time it depicts God giving appropriate responses and handing Job over to the various trials that will befall him. You will, therefore, do rightly if you also now think in this way with me.

"That he should deceive the nations no more," it says, "till the thousand years were ended." It was necessary that the sojourn of the Lord on the earth have a somewhat greater support and protection, to prohibit the unclean demons from attacking it in the same way as they did against humankind before the time of the incarnation. "And that after this the devil must be loosed for a little while." What does he mean by "a little while"? He means the time between the incarnation of the Lord and the consummation of the present age. When measured and compared with that which is past and that which is future, this present age is little, even though it should seem to be great. For

[62]Ps 118:24 (117:24 LXX). [63]Ps 5:3 (5:4 LXX). [64]Ps 46:5 (45:5 LXX). [65]Mal 4:2. [66]Hos 10:12. [67]Lk 1:78-79. [68]Ps 118:27 (117:27 LXX). [69]Oecumenius probably has in mind the miracles of Christ. [70]Mt 8:29. [71]Mt 12:29.

if our Lord appears bodily at the "last" hour,[72] indeed at the "eleventh" hour, as the faith of the holy writings claim, the time until the consummation is properly called little. After this the devil will again be bound, this time with an eternal and never-ending bond. However, although he has been loosed, bind yet again, O Lord, his works of cunning against us. For you are our King, and it is proper to give you glory forever. Amen.

Eleventh Discourse

Revelation continues with the same thought in mind, for it says:

[20:4-8] ***Then I saw thrones, and seated on them were those to whom judgment was committed. Also I saw the souls of those who had been beheaded for their testimony to Jesus and for the word of God, and who had not worshiped the beast or its image and had not received its mark on their foreheads or their hands. They came to life and reigned with Christ a thousand years. This is the first resurrection. Blessed and holy is he who shares in the first resurrection! Over such the second death has no power, but they shall be priests of God and of Christ, and they shall reign with him a thousand years. And when the thousand years are ended, Satan will be loosed from his prison and will come out to deceive the nations that are at the four corners of the earth.***

In the previous section I said that having begun to mention the devil, the vision, as it were, preserved the storyline and explained not only that which the devil was to suffer at the consummation of the present age but also what he spiritually suffered when the Lord was made incarnate. Continuing this storyline, he explains yet more of the life of the incarnate Lord, namely, that which now meets us in the vision.

For it says, "Then I saw thrones, and seated on them were those to whom judgment was committed." He sees the holy apostles to whom the promise was made that they would "sit on twelve thrones, judging the twelve tribes of Israel."[1] Although this will be fulfilled more completely in the coming age, it happened partially at the time of the incarnation. For when they believed in the Lord and so shared in a multitude of blessings, they condemned those who did not wish to come to the faith and who, although they had been taught by the grace given to the apostles, did not advance to the same piety but rather plotted the death of Christ on the cross. And it says, "and the souls of those who had been beheaded for their testimony to Jesus and for the word of God." These, in common with the others, he saw sitting on thrones and judging the rest of humankind. It says that they were beheaded, for they had been killed by the axe. He is speaking figuratively about those who have offered their members up to death for the sake of their faith in Christ and especially of those who endured martyrdom for the faith. For to be sure, the Jews caused them to be thrown outside the synagogues with much revilement and they confiscated for themselves their property, as the wise apostle testifies,[2] for they believed completely in Christ. The Lord also spoke about these persons: "Blessed are you when people revile you and persecute you and utter all kinds of evil against you falsely on my account."[3] And following the thought of the narrative and holding captive every idea in obedience to the holy Scriptures, you will consider those who do not worship the beast or receive his mark and his image to be those who did not conspire with the rest of the Jews in their plots against the Lord or obey the suggestions of the devil, who is hated of God. For this would be to worship him and also his image. The imprint of his will on the hearts of

[72]See Jn 6:39, 40; 12:48; Acts 2:17; 2 Tim 3:1. **Eleventh Discourse** [1]Mt 19:28. [2]See Heb 10:34. [3]Mt 5:11.

the Jews he calls an image, which he also calls a mark, which encompasses both their guiding and their active principles.[4] For the head, of which the forehead is a member, is representative of the guiding principle, while the hand is representative of the active principle.

"They came to life and reigned with Christ a thousand years." He again speaks of a thousand years to indicate, as I said above, the sojourn of the Lord on the earth. During this time they lived the spiritual life and reigned with Christ, confronting demons and giving honor to suffering and bringing about a great many miracles. Not that one is only to be present with Christ, the King of glory; one should also reign with him. And so it is spoken by the prophet concerning them: "When the heavenly One scattered kings on it, they will become white as snow on Zalmon."[5] "The rest of the dead did not come to life," it says, "until the thousand years were ended." He calls those dead who remained in unbelief. The Lord spoke of these when he said, "Let the dead bury their own dead."[6] To be sure, the unbelievers did not live the spiritual life until the time of the incarnation, which is the thousand years, was completed. But after this they lived. How so? By the visitation and presence of the Holy Spirit. For then most of the Jews believed in Christ, as many as did not believe in him when he was living among them in the flesh. And this was accomplished[7] in a most divine manner, and not as the human mind might have expected. For while in the Old Testament the Son was proclaimed and was made known through his incarnation and his many signs and wonders, the Holy Spirit was not yet clearly revealed to humankind. In the Old Testament there was only talk concerning him but there was no manifest and perceptible activity, which especially leads people to faith, as there was of the Son. He was, however, perceived by those who progressed into the depths of the divine purpose. For to be sure, everything that is done and accomplished is effected by the holy Trinity. The Lord establishes this clearly when he says somewhere, "The Father has given me commandment what to say and what to speak,"[8] and again, "I am able to do nothing from myself,"[9] referring whatever happens to the Trinity; and again from John, "The Son of man can do nothing from himself, unless he sees his Father doing it,"[10] and somewhere Jesus vigorously claims, "If I by the Spirit of God throw out demons."[11] Since, as I said, there was no perceptible activity of the Holy Spirit among humankind, it was determined by plan that virtually all people would receive faith in Christ by the coming and power of the Paraclete and of God the Father, so that it might be clearly evident to all that he also is of the same substance and of equal power with the Father and the Son. To be sure, we are given no information that during the time of the incarnation any more than 120 persons had come to faith. The Acts of the Apostles numbers those who had gathered together in the upper room to have been so many.[12] But since the power of the Christ's teaching had reached many, then certainly faith would have been preserved for this very coming of the Spirit. Just as when seed is scattered on the ground and the rains come and the sun shines upon it, all the seeds that had remained hidden and concealed in the ground until this time now start to spring up and become visible, for they had been simply kept in the earth, so also did it happen at the visitation of the Holy Spirit. All those to whom the teaching of the Lord had been thrown as seed began to spring up to faith. Therefore, it is said with greater accuracy in Revelation, "the rest of the dead did not come to life until the thousand years were ended."

"This is," it says, "the first resurrection,"

[4]Translating ἡγεμονικόν and πρακτικόν. [5]Ps 68:14 (67:15 LXX). [6]Mt 8:22. [7]The verb corresponds to the noun οἰκονμία, the plan according to which God fulfills his purposes. [8]Jn 12:49. [9]Jn 5:30. [10]Jn 5:19. [11]Mt 12:28. [12]Acts 1:15.

clearly that of faith. For the second resurrection will be the universal resurrection of the body. Therefore, "blessed is he who shares in the first resurrection!" For we will all take part in the second resurrection, even those who are unwilling. On those who share in the first resurrection, that is, on the faithful, "the second death will have no power." What sort of death is this second death? Clearly it is that of sin and of the subsequent punishment. For just as he spoke of a first and a second resurrection, so also there is a first and a second death. The first death is physical and results in the separation of the soul and the body. The second death, by contrast, is spiritual and is caused by sin. Of this death also the Lord spoke: "Do not fear those who kill the body; rather fear him who can destroy both soul and body in hell."[13]

The faithful, it says, "shall be priests of God and of Christ." For all the faithful were appointed priests of the word of the gospel, and concerning these the prophet, playing the prophetic lyre, said, "You will make them princes over all the earth."[14] "And they shall reign with him a thousand years," the thousand years of the incarnation, as we have often noted. "And when," it says, "the thousand years are ended." That is, when the Lord completed the economy according to the flesh and ascended into heaven, the devil was to be released from his spiritual chains again to deceive the nations. In previous passages it was said that the Lord's sojourn among humankind destroyed the work of the devil. But when the Lord had ascended into heaven, the devil once more effected that which is proper and customary to him, and the people on the earth were again subject to his authority as was their custom. For the devil attempts to lead all astray. Although some are persuaded by him, others are not persuaded and struggle against the evil one.

However, perhaps someone might say, "Why is it that when the devil was restrained and his own assaults were repulsed by the coming of the Lord in the flesh, that he was let loose again against us, to lead those on earth astray? Were it not better had he been bound and humankind left free of further deception?" To such a person it must be said: Why do you not rather inquire after the existence of the devil at the beginning? Or, why do you not inquire why he was not utterly destroyed when he first existed and had become a transgressor, so that he would have no access at all to humankind? But, O friend, how would athletes continue to receive vigorous exercise were there no one to wrestle against? And how would athletes demonstrate their strength were there no opponent? For some people are lazy and subject to pleasure and are perverse from themselves, whether or not the devil is present and prodding them on. But the people of God, who are noble athletes, would be wrongly treated were their courage against the passions not put to public display. So, as it happens, the lazy would receive no benefit and the zealous would be very greatly wronged were there no Satan. In a way, Satan serves as an athletic trainer for humankind, providing for those who contend an opportunity for victories.[15] For as I said, those enamored with sin are in no way harmed, since, even were the devil not present, they would use their own sluggishness in place of him. And so, although unwilling, the devil does good to those strong athletes, while he harms these not at all, or very little. But for my sake and yours, lest we be further injured by the work of the devil in any manner small or great, you [O friend] were willing that the slaves of sin be left unconstrained by any discipline and in a state of defeat and that the patriarchs and the prophets be despoiled of the glory of their victories, along with the apostles, the Evangelists and those who had remained steadfast even to the point of blood

[13]Mt 10:28. [14]Ps 45:16 (44:17 LXX). [15]"Victories" translates στεφάνων ("crowns"), referring to crowns given to the victor.

for the witness of Christ and had preserved their nobility for him. Furthermore, you would have the confessors and those pastors who govern the churches well to be deprived of their glory, together with the ascetics, who endure very great hardships, and every righteous person who is perfected by faith in Christ. "Of none of these is this world worthy."[16] As a result, those noble and virtuous combatants mitigate to some extent the penalty of sinners who are altogether responsible for their hurts. For one who is upright is honored more by God than are thousands of those who do evil.

Therefore, both of these actions were exceptionally good and inspired, that at the coming of the Lord the impious attacks of the devil were stopped and that after his ascension into heaven the devil was loosed to tempt humankind. For had Satan been allowed to display all of his spiritual power while the Lord sojourned on the earth, he would not have allowed anyone to become a hearer of the divine teaching. Nor would anyone have learned who is the true God by nature and what is the pure worship of him and what is vice and what is virtue. Rather, the devil would have prepared the cross for Christ prematurely, even before the Lord had begun to teach. And had this happened, such a great and admirable mystery as the Lord's incarnation would have been ineffective and without any benefit. But as it was, by the constraint of the devil, those on earth were taught these things and moreover put away the use of their free will and the struggle against the adversary concerning behaviors of vice and virtue in which there is consensus and agreement. For the person who knows good and evil simply chooses one or the other by his own impulses. However, the person who does not even know what to do is like one wounded in a night battle who is unaware that he has been hit and does not know of his own destruction. The person who has knowledge of the choices has opportunity to choose by his own volition what he wishes. However, there is no such opportunity for the person who does not know [the choice of good and evil]. From the beginning God made man with his own free will and as one who is governed by the power of his own reason and thought. And that one must first know virtue and vice so that there might be opportunity for the use of one's own free will, see what the holy Moses says in Deuteronomy to the disobedient people of Israel: "See, I have set before you this day life and death, good and evil."[17] He said this so that what was chosen might be selected from both of these choices. Again in Exodus Moses says, "But if you hearken attentively to my voice and do all that I say."[18] And what does Isaiah say? Does he not assert the same teaching at the beginning of his prophecies when he speaks in the person of God and says, "If you are willing and listen to me, you shall eat the good of the land. But if you refuse and do not listen to me, you will be devoured by the sword; for the mouth of the Lord has spoken"?[19]

However, enough of these things. Since he said in the preceding that the devil "will come out to deceive the nations," he now speaks of the character of these nations and which of them will be their vanguard. It says "Gog and Magog to gather them for battle," namely, that battle that is against the saints. For having completed his discourse concerning the incarnation that is for our salvation, he returns again to the point from which he digressed, that is, from the discussion of the defeat and punishment of the devil and of the antichrist and of those nations that had gathered with them. Completing now what it had previously left undone, the text continues with the other nations who fight with the antichrist, that is, Gog and Magog, and it speaks as follows:

[16]Heb 11:38. [17]Deut 30:15. [18]Ex 23:22. [19]Is 1:19-20.

[20:8-10] ***And he came out to deceive all the nations that are at the four corners of the earth. After this he says: That is, Gog and Magog, to gather them for battle; their number is like the sand of the sea. And they marched up over the broad earth and surrounded the camp of the saints and the beloved city; but fire came down from God out of heaven and consumed them, and the devil who had deceived them was thrown into the lake of fire and sulfur where the beast and the false prophet were, and they will be tormented day and night forever and ever.***

The holy prophet Ezekiel also spoke concerning Gog and Magog, relating how evil persons perish in an evil way. These are certain nations that shall lead the nations at the time of the consummation. These nations do not at present exist, or they are certain nations that do at present exist but that are called different names by the divine Scripture. These, therefore, will fight alongside that God-hated Satan against the servants of Christ. "And they surrounded the beloved city," that is, the church. However, "fire brought from heaven" will destroy all of them, and moreover when the consummation has occurred, Satan, the originator of evil, together with the devil and the antichrist, will be thrown into the lake of fire, that is, Gehenna. Let the one who reads take note that in earlier material Revelation transmitted information about three figures: the first was the dragon, who was shown in heaven and who is the originator of evil; the second is the beast who rose from the sea and whom I claimed was second to Satan but prominent among the rest of the demons; and the third was the antichrist, who is also called the false prophet.[20] However, it was stated a little earlier that the second, the devil, and the antichrist were "thrown into the lake of fire which burns with brimstone."[21] But now it speaks of Satan, or the devil, who earlier it had called "dragon."

"And they will be tormented," it says, "day and night forever and ever." You who read this book know that I have interpreted the phrase "the thousand years," in which the devil was bound and thrown into the bottomless pit and again loosed, to refer very precisely to the incarnation of the Lord and his life on the earth, during which the devil's activity was for a short time impeded. But now it is revealed that his punishment and that of those deceived by him is not a thousand years after which there is a loosing of the evil one. Rather, this punishment is "forever and ever."

[20:11-12] ***Then I saw a great white throne and him who sat on it; from his presence earth and sky fled away, and no place was found for them. And I saw the dead, great and small, standing before the throne, and books were opened, and another book was opened, which is the book of life. And the dead were judged by what was written in the books, by what they had done.***

By the words "white throne" it speaks of a throne that is bright and radiant. By the figure of the flight of the heaven and the earth, the passage indicates their change and transformation. For if "the heavens will pass away with a loud noise," as the holy Peter says,[22] and as the prophet who says, "In the beginning, O Lord, you did lay the foundation of the earth, and the heavens are the works of your hands; they shall perish, but you remain, and they all shall grow old as a garment, and as a vesture you shall fold them, and they shall be changed,"[23] then rightly does Revelation speak of their passing away and their destruction, which signify their change, as a flight, since no place was found for them. For where would one find that corruption that had been cast off? There-

[20]See the comments on Rev 12:3; 13:1, 11. [21]Rev 19:20. [22]2 Pet 3:10. [23]Ps 102:25-26 (101:26-27 LXX).

fore, in the present passage he speaks of their change, while a little further on he says that they shall become new.[24]

"And I saw," it says, "the dead, great and small, standing before the throne." By "great" he speaks of the just, not because they are great by any physical measurement but because of their glory and the brightness of their virtue. By "small" he means the sinners, since they have become as nothing through their baseness and worthlessness. "And books were opened, and another book was opened, which is the book of life." In the Gospels, the Lord says that the way that leads to destruction is broad and wide and that many walk on it, but that the way that leads to life is narrow and cramped and that not only are there few who are walking on it, but few who even find it.[25] For this reason he saw many books and one book. There are many books because all of humankind is inscribed in them, and there is a great number in them. There is but one book of life, because in it are inscribed those who are the elect, that is, those blameless in virtue, who have trodden every rugged and steep path of virtue. Everyone in the books, it says, were judged deservedly according to their works. At the beginning of the sixth discourse, mention was also made of another book, which was called a "little scroll."[26] But now he speaks of a "book" and of a "book of life," as if there were three different ones. He speaks of a "little scroll" in which are listed the most impious according to my interpretation above. He also speaks of the "book of life" in which are listed the most pious and righteous. And finally he speaks of "books" in which all those are listed who are, as it were, in between evil and virtue.[27]

Having spoken of matters pertaining to the resurrection—for to say, "I saw the dead before the throne" receiving their reward and being judged "according to their works" is to speak about the resurrection. For he saw the dead rising up and receiving their reward—it remains for the text to describe the manner in which the resurrection occurred. And it says:

[20:13–21:2] ***The sea gave up the dead in it, death and hades gave up the dead in them, and each was judged by what they had done. And death and hades were thrown into the lake of fire. And if anyone was not found written in the book of life, he was thrown into the lake of fire. And I saw a new heaven and a new earth. For the first heaven and the first earth had passed away, and the sea was no more. And I saw the holy city, new Jerusalem, coming down out of heaven from God, prepared as a bride adorned for her husband.***

Those who do not believe in the resurrection of the body smile at us and at our teaching, which asserts that these very bodies are to rise again, as though this were not only difficult but altogether impossible. They say moreover that every earthly body consists of the four elements of fire, water, earth, air, and that on death bodies return to those elements from which they were constituted in the first place. So that which is of fire in us returns to that which is naturally and wholly fire; that which is of water returns to water, and the other two return to what belongs to them. "Since these elements," they may argue, "have been mixed and compounded with their own substances, how is it possible that that which has become one simple, indistinguishable substance by mixture be restored as bodies, as you say, unless you would say that different bodies are arising instead of the other [previous] ones?" To such persons one might quote

[24]Oecumenius may have had Origen in mind, who claimed that rational creatures will return to their original, primordial existence (*Princ.* 2.1.1-2). However, no polemical intention is evident in the text. [25]See Mt 7:13-14. [26]See Rev 10:2, 10. [27]Oecumenius distinguishes between βιβλιδάριον ("little scroll"), βιβλίον ζωῆς ("book of life") and βίβλοι ("books").

the holy Scripture: "You are wrong, O people, because you do not know the power of God,"[28] by whose will all things received their being, since for him only to will a work is for it to be accomplished, as I said before.[29] For what is easier, to bring substances out of nothing, or, having once brought them forth and mixing them either with themselves or with other things, again to dissemble them and assign to each what is its own? Furthermore, even we are often successful by a certain technique in separating wine that has been mixed with water. Moreover, even the sun draws up through the mists and vapors what is fresh and sweet from the sea, while it leaves that which is heavy, earthy, salty and bitter. But the primary consideration is that God alone is able to do whatever he wishes. If, therefore, God has brought that which had no existence into existence, how is it not easier for him to separate again what had been mixed completely with the elements simply by willing to do so and to assign to each body what belongs to it, even though for humans this would be impossible? It is impossible for you and for me to divide the brilliance of fire from its heat, yet this is possible with God—for it says, "There is a voice of the Lord who divides flames of fire."[30] In the same way it is impossible for you and me to separate what has been mixed together, while for God it is easy and readily done.

The present passage of Revelation now offers to us this marvelous doctrine [of the resurrection of the body], saying, "The sea gave up the dead in it" from the sea. This concerns the element of water. Signifying every watery substance, it says that the watery substance gave up everything that had been mixed with it from what was of water in human bodies. "And death and hades," it says, "gave up the dead in them." By "death" it means the earth, since our bodies had decayed in it. And so the holy prophet also speaks periphrastically of death as the "dust of death," saying, "He has brought me down to the dust of death."[31] And so the earth gave up everything in it which had been earthly of our bodies. In addition, hades gave up the dead in it. By "hades" he speaks of air and fire, for they are formless and invisible. For to be sure, because it is so fine, air is invisible, unless it becomes dense, and fire that smolders in wood is invisible, unless it burst into flame. Moreover, that element of fire, the ether, is invisible to us because it is obscured by the interposition of much air. And too, by "hades" he speaks of fire because of the destruction and formlessness it wreaks on that which it touches. And so many sayings name it "Unknown." Therefore, when each element has given back whatever was mixed with it of the human being, the resurrection is accomplished.

When this has occurred, "all were judged by what they had done. Then death and hades," it says, "were thrown into the lake of fire." This is to say, once the resurrection has happened and each soul has received its own body, death, namely, the formless, disembodied life of souls in death is destroyed. The passage describes this in a figurative manner and speaks of their destruction symbolically when it says that death and hades were thrown into the lake of fire. The prophet Hosea also speaks similarly, saying, "Where is your penalty, O death? Where, O hades, is your sting?"[32] "This is," it says, "the second death, the lake of fire." In previous passages it spoke of the physical death, that is, the separation of the soul and the body as the first death,[33] while the second death was the spiritual death, punishment and torment, which has sin as its cause. But, it says, all those who remained in sins and were not accounted worthy to be in the book of life suffered the same fate. Do not marvel that it says that even those who had sinned moderately were thrown into the lake of fire together with the devil and the antichrist, for he said

[28]See Mt 22:29. [29]See his comments on Rev 16:2-7. [30]Ps 29:7 (28:7 LXX). [31]Ps 22:15 (21:16 LXX). [32]Hos 13:14.

this earlier.[34] For even there, there is a distinction of punishments. Just as in a fire there is a part that is continuously very hot and a part that is not so hot and is somewhat temperate, yet every part is called fire, so you might, as I do, consider this also to be like that.

"And I saw," it says, "new heavens and a new earth; for the first heaven and the first earth had passed away, and the sea was no more." In his second letter, Peter speaks in a similar way: "According to his promise we wait for new heavens and a new earth."[35] They do not say this as though heaven and earth and sea are destroyed and pass into nonexistence and that other things come into being in their place. Rather, they mean that the present realities have cast off their corruption and become new, putting off their filth as though it were an old and dirty garment. For that is called new that is not such as it was formerly but is as it has now become. The creation shall then be free of every corruption that it contracted through the transgression of humankind. The holy apostle is also a very trustworthy witness to these things when in his letter to the Romans he writes this about the new creation: "For the creation waits with eager longing for the revealing of the sons of God; for the creation was subjected to futility, not of its own will but by the will of him who subjected it in hope, because the creation itself will be set free from its bondage to decay unto the glorious liberty of the children of God."[36] And not only he but also the holy prophet sang of the heaven and the earth in the testimony just presented: "They will all wear out as a garment, and as a vesture you will fold them, and they will be changed."[37]

"And I saw the holy city," it says, "new Jerusalem, coming down out of heaven from God prepared as a bride adorned for her husband." By "Jerusalem" he symbolizes the blessed destiny and dwelling of the saints, which it figuratively calls Jerusalem both here and in the following passages. He has described her adornment magnificently and becomingly, so that we might lead our minds from perceptible realities to the spiritual bliss of the life of the saints.

[21:3-5] ***And I heard a loud voice from heaven, saying, "Behold, the dwelling of God is with people. He will dwell with them, and they shall be his peoples, and God himself will be with them and will be their God; he will wipe away every tear from their eyes, and death shall be no more, neither shall there be mourning nor crying nor pain any more, for the former things have passed away." And he who sat on the throne said, "Behold, I make all things new." And he said, "Write, for these words are trustworthy and true."***

In the preceding discussion did I not aptly state that the vision symbolically calls the destiny of the saints and their spiritual habitation there as Jerusalem? Note, he now unveils the symbolism [of the new Jerusalem as the destiny of the saints] and says, "Behold, the dwelling of God is with people, and he will dwell with them, and they shall be his people,[38] and God himself will be with them and will be their God." The apostle indicated this even more clearly when he said, "Then we who are alive, who are left, shall be caught up in the clouds to meet the Lord in the air; and we shall always be with the Lord."[39]

"And he will wipe away every tear from their eyes," it says. The prophet Isaiah says something similar to this: "Death has prevailed and swallowed people up, but again God has taken every tear away from every face."[40] For if, as the holy apostle says, "pain and sorrow and sighing have fled away" in that blissful life

[33]See the comments on Rev 2:11; 20:6. [34]Rev 19:20. [35]2 Pet 3:13. [36]Rom 8:19-21. [37]Ps 101:27 (LXX). [38]Oecumenius uses the singular here; in the biblical quotation above he used the plural. [39]1 Thess 4:17. [40]Is 25:8.

of the saints,[41] how would any tears remain, in the absence of those things? "The former things have passed away," it says. By this he means that the suffering of the saints has come to an end. Now the rewards for their toils have come. "Behold," it says, "I make all things new." If the heaven, earth and the sea are new, and moreover if humankind and that which pertains to their joy and glory are new and in no way interrupted by tears or pains or sins, then indeed all things are new. "Do not think, O John," [the one on the throne] says, "that because of their surpassing greatness what has been said and revealed to you is false or fantasy. All of these things are trustworthy and true. Therefore, write them down."

[21:6-8] ***And he said to me, "They are done! I am the Alpha and the Omega, the beginning and the end. To the thirsty I will give from the fountain of the water of life without payment. He who conquers shall have this heritage, and I will be his God and he shall be my son. But as for the rest, the faithless, the polluted, the murderers, the fornicators, the sorcerers, the idolaters, and all lies, their lot shall be in the lake of fire that burns with fire and sulfur, which is the second death."***

"They are done!" it says. What is done? These things, namely, that are here spoken, and nothing in them is false. He has written "they are done," instead of "they shall be done." "I am the Alpha and the Omega, the beginning and the end," he says. Since he repeats what he had earlier said, also we, as it were following in his footsteps, repeat what we have said in previous passages.[42] The phrase "Alpha and Omega, the beginning and the end" signifies that God is without any beginning and without any end. Since nothing in this life is without a beginning, he used the terms "beginning" and "end," as common among us, instead of "without beginning" and "without end."

"To the thirsty," it says, "I will give from the fountain of the water of life without payment." In the Gospels the Lord says, "Blessed are they who hunger and thirst after righteousness, for they shall be filled."[43] Therefore, to one who thirsts after such a thirst, I shall give life without payment. But how is it that he said "without payment," since the saints attain to the future life with very great hardships? Why, therefore, does he say that he gives it without payment? He says this to indicate that one never bears anything worthy of the blessings of that future time, no matter how much one might labor. And the apostle made the same point when he said, "For I consider that the sufferings of this present time are not worth comparing with the glory that is to be revealed to us."[44] "He who conquers," it says, these sufferings and the evil beast, the devil, "shall have this heritage." So those who conquer shall have such a heritage. But "for the cowardly and the unfaithful" and such as those, there will be a lot "in the lake of fire." He calls those cowardly who are weak to every good work, because the endurance of hardship is a matter of one's own willpower. "And all lies," it says. He did not say "for all liars" but "for all lies,"[45] that is, those who behave contrary to nature and falsify the natural beauty of virtue into the base and counterfeit appearance of evil. That that fire will be "the second death" was discussed earlier.[46]

[21:9-14] ***Then came one of the seven angels who had the seven bowls full of the seven last plagues and spoke to me, saying, "Come, I will show you the wife of the Lamb." And in the Spirit he carried me away to a great, high***

[41]Is 51:11. Interestingly, Oecumenius calls Isaiah the "holy apostle," revealing the early church view that Isaiah was above all others the Old Testament prophet who foretold the gospel story. [42]See the comments on Rev 1:8. [43]Mt 5:6. [44]Rom 8:18. [45]Oecumenius observes that the text uses τὸ ψεῦδος not ὁ ψεύστης. [46]See the comments on Rev 20:14.

mountain, and showed me the holy city Jerusalem coming down out of heaven from God, having the glory of God, its radiance like a most rare jewel, like a jasper, clear as crystal. It had a great, high wall, with fifteen[47] gates, and at the gates twelve angels and the names of the twelve tribes of the sons of Israel were inscribed; on the east three gates, on the north three gates, on the south three gates.[48] And the wall of the city had twelve foundations, and on them the twelve names of the twelve apostles of the Lamb.

"Then came one of the seven angels," it says. Who are these seven? Certainly those about whom there was much discussion earlier.[49] "Come," it says, "I will show you the wife of the Lamb." The angel intends to show the church of the "firstborn who are enrolled in heaven," which he also calls the "heavenly Jerusalem." Paul spoke to the Hebrews of this church, writing, "For you have not come to a mountain that may be touched, to a blazing fire, darkness, and gloom, and a tempest and the sound of a trumpet, and a voice whose words made the hearers entreat that no further message be spoken to them. For they could not endure the order that was given, 'If even a beast touches the mountain, it shall be stoned.' Indeed, so terrifying was the sight that he said, 'I tremble with fear.' But you have come to Mount Zion and to the city of the living God, the heavenly Jerusalem, and to innumerable angels in festal gathering, and to the assembly of the firstborn who are enrolled in heaven, and to a judge who is God of all."[50] In the gathering or the assembly of all the saints into one, that is, by the image of the heavenly Jerusalem, the passage depicts the blessedness of the saints and the life that they will have in God and with God. As I indicated, the passage adorns the city with physical and magnificent imagery in order to guide our mind to some extent from its depiction to its spiritual glory and splendor.

"And in the Spirit he carried me away to a high mountain," it says, "and showed me the holy city Jerusalem coming down out of heaven from God, having the glory of God." Without spiritual grace no human mind was ever lifted up so that it might comprehend the glory of the saints. This clearly refers to the church since it speaks of the life of righteousness, and their citizenship both here and also there [in the heavenly city] is as "a great, high mountain." For among the saints there is nothing inferior and debased. Rather, everything among them is sublime and exalted. Concerning them it is written, "God's mighty ones of the earth have been greatly exalted."[51]

"Its radiance," that is, Christ, the "sun of righteousness,"[52] it says, was "like a jasper." As I noted earlier,[53] jasper has a certain green quality and so exhibits the life-bearing and life-giving nature of Christ, who "opens his hand and satisfies the desire of every living thing."[54] Indeed, green plants are the chief form of earthly food. However, the jasper was also as crystal and so symbolizes the purity and the holiness of Christ, for he "did no sin, and there was no deceit in his mouth," as the prophecy of Isaiah says.[55] And, again, the wall of the saints, or of the church, is Christ, since he is our bulwark, our fence and our help. "It had," it says, "twelve gates." This symbolizes the holy apostles who proclaimed to us the way of faith in Christ. "And at the gates there were twelve angels." I am convinced that there were also holy angels who worked with the holy apostles for the faith of the world. For if the law that came from Moses was proclaimed by angels, as the apostle says, "For if the message

[47]The preferred ms tradition reads "fifteen." However, as the use of "twelve" below indicates, this must have been a scribal error. [48]The text of Oecumenius does not include the three gates in the west wall. [49]The seven angels of Rev 15–17. [50]Heb 12:18-23. [51]Ps 46:10 (LXX). [52]Mal 4:2. [53]See the comments on Rev 4:1-3. [54]Ps 145:16 (144:16 LXX). [55]Is 53:9.

declared by angels was valid,"[56] how much more would not the proclamation of the gospel possess the cooperation of angels? "And names inscribed," it says, "that are the names of the twelve tribes of Israel." In a material sense, Israel is those who were begotten from Jacob the patriarch. However, spiritually, Israel is those who walk by the faith of our father Abraham. Of this the apostle is a witness, saying, "The father of the circumcision not only for those who are of the circumcision but also for those who follow the example of the faith of our father Abraham."[57] For Israel interpreted means "a mind that beholds God" or a mind that has spiritual discernment. And who, other than the faithful, have seen God with the mind or have acquired spiritual discernment by the abundant working of the Spirit? Therefore, their names are written on the gates of the city. To be sure, the twelve tribes symbolize the fullness of the saints. For having once called the faithful Israel, he mentions also the number that signifies their fullness, saying, "twelve tribes." And it says that there were three gates on each of the four corners of the world. For the holy apostles conceived all things in threes, proclaiming the consubstantial Trinity to the nations and "baptizing them in the name of the Father and of the Son and of the Holy Spirit."[58]

"The wall of the city," it says, "had twelve foundations." Christ, whom we considered to be the wall, rests on the preaching of the apostles, and he is placed on them as "a precious cornerstone," as it is written.[59] On them, that is, on the foundations, are the "twelve names of the twelve apostles of the Lamb." It has clearly revealed the symbol, saying explicitly that the apostles are the gates and the foundations of the holy city, the church. "Avoiding the profane chatter of what is falsely called knowledge"[60] by the heretics, may we all remain in their teaching by the grace of Christ, our guide and chief shepherd, to whom be glory forever. Amen.

Twelfth Discourse

The blessed Evangelist continues his description of the holy city, the heavenly Jerusalem, now describing its greatness, its size, its ornamentation, and other arrangements. The text says:

[21:15-22] ***And he who talked to me had a measuring rod of gold to measure the city and its gates and wall. The city lies foursquare, its length the same as its breadth and its height; and he measured the city with his rod, twelve thousand stadia; its length and breadth and height are equal. He also measured its wall, a hundred and forty-four cubits by a man's measure, that is, an angel's. The structure of the wall was built of jasper, while the city was pure gold, clear as glass. The foundations of the wall of the city were adorned with every jewel; the first foundation was jasper, the second sapphire, the third chalcedony,[1] the fourth emerald, the fifth sardonyx, the sixth carnelian, the seventh chrysolite, the eighth beryl, the ninth topaz, the tenth chrysoprase, the eleventh jacinth, the twelfth amethyst. And the twelve gates were twelve pearls, each one, each of the gates made of a single pearl, and the street of the city was pure gold, transparent as glass. And I saw no temple in it, for the Lord God, the Almighty, is its temple, and the Lamb.***

The measuring rod by which he measured the holy city was that of a surveyor. It was gold on account of the honor of both the angel who was measuring and the city that was being measured. "And the city," it says, "lies foursquare, its length the same as its breadth and its height." The foursquare shape is called by the experts a cube. It is a flat surface of four

[56]Heb 2:2. [57]Rom 4:12. [58]Mt 28:19. [59]Is 28:16. [60]1 Tim 6:20. **Twelfth Discourse** [1]Oecumenius's text reads καρχηδών rather than χαλκηδών. However, it makes no sense in this passage.

square corners, and when it is foursquare and equal in all of its dimensions, they say that the cube exhibits great stability. For the blessings of the saints are permanent and unchangeable, since there is no change to corrupt their bliss. And, indeed, the grandeur of the city and the magnificence of the saints signify that although they are considerably less in number than the sinners, they are not so small in number as not to fill such a city.

"And he measured its wall, a hundred and forty-four cubits by a man's measure, that is, an angel's." It is often the habit of the holy Scripture to use the word *men* when speaking of angels. This is clear from those passages in which the archangel Gabriel is interpreted as "man of God."[2] Moreover, the prophet said, "You will preserve men and beasts, O Lord,"[3] by "men" referring to angels and by "beasts" referring to human beings. For compared with the thoughts of the angels, human beings are irrational and like animals. The prophet did not say "men" and "beasts," as someone might think, meaning real men and real beasts. For concerning beasts the apostle says, "Is it for oxen that God is concerned?"[4] Therefore, the beasts mentioned by the prophet are to be regarded as human beings and the men regarded as angels. In addition, according to Luke, the Lord also called angels men when he said, "Let your loins be girded and your lamps burning, and be like men who are waiting for their master to come home from the marriage feast."[5] Therefore, since angels are often called men, as I have said above, their gaze is directed toward God. For this reason it says here "by a man's measure, that is, an angel's." By this language is signified that what is divine is wholly incomprehensible—above I have interpreted the wall of the city to be Christ[6]—but rather by the contemplation of the greatness of God men become angels. And so, the wall of the city is measured by an angelic cubit, not a human one. That the wall measures a 144 cubits indicates a certain mystical number determined by the wisdom and the discerning measurement of the angels.

"And the structure of the wall was built of jasper," it says. I have already indicated that jasper suggests the life-bearing and life-giving quality of Christ. "And the city," it says, "was pure gold, clear as glass." Along with the splendor and clarity of the saints, the gold serves also to manifest their honor and their purity in deed and word. "And the foundations of the wall of the city were adorned with every jewel." I have claimed already that the foundation of the wall—the wall is the Lord, as I have often said—is the holy apostles,[7] since Christ rests on their teaching and remains over them according to the promise that he gave when he said, "And lo, I am with you always, to the close of the age."[8] Therefore, these foundations, that is, the apostles, are adorned with every virtue—for the precious gems represent virtue. For by their work and by their preaching the apostles have become pure, as well as by their struggles for the sake of Christ and by their devotion to him even to blood. Should someone desire a more exact explanation concerning the stones—such an exposition is possible—one must begin a little further back. According to the law of Moses, the chief priests were arrayed in an intricate way, being clothed with a full-length robe, a shoulder strap, a belt, a turban, a girdle, and other things.[9] It presented an awesome and terrifying sight, but by means of these vestments there was signified a mystical symbolism. They also had an oracle of judgment, which was woven to the shoulder strap by a multicolored embroidery.[10] And the form of the oracle was that of a double cloth, a span in length, and square, and on it twelve stones were laid in four rows with

[2]See Dan 9:21. [3]Ps 36:6 (35:7 LXX). [4]1 Cor 9:9. [5]Lk 12:35-36. [6]See the comments on Rev 21:12. [7]See the comments on Rev 21:9-14. [8]Mt 28:20. [9]See the full description in Ex 28:1-39. [10]Ex 28:15.

the names of the sons of Israel. Some of these stones are also placed here in the foundations of the wall, while some angular stones are not arranged and placed among them. Eight of the stones placed in the foundations [of the city] are also mentioned in this passage concerning the oracle of judgment. These eight are jasper, sapphire, emerald, carnelian, chrysolite, beryl, topaz and amethyst. The four stones in the foundations not numbered with those on the oracle of judgment were chalcedony, sardonyx, chrysophrase and jacinth.

And the gates of the city, which I have interpreted to represent the apostles, "each was of a single pearl." And so the pearl is now placed here as something new, for it was not numbered with the stones of the oracle. It is possible, then, to see that the stones just now enumerated are more precious than those listed by the Old Testament as woven in the oracle. Through this it is signified that the apostles understood the Old Testament and were well-versed in the laws and customs in it—and for that reason the wise apostle said "as to righteousness under the Law blameless."[11] However, it also signified that they had become well-versed in the commandments of the New Testament and were rich in the knowledge of it. For it was much clearer, and as it were more precious than the knowledge of the Old Testament, since in the Law there was a kind of shadow, while in the New Testament reality had come. And this is symbolized by the mingling of the jewels of the Old Testament and those of the New Testament that are in the foundations of the city, which, as I have said, indicate the apostles. In the Gospels the Lord also said the same thing: "Therefore every scribe who has been trained for the kingdom of heaven is like a householder who brings out of his treasure what is new and what is old."[12] And the gates of the city, which I have interpreted as the apostles, were each from a single pearl, indicating their honor, purity and splendor. "And the street of the city," it says, "was pure gold, transparent as glass." I have said that the gold and the purity and transparency of the glass signify the honor and purity of the life of the saints.

"And I saw no temple in it," it says, "for its temple is the Lord, God the Almighty, and the Lamb." For what need is there of a temple when God is present and in some manner lives with the saints and when God's face is to some extent made visible? For the holy apostle has said that in the present age the knowledge of God is "in a mirror" and "in darkness" but that in the coming age such knowledge will be "face to face."[13] Someone might reasonably ask, "Why did he mention God the Almighty, that is, the Father of the Lord and the Lamb, the Son of God, but did not yet mention the Holy Spirit?" To such a person one must respond: "When he says 'the Lord' and 'God,' he is naming the Father and the Son and the Holy Spirit, for these are God. And further, when he says 'the Lord God the Almighty' he indicates the holy Trinity by the three designations." But someone might inquire further, "Why, then, having mentioned the venerable Trinity by the words 'the Lord, God the Almighty is its temple,' does he make special mention of the Lamb, who is Christ, so that we no longer are considering the Trinity?" Let it not seem to him to be so, for we are not taught to think that! Rather, when it mentions the holy Trinity and the Lamb, the passage indicates that one of the holy Trinity has become incarnate and that with his flesh the Son fills the holy Trinity and even now in heaven is not without his flesh. For periphrastically he signified the Son who became flesh through the name "God," who is the Son, while by "Lamb" he indicated the very same Christ incarnated, consubstantial with us and endowed with a rational soul, to which

[11]Phil 3:6. [12]Mt 13:52. [13]See 1 Cor 13:12.

flesh the Word was united hypostatically.

[21:23-25] ***And the city has no need of sun or moon to illuminate it, for the glory of God is its light, and its lamp is the Lamb. By its light shall the nations walk; and the kings of the earth shall bring their glory and their honor into it, and its gates shall never be shut by day, for there shall be no night.***

"And the city," it says, "has no need of sun." There is no need of physical light for those who enjoy the spiritual light of God. For to behold spiritual realities is the lot of the saints at that time. "By its light shall the nations walk," it says. The passage speaks not only of the Gentiles but also of the saints from Israel who came to faith. For since the saints from the Gentiles are more numerous by far, it indicates also those from Israel in speaking of those who are more numerous. "And the kings of the earth shall bring their glory and their honor into it." By "kings of the earth" it means all the saints, of whom it is written, "When the heavenly One scatters kings on it, they shall be made white as snow in Zalmon," as I quoted also above.[14] Therefore, since these possess a certain glory and honor—he speaks of that honor that comes from virtue—they shall carry it into that holy city. This is as though he said, the blessings arising from virtue shall dwell with the saints. "And its gates," it says, "shall never be shut by day." This has two possible meanings. It may mean that there will be peace and security so that there will be no need for the city to set a sentry for itself or to ever close its gates and make them secure with bars. Or the words may say that the apostolic teachings—for I have noted that the gates are the apostles—will never fall silent there but rather that even there the apostles will be teachers of new and more divine teachings for the saints. For being "sons of day and of light,"[15] the righteous shall revel in the divine illumination of the praises and the mysteries, since the day and the light of divine illumination is perpetually around them. "For there shall be no night," it says. For were the divine illumination ever to be interrupted, there would be also night. But since it is impious to say this, for the divine light shines without interruption, how shall there be night for the saints?

[21:26–22:5] ***And they shall bring into it the glory and the honor of the nations. But nothing unclean shall enter it, nor anything that practices abomination or falsehood, but only those who are written in the Lamb's book of life. And he showed me the river of the water of life, bright as crystal, flowing from the throne of God and of the Lamb through the middle of its street; and on either side of the river, the tree of life with its twelve kinds of fruit, yielding its fruit each month; and the leaves of the tree were for the healing of the nations. There shall no more be anything accursed, but the throne of God and of the Lamb shall be in it, and his servants shall worship him; they shall see his face, and his name shall be on his forehead. And night shall be no more; they shall need no light of a lamp or light of the sun, for the Lord God will illuminate them, and they shall reign forever and ever. Amen.***

When it mentions the "glory and honor of the nations" that are carried into the holy city, it is speaking periphrastically of those from the Gentiles who were reputable and who had performed works worthy of life. For these shall be brought into the heavenly Jerusalem and shall live together with the saints there. "But nothing unclean shall enter it, nor anything that practices abomination, but only those who are written in the Lamb's book of life." For "what fellowship has light with darkness,"[16] or the sinner with the righteous of God, for the Lord instructs us in the Gospels that these are

[14]Ps 68:14 (67:15 LXX). [15]See 1 Thess 5:5. [16]2 Cor 6:14.

separated by a wide chasm?[17]

"And he showed me," it says, "the river of the water of life, bright as crystal, flowing from the throne of God and of the Lamb through the middle of the street of the city." The "river of life" is the abundant and plenteous gifts of the grace of Christ that are everlastingly poured out on the saints. These gifts sweep and flow on them much like a river. "And on either side of the river," it says, "the tree of life," full of fruit, producing fruit each month. As the author of the Proverbs writes concerning wisdom, the Lord is the "tree of life." He says, "She is a tree of life to those who lay hold of her."[18] And the wise Paul has taught us that "Christ is the power of God and the wisdom of God."[19] He says that the saints are not only rich in the gracious gifts of Christ but also that they have him as one who lives in them and among them,[20] and that this is the pinnacle of the highest blessedness. Continuously and without cessation the tree of life, namely, Christ, produces ripe fruit and gifts for the saints, as though he were heaping generosity on generosity, and so they never become bereft of God's benefits. "And the leaves of the tree," it says, "were for the healing of the nations." The leaves of life are those who hang from Christ and cling to him: patriarchs, prophets, apostles, evangelists, martyrs and also confessors, those who perform the rites of the gospel at the proper time, the shepherds of the church and every righteous person, those who even now heal souls and will be for the saints the source of additional blessings.

"There shall no more be anything accursed," it says. Even were now curses especially put to flight, we are nonetheless tossed about by them, with thousands of allegations brought up against us with our knowledge and even without our knowledge. But then the saints will be clean and untainted of any stain of the soul as well as of the body. And the rule of God will exist in the city, for this is the meaning of "the throne." And the saints "shall worship him," it says, not with a worship that is laborious but that done with joy and spiritual gladness. Such worship comes from the vision of his face. "And they shall see his face," it says. They will behold the face of God to the extent possible by human nature. "And his name," it says, "shall be on their foreheads." These words symbolize the abiding memory they have of God and their union with him. For just as God rests on them and is imprinted on them, so he is always present with the saints. And this is evident also from what Paul said: "And we shall always be with the Lord."[21] "And night shall be no more," it says. The saints shall never have need of the light of the sun or that from a lamp, since the light of God will provide never-ending illumination. "And they shall reign," clearly the saints, "forever." The all-wise Daniel testified of these things, saying, "And the saints of the Most High shall receive the kingdom and possess it forever and ever."[22]

[22:6-9] ***And he said to me, "These words are trustworthy and true. And the Lord of the spirits of the prophets has sent his angel to show his servants what must soon take place. And behold, we are coming soon.[23] Blessed are they who keep the words of the prophecy of this book."***

I John am he who heard and saw these things. And when I heard and saw them, I fell down to worship at the feet of the angel who showed them to me; but he said, "You must not do that! I am a fellow servant with you and your brethren and the prophets and with those who keep the words of this book. Worship God!"

"These words are trustworthy," it says, that is, they are true. "And the Lord of the spirits of the prophets." By "spirits of the prophets" he

[17]See Lk 16:26. [18]Prov 3:18. [19]1 Cor 1:24. [20]See 2 Cor 6:16. [21]1 Thess 4:17. [22]Dan 7:18. [23]The text of Oecumenius has the plural.

means the prophetic gifts, as we learn from the all-wise Paul, who said, "and the spirits of the prophets are subject to prophets,"[24] and from the holy prophet Isaiah, "We have conceived, O Lord, because of fear of you, and we have been in birth pangs and have brought forth the breath[25] of your salvation that you have wrought on the earth."[26] "To show his servants what must soon take place," it says. By means of John and his writings, all have learned what he saw. And appropriately he says "soon," for as I have noted earlier,[27] in comparison with the everlasting ages that are coming, all time is short, even if someone might think it a very long while. And therefore he added, "Behold, I am coming soon. Blessed are they who keep these words of this prophecy." For those who keep these words are eager by a God-pleasing life not to fall into the punishments mentioned in it. "And when I heard and saw them I fell down to worship at the feet of the angel." I interpreted this earlier when I explained that the teachings of the Greeks about their native gods have nothing in common with the most pure doctrines of the church.[28]

[22:10-14] ***And he said to me, "Do not seal up the words of the prophecy of this book, for the time is near. Let the evildoer still do evil, and the filthy still be filthy, and the righteous still do righteousness, and the holy still be holy. Behold, I am coming very soon, bringing my recompense, to repay every one for what he has done. I am the Alpha and the Omega, first and last, beginning and end." Blessed are those who wash their robes, that they may have the right to the tree of life and that they may enter the city by the gates.***

"Do not seal up these words," it says. That is, you ought not keep these words to yourself or lock them up in the treasury of your mind. Rather, make them known to everyone. "For the time is near," it says. He is saying something like this: While the right time when they will have need to hear these words is not far distant, as it was once, that time is not yet present either. For it is not good that the exhortation of these words be, as it were, superfluous—for what need of exhortation do those have who are still acquainting themselves with evil and good?—for it is untimely to instruct by word those who are learning from experience. But why does he say it is near? Because it is neither a long time away, nor is it already present.

"Let the evildoer still do evil, and the filthy still be filthy," it says. He is not urging or commanding anyone to do that which is wicked or to defile themselves. Rather, he is saying that the short time remaining gives humankind yet an opportunity. Therefore, let each person do that which is pleasing, and let people use their free will as they choose, whether for that which is evil or for that which is good. And so he continues, "Let the righteous still do righteousness and the holy still be holy. Behold, I am coming soon, bringing my recompense, to repay every one for what he has done." "I am coming," says the Lord, referring to his second coming. And he is bringing with him whatever is necessary for the rewarding of each person, whether that is good or evil. He says, "I am the Alpha and the Omega, first and last, beginning and end." These words have been sufficiently discussed in earlier material.[29] Therefore, let us continue. "Blessed are those who wash their robes, that they may have the right to the tree of life," it says. By "robes" he means our bodies. Therefore, blessed are those who live well and cleanse themselves from every stain of sin. For those who have lived in such a manner will have the right to lean on the tree of life and to rest on it. The tree of life is the Lord, as I have

[24]1 Cor 14:32. [25]"Breath" translates πνεῦμα, which allows Oecumenius to see in Isaiah a reference to the "spirits of the prophets." [26]Is 26:18. [27]See his comments on Rev 1:1-2; 13:4-8. [28]See the comments on Rev 19:10. [29]See the comments on Rev 1:8; 21:6-8.

noted earlier. "That they may enter the city by the gates." Through the gates, that is, by the apostolic doctrines and teachings they become partakers of the life and blessedness of the saints.

[22:15-19] ***Outside are the dogs and sorcerers and fornicators and murderers and idolaters, and everyone who loves and practices falsehood. "I Jesus have sent my angel to you with this testimony for the churches. I am the root and the offspring of David, the bright morning star." The bride says, "Come."[30] And let him who hears say "Come." And let him who is thirsty come, let him who desires take the water of life without price. I warn everyone who hears the words of prophecy of this book: if anyone adds to them, God will add to him the plagues described in this book, and if anyone takes away from the words of the book of this prophecy, God will take away his share in the tree of life and in the holy city, which are described in this book.***

"Outside are the dogs," it says. It is customary in the holy Scriptures to call homosexuals "dogs" because they are shameless and impure. In Deuteronomy the law of the holy teacher Moses says, "You shall not bring the hire of a harlot or the wages of a dog into the house of the Lord your God in payment for any vow,"[31] since indeed such persons are similar to dogs because of their shamelessness. Even a wise man outside the church gives witness to the same view, saying, "Flee every murder and adulterous couch of a woman, and also the oaths of the rich and shameless beds of boys."[32] Therefore, such dogs are outside the holy city and apart from the life with the righteous. For what do they have in common with the righteous of God?

"And everyone who loves and practices falsehood" will be outside, it says. Everything against nature is false. Virtue is according to nature, since from the beginning the Creator has implanted in our makeup the seed of virtue, and so vice is against nature. For just as health is natural to our bodies and sickness is unnatural, and just as seeing and hearing are natural while blindness and deafness are unnatural, so also virtue in our souls is natural and evil is unnatural. Health is, then, analogous to virtue, and vice analogous to sickness. In a corresponding way, falsehood is evil, for it often falsely presents itself as virtue. Temerity masquerades as courage, dishonorable conduct as prudence, sloth as wisdom and false modesty as righteousness. All of these things are evils, cloaking themselves with a mask of virtue to those who fall in with them, and therefore he casts outside the divine walls those who pursue such lying deceit.

"I Jesus have sent my angel to you with this testimony for the churches," it says. "To testify" means to bear witness, not in private or in secret but so that the churches everywhere will hear and no one, feigning ignorance, will with evil intent do evil. "I am the root and the offspring of David," it says. We might think that it would have been more consistent had he said, "I am the branch that has sprung from the root of David," However, on the contrary he has here called himself the root of David, and not only "root" but also the "offspring," as I noted above. He is root and cause of all things, including David, insofar as he is and is known to be God, while he is offspring of David and has sprung from him according to the flesh, insofar as he is and is known to be man. And so he is—as the holy apostle somewhere says of his own words, "it is not irksome to me to say the same things" often, and for those who read them it is safe[33]—and so he is the Immanuel, both of divinity and of humanity,

[30]Oecumenius does not mention the Spirit here, but he includes it in the discussion below. [31]Deut 23:18. [32]It is unknown who this non-Christian source is. [33]See Phil 3:1.

possessing both perfectly according to their own proper quality, unconfusedly, unchangeably, immutably, really.[34] We are convinced that after the inexpressible union there is one person, one hypostasis and one energy, "even if the difference of the natures, from which we state the ineffable union has been made is not perceived," nor the characteristic of each according to their natural quality, as our holy father, Cyril, says.[35]

"The morning star," it says. He means either the sun, since he is called "sun of righteousness" in Malachi,[36] and further by the prophet who sings, "fire has fallen on them," that is, on the chief priests of the Jews, "and they did not see the sun," that is, him who is the "sun of righteousness," namely, Christ.[37] Or he means the morning star. For he is also called this by Peter in his second letter: "until the day dawns and the morning star rises in your hearts."[38] "And the Spirit," that is, the prophetic Spirit, "and the bride," the church that is universal and in every place, say, "Come!" We are instructed to seek the second coming of the Lord, and indeed to pray for it. For to be sure, whoever prays "thy kingdom come"[39] to God seeks the kingdom of Christ, which is also the kingdom of the Father and of the Spirit. "And let him who hears say, 'Come,' " it says. Everyone who hears these words, even you, John, ought to pray for the kingdom of the coming of Christ. He says this to exhort everyone to the works and practices of righteousness. For no one who is not fully aware of righteousness in himself would pray for the coming of Christ, at which he will demand an accounting of the life of all.

"And let him who is thirsty come, let him who desires take the water of life without price." Since the time of my coming will come, says the Lord, place your mouth on the fountain of life, that is, on the practice of virtue. Already before the Lord came, Isaiah had said the same thing when he urged, "All who have no money, go and buy, and drink without money and without price."[40] And in earlier discussion[41] I noted that the acquisition of virtue through struggles and labors is received as a free gift, since "the sufferings of this present time are not worth comparing with the glory that is to be revealed to us," as the all-wise Paul says.[42]

"I warn every one who hears these words," that is, I bear witness that nothing be added, lest one bring on oneself the plagues mentioned here, and that nothing be taken away, lest one be removed from partaking in the tree of life and in the holy city that have been described. For both are contained in this book. Then, to make his own words trustworthy and venerable, see what the Evangelist added:

[22:20] ***He who testifies to these things says, "Surely I am coming soon."***

John says here what Paul had earlier said: "For I am already on the point of being sacrificed, and the time of my departure has come."[43] John is saying in effect, "I who am finally at the end of this life teach these things and attest to their truth, so that no one will forsake the word [of the revelation] through doubt. For what person would choose to make up words as though they were from God and as though he were not going to die and depart into the hands of God any more evidently than is the case with everyone else who is still alive? Certainly it would not be such a case with a person like John! Therefore he says, I am writing these things all but speaking to Christ who

[34]Oecumenius is most likely referring to the *Definition of Faith* of the Council of Chalcedon (451). Chalcedon confessed that the two natures of Christ were united "unconfusedly" (ἀσυγχύτως), "immutably" (ἀτρέπτως), "indivisibly" (ἀδιαιρέτως), "inseparably" (ἀχωρίστως). Oecumenius mentions the first two adverbs but then uses the adverbs "unchangeably" (ἀναλλοιώτως) and "really" (ἀφαντασιάστως), that is, not merely in appearance only. [35]Cyril of Alexandria *Letter* 39.6 (FC 76:151). [36]Mal 4:2. [37]See Ps 58:8 (57:9 LXX). [38]2 Pet 1:19. [39]Mt 6:10. [40]See Is 55:1. [41]See the comment on Rev 21:6-8. [42]Rom 8:18. [43]2 Tim 4:6.

is calling me to a change of place, "Yes, I am coming soon!"

[22:20] ***Amen. Come, Lord Jesus!***

Since the prophetic Spirit said to him in the preceding material, "And he who hears, let him say to the Lord, 'Come!' " obedient to what had been commanded him, he says, "Come, Lord Jesus!" This is as though he said, "Yes, Lord Christ, quickly bring your second coming, which is our salvation."

[22:21] ***The grace of the Lord Jesus be with all the saints. Amen.***

The worldly have already been banished from the life of the saints and from any entry into the spiritual Jerusalem. For how would the grace of Christ, our God, come on those who had been declared excluded? Make us, O Christ, to be partakers of this grace through your goodness alone. For it is proper to glorify you now and always and forever. Amen.

With bold and ignorant talk, some say that the holy Revelation was not written by John himself, both evangelist and theologian. Giving heed to this opinion, they find themselves, as it were, in a tight spot. I believe that this opinion arises not from ignorance or from a revelation but only from a simplicity of mind, and if I might speak boldly, from a love of this life and an inordinate attachment to earthly things. It is a crude opinion and is not to be opposed by anxious denials. For since the saintly and holy Fathers explicitly give witness to this writing, who is capable to repudiate these things or in any way reach such a conclusion that these things are not so? For in his writing *Against Eunomius*, the great Basil presents a refutation of the heretic's detestable blasphemies and his nonsensical arguments. The holy theologian mentions these in his fourth book in which he discusses "the difficulties and their solutions drawn from the inspired Scriptures of the New and Old Testament in the controversy concerning the Son."[44] He begins like this: "If the Son is God by nature, and the Father is God by nature, then the Son is not one God and the Father another, but the same God."[45] And after other comments he continues: "Moses proclaimed of the Son, 'He who is has sent me,'[46] and the Evangelist John said, 'In the beginning was the Word,'[47] and he did not say 'was' only one time but four times, and again elsewhere, 'He who is is from God'[48] and 'He who is is in the bosom of the Father,'[49] and in other passages, 'He who is is in heaven,'[50] and in Revelation, 'He who is and who was and who is coming'."[51] He did not place Revelation in a special category of writings but continued by taking up the witness of Paul. If Revelation itself were written by a certain other John, as the idle talk of many would have it, the great Basil would have written the words from Revelation in the name of that author. However, having quoted first words of Moses and then words of the apostle and theologian [John] and then also words of the apostle Paul, he had no need to add the testimony of any other to these. Now these things are from the refutations of the great and holy Basil.

And the great Gregory, who is called the Theologian, gave a defense of himself in the presence of 150 bishops, the so-called Valedictory, in which he openly wrote: "How long will you inherit my holy mountain?" and a little later, "I am convinced that various angels are guardians of various churches, as John

[44]This is the title of *Against Eunomius* 4 (PG 29:671-72). [45]Basil of Caesarea *Against Eunomius* 4.1 (PG 29:672). Although we retain Oecumenius's ascription of *Against Eunomius* to Basil, scholars now largely doubt the authenticity of the work. DeGroote refers the writing to Pseudo-Basil (TEG 8:290-91). [46]Ex 3:14. [47]Jn 1:1. [48]Jn 8:47. [49]Jn 1:18. [50]Jn 3:13. [51]Rev 1:8. Basil of Caesarea *Against Eunomius* 4.2 (PG 29:677).

teaches me in the Revelation."[52] And finally, in the third book of his *Ecclesiastical History,* Eusebius of Pamphilus spoke as follows: "Such, then, was the plight of the Jews at that time."[53] And after some further discussion: "It is recorded that at that time the apostle and evangelist John, being still alive, was condemned to dwell on the island of Patmos for his testimony to the divine word by Domitian, son of Vespasian. Indeed, Irenaeus, in writing about the number of the name of the antichrist which is to be found in the Revelation of John, as it is called, uses these very words in the fifth book of his work *Against the Heresies,* with reference to John: 'But if it were necessary that his name should be announced openly at this present time, it would have been stated by him who also saw the revelation.' "[54]

[52]Gregory of Nazianzus *Or.* 42:8-9 (NPNF 2 7:388-89). [53]Eusebius *Hist. eccl.* 3.1.1. [54]Eusebius *Hist. eccl.* 3.18.1-3. See Irenaeus *Haer.* 5.30.3 (ANF 1:559).

ANDREW OF CAESAREA
Commentary on the Apocalypse

A Listing of the Chapters of the Interpretation of the Revelation of Saint John the Apostle

[1]Andrew of Caesarea seems to be the first to divide Revelation according to a distinct interpretative order. He divides Revelation into twenty-four books (λόγοι) and seventy-two chapters (κεφάλαια), three chapters to each of the books.

BOOK TWENTY-THREE

BOOK TWENTY-FOUR

The Interpretation of Andrew, Archbishop of Caesarea of Cappadocia, of the Revelation of John the Theologian

To my lord, brother and fellow servant.[1] Although I have often been asked by many who out of love have a higher opinion of me than my ability allows to give an explanation of the Revelation of John the Theologian and to fit the prophecies to the times after the vision, I have delayed undertaking this which is beyond me. For I know that to render an account of those things that have been mystically seen by the saints and that will occur in the future demands a great understanding that is enlightened by the divine Spirit. For if the books of the ancient prophecies that have received the interpretation of many still possess unseen depths of the mysteries in them until that day when the perfection of that partial knowledge that is passing away will be revealed—although most of these mysteries proclaim "the first appearance of our great God and Savior,"[2] and together with these certain of them also announce his second coming—how would anyone not be shown overly daring who, not partaking of the prophetic Spirit, would undertake the explanation of those things whose end is not yet seen? However, since "a good obedience is better than sacrifice,"[3] and "hope shall not be ashamed,"[4] and "love does not fail,"[5] as the apostle says, I will complete in brief the task that is laid on me, with the aid of God who makes wise, hoping to fill up that which is lacking through your God-pleasing soul with which I am bound and to acquire the reward of obedience that I believe is the fruit of love.

First, therefore, as you yourself know, all inspired Scripture is given from the grace of God in a tripartite manner corresponding to the tripartite nature of humankind. As it were, the body of Scripture is the letter and the story according to its literal meaning.[6] As if it were the soul, the tropological meaning leads the reader from that which is of the sense to that which is intellectual.[7] And as is the spirit, the anagogical and spiritual meaning[8] reveals that which is coming and the higher things. The first is proper to those who are taught of the Law; the second is proper to those who live in grace; the third is proper to that blessed lot in whom the Spirit rules since all fleshly thoughts as well as movements are submitted to him. The first corresponds to the stories of things that have already happened, although it is embellished often and in many places by types that precede the truth. The second is characterized by proverbial exhortations and other such forms of didactic speech, such as, "thorns growing in the hand of a drunkard,"[9] and "Be ashamed, O Sidon, for the sea has spoken,"[10] and other similar statements. The third meaning, namely, the spiritual, is found with abundance in the Revelation of the Theologian, often with the historical form and figurative statement, as was seen in other prophecies. But in this work the spiritual meaning is especially prevalent, in as much as it discourses to the more perfect about that knowledge that has been commanded of God. Therefore, also we provide an explanation of the visions seen by the saint, without claiming to have comprehended the depths of the Spirit that are hidden within. We do not undertake to understand everything according to the letter, nor do we make claims on the basis of our conjectures. Rather, as though a mental exercise for greater skill we offer contempt for present things, since they are passing away, and a desire for that which is to come, since they will endure. We leave the deep knowledge of

Interpretation [1]It is unknown who this brother and fellow servant is. The address suggests that he was also a bishop. [2]See Tit 2:13. [3]See 1 Sam 15:22. The LXX reads ἀκοὴ ὑπὲρ θυσίαν ἀγαθή "a good report is better than sacrifice." The text of Andrew reads ὑπακοὴ ὑπὲρ θυσίαν ἀγαθή. [4]Rom 5:5. [5]1 Cor 13:8. [6]Translating κατ' αἴσθησιν, literally "according to sense perception." [7]Translating ἐξ αἰσθητῶν ἐπὶ τὰ νοητά. [8]Translating ἡ ἀναγωγὴ καὶ θεωρία. [9]Prov 26:9. [10]Is 23:4.

these things to the divine wisdom that comprehends the times during which these prophecies will take place. Moreover, through the apostles the divine wisdom discourages us from seeking after these times.[11]

We have accomplished this through obedience, dividing the present work into twenty-four books and seventy-two chapters. Such a division corresponds to the tripartite constitution of body, soul and spirit of the twenty-four elders who represent the fullness of those who have pleased God from the beginning until the consummation of the age, as this will become clear in what follows. It would be superfluous to expend words concerning the inspired nature of the book, since the blessed Gregory the Theologian and Cyril and in addition to them the more ancient witness of Papias, Irenaeus, Methodius and Hippolytus have testified to the trustworthiness of the book.[12] We too have come to this opinion, receiving much inspiration from these testimonies, since in certain places we make use of them. And you, O man of God,[13] with prayer requite this labor, which is not small, as I think, bringing it to completion with contrition by remembering that which will be granted to the righteous as well as that recompense and reward that will be given to the sinners.[14]

BOOK ONE

Chapter 1
The revelation of Jesus Christ

[1:1] ***The revelation of Jesus Christ, which God gave him to show to his servants what must soon take place.***

A revelation is the manifestation of hidden mysteries, with the guide being enlightened either through divine dreams or through a divine illumination received while awake. He says that the revelation was given to Christ. By this expression concerning him John is thinking more of Christ's humanity,[1] since in his Gospel John more than all others dwells on those things that are sublime and proper to God. But also here by means of the ministering angel and the mention of the servants who are instructed he makes known the greatness of the deity of Christ. For all things are his servants. That events must take place soon indicates that some of these things will happen at once on the reading concerning them and that those things that will be at the consummation are not delayed. For with God a thousand years is reckoned "as yesterday when it is past."[2]

[1:1-2] ***And he made it known by sending his angel to his servant John, who bore witness to the Word of God and to the testimony of Jesus Christ, whatsoever he saw, namely, all things that are and that which must happen after them.***[3]

Christ showed these things to me through an angel as a lord to his own servant who bore witness through a confession of him.[4] This occurred that through the revelations given to me I might testify and proclaim for the conversion of those who hear those things that are and lie hidden to humankind and those things that will come in the future. For he saw both of these by way of prophecy, as is clear from what is said: "All things that are and that which must happen." These words are indicative of

[11]See 1 Thess 5:1. [12]For Gregory of Nazianzus *Or.* 29:17; 42:9; Cyril of Alexandria *Adoration in Spirit and Truth* 6; Irenaeus *Haer.* 1.26.3; 4.14.2; 4.17.6; 4.18.6; 4.20.11; 5.26-34; Methodius *Res.* 2.28; *Symp.* 1.5; 5.8; 6.5; Hippolytus *Antichr.*, where Revelation is thoroughly used. [13]1 Tim 6:11. [14]Andrew says that if his reader is brought to repentance through the reading of his commentary, then its primary purpose has been achieved and he has his suitable reward for writing it. **Book One** [1]Christ receives revelation according to his humanity; according to his deity he is himself the revealer. [2]Ps 90:4 (89:4 LXX). [3]The textual tradition of Revelation is quite different from the rest of the New Testament. The text of Andrew was followed by much of the Majority Text, the Byzantine text tradition. The text of Andrew and of those manuscripts that follow him are indicated in Nestle-Aland's Greek text by the *siglum* $\mathfrak{M}^A$. [4]The reference is to John's confession of Jesus that occasioned his banishment to Patmos.

both present and future time.

[1:3] ***Blessed is he who reads and those who hear the words of the prophecy and who keep what is written therein; for the time is near.***

He calls those blessed who read and hear by means of their works. For the present time through which it is possible to obtain blessedness is short, and this time lies available for everyone that they might work. As the Lord says, "Work while it is day."[5] There is also another interpretation. "The time is short" for the distribution of rewards, because this life is short in comparison with the coming age.

[1:4] ***John to the seven churches that are in Asia: Grace to you and peace from him who is and who was and who is to come, and from the seven spirits who are before his throne.***

Although there are many churches in every place, he wrote to seven only. For through the number seven he indicates the mystery of the church that exists everywhere and that which corresponds to the present life in which there is a sevenfold period of days. And therefore he makes mention of seven angels and seven churches to which he says, "Grace to you and peace from the tri-hypostatic deity."[6] Through the phrase "who is" the Father is indicated, who spoke to Moses: "I am who I am."[7] Through the phrase "who was" the Word is indicated, who "was in the beginning with God."[8] And through the phrase "who is to come" the Paraclete is indicated, who always visits the children of the church in holy baptism but will come more perfectly and more clearly in the age to come. It is possible to recognize in the seven spirits the seven angels who have received the governance of the churches. These are not numbered with the most divine and royal Trinity but are mentioned together with it as servants, even as the divine apostle says: "I testify to you before God and the elect angels."[9] These phrases may be understood also in another manner.[10] The phrase "who is and who was and who is to come" may signify the Father who encompasses in himself the beginning, the middle and the end of all things. "The seven spirits" may indicate the energies of the life-giving Spirit. Then follows Christ, our God, who for us became man. For in many places each of the divine persons are quite indiscriminately ordered, now before and now after. And so he says here:

[1:5] ***And from Jesus Christ, the faithful witness, the firstborn from the dead and the ruler of the kings on earth.***

Having testified under Pontius Pilate, he is himself faithful in all his words. He is the firstborn from the dead, since he is life and resurrection,[11] for those over whom he rules will no longer see death, as did those who formerly died and rose again, but will live eternally.[12] And as King of kings and Lord of lords[13] he is the ruler of kings, for he is equal in strength to the Father and of one essence[14] with him. Another interpretation is that he is called "ruler of the kings of the earth" because he rules over the earthly passions.

According to the blessed Gregory, the phrase "who is and who was and who is to come, the Almighty" refers to Christ.[15] Nor is there anything strange when words similar to these[16] are spoken a little later and there refer to Christ, and to these also the phrase

[5]Jn 9:4. [6]One God in three persons. Andrew uses the traditional Greek term ὑπόστασις for "person." [7]Ex 3:14. [8]Jn 1:1, 2. [9]1 Tim 5:21. [10]The first interpretation was that of Oecumenius. Now Andrew gives another interpretation that perhaps he prefers and believes to be the correct one. [11]Jn 11:25. [12]See Jn 5:24; 8:51. [13]See 1 Tim 6:15. [14]Translation of ὁμοούσιος, the term in the Nicene Creed to affirm the equal deity of the Son with the Father. [15]See Gregory of Nazianzus *Or.* 29.17, quoting Rev 1:8, which Gregory adduces as a title of the divine majesty of the Son (NPNF 2 7:307). [16]That is, the "who is and who was and who is to come" in Rev 1:4.

"the Almighty" is attached without thereby any other person being mentioned for the first time or by way of repetition.[17] The introduction in this verse of the phrase "and from Jesus Christ" seems to lend support to the interpretation offered by us. For it would be superfluous to add immediately the words "and from Jesus Christ" to a discussion concerning the divine Word and the person of the Son alone, as though the one seemed to be distinct from the other. Terms and phrases that befit God may refer equally to each divine person, to that which is common to the three, but not to the personal properties, or relations, as Gregory the Theologian says,[18] or to the incarnation of the Word.[19] From these considerations it is clear why we learn in the Gospel that the thrice-holy hymn of the seraphim is spoken to the Son,[20] while we learn in the speech of Paul in Acts that it is addressed to the Holy Spirit,[21] and while in the offering of the awesome mysteries we address it to the Father, to whom we are wont to make such a prayer,[22] as also the blessed Epiphanius says in his book On the Holy Spirit.[23] We have made these comments to demonstrate that our interpretation is not opposed to the testimonies of the Fathers.[24] With God's help we attend as closely as possible to the sequence of the text.

[1:5-6] ***To him who loved us and has freed us from our sins by his blood and made us kings and priests to his God and Father, to him be glory and dominion forever and ever. Amen.***

It is fitting, he says, to give glory to him who through his love has freed us from the chains of death and has washed us from the filth of sin by the outpouring of his life-giving blood and water[25] and has made us a royal priesthood[26] bringing to the Father the living sacrifice of a reasonable service, rather than the sacrifice of irrational beasts.[27]

[1:7] ***Behold, he is coming with the clouds, and every eye will see him, everyone who pierced him; and all tribes of the earth will wail on account of him. Even so, Amen.***

Here it says that as a lamb slain he will come on the clouds in the glory of the Father to be judge.[28] These "clouds" are to be understood either as incorporeal powers[29] or as clouds such as those that hid him on Mount Tabor when he was with his disciples.[30] Although every eye will see him coming with glory, those who pierced him and all the tribes of the earth that have remained in unbelief will grieve. "Even so, Amen" is the equivalent of "most certainly." And so he gives the same

[17]Andrew interpreted the "who is and who was and who is come" in Rev 1:4 as a reference to the holy Trinity. It not strange that the same phrase should in Rev. 1:8 refer to Christ alone, since that which is ascribed to one of the divine Trinity is ascribed equally to all three. [18]"Personal properties" translates ἰδιότητες, while "relations" translates σχέσεις. See Gregory of Nazianzus *Or.* 29.12; 34.13 (NPNF 2 7:305, 337). [19]Characteristics such as "holy" are true of deity and therefore may refer to all three of the divine persons. Characteristics such as "begetter" and "begotten," however, are personal properties because they can refer only to one of the persons. Such characteristics as "to be born" or "to have suffered" can refer only to the incarnate Word. [20]The "holy, holy, holy" comes from Is 6:3. The Gospel reference is apparently to Mt 13:13-15; Mk 4:12; Jn 12:39-41, which quote Is 6:9-10 and seem to imply that the Son was the original speaker of these words and therefore is the one to whom the Trisagion was spoken. [21]The reference is apparently to Acts 28:25-27, which quotes Is 6:9-10 as spoken by the Holy Spirit, and therefore implicitly as the one to whom the Trisagion of Is 6:3 was spoken. [22]Andrew is probably referring to the Eucharistic prayer that was addressed to God the Father and included a prayer of thanksgiving to him for creation and salvation that in turn introduced the Trisagion. [23]Andrew apparently refers to a work of Epiphanius that is no longer extant. [24]Andrew has a reason for his desire to be regarded as in agreement with the Fathers. By his time the Trisagion had become a point of controversy. The Monophysite bishop of Antioch, Peter the Fuller (d. 488), had added the theopaschite clause "who was crucified for us" to the Trisagion, clearly making the hymn a hymn to Christ and emphasizing the reality of the incarnation of the divine Word. The supporters of the Council of Chalcedon insisted rather that the hymn was addressed to the Trinity, and this is the view adopted by Andrew. Eventually the theopaschite addition would be anathematized by Canon 81 of the Quinisext Council (692) (NPNF 2 14:400). [25]See Jn 19:34. [26]See 1 Pet 2:9. [27]See Rom 12:1. By the "washing" and the "bringing of sacrifice" Andrew most likely has baptism and the Lord's Supper in mind. [28]See Mt 16:27; Lk 9:26. [29]See Mt 24:30; Mk 13:26; Lk 21:27. [30]See Mt 17:1-8; Mk 9:2-8; Lk 9:28-36.

meaning in both the Greek and the Hebrew tongue. For "Amen" is interpreted "let it be so."[31]

[1:8] ***I am the Alpha and the Omega, the Beginning and the End, says the Lord God, who is and who was and who is to come, the Almighty.***

Here Christ is shown to be God who rules all things, who is without beginning and similarly without end, who is and who was before and who is without limit, since he is eternal with the Father. For this reason he gives to each the wages of their deeds.[32]

[1:9] ***I, John, your brother and fellow participant in the tribulation and in the kingdom and the patient endurance of Jesus Christ, was on the island called Patmos on account of the word of God and the testimony of Jesus.***

Since I am your brother, he says, and a fellow participant in the sufferings for Christ's sake, I am rightly regarded as trustworthy among you. For, having been condemned to live on the island of Patmos "because of the testimony of Jesus," I will announce to you the mysteries that I was given to see on it.

Chapter 2
The vision in which he beholds the Lord

[1:10-11] ***I was in the Spirit on the Lord's day, and I heard behind me a loud voice like a trumpet saying, "I am the Alpha and the Omega, the First and the Last. Write what you see in a book and send it to the seven churches, to Ephesus and to Smyrna and to Pergamum and to Thyatira and to Sardis and to Philadelphia and to Laodicea."***

Overcome by the Holy Spirit and possessing an ear attuned to spiritual realities,[33] he heard on the Lord's day—called this in honor of the resurrection—a voice similar to a trumpet made loud through a megaphone, for "their sound has gone out into all the earth."[34] Through the Alpha and the Omega the voice reveals that God is without beginning and without end. Through the voice he is commanded to send to the seven churches all that he has seen. As we have already said,[35] the number seven indicates the period that ends in the sabbath rest of the coming age. Therefore, the great Irenaeus wrote that also the seven heavens and the seven angels that are superior to the rest had been created by God.[36]

[1:12-13] ***And I turned to see the voice that was speaking to me, and on turning I saw seven golden lampstands, and in the midst of the lampstands one like a son of man, clothed with a long robe and with a golden girdle round his breast.***

He shows that the voice was not sensory when he says "I turned," not to hear but "to see the voice." For spiritual hearing and spiritual seeing are the same thing. Having turned, he says, I saw seven lampstands—which later he calls the churches—and in the midst of them he saw Christ like to a man. [John speaks in this manner] since Christ is also God and not a mere man. He was clothed with a long robe, as a high priest of those things above "according to the order of Melchizedek."[37] Moreover, he was girded with a golden girdle, not around the loins, as other men are, to check desires (for the divine flesh is not accessible to these), but at the chest, around the breasts, so that the boundlessness of the righteous wrath of God might be restrained

[31]"Most certainly" translates πάντως; "let is be so" translates γένοιτο. [32]See Ps 62:12 (61:12 LXX); Prov 24:12; Mt 16:27; 2 Cor 5:10. [33]Translating πνευματικὸν οὖς. [34]Ps 19:4 (18:4 LXX). [35]See the comments on Rev 1:4. [36]Irenaeus *Haer.* 1.5.2 (ANF 1:322). Irenaeus attributes this view to the Valentinians, who, he says, claim that the seven heavens are intelligent and so also call them angels. [37]Ps 110:4 (109:4 LXX); Heb 5:6, 10; 6:20; 7:17.

by benevolence and that the truth might be revealed girding about the two Testaments that are the dominical breasts through which the faithful are nourished. It is a golden girdle to indicate its excellence and purity and genuineness.

[1:14] ***His head and his hair were white as white wool, white as snow; his eyes were like a flame of fire.***

Although for our sake he was of recent origin, he is ancient and indeed eternal, and the white hair is symbolic of this. "His eyes are as flames of fire," enlightening the saints even as they burn those who are defiled.

[1:15] ***And his feet were like burnished bronze, refined as in a furnace.***

The divine Gregory interpreted the feet to refer to the economy according to the flesh. For the feet, having been added to Christ's deity, effected our salvation.[38] And the feet are also the foundations of the church. And they are "like bronze incense," which, the medical people say, possesses a good smell when burned and which is called by them masculine incense. There is another interpretation: since the bronze refers to the human nature and the incense refers to the divine nature, through these is indicated the sweet odor of the faith and the unconfusedness of the unity.[39] Or another interpretation: the bronze shows the euphony of the proclamation, while the incense shows the conversion of the nations, from which the bride is commanded to come.[40] The feet of Christ are also the apostles who have been purified in the furnace of temptations according to the imitation of their teacher.

[1:15] ***And his voice was like the sound of many waters. In his right hand he held seven stars, from his mouth issued a sharp two-edged sword, and his face was like the sun shining in full strength.***

He speaks in an appropriate manner. For the voice of Christ is common with that of the Spirit, from whom rivers of living water flow from the belly of the faithful and that sounds throughout into all the earth.[41]

[1:16] ***In his right hand he held seven stars, from his mouth issued a sharp two-edged sword, and his face was like the sun shining in full strength.***

A little later he will call the seven stars "the angels of the churches."[42] He speaks of a "two-edged sword," which is the condemning judgment against the impious and is "sharper than any two-edged sword."[43] Or, this sword is the "sword of the Spirit"[44] that circumcises our inner person. His face shines "as the sun," not referring to the sun perceived by the senses but to the intellectual sun. For he is the "sun of righteousness,"[45] who shines by his own power and strength, not as the perceptible sun, which is a creature and shines only by that power given to it from God and by divine command.

[1:17-18] ***When I saw him, I fell at his feet as though dead. But he laid his right hand on me, saying, "Fear not, I am the first and the last, and the living one; I died, and behold, I am alive for evermore. Amen."***

Christ revived the apostle who was suffering on account of the weakness of the human nature the same as he did to Joshua, son of

[38]This opinion cannot be located in the extant works of Gregory of Nazianzus. [39]Translating τὸ ἀσύγχυτον τῆς ἑνώσεως, language perhaps reflecting the *Definition of Faith* of the Council of Chalcedon (451) that the two natures of Christ were united unconfusedly (ἀσυγχύτως). [40]That is, the church will be the union of peoples from the nations. [41]Jn 7:38. Andrew represents the opinion that the rivers of living water are the spiritual teaching of the church. [42]See Rev 1:20. [43]Heb 4:12. [44]Eph 6:17. [45]Mal 4:2.

Nun,[46] and to Daniel,[47] saying to him, "Fear not," for I did not come that you should die, but I who am without beginning and without end became dead for your sake.

[1:18] ***"And I have the keys of hades and death."***

He speaks here of his authority over physical and spiritual death.

[1:19-20] ***"Therefore write what you see, what is and what is to take place after these things. As for the mystery of the seven stars that you saw in my right hand, and the seven golden lampstands, the seven stars are the angels of the seven churches, and the seven lampstands that you saw are the seven churches."***

Since Christ is the true light, those who are made rich in his brightness are because of him lamps, and they make bright the nighttime of the present life. Rightly too are the churches called "lampstands," for they have lights who "hold fast the word of life," as the apostle says.[48] And these lamps and lampstands are golden because of the precious and pure character of the faith that is in them. Over each of these an angel is established as protector, as the Lord says.[49] Indeed, Gregory the Theologian understands the present passage as follows: those whom he has figuratively named "stars" are so-named because of the brightness and purity of their nature.[50]

Chapter 3
The letter to the angel of the church at Ephesus

[2:1] ***"To the angel of the church in Ephesus write: The words of him who holds the seven stars in his right hand, who walks among the seven golden lampstands."***

He converses with the church through the angel, just as someone might speak to the student through a pedagogue. The teacher naturally assumes as his own that which pertains to the student, whether that is failures or accomplishments, that is, he is zealous that the student become like himself. It is possible, as Irenaeus and Epiphanius claim,[51] that through the seven stars—that is, angels—it is revealed that the arrangement of the spiritual orders that exist in the seven intelligent heavens are in the right hand of Christ, in which are also "the ends of the earth."[52] According to his own promise and work Christ "is walking in the midst of the churches."[53]

[2:2-5] ***"I know your works, your toil and your patient endurance, and how you cannot bear evil men but have tested those who call themselves apostles but are not, and found them to be false; but you have borne up and are patiently enduring for my name's sake, and you have not grown weary. But I have this against you, that you have abandoned your first love. Remember then from where you have fallen, repent, and do the works you did at first."***

Although in two matters he approves of the church, in one particular he finds fault with her. He mentions her fault in the middle of his comments, while placing the accomplishments of the church on either side. He praised the church's labor and her patient endurance for the faith and her separation from evil people, for she did not believe every spirit[54] but tested the false apostles, and when the church found

[46]Josh 5:14. [47]See Dan 8:17; 10:9. [48]Phil 2:16. [49]See Mt 18:10. [50]Gregory of Nazianzus *Or.* 42.9 (NPNF 2 7:389). [51]Irenaeus *Haer.* 1.5.2 (ANF 1:322); Epiphanius *Pan.* 31.18.8 (GCS 25:431). For "intelligent" Irenaeus and Epiphanius use νοερός and νοητός. Andrew uses μακάριος "blessed" for these seven heavens. Being intelligent was associated with being blessed. [52]Ps 95:4 (94:4 LXX). [53]See Lev 26:12. [54]See 1 Jn 4:1.

them to be false, she sent them away. And to this he adds that the church hated the works of the evil-doing Nicolaitans.[55] However, he blames the church because she has become tepid in her love and good works toward the neighbor, and in addition he summons the church again through the following words: "Do the works that you did at first."

[2:5-6] *"If not, I will come to you quickly and remove your lampstand from its place, unless you repent. Yet this you have, you hate the works of the Nicolaitans, which I also hate."*

To remove the church is to deprive her of the divine grace. In this manner distress and turmoil by evil spirits and by evil people who are in their employ are brought on the church. However, some interpret the removal of the lampstand to refer to the transfer of the episcopal throne of Ephesus to the royal city.[56] But whoever reads this will know by their loathsome heresy the works of the Nicolaitans that are hated by God.

[2:7] *"He who has an ear, let him hear what the Spirit says to the churches. To him who conquers I will grant to eat of the tree of life, which is in the midst of the paradise of God."*

Every person has a physical ear, but only the spiritual person has a spiritual ear, such as was granted to Isaiah.[57] And to such as conquer in the struggle against the demons, he promised to give "to eat from the tree of life," that is, to grant them to share in the blessings of the future age, for eternal life is figuratively depicted through the tree. And Christ is said to be both, as is clear from what Solomon says and what our apostle writes in another passage. For concerning wisdom, Solomon says, "She is the tree of life,"[58] while John writes about Christ, "This is God and eternal life."[59] If, therefore, we are allowed to attain to these things, let us accomplish the victory over our sufferings. For most certainly proper recompense will follow our trials, by the grace and beneficence of our Lord, Jesus Christ, with whom be glory to the Father together with the Holy Spirit forever and ever. Amen.

BOOK TWO

Chapter 4
What was revealed to the angel of the church at Smyrna

[2:8] *"And to the angel of the church in Smyrna write: The words of the first and the last, who died and came to life."*

Christ is first as God, but he is last since in the last times he became man and through his death of three days opened for us eternal life.

[2:9] *"I know your works and your tribulation and poverty, but you are rich."*

In the things of the flesh you have tribulation and poverty, which you endure for my sake, being beaten by unbelievers and being deprived of present goods. But in the things of the Spirit you are rich, for you have the "hidden treasure in the field"[1] of your heart.

[55]John mentions the Nicolaitans in the letters to Ephesus and Pergamum, and most likely also in the letter to Thyatira. According to Irenaeus, the Nicolaitans were followers of Nicolaus, one of the seven deacons mentioned in Acts 6:5. They led lives of "unrestrained indulgence" and taught that "it is a matter of indifference to practice adultery and to eat things sacrificed to idols" (*Haer.* 1.26.3 [ANF 1:352]). According to Clement of Alexandria, however, Nicolaus was an "admirable man" who practiced a rigorous asceticism. His saying, "One must misuse the flesh," was perverted by the Nicolaitans to justify their own vice (*Strom.* 2.118.3-5 [FC 85:234-35]). [56]This apparently refers to the implementation of Canon 28 of the Council of Chalcedon, which ordered that the metropolitans of Pontus, Asia and Thrace be ordained by the archbishop of Constantinople. For a full discussion of Canon 28, see Peter L'Huillier, *The Church of the Ancient Councils: The Disciplinary Work of the First Four Ecumenical Councils* (Crestwood, N.Y.: Saint Vladimir's Seminary Press, 1996), 267-96. [57]See Is 50:4. [58]Prov 3:18. [59]1 Jn 5:20. **Book Two** [1]Mt 13:44.

[2:9] *"And the slander of those who say that they are Jews but are not, but are a synagogue of Satan."*

The word "to know" is according to common usage. And so he says, I am very well aware of "the blasphemy of the synagogue of Satan," for they are not what they say they are. For he is not a Jew who is one openly but who is one inwardly.[2] For Judah is interpreted as "confession."[3]

[2:10] *"Do not fear what you are about to suffer. Behold, the devil is about to throw some of you into prison, that you may be tested, and for ten days you will have tribulation. Be faithful to death, and I will give you the crown of life."*

Do not fear, he says, the trial that comes from those who fight against God through tortures and temptations. For this trial will be of ten days duration, not long-lived. Therefore, death is to be despised, since in a short time you will procure the unfading crown of life.[4]

[2:11] *"He who has an ear, let him hear what the Spirit says to the churches. He who conquers shall not be hurt by the second death."*

One who hears spiritually and overcomes the evil suggestions of the devil, although he may be subject to the first death according to the flesh, he will not be harmed by the second death of Gehenna.

Chapter 5
What was revealed to the angel of the church at Pergamum

[2:12-13] *"And to the angel of the church in Pergamum write: The words of him who has the sharp two-edged sword. I know your works and where you dwell, where the throne of Satan is."*

The city to which this is said was given to idolatry, but he is expressing approval of those in it who remained faithful through the endurance of trials. The "two-edged sword" is either the word of the gospel, which cuts the heart and separates the faithful from the unfaithful, or it is the relentless judgment against the impious.

[2:13] *"You hold fast my name, and you did not deny my faith in the days of Antipas, my faithful witness (for every witness is faithful), who was killed among you, where Satan dwells."*

Antipas was a most courageous martyr in Pergamum, whose martyrdom I have read.[5] Here the Evangelist recalls his memory as a demonstration of their endurance, as well as of the cruelty of those who were deceived.

[2:14-15] *"But I have a few things against you; you have some there who hold the teaching of Balaam, who through Balaam taught Balak to put a stumbling block before the sons of Israel, that they might eat food sacrificed to idols and practice immorality. So you also have some who hold the teaching of the Nicolaitans, which I hate."*

It seems that this city had two evils. There were a good number of Greeks, and among those regarded as faithful the shameful Nicolaitans were sown as evil weeds among the wheat.[6] And therefore he reminds them of Balaam, saying, "who through Balaam taught

[2]Rom 2:28-29. [3]Translating ἐξομολόγησις, which could also be rendered "thanksgiving." See Gen 29:35. [4]1 Pet 5:4. [5]This account, which Andrew had read, is no longer extant. According to tradition, Antipas was a disciple of the apostle John and a bishop of Pergamum during the time of the emperor Domitian. Especially effective against demons, he was eventually burned in a bronze bull used to burn incense to the emperor. His death is traditionally dated to A.D. 92, and his martyrdom celebrated on April 11. [6]Mt 13:24-30.

Balak."[7] Through these words it is clear that he refers to the mental Balaam, that is, the devil, who through the sensual Balaam taught Balak to throw a stone of stumbling before the Israelites, namely, to sacrifice to idols and to commit fornication. Through the pleasure of this heresy, they fell so low that they offered sacrifices to Beelphegor.[8]

[2:16] ***"Repent. But if not, I will come to you quickly and war against them with the sword of my mouth."***

What goodness, even in this threat! For he did not say, "I will war against you," but "I will war against them," namely, against those who are incurably sick.

[2:17] ***"He who has an ear, let him hear what the Spirit says to the churches. To him who conquers I will give to eat some of the hidden manna, and I will give him a white stone, with a new name written on the stone, which no one knows except him who receives it."***

The "hidden manna" is "the Bread of Life" who came down from heaven for us and became edible.[9] Figuratively, those good things are also called "manna" that are in the future going to come down from heaven from where comes also the "new Jerusalem."[10] Those who conquer the devil, he says, shall attain these things. They shall also receive a "white stone," that is, having conquered, they shall be regarded as worthy of a portion at the right hand. And they shall receive a "new name" that is unknown in the present life. "For eye has not seen, nor has ear heard," nor has the mind thought of the good things that are coming, including the new name that the saints will inherit.[11]

Chapter 6
What was revealed to the angel of the church at Thyatira

[2:18] ***"And to the angel of the church in Thyatira write: The words of the Son of God, who has eyes like a flame of fire and whose feet are like burnished bronze."***

The text speaks of the fiery likeness of the eyes, which signifies the illumination of the righteous and the punishment of the sinners. The feet and the burnished bronze symbolize the fragrance of Christ, the spiritual ointment, among those who are being saved.[12] They symbolize as well the undivided and unmixed unity of the divinity and humanity. For this unity, as though hardened in fire by the Holy Spirit, is incomprehensible to human reasoning.

[2:19-20] ***"I know your works, your love and faithfulness and service and patient endurance, and that your latter works exceed the first. But I have much against you, that you tolerate the woman Jezebel, who calls herself a prophetess and is teaching and deceiving my servants to practice immorality and to eat food sacrificed to idols."***

Although on account of your faithfulness and your service for those in need I acknowledge your piety and your endurance, nonetheless I rightly blame you because you allow the heresy of the Nicolaitans to exist openly. This heresy is figuratively called "Jezebel" because of its impiety and licentiousness. Because of this heresy my servants, through their simplicity of mind, are presented with a stone of stumbling and are drawn toward idolatrous practices from which they had previously fled. You must

[7]The text of Andrew reads ὅς ἐδίδασκεν ἐν τῷ Βαλαὰμ τὸν Βαλάκ. Andrew interprets ὅς to refer to the devil, while Balaam is his human instrument. [8]The name given to the god Baal on Mount Phegor in Moab. See Num 25:1-13; Deut 4:3; Ps 106:28 (105:28 LXX). [9]Jn 6:35, 48, 50. He is thinking of the Eucharist. [10]Rev 21:2, 10. [11]1 Cor 2:9. [12]2 Cor 2:15.

curb this heresy, because it deceitfully calls itself a prophetess, being moved by an evil spirit.

[2:21] ***"I gave her time to repent from her fornication."***

Although this evil heresy was given an opportunity to repent, it did not take advantage of this.

[2:22-23] ***"Behold, I will throw her on a sickbed, and those who commit adultery with her I will throw into the great tribulation, unless they should repent from their works. And I will slay her children with death."***

He continues to speak figuratively and compares the union with heretics to that with a harlot, and he threatens to throw her into sickness and death as well as those who have become defiled with her and have committed fornication before God, unless they should turn to him through repentance.

[2:23-25] ***"And all the churches shall know that I am he who searches mind and heart, and I will give to each of you as your works deserve. But to the rest of you in Thyatira, who do not hold this teaching, who do not know the deep things of Satan, as they say, I do not lay on you any further burden; only hold fast what you have, until I come."***

He says these things against the heretics who have been deceived and who deceive others. But to the more simple, the Lord says, "Since on account of your simplicity you are not able to withstand those who are evil and have a facility with words," namely, that you do not know "the deep things of Satan," as you call it, I will not expect from you any war through words, but only that you preserve the teaching that you received until I remove you from there.

[2:26-28] ***"He who conquers and who keeps my works until the end, I will give him authority over the nations, and he shall rule them with a rod of iron, as when earthen pots are broken in pieces, even as I myself received authority from my Father."***

"To him who does my works," the Lord says, "I will give authority over five or ten cities," as he said in the Gospel.[13] Or, this passage refers to the judgment of the unfaithful, through which the deceived will be crushed, as though beaten with a rod of iron, and will be judged by those among them who have believed in Christ, as the Lord said: "The men of Nineveh will rise and condemn this generation."[14] The words "as I myself received from the Father" refer to his human nature, which he assumed through the flesh.

[2:28-29] ***"And I will give him the morning star. He who has an ear, let him hear what the Spirit says to the churches."***

By "morning star" he means either that one of whom Isaiah spoke: "How have you fallen from heaven, O Day Star, O Morning Star?"[15] and of whom it is promised that he will be "crushed under the feet of the saints,"[16] or the Lord means that one of whom the blessed Peter speaks, of the "morning star who rises in the hearts of the faithful,"[17] clearly meaning the illumination of Christ. Both John the Baptist and Elijah the Tishbite were called light bringers. For the one foretold of the first rising of the "sun of righteousness,"[18] and the other is known as the forerunner of the second rising. And after these, we believe that those who have conquered the devil will receive their inheritance. Nor is it surprising that we should interpret this in so opposite a fashion. For we learn from the holy Scriptures that the "lion" from Judah is Christ, while the "lion" from Bashan is the antichrist,

[13]Lk 19:17. [14]Mt 12:41. [15]Is 14:12. [16]Rom 16:20. [17]2 Pet 1:19. [18]See Mal 4:2.

the same image signifying both.[19] And so is noted the rising of the coming day, in which the darkness of the present life will be hidden, and the angel proclaims this. For this precedes the "sun of righteousness" that will shine on the saints and dispel the gloom of the present life, by whose rays may also we be made bright, by the good pleasure of the Father with the all-holy Spirit, to whom be glory forever. Amen.

BOOK THREE

Chapter 7
What was revealed to the angel of the church at Sardis

[3:1] *"And to the angel of the church in Sardis write: The words of him who has the seven spirits of God and the seven stars. I know your works; you have the name of being alive, but you are dead."*

We have said before that the "seven stars" are divine angels.[1] The "seven spirits" are either the selfsame angels or the energies of the life-giving Spirit. Either way, both are in the hand of Christ, for he governs the former as Lord, and as the ὁμοούσιος[2] he is the supplier of the Spirit. However, he rebukes the church, since while it possesses the name of a living faith, it has died in respect to good works.

[3:2] *"Be watchful, and strengthen what remains and is on the point of death, for I have not found your works perfect in the sight of God."*

He tells the angel to shake off the slumber of indifference and to strengthen your[3] members who are going to die through disbelief. For it is not the beginning of good works that crowns the worker, but rather their completion.

[3:3] *"Remember then what you received and heard; keep that and repent."*

Hold fast the tradition that you received from the apostles, and repent of your indifference.

[3:3] *"If you will not awake, I will come like a thief, and you will not know at what hour I will come on you."*

This is reasonably written. For neither the time of death of any individual nor the common consummation[4] is known to anyone. To those who are prepared, it will be the cessation of toil; however, to those who are unprepared, like a "thief" he will bring on spiritual death.

[3:4] *"Yet you have a few names in Sardis, people who have not soiled their garments; and they will walk with me in white, for they are worthy."*

He says that the church possesses this good thing: she has some who have not defiled the vestment of their flesh with sordid deeds. These will shine brilliantly with me at the regeneration, since they have preserved spotless their garment of incorruptibility.[5]

[3:5-6] *"He who conquers will be clad in white garments, and I will not blot his name out of the book of life; I will confess his name before my Father and before his angels. He who has an ear, let him hear what the Spirit says to the churches."*

[19]See Deut 33:22; Gen 49:9-10; Rev 5:5. That the lion from Judah and the lion from Bashan were images of the Christ and the antichrist was primitive Christian conviction. See Hippolytus *Antichr.* 6–15 (ANF 5:206-7). **Book Three** [1]See the comment on Rev 1:4. [2]The term comes from the Nicene Creed and confesses that the Son possesses the same deity as does the Father. Along with the Father, the Son is the giver of the Spirit. [3]Translating the singular σου. Andrew does not abandon the aspect of direct discourse, even in his own comments. [4]That is, the time of the general resurrection. [5]The language of "vestment" and "garment" probably refers to the white robe in which the newly baptized were clothed. This robe represented purity of body and mind.

One who wins this victory shall shine as the sun because of the garments of his virtuous deeds, and his name will be indelibly entered into the book of the living. And he will be confessed before my Father and his holy powers, just as it is for the triumphant martyrs.[6] For, as he says in the Gospel, "the righteous will shine as the sun."[7]

Chapter 8

What was revealed to the angel of the church at Philadelphia

[3:7] ***"And to the angel of the church of Philadelphia, write: The words of the holy one, the true one, who has the key of David, who opens and no one shuts, and who shuts and no one opens."***

His kingdom is called "the key of David," for this is a symbol of authority. And, moreover, the Holy Spirit is the key of the book of the Psalms and of every prophecy, for through him the treasures of knowledge[8] are opened. He received the first key according to his humanity, but the second key he possesses according to his deity, which has no beginning. In some of the copies "hades" is written instead of "David." Through the image of the "key of hades" the authority of life and death is ascribed to Christ. He is the "holy one" and the "true one" because he possesses holiness in himself and according to his own essence he is truth.

[3:8] ***"I know your works. Behold, I have set before you an open door, which no one is able to shut. I know that you have but little power, and yet you have kept my word and have not denied my name."***

Through these words we learn that although this city was small in size, it was great in faith. For this reason he says to it, "I know your works," that is, I approve of them. He spoke in a similar way also to Moses: "I know you above all others."[9] And I have opened before you the door of the teaching of the gospel, which cannot be closed through persecutions. It is enough that I lay this on you, and I will not demand from you anything beyond what you are able.

[3:9] ***"Behold, I give those of the synagogue of Satan who say that they are Jews but are not but lie—I will make them come and bow down before your feet, and know that I have loved you."***

As reward for your confession of my name, he says, you will have the conversion and repentance of the Jews. These will fall before your feet beseeching approach to me and enlightenment from me, and they will no longer be Jews[10] in the open but in the hiddenness of the heart.

[3:10-11] ***"Because you have kept my word of patient endurance, I will keep you from the hour of trial that is coming on the whole world to try those who dwell on the earth. I am coming soon; hold fast what you have, so that no one may seize your crown."***

By the "hour of trial" he speaks either of the persecution against the Christians that occurred almost immediately by those who ruled Rome badly at that time, from which he promised that the church would be freed,[11] or he speaks of the universal coming of the antichrist against the faithful at the end of time. From this coming he pledges to free those who are zealous, for they will beforehand be seized upward by a departure from there, lest

[6]See Mt 10:32; Lk 12:8. [7]Mt 13:43. [8]See Col 2:3. [9]Ex 33:12, 17. [10]Translating ἰουδαΐζοντες, which has the idea of living according to Jewish practice. [11]Presumably Andrew has persecution under Domitian in mind.

they be tempted beyond what they are able to endure. He says well, "I am coming soon," for "after the tribulation of those days, the Lord will immediately come," as it says.[12] Therefore, he exhorts them to keep the treasure of their faith safe, so that no one lose the crown of endurance.

[3:12] *"He who conquers, I will make him a pillar in the temple of my God; never shall he go out of it."*

He speaks correctly. For he who conquers against the opposing powers is established as a "pillar and foundation of the truth," having in it an immoveable foundation, as the apostle says.[13]

[3:12] *"I will write on him the name of my God and the name of the city of my God, the new Jerusalem that comes down from my God out of heaven, and my new name."*

On the heart of such a pillar, he says, I will inscribe the knowledge of the divine name and of the Jerusalem that is above, so that with the eyes of the Spirit you might see the blessings that are in it. And I will inscribe "my new name," which is to be made known to the saints in the coming age. When he says "of my God," he is speaking concerning the Father in a human way, since without any change he became flesh for us.[14] He speaks of "the Jerusalem that comes down from above," since the divine knowledge finds its beginning with the angels and comes down to meet us, both they and we being united through Christ, our head.

[3:13] *"He who has an ear, let him hear what the Spirit says to the churches."*

Let us pray that also we might acquire such an ear.

Chapter 9
What was revealed to the angel of the church at Laodicea

[3:14] *"And to the angel of the church in Laodicea write: The words of the Amen, the faithful and true witness."*

Through his faithfulness the truth of Christ is revealed, or rather that he is himself the truth according to essence.

[3:14] *"The beginning of God's creation."*

He writes "beginning" instead of "kingdom," for he is the beginning of all things as the one who governs all created things. He is "the beginning of creation" as the one who is its immediate and uncreated cause.[15]

[3:15-16] *"I know your works; you are neither cold nor hot. Would that you were cold or hot! So, because you are lukewarm, and neither cold nor hot."*

Gregory the Theologian says, "It is necessary to be truly hot or to be truly cold."[16] This is well said. For there is often hope that the person who is cold and has never tasted living faith might attain it. But the person who was hot through baptism by the Spirit and has later cooled off through indifference, disadvantaged by a faith that has been lost, cuts himself off from the hopes of salvation. For moderation is not unknown where works are considered, just as in a lawful marriage there may be moderation in chastity, and even fornication may not be wholly absent. However, in faith modera-

[12]Mt 24:29. [13]1 Tim 3:15. [14]The incarnation did not effect any change in the deity of the Son. In becoming one of us, the Son remained what he was, God the Son. [15]Andrew is taking advantage of the multiple nuances of the term ἀρχή. Generally the term means "first," and so it can refer to a beginning of time, a cause or a leading and governance. [16]This saying of Gregory of Nazianzus cannot be located.

tion and being lukewarm are not acceptable.

[3:16-17] ***"I will spew you out of my mouth. For you say, I am rich, I have prospered, and I need no one; not knowing that you are wretched, pitiable, poor, blind and naked."***

Just as that which is lukewarm induces vomiting in those who take it in, so also, he says, I will vomit you out through the word of my mouth into eternal destruction, as though you were rotten food. For mixing together the seed of the divine word with the thistles of wealth, you have become unaware of your poverty in spiritual matters and of the blindness of your spiritual eyes and of your nakedness in good works.

[3:18] ***"I advise you to buy from me gold refined by fire, that you may be rich, and that you might wear white garments, and that the indecency of your nakedness might not be seen, and buy salve to anoint your eyes that you might see."***

If you wish to be rich, he says, with a zealous intent and a willing heart obtain from me, who makes rich, gold that has been purified in fire, namely, the word of teaching that is made brilliant in the fire of temptations. And through this you will have in your heart a treasure that is secure, and you will wear the bright stole of virtue, through which the nakedness, which has come to you by sin, will be clothed. The salve is certainly poverty. For if "gifts make blind the eyes of those who see,"[17] then certainly that which is incorruptible will open them.

[3:19] ***"Those whom I love, I reprove and chasten; so be zealous and repent."***

Oh, the depths of the divine benevolence! With what goodness is this reproof mixed!

[3:20] ***"Behold, I stand at the door and knock; if anyone hears my voice and opens the door, I will come in to him and eat with him, and he with me."***

My presence, he says, is without compulsion. I knock at the door of the heart, and to those who open I rejoice with them at their salvation. For I regard this as food and supper, that as I am nourished even so they are nourished; they banish the famine of hearing the word of God[18] and the darkness of deceit.

[3:21-22] ***"He who conquers, I will grant him to sit with me on my throne, as I myself conquered and sat down with my Father on his throne. He who has an ear, let him hear what the Spirit says to the churches."***

"The throne" indicates the kingdom and the rest of the coming age. Therefore, he says that those who have conquered the enemy "will be glorified with me and will rule with me."[19] When he says "as I myself have conquered," he is speaking in a human manner on account of the assumption of the flesh. For God the Word did not acquire the kingdom as a prize for virtue, for he has this essentially as an eternal possession. For if this were not so, he would not be able to share it with others. But according to the Theologian and the "son of thunder," he shared from his fullness with all the saints.[20] For this reason also he promised to his holy apostles that they would sit on twelve thrones and judge the future twelve tribes of Israel.[21] For when he who is God and the eternal King became man for us, he shared everything that is ours, except only sin,[22] and shared everything of his with those who had conquered the devil as it was possible for human nature to receive. Therefore, having made a cloud the chariot of his ascension into heaven, he said through the apostle

[17]Ex 23:8; Deut 16:19; Sir 20:29. [18]See Amos 8:11. [19]Rom 8:17. [20]Jn 1:16. [21]Mt 19:28; Lk 22:30. [22]Heb 4:15.

that the saints would be snatched up to meet him on the clouds.[23] And when he, who is the Creator and Lord of creation, shall come as judge, he will allow the saints to judge those who had rebelled against the truly divine and blessed service. As the apostle says, "Do you not know that we are to judge angels?"[24] that is, the principalities of the darkness. Since, therefore, we have such a benefactor of humankind as judge, let us be zealous to receive his favor, fulfilling at all times the word of Solomon, "Let your garments be always white,"[25] not making them filthy through evil deeds. For in this way, having decorated our souls in a way fit for marriage, we shall present ourselves lovely for union with the King, and we shall receive the eternal blessings in Christ, our God, the supplier of these things, with whom glory, honor and worship be to the Father, together with the all-holy Spirit, forever and ever. Amen.

BOOK FOUR

Chapter 10

Concerning the door seen in heaven and the twenty-four elders and what follows

[4:1] *After this I looked, and lo, in heaven an open door! And the first voice, which I heard speaking to me like a trumpet, said, "Come up here, and I will show you what must take place after this."*

The opening of the door signifies the revelation of the hidden mysteries of the Spirit. The trumpet represents the sonorous voice of the Revealer. "Come up here" indicates that the mind of the hearer is to turn away completely from the things of the earth and be turned toward heaven.

[4:2-3] *At once I was in the Spirit, and lo, a throne stood in heaven, with one seated on the throne who appeared like jasper and carnelian, and round the throne was a rainbow that looked like an emerald.*

Having heard the voice and being conformed to the Spirit, I beheld the sovereign throne that symbolizes the repose of God among the saints, for God is enthroned among them. When in this passage he presents a vision of the Father, he does not present him in any bodily form as was the case in the previous vision of the Son, but he likens him to precious jewels. The jasper, which is green, symbolizes the ever-green, life-bearing and nourishing supply of the divine nature, since every seed brings forth a green shoot. Yet, in addition it is fearful to that which is in opposition, for they say that jasper is fearful to the beasts and monsters.[1] And furthermore, [there is the sardion stone], which has the therapeutic quality of physical healing for those who receive it. The great Epiphanius says that when applied this stone heals swellings and wounds that are caused by iron.[2] The rainbow has the appearance of an emerald and reveals the manifold brilliance of the virtues of the angelic orders.

[4:4] *Round the throne were twenty-four thrones, and seated on the thrones were twenty-four elders, clad in white garments, with golden crowns on their heads.*

One of the interpreters before us has understood the twenty-four elders to represent Abel along with twenty others from the Old Testament and three from the New Testament.[3] Whether this is so, or whether what is indicated through the number twenty-four are those who have excelled in deeds and word,

[23]Acts 1:9; 1 Thess 4:17. [24]1 Cor 6:3. [25]Eccl 9:8. **Book Four** [1]See Epiphanius *On the Twelve Gems* 6 (PG 43:297). On the jasper, which is "fearful," Epiphanius says that it is called "ancient" and is similar "to snow or the foam of the sea." [2]Epiphanius *On the Twelve Gems* 1 (PG 43:293). [3]Andrew is referring to Oecumenius.

let the reader decide. It makes better sense, however, to regard twelve of the elders to be illustrious men from the Old Testament and the other twelve elders to be men of eminence from the New Testament. To be sure, in the Old Testament the leading men were the twelve patriarchs, and in the New Testament the most eminent were the twelve apostles, who the Lord promised were to sit on twelve thrones.[4] The white garments are symbols of the pure life and of unceasing festivity and gladness. The crowns signify the victory that they achieved through their courage against the evil demons.

[4:5] ***From the throne issue flashes of lightning and voices and thunder.***

This passage shows how fearful and terrible God is to those unworthy of his longsuffering. However, the lightning and the thunder become, to those worthy of salvation, their enlightenment. The lightning enlightens the eyes of the mind, and the thunder falls on spiritual ears.

[4:5-6] ***And before the throne burn seven lamps of fire, which are the seven spirits of God; and before the throne there is as it were a sea of glass, like crystal.***

These spirits must either be regarded as the seven angels that are above all the others, as Irenaeus believes,[5] or they are the energies of the life-giving Spirit, which are mentioned by Isaiah.[6] The "sea of glass" signifies the multitude of the holy powers and the purity, spotlessness and utter quiet of the life that is to come. Perhaps the sea also represents the heavenly chambers that are inaccessible to us and covered by water, as the psalmist says.[7] And since to some it seems that the nature of heaven is like crystal,[8] it behooves us to consider whether the essence of that pavement trodden by God, having at once brightness and transparency, is not signified through these things. However, it is laughable to investigate those things that lie beyond our comprehension.

[4:6] ***And in the midst of the throne, and around the throne, are four living creatures, full of eyes in front and behind.***

Through this image the throne is shown to symbolize the kingdom of God and the final rest. In the midst of the throne and around the throne he saw the seraphim. Through the multitude of their eyes, he is taught that in the divine light they have the capacity to see God, and moreover that they are enlightened by God with the knowledge of those things that are future and of those things that are past.

[4:7] ***And the first living creature was like a lion, the second living creature like an ox, the third living creature had the face of a man, and the fourth living creature like a flying eagle.***

We know that Isaiah also saw these living creatures.[9] Some are of the opinion that these four shapes indicate the governance and preservation of the four elements by God or the dominion of God over the regions of the heaven, the earth, the sea and the underworld.[10] A more likely opinion is that of others who think that the four virtues or the four Evangelists are represented. According to the opinion of Irenaeus,[11] the lion shows fortitude and represents the Gospel of John, which speaks of the preexistent kingdom of Christ when it proclaims that "in the beginning was the Word."[12] Since it is satisfied with its own labors, the ox reveals righteousness and

[4]Mt 19:28. [5]Irenaeus *Haer.* 1.5.2 (ANF 1:322). [6]Is 11:2. [7]Ps 104:3 (103:3 LXX). [8]Andrew seems to have Oecumenius in mind. [9]Is 6:2. [10]Andrew has Oecumenius in mind. [11]Irenaeus *Haer.* 3.11.8 (ANF 1:428). [12]Jn 1:1.

represents the Gospel of Luke, for it presents the genealogy of Christ according both to the order of the Law and of the priesthood.[13] The eagle suggests temperance, for that virtue is characteristic of that creature, and so it represents the Gospel of Mark, which is brief and makes its beginning from the prophetic Spirit.[14] The image of the man indicates prudence and represents the Gospel of Matthew, which proclaims the birth of Christ as by nature and not by the Law.[15] These living creatures might similarly signify the economy of Christ. Through the lion Christ is represented as a king, through the ox as a priest or rather as sacrifice, through the man as the one who became man for us and through the eagle as the one who provides the life-giving Spirit that descends on us from above.

[4:8] *And the four living creatures, each of them with six wings, are full of eyes all round and within.*

According to the great Dionysius, these creatures hide their faces with two wings and hide their feet with two wings and with two fly,[16] so that their reverence concerning whatever is higher and deeper than their own understanding might be evident, yet according to the divine constraints they are uplifted through the middle wings of their understanding to the divine rays.[17]

[4:8] *And they have no rest by day or night, saying, "Holy, holy, holy, is the Lord God Almighty, who was and is and is to come!"*

There is no rest for these holy powers, for they never cease from their divine hymnody but proffer the threefold acclamation of holiness to the tri-hypostatic deity. For we have said that the phrase "who was and is and is to come" indicates the holy Trinity.[18]

[4:9-10] *And whenever the living creatures give glory and honor and thanks to him who is seated on the throne, who lives forever and ever, the twenty-four elders fall down before him who is seated on the throne and worship him who lives forever and ever.*

Through this verse it is shown that the aforementioned twenty-four elders participate in the hymnody of these heavenly powers, confessing that the power to achieve victory over their spiritual enemies was received from God.

[4:10-11] *And they cast their crowns before the throne, saying, "Worthy are you, our Lord and God, to receive glory and honor and power, for you did create all things, and by your will they exist and were created.*

You, O Master, he says, are the cause and the giver of the crowns of victory, and to you thanksgiving is owed by all things, for they are your creatures.

Chapter 11
Concerning the book sealed with seven seals that no creature can open

[5:1] *And I saw in the right hand of him who was seated on the throne a book written on the inside and on the outside, sealed with seven seals.*

We recognize the book to be the all-wise memory of God in which, according to David, all people are recorded,[19] as well as the depths of the divine judgments.[20] Those things written on the outside through the letter are more easily comprehended. Those things written on the inside through the Spirit are more difficult

[13]Lk 1:5-9; 3:23-38. [14]Mk 1:2-3. Andrew refers to the quotations from Mal 3:1; Is 40:3 at the beginning of Mark. [15]Mt 1:18-25. [16]See Is 6:2. [17]Pseudo-Dionysius *The Ecclesiastical Hierarchy* 4.3.8 (PG 3:481). [18]See the comment on Rev 1:4. [19]Ps 139:16 (138:16 LXX). [20]Ps 36:6 (35:6 LXX).

to decipher. The seven seals signify either the obscurity of the book that is known to no one or the economies of him "who searches the depths of the Spirit of God."[21] No created being is able to open these seals. The book also is understood to be the prophecy that Christ said in the Gospel of Luke was being fulfilled,[22] but the rest of the prophecy will be fulfilled in the last days.

[5:2-3] ***And I saw a strong angel proclaiming with a loud voice, "Who is worthy to open the book and to break its seals?" And no one in heaven or on earth or under the earth was able to open the book or to look into it.***

Through these words it is indicated that neither angels, nor persons who are in the flesh, nor the saints who have already departed the flesh can with certain knowledge comprehend the divine judgments. This is possible only by the Lamb of God who through his coming loosed the obscurity of those things prophesied long ago concerning him.

[5:4] ***And I wept much that no one was found worthy to open and to read the book or to look into it.***

"I wept," he says, perhaps because the purest order of the angelic beings had fallen into ignorance.

[5:5] ***And one of the elders said to me, "Weep not; behold, the Lion of the tribe of Judah, the Root of David, has conquered, so that he can open the book and its seven seals."***

Although the book is incomprehensible even to angels, he says, it is not to God who for the sake of humankind became man, who as the Creator is the Root of David according to his deity but is from the root of David according to his humanity.

Chapter 12
Concerning the vision in the midst of the throne and of the four living creatures

[5:6] ***And between the throne and the four living creatures and among the elders, I saw a Lamb standing as though it had been slain, with seven horns and with seven eyes, which are the spirits of God sent out into all the earth.***

The seven eyes and the seven horns of the Lamb indicate the seven spirits of Christ that Isaiah mentioned,[23] as did also the prophet Zechariah.[24] The phrase "as though slain" suggests the life he received after the slaughter, for in truth after the resurrection from the dead, as one who had been slain, he showed the tokens of his passion.[25]

[5:7-8] ***And he went and took the book from the right hand of him who was seated on the throne. And when he had taken the book, the four living creatures and the twenty-four elders fell down before the Lamb, each holding a harp, and with golden bowls full of incense, which are the prayers of the saints.***

The harps indicate the harmonious and melodious divine doxology, while the incense indicates the sweet-smelling sacrifice of the faithful that is offered through a most pure life, as the apostle says: "We are the aroma of Christ."[26] The bowls are symbolic of the thoughts from which the sweet aroma of good works and pure prayer come.

[5:9-10] ***And they sang a new song, saying: "Worthy are you to take the book and to open its seals, for you were slain and by your blood you ransomed us for God from every tribe and***

[21]See 1 Cor 2:10. [22]Lk 4:21. [23]Is 11:2. [24]Zech 4:10. [25]Lk 24:39; Jn 20:20. [26]2 Cor 2:15.

tongue and people and nation, and have made them kings and priests for our God, and they shall reign on earth."

Through this passage it is revealed that the elders, both those in the Old Testament and those in the New Testament, were well-pleasing to God, and that on behalf of the whole world they bring forth a hymn of thanksgiving to the Lamb of God who was slain and redeemed us. It is a "new song," which we have been taught to sing, who from every tribe and tongue have been freed from the antiquity of the letter and through the Spirit have received light. He says that these will rule the new earth, which the Lord promised to the humble.[27]

[5:11-13] ***And I looked, and I heard around the throne and the living creatures and the elders the voice of many angels, numbering myriads of myriads and thousands of thousands, saying with a loud voice, "Worthy is the Lamb who was slain, to receive power and wealth and wisdom and might and honor and glory!" And I heard every creature in heaven and on the earth and under the earth and in the sea, and all therein, saying, "To him who sits on the throne and to the Lamb be blessing and honor and glory and might forever and ever! Amen."***

From all beings, whether intelligent or sensible, whether living or simply existing in some way, God, as the creator of all things, is glorified by words proper to their natures. Also praised is his only-begotten and consubstantial Son who graciously renewed humankind and the creation that was made through him. And it is written that, as man, he received authority over all things in heaven and on the earth.[28]

[5:14] ***And the four living creatures said, "Amen!" and the elders fell down and worshiped.***

Through these words, one flock and one church from angels and from humankind is indicated that has been formed through Christ, the God who united that which was separate and has destroyed the partition wall of separation.[29] And so, as we have heard, with the four living creatures who surpass the other angelic ranks, also the elders, who represent the fullness of those who are being saved, are worthy of the hymn and worship of God. Of which may also we be found worthy in Christ, the giver of peace and our God, with whom together with the Father and the Holy Spirit be glory and might forever and ever. Amen.

BOOK FIVE

Chapter 13
The loosing of the first seal

[6:1] ***And I saw when the Lamb opened one of the seven seals, and I heard one of the four living creatures say, as with a voice of thunder: "Come!"***

Indeed, here is indicated the good order of those in heaven, which descends from the first ranks to the second. And therefore from one figure of the four-formed living creatures, namely, from the lion, he heard the first voice that gave the command "Come!" to the angel who mystically symbolizes the vision. The first living creature, the lion, seems to me to signify the royal intention of the apostles against the demons. Concerning them it is said, "Behold, the kings of the earth have gathered together."[1] And again: "You will establish them as rulers over all the earth."[2]

[6:2] ***And I saw, and behold, a white horse, and the one sitting on it had a bow; and a crown was given to him, and he went out conquering and to conquer.***

[27]Mt 5:5. [28]Mt 28:18. [29]Eph 2:14. **Book Five** [1]Ps 48:4 (47:4 LXX); also Ps 47:9 (46:9 LXX). [2]Ps 45:16 (44:16 LXX).

Some have interpreted the loosing of the present seal and all those that follow thereafter to refer to the incarnate economy of God the Word: the first seal referring to his birth, the second to his baptism, the third to the miracles after this, the fourth to his appearance before Pilate, the fifth to the cross, the sixth to the burial in the tomb, the seventh to the plundering of hell.[3] But we have read Methodius and note how he spoke concerning this text: It is not necessary to think "that Christ is the one who has been born; for the mystery of the incarnation of the Word was fulfilled long before the Apocalypse, whereas John speaks of things that are present or future."[4] In this passage Methodius is expounding the fall of the red dragon as though he were already subdued.[5] And so we understand the loosing of the first seal to signify the generation of the apostles. For, as though it were a bow, they stretched forth the gospel message against the demons and led to Christ those wounded by the arrows of salvation. And because they conquered the leader of deceit through the truth, they received a crown, and in hope they awaited a second victory, namely, the confession of the name of the Master to a violent death. Therefore, it is written, "he went out conquering and to conquer." For the first victory is the conversion of the nations; the second is the willing departure from the body in persecution for the sake of that conversion.

Chapter 14
The loosing of the second seal

[6:3] ***When he opened the second seal, I heard the second living creature say, "Come!"***

I suppose that the second living creature is the bull to depict the sacred sacrifices of the holy martyrs, since the first creature signified the apostolic authority, as we said.

[6:4] ***And out came another horse, bright red; it was permitted to its rider to take peace from the earth, so that people should slay one another; and he was given a great sword.***

We suggest that this second seal is to be interpreted as the succession of the apostles that is fulfilled through martyrs and teachers. During this succession, as the proclamation is extended abroad, the peace of the world is taken away, creation being divided against itself, as was spoken by the Lord: "I have not come to bring peace on earth, but a sword."[6] And by this sword the sacrifices of the martyrs are offered on the heavenly altar. The "red horse" is symbolic either of the shedding of blood or of the red-hot disposition of those who suffer for Christ. The words "it was permitted to its rider to take peace" show the all-wise permission of God that tests his faithful servants through temptations.

Chapter 15
The loosing of the third seal

[6:5] ***When he opened the third seal, I heard the third living creature say, "Come!"***

I believe that the third living creature here is the man and that this passage shows the fall of humanity, and for this reason their punishment because of their inclination toward sin by the power of free will.

[6:5-6] ***And I saw, and behold, a black horse, and its rider had a balance in his hand; and I heard what seemed to be a voice in the midst of the four living creatures saying, "A quart of wheat for a denarius, and three quarts of barley for a denarius; but do not harm oil and wine!"***

It is likely that an actual famine existed at that

[3]Andrew is referring to the interpretation of Oecumenius. [4]Methodius *Symp.* 8.7 (ACW 27:112). [5]Andrew is referring to the red dragon of Rev 12:3. [6]Mt 10:34.

time, as will be mentioned in comments that follow. We think that the "black horse" depicts the sorrow that comes on those who have fallen away from faith in Christ on account of the abundance of torments. The "balance" is he who tests those who either by inconstancy of mind or by vainglory have fallen from the faith through weakness of the body. The phrase "a quart of wheat for a denarius" figuratively indicates those who have struggled lawfully and have carefully preserved the divine image given to them. The phrase "three quarts of barley for a denarius" speaks of those who like cattle have through cowardice bowed the neck to persecutors but have later repented and have washed their defiled image with tears. The command "do not harm wine and oil" indicates that the healing of Christ through repentance, which healed him who fell among the thieves,[7] ought not be rejected, nor that those be allowed to be seized prematurely by death who through patience would be retrieved from defeat. Therefore, that we also might possess God as our beneficent physician for the suffering of our souls, let us be zealous to be such to our brothers who have fallen, bringing to them the wine of consolation mixed with the oil of compassion, "so that what is lame may not be put out of joint but rather be healed," as the apostle says.[8] And so becoming fellow workers with God, we may eternally enjoy his blessings by the grace and good will of our Lord, Jesus Christ, with whom to the Father together with the Holy Spirit be glory forever and ever. Amen.

BOOK SIX

Chapter 16

The loosing of the fourth seal revealing the tribulations coming on the impious

[6:7] ***When he opened the fourth seal, I heard the voice of the fourth living creature say, "Come!"***

The soaring flight and the swiftness on its prey of the fourth living creature, namely, the eagle, suggests those plagues that come from above, from the divine wrath for the vindication of the pious and for the punishment of the impious, unless these should turn from their sins through improvement.

[6:8] ***And I saw, and behold, a pale horse, and its rider's name was Death, and Hades follows him; and they were given power over a fourth of the earth, to kill with the sword and with famine and with death and by the beasts of the earth.***

This sequence of events has happened before and reflects also contemporary occurrences. For as Eusebius says in the eighth chapter of the ninth book of his Ecclesiastical History, at the height of the persecution, when Maximinus was Roman emperor, both famine and pestilence along with other things fell on them, so that such an innumerable multitude perished that they could not be buried. At that time indeed the Christians zealously undertook the task of burying the dead and by their love of humanity led those who had been deceived to the recognition of the truth. Moreover, the Armenians resisted the Romans, he says, so that many were killed with the sword and the bodies of the dead were eaten by dogs. Finally, those left alive began to kill the dogs, fearing that they themselves might die and that the living would become their tombs. For it was not impossible that even wild animals shared the same meal with dogs on account of the abundance of food.[1] We know that even in our

[7]Lk 10:30. [8]Heb 12:13. **Book Six** [1]Eusebius *Hist. eccl.* 9.8.1-12 (NPNF 2 1:361-62). Maximinus II Daia was a strong supporter of the traditional gods and a brutal persecutor of Christians. A member of the tetrarchy of Roman rulers, he initiated civil war against Licinius in 313 but was decisively defeated, dying in August 313. The war with the Armenians most likely occurred in November or December 312.

own times similar things have happened.

Chapter 17

The loosing of the fifth seal showing the entreaty of the saints to the Lord concerning the consummation

[6:9-10] ***When he opened the fifth seal, I saw under the altar the souls of the persons who had been slain for the Word of God and for the witness that they had; they cried out with a loud voice, "O sovereign Lord, the holy and true, how long before you will judge and avenge our blood from those who dwell on the earth?"***

Should anyone attempt to refer the loosing of the four seals to the previous works of Christ, he could rightly refer also this seal to the prophets and the other saints who had beforehand been sacrificed and cry out for the divine mercy, which from these martyrs until the cross had patiently endured the evil treatment from the Jews. But should one follow the teachers of the church and interpret these seals as prophecy of future events, he will regard such a plea as proper for those who have been slain for the sake of Christ and cry out against their persecutors, so that by it the worthy might repent and the impiety of the disobedient might be ended by the universal consummation, "lest the righteous put forth their hands to do wrong."[2] For if the ungodly had already at that time experienced the divine wrath, as it is said, their bodies would nonetheless have need of sufferings either for their correction or their punishment.

[6:11] ***And they were each given a white robe and told to rest a little longer, until the number of their fellow servants and their brothers should be completed, who were to be killed as they themselves had been.***

In this passage the saints are shown praying for the consummation of the world. Therefore, they are told to have patience until the completion of the brethren, so that "apart from them they would not be made perfect," as the apostle says.[3] The white robes reveal the brightness that appears on them because of their virtues, in which they are clothed, although they "had not yet received the promises."[4] And so, putting away every dullness, in the hope for these things, which they see in the spirit, they rightly rejoice, resting in the bosom of Abraham. For by many of the saints it is said that each receives a place worthy of the doer of virtue through which they are judged for their future glory.

Chapter 18

The loosing of the sixth seal showing the plagues that will come at the end of time

[6:12-13] ***And I looked, and when he opened the sixth seal, there was a great earthquake; and the sun became black as sackcloth, and the moon became like blood; and the stars of the sky fell to the earth as the fig tree sheds its fruit when shaken by a great wind.***

Some have understood all these things to refer to the siege under Vespasian, interpreting allegorically everything that is spoken.[5] However, we think that this passage presents the transition from the times of the persecutions to the time before the arrival of the false Christ. For it has been prophesied that at that time there would be such tribulations, such as we know have never happened before. Perhaps such prophecy was made so that those involved in them will not apostatize when the torments from the antichrist occur. Indeed, throughout the Scriptures "earthquake" often signifies the change of things. The phrase "once again I will shake"[6] signifies "the removal of what is

[2]Ps 125:3 (124:3 LXX). [3]Heb 11:40. [4]Heb 11:39. [5]Andrew apparently has Oecumenius in mind. [6]Hag 2:6; Heb 12:26.

shaken," as the apostle says.[7] And in the Old Testament it is said concerning the crossing of the Israelites from Egypt, "the earth quaked, the heavens poured."[8] The blackness of the sun and the dark, bloody appearance of the moon signify the darkness that will come on those overtaken by the wrath of God, as also the blessed Cyril often interpreted these things.[9] The phrase "the stars fell" was already written of those who were deceived by Antiochus.[10] It refers also to those who think themselves to be lights of the world but who will fall, being crushed by the events of that time, even as the Lord said, "to lead astray, if it were possible, even the elect by the great tribulation."[11] This is perhaps the reason the fig tree is taken as a parable, for when the wind of the devil shakes it, it casts down its immature fruit that is not yet ripened by the heat of temptations or made sweet by grace. We know that this can be understood in either a good or in a bad sense, whether from the two baskets of good and evil figs that appear in Jeremiah[12] or from the fig tree that Christ made to wither[13] or that mentioned in the Song.[14] But whether these things will occur in a visible manner when Christ comes in glory as judge, only he knows who has the hidden treasuries of wisdom and knowledge.

[6:14] ***The sky vanished like a scroll that is rolled out.***

That heaven is rolled out as a scroll symbolizes either that the second coming of Christ is unknown—for the book is opened noiselessly and quickly—or that even the heavenly powers grieve for those who have fallen from faith as though they experience a certain rolling out through sympathy and grief. However, this image symbolizes also something else, namely, that the substance of heaven does not disappear, but as though by a certain rolling up changes into something better. As Irenaeus says in the fifth book of his Overthrow of Falsely-Named Knowledge, "For neither is the substance nor the essence of the creation annihilated—for faithful and true is he who has established it—but 'the fashion of this world passes away,'[15] within which the transgression occurred, as the elders say."[16] While the great Irenaeus thinks these things, we think that the apostle is using the image of an old custom. For the Hebrews used scrolls rather than the codices, which are common among us. The rolling out of a scroll did not cause anything to disappear but effected the appearance of that written within. So also the opening of the heavenly body shows the revelation of the blessings that lie in wait for the saints. We have understood this passage in a fourfold manner in proportion to that which has been supplied to us from God. We follow closely now what follows.

[6:14-17] ***And every mountain and island was removed from its place. Then the kings of the earth and the great men and the rich and the generals and the strong, and everyone, slave and free, hid themselves in the caves and among the rocks of the mountains, calling to the mountains and rocks, "Fall on us and hide us from the face of him who is seated on the throne and from the wrath of the Lamb; for the great day of his wrath has come, and who can stand before it?"***

Our Lord asked the disciples concerning the destruction of the temple in Jerusalem and concerning the consummation of the world, and as they were able to receive, he foretold of the coming events. To some extent these

[7]Heb 12:27. [8]Ps 68:8 (67:8 LXX). [9]See Cyril of Alexandria *Adoration in Spirit and in Truth* 9 (PG 68:641). [10]See 2 Macc 4:7–5:27. [11]Mt 24:24. [12]Jer 24:1-5. [13]Mt 21:19-20. [14]Song 2:13. [15]1 Cor 7:31. [16]Irenaeus *Haer.* 5.36.1 (ANF 1:566). See also Tertullian *Against Hermogenes* 34 (ANF 3:496-97). See Rev 20:11 below.

events have already happened to the Jews who killed Christ during the siege under Vespasian and Titus, as the Jew, Josephus, recounts it.[17] But at the end, with a superabundance beyond everything, so to speak, these things will come on the world at the coming of the antichrist, as he is called. At that time, the great men, whether those who hold office in the church or those who possess worldly power—here figuratively called "mountains"—and the churches of the faithful—metaphorically called "islands"—that "are keeping a feast to God," as Isaiah said,[18] they will flee from their places, changing from place to place on account of the false christ. And these things also we have benevolently experienced on account of our sins before his coming.

"The kings of the earth," that is, those who exert power over it[19] and possess nothing in heaven, they too shall pray with all the great and with those who are rich in the things below and with the servants of the things below and those free of the service of Christ, that they be hidden by the caves and the rocks and the mountains. For they do not want to experience the divine wrath that with divine consent will pour down on them either at the coming of the antichrist in the form of punishments from famine and other plagues or in endless torments that are expected after the resurrection. For then the divine anger will burn righteously as a furnace,[20] consuming those who built on the foundation of faith with wood and chaff and stubble,[21] as though food for the fire. From this may the benevolent God redeem us and make us to be partakers in the eternal rewards that are prepared for his saints, arranging us with the fullness of those who are being saved by the grace of his only-begotten Son, with whom be glory and worship to the Father together with the Holy Spirit forever. Amen.

BOOK SEVEN

Chapter 19

Concerning the 144,000 saved from the plagues of the four angels

[7:1] ***After these things I saw four angels standing at the four corners of the earth, holding back the four winds of the earth, that no wind might blow on earth or sea or against any tree.***

These things are thought by some to have occurred long ago to the Jews at the hands of the Romans. They think that the four divine angels reveal the impossibility for those who were experiencing the wrath to escape either on the land or on the sea.[1] However, how much more will these things occur at the coming of the antichrist, and not only partially in the land of the Jews, but over the whole world at whose four corners the angels stand fulfilling a service assigned to them by God, but unknown to us. The holding back of the winds reveals clearly the dissolution of the good order of creation and the inevitability of evil. For by means of wind the plants of the earth are nourished and ships sail the sea.

[7:2-3] ***And I saw another angel ascend from the rising of the sun, with the seal of the living God, and he called with a loud voice to the four angels who had been given power to harm earth and sea, saying:***

This was revealed long ago to Ezekiel concerning him who was clothed in a fine linen robe and who sealed the foreheads of those who mourned so that the righteous would not be destroyed along with the wicked,[2] since the virtue of the saints is hidden and is unknown even to the angels. This is shown also here

[17]Josephus *J.W.* 5–6. [18]Is 41:1; 45:16 (LXX). [19]Mt 20:25. [20]Mal 4:1. [21]1 Cor 3:12. **Book Seven** [1]Andrew has the interpretation of Oecumenius in mind. [2]Ezek 9:2-11.

to the blessed John, that a preeminent holy power encourages the avenging holy angels to do nothing until they might recognize the servants of the truth by virtue of their having been sealed. Although this has happened partially long ago when those who believed in Christ fled from the siege of Jerusalem by the Romans into very many destinations, the great James having showed to blessed Paul their great number,[3] then, as has been said, this will especially occur at the coming of the antichrist when the seal of the life-giving cross will separate from the faithless the faithful who bear without shame and with boldness the sign of Christ before the impious. Therefore, the angel says,

[7:3] ***"Do not harm the earth or the sea or the trees, until we have sealed the servants of our God on their foreheads."***

Just as the creation, created for our sakes, shares in the torments with us who are being chastised, so too it will be made clean with the saints who are being glorified.[4] Through these words we learn that the virtuous will require the power of angelic assistance before the arrival of the trials by way of the seal of the Spirit that is given to us. This seal will reveal its power to that extent that we add our own work to it, for everything remains without aid that by its own will wills not to be aided.

[7:4-8] ***And I heard the number of the sealed, a hundred and forty-four thousand sealed, out of every tribe of the sons of Israel; twelve thousand sealed out of the tribe of Judah.***

Judah is interpreted "confession."[5] Through him those are manifested who are being saved through the confession to Christ who came forth as a branch from Judah.

Twelve thousand sealed out of the tribe of Reuben.

Reuben is interpreted "son of vision."[6] Through him those are shown who possess spiritual sight through purity of heart.[7]

Twelve thousand of the tribe of Gad.

Gad is interpreted "temptation."[8] Through him those are shown who through the endurance of temptations are being crowned, after the example of Job.[9]

Twelve thousand of the tribe of Asher.

Asher is interpreted "blessing."[10] Through him are revealed those who are worthy of dominical blessings because of their life and are made worthy of standing at the right hand of Christ[11] and are shown to be children of the light and of the day.[12]

Twelve thousand of the tribe of Naphtali.

Naphtali is interpreted "prayer." Through him those are characterized who are bound to God through unceasing prayer.

Twelve thousand of the tribe of Manasseh.

Manasseh is interpreted "forgetfulness."[13] He represents those who, on account of love for God, have forgotten the things from the past and their paternal homes.[14]

Twelve thousand of the tribe of Simeon.

Simeon is interpreted "obedience."[15] He clearly refers to those who are becoming righteous through obedience to the divine commandments.

[3]Acts 21:20. [4]Rom 8:19-22. [5]Philo *Somn.* 2.34. [6]Philo *Somn.* 2.33; *Mut.* 98. [7]See Mt 5:8. [8]Philo *Somn.* 2.35. [9]See Job 42. [10]Philo *Somn.* 2.35. [11]See Mt 25:33-34. [12]See 1 Thess 5:5. [13]Philo *Mut.* 99–100. [14]See Gen 41:51. [15]Philo *Somn.* 2.34; *Mut.* 99.

Twelve thousand of the tribe of Levi.

Levi is interpreted "having been taken up."[16] Through him those are indicated who have been taken up by Christ through a life proper to the priesthood. Levi is listed eighth, since by the eighth day of the resurrection the true priesthood is made known.

Twelve thousand of the tribe of Issachar.

Issachar is interpreted "reward."[17] He represents those who for the sake of the rewards from God have lived virtuously.

Twelve thousand of the tribe of Zebulun.

Zebulun is interpreted "abode of power" or "fragrance." Through him those are indicated who by the indwelling of Christ have been made firm against sufferings and have become his sweet smell, as Paul says.[18]

Twelve thousand of the tribe of Joseph.

Joseph is interpreted "addition."[19] That is, he represents those who in addition to the kingdom of heaven receive those things necessary for eternal life, as the Lord says.[20]

Twelve thousand sealed out of the tribe of Benjamin.

Benjamin means "son of sorrow"[21] or "son of day"[22] or "son of my right hand." He indicates those with sorrow in their heart. This refers either to those believers from the Jews who fled the siege of the Romans and equaled this number, or, what is rather more likely, to those from the Jews who are saved at the consummation when, as the apostle puts it, after "the full number of the Gentiles come in, all Israel will be saved."[23] Either interpretation is acceptable. The exact equality of each tribe seems to me to show the utter fruitfulness of the apostolic seed, since twelve multiplied by twelve and multiplied by the perfect number of a thousand yields the thousands here indicated. For these were the disciples of that seed that out of love for humankind fell on the earth and brought forth the various fruits of universal salvation.

And this is to be noted, that the tribe of Dan, out of which the antichrist is to be born, is not arranged with the other tribes.[24] Instead of it the tribe of Levi is mentioned, which as the priestly tribe of old had not entered into the division among the tribes.[25]

From the interpretation of the names there is a certain understanding that is suitable to each of the tribes, as is provided in the next examples. He has listed Joseph instead of Ephraim, his son. As we have said, the number given is suitable to these, as it is said, both because of the twelve patriarchs of the ancient Hebrews and because of the holy apostles who instead of them "were established as rulers on all the earth," as it is written,[26] and through whom the Jews in the diaspora of the earth are saved in the last days.

[This is an opportunity to complete the task, for we often find in holy Scriptures that parents give names to their offspring because of things that have either occurred or have been said.[27] About Leah it is written that when she was giving birth she said, "The Lord has seen my humiliation," and named the child Reuben, which means "son of vision."[28] And when she gave birth a second time, she said, "The Lord has heard that I am hated," and she

[16]Philo *Somn.* 2.34. [17]Gen 30:18; Philo *Somn.* 2.34. [18]2 Cor 2:15. [19]Gen 30:24; Philo *Somn.* 2.47; *Mut.* 89–90. [20]Mt 6:33. [21]Gen 35:18; Philo *Mut.* 94–96. [22]Philo *Somn.* 2.36; *Mut.* 92–93. [23]Rom 11:25-26. [24]See Irenaeus *Haer.* 5.30.2 (ANF 1:559); Hippolytus *Antichr.* 14 (ANF 5:207). [25]See Deut 10:9; 12:12. [26]Ps 45:16 (44:16 LXX). [27]Some manuscripts of Andrew's commentary give this second, and probably less authentic, interpretation of the twelve names of the patriarchs. Some manuscripts provide both versions. [28]Gen 29:32.

named the child Simeon, which means "having heard."[29] He read also that when Rachel was in hard labor, she named the child "son of sorrow" from what had happened.[30] And there are other such names that are familiar to those well-versed in the divine texts.

For this reason, we have considered the explanation of the patriarchal names and think that the tribe of Judah, which means "confession," symbolizes those who are being saved through repentance and love of the Lord who sprouted from Judah and who justified a tax collector and a prostitute and a thief.[31] The tribe of Reuben, which means "son of one who sees" or "son of vision," represents those who are pure in heart and see by the Spirit.[32] The tribe of Gad, which means "temptation" or "ordeal," symbolizes those who through trials and tribulations are being "refined as gold" and crowned by the "genuineness of faith."[33] The tribe of Asher, which signifies "blessing," indicates those who by holding fast to the blessings that are taught of God will attain the everlasting bliss of the eternal praises. The tribe of Naphtali, which is interpreted "understanding" or "stump,"[34] represents those who cling with understanding to the stump of the Lord's cross and by it crush the demons. The tribe of Manasseh, which is interpreted "from forgetfulness," symbolizes those who for the sake of Christ "forget the father's house" so that "the king might desire the beauty"[35] of their souls and find them worthy to be invited to the mystical wedding. The tribe of Simeon, which indicates "attentiveness," represents those who through good works are attentive to the commandments of God. The tribe of Levi, which indicates "one who is accepted," symbolizes those who "are chosen and accepted by God," as the psalm says, and "will dwell in the courts of God."[36] Since they will serve as priests on the eighth day that is after the present age of seven days, the tribe of Levi is numbered in eighth place. The same is also first, since everyone does not attain one continuous path.

The tribe of Issachar, which means "reward," represents those who dedicate themselves to works of virtue for the reward of future prizes and sincerely pursue them for the sake of good itself. The tribe of Zebulun, which is interpreted "change is accepted," symbolizes those who give up their transient wealth to the poor and "are received by Christ,"[37] and who heal the mutability of material gain, which is born of vanity, by remembering the fire of Gehenna. The tribe of Joseph, which means "the Lord is gain," symbolizes those who along with the kingdom of heaven receive as though by addition all the necessities of life from the true Lord.[38] Such are indicated by the divine name Jaoth.[39] The tribe of Benjamin, which is interpreted "son of sorrow" or "son of day," represents those who because of "the multitude of sorrows in the heart," as the psalm says,[40] and moreover because of the abundance of bodily sufferings they have displayed for the sake of Christ, have become "sons of light and sons of day."[41] Such interpretations on the basis of the names are for an exercise for those more skilled in the discernment of the Scriptures.[42] In our opinion the tribe of Dan is omitted not only because the antichrist was to arise from it, as we noted, but also because it is a burdensome thing "to judge the servant of another."[43] For this reason the Lord says, "Judge not, that you be not judged."[44] For "there is one lawgiver and judge," as the great James says.[45] Dan is interpreted "judgment."]

[29]Gen 29:34. [30]Gen 35:16-18. [31]Lk 7:31-50; 18:9-14; 19:1-10; 23:39-43. [32]Mt 5:5. [33]1 Pet 1:7. [34]Gen 49:21. [35]Ps 45:10-11 (44:10-11 LXX). [36]Ps 65:4 (64:4 LXX). [37]Rom 15:7. [38]See Mt 6:33. [39]The divine name is ιαωθ. Most likely for Andrew the name indicates "the Lord of hosts," or "the Lord almighty." The form ιαωθ probably reflects "God Sabaoth" (ιαω σαβαωθ). According to Irenaeus, ιαωθ was a name for God among the Gnostics (*Haer.* 2.35.3). [40]Ps 94:19 (93:19 LXX). [41]1 Thess 5:5. [42]Translating πρὸς γυμνασίαν τοῖς ἐντρεχεστέροις τὴν διάνοιαν. [43]Rom 14:4. [44]Mt 7:1. [45]Jas 4:12.

Chapter 20
Concerning the numberless throng from the nations who wear bright robes

[7:9-10] ***After this I looked, and behold, a great multitude that no one could number, from every nation, from all tribes and peoples and tongues, standing before the throne and before the Lamb, clothed in white robes, with palm branches in their hands, and crying out with a loud voice, "Salvation belongs to our God who sits on the throne, and to the Lamb!"***

These are the ones of whom David spoke: "I shall number them, and they will be more than the sand."[46] Namely, these are those who long ago struggled as martyrs for the sake of Christ and those from every tribe and tongue who will fight valiantly at the end of time. By the outpouring of their own blood for the sake of Christ, some have made white and others will make white the robes of their deeds. And they have in their hands palm branches, which are symbolic of victory and which are good, straight and white as are their hearts. And they form a chorus around the divine throne of the godly rest, as grateful family members ascribing the victory over the demons to him who provides it.

[7:11-12] ***And all the angels stood round the throne and round the elders and the four living creatures, and they fell on their faces before the throne and worshiped God, saying, "Amen! Blessing and glory and wisdom and thanksgiving and honor and power and strength be to our God forever and ever! Amen."***

Behold the one church of angels and of people! Long ago angels appeared amazing to persons who were equal to the angels, as we know from Daniel.[47] Then in the future they will become the fellow ministers of people, whether, as some of the saints say, being manifested in their own bodies, which are spatially circumscribed, or, as others say, not appearing in their own nature, not having the threefold distinction of length and width and depth, which is common to bodies.[48] Rather, they will be modeled and given a form that seems good to God. However, standing around the seraphim and the elders they display by that position the greatness of the dignity they enjoy. Those who are represented by the number of the elders are given honor by this dignity. Through them all thanksgiving on our behalf will be sent up to God for those works that he has done according to his own nature toward his creation.

[7:13-14] ***Then one of the elders addressed me, saying, "Who are these, clothed in white robes, and from where have they come?" I said to him, "My lord, you know."***

Through his question one who was seen in the vision arouses the saint to ask about those things that were seen. And he who prudently acknowledges his ignorance is made wise by the one in the vision.

[7:14-15] ***And he said to me, "These are they who have come out of the great tribulation; they have washed their robes and made them white in the blood of the Lamb. Therefore are they before the throne of God and serve him day and night within his temple; and he who sits on the throne will dwell on them."***

Blessed are those who through temporary sufferings receive the fruit of eternal rest, and by suffering with Christ also reign with him and serve him continuously. In this passage, the words "day and night" indicate the absence of cessation or end, for then there will be no night.[49] Rather, there will be one day that is illumined by the Sun of righteousness, not by

[46]Ps 139:18 (138:18 LXX). [47]Dan 10:4-9. [48]Andrew probably has Origen in mind. [49]See Rev 21:25; 22:5.

the sun that we see with our eyes. In like manner, "night" refers to the hidden and deep mysteries of knowledge, while "day" refers to the mysteries that are open and easily obtained. "His temple" is the entire creation, which is being renewed through the Spirit, but especially it is those who have preserved the living and unquenchable guarantee of the Spirit,[50] for among them he has promised to dwell and to walk.[51]

[7:16] *"They shall hunger no more, neither thirst any more."*

This is rightly spoken. For they will have the bread from heaven[52] and the water of life.[53]

[7:16] *"The sun will not fall on them, nor any scorching heat."*

They will no longer be oppressed by temptations, which are here symbolized by the sun and its heat, since the time of struggles has passed away.

[7:17] *"For the Lamb in the midst of the throne will feed them as a shepherd and will guide them to springs of living water; and God will take away every tear from their eyes."*

He says that those who at that time are led by Christ as their shepherd will not fear the attacks of the wolves, since the wolves will be sent to the unquenchable fire. Rather, they will be led to the pure and clear fountains of divine thoughts, for the image of water already indicates the abundant stream of the divine Spirit. For concerning the one who believes in him in a pure way the Lord said, "Rivers of living water will flow from his belly."[54] From this fount the saints will at that time drink abundantly, and they will be in infinite joy and gladness, possessing perfect knowledge after being rid of partial knowledge and having become rid of the change that comes with corruption.

Chapter 21

The loosing of the seventh seal showing the angelic powers bringing to God the prayers of the saints as incense

[8:1-2] *When he opened the seventh seal, there was silence in heaven for about half an hour. Then I saw the seven angels who stand before the throne of God, and seven trumpets were given to them.*

Often the number seven is taken by this saint to correspond to this age and the sabbath rest of the saints. Therefore, also here at the loosing of the seventh seal, the dissolution of the earthly city is signified, the seven angels administering the torments against those people who are deserving of chastisement or punishment. The silence reveals the good order and piety of the angels as well as the fact that the second coming of Christ is unknown, even to angels. The half hour shows the shortness of time, for when as the plagues come and the events of consummation on the earth are occurring, the kingdom of Christ will appear.

[8:3] *And another angel came and stood at the altar with a golden censer.*

Although what is revealed to the saints is depicted in material form and with colors, whether it is the altar or the censer or something else, in reality these things are invisible and intellectual. And it is at such an altar that the angel stands and swings the censer (that is, that bowl that receives incense) bearing to God the prayers of the saints as though they were incense. The saints pray that God would lessen the avenging torments of the wicked and trans-

[50]See 2 Cor 1:22; 5:5. [51]2 Cor 6:16. [52]Jn 6:31-51. [53]Jn 4:10; 7:38; Rev 21:6; 22:1, 17. [54]Jn 7:38.

gressors at the consummation of all things and that at his coming he would reward those who had labored for Christ. And this is shown by what follows.

[8:3] ***And he was given much incense so that he might place the prayers of the saints on the golden altar before the throne.***

The altar is Christ, on which every ministering and holy power is established and on which the sacrifices of the martyrs are offered. This altar was prefigured in the altar that was shown to Moses on Mount Sinai together with the tabernacle.[55] The incense is the prayers of the saints, which to God are as a sweet-smelling fragrance, as has been said.[56] He says that the altar, namely, Christ, is "before the throne," that is, before the most eminent and holy of powers who are there because of the abundance of the divine love and of the pure wisdom and knowledge in them. This is shown by the interpretation of the names of those most high powers that are closest to God.

[8:4-5] ***And the smoke of the incense rose with the prayers of the saints from the hand of the angel before God. Then the angel received the censer and filled it with fire from the altar and threw it on the earth.***

The prayers of the saints offered through an administering angel cause the censer filled with the avenging fire to be poured out on the earth. This is just as it was revealed long ago to Ezekiel by one of the cherubim, that he should receive from such a fire and give it to the angels that they might send the fire for the punishment of the wicked inhabitants of Jerusalem.[57] And every high priest is representative of such an angel, for as a mediator between God and people, he carries up their petitions and brings down God's redemption, and he turns some sinners to repentance either by word or by a harsher discipline.

[8:5-6] ***And there were voices, peals of thunder, flashes of lightning and an earthquake. And the seven angels who had the seven trumpets readied themselves to blow them.***

Through all of these the horrors that are to occur before the consummation are indicated. It was the same on Mount Sinai when such wonders were symbols making known the divine presence, frightening everyone and persuading the more sensible of them to repentance. By such things the angels render their service. They are like empathetic physicians who by cauteries and surgery heal, in imitation of Christ, those who have become weak by that fearful disease of sin. Or in an appropriate manner they ameliorate the coming punishment for the indifferent, if in some way they demonstrate thankfulness. That he might not give us over to the death of sin, however, our beneficent Lord chastens us who have been sealed by the precious name of Christ and who desire the glory of the saints and pray for escape from the suffering and pains that will come at that time. Rather, as it is written, he will "give to us rest from the evil days" of eternal torments, when a "pit is dug" for the inventor of sin,[58] namely, the dark and exceedingly deep pit of Gehenna. We, however, will receive "the dwelling of all who rejoice,"[59] for dwelling with the saints we will be with the Savior, Christ, our God, to whom be all praise, honor and worship, together with the Father and the all-holy Spirit, now and always, and forever and ever. Amen.

BOOK EIGHT

Chapter 22

Concerning the seven angels who at the

[55]Ex 25:1–27:19. [56]2 Cor 2:15. [57]Ezek 10:6-7. [58]Ps 94:12-13 (93:12-13 LXX). [59]Ps 86:7 (LXX).

sound of the first trumpet throw hail, fire and blood on the earth

[8:7] ***The first angel blew his trumpet, and there was hail and fire mixed with blood. And it was thrown down on the earth, and a third of the earth was burned up, and a third of the trees were burned up, and all green grass was burned up.***

Some have interpreted these things to depict the punishment of sinners in Gehenna, which is symbolically described as various kinds of physical torment.[1] However, we think it more likely that the third portion is not of those punished from the totality of people who will be punished in the coming age but rather—"for the way that leads to destruction is broad"[2]—this passage shows the plagues that will occur before the consummation. The hail indicates the scourgings that will come from heaven for righteous judgment, and the fire mixed with blood indicates the destruction by fire and slaughter at the hands of the barbarians that will occur almost daily.[3] And, as we see, by these torments not less than one third of all the creatures on earth will be physically killed, for wars destroy not only human beings but also everything produced on the earth. And the blessed Joel confirms our understanding of what will come when he says, "Blood and fire and vapor of smoke will come before the great day."[4]

Chapter 23

Concerning the second angel and the destruction of living things in the sea

[8:8-9] ***The second angel blew his trumpet, and something like a great mountain burning with fire was thrown into the sea; and a third of the sea became blood, a third of the living creatures in the sea died, and a third of the ships were destroyed.***

We are aware that according to the opinion of some this shows the sea with those in it burning by a purifying fire after the resurrection.[5] However, the mention of a third seems to us ill-suited for this interpretation. For, as it is said, those who are being punished are more than those being saved. But according to the anagogical sense there is nothing wrong with thinking that the present life is figuratively called a sea. Through the depths of the divine judgments it supports some and destroys with plagues the third of those in it, punishing some immediately but showing longsuffering to others for their change and repentance. As some of our teachers think, we think that the great mountain is the devil,[6] who burns with the fire of wrath against us but who will be bound in Gehenna. But during the time allowed to him he will destroy a third of the islands and ships in the sea and that which swims in it, even as long ago he did to Job.[7] For he is an enemy and an accuser against the righteous judgment of God. For "to that which one is submitted, to that one is a slave."[8] It would not be foreign or contrary to the intention of this passage to say that the death of the soul comes on those who in the sea of life blaspheme the Trinity through works or words.

Chapter 24

Concerning the third angel and the bitterness of the waters of the rivers

[8:10-11] ***And the third angel blew his trumpet, and a great star fell from heaven burning like a torch, and it fell on a third of the rivers and on the fountains of waters. The name of***

Book Eight [1]Andrew has the interpretation of Oecumenius in mind. [2]Mt 7:13. [3]Andrew is perhaps referring to the invasion of the Huns in 515. [4]Joel 2:30-31 (3:3-4 LXX). [5]Andrew is referring to Oecumenius. [6]Andrew is the first Greek commentator to give this interpretation of the mountain. We do not know who these teachers are. Among Latin commentators of Revelation, the Venerable Bede and Beatus of Liebana also interpret the mountain to be the devil. [7]See Job 1:1–2:13. [8]See 2 Pet 2:19.

the star is Wormwood. A third of the waters became wormwood, and many people died of the water, because it was made bitter.

Some say that the bitterness revealed through the wormwood is symbolic of the torment that comes to those sinners being punished in Gehenna, who, on account of their number, are reasonably called "waters."[9] But we think that these depictions signify the sufferings at the time that has been revealed. The star indicates either that these things come on people from heaven, or it refers to the devil, of whom Isaiah says: "How has the Day Star, which rose in the morning, fallen from heaven."[10] For through pleasure he gives people a foul and bitter destruction to drink and through this he is allowed at that time to bring on them punishing torments. However, he does not bring torment on everyone, but by the longsuffering of God to a third part lest harboring doubt about the coming retribution become a cause of spiritual death to those who fail to endure. For especially the Lord made clear the certainty that these bitter torments would occur to those who are living before the consummation,[11] of which those who are seen in the vision are precursors. It is necessary, therefore, that we examine ourselves lest we be judged. As the holy apostle says, "For if we judged ourselves, we would not be judged, but when we are judged by the Lord, we are chastened,"[12] and we receive the sufferings that come on us with thanksgiving. For we notice that those who are concerned about sicknesses in the body bear patiently the cuts and cauteries of the physician, for they desire to be healed. Therefore, we should examine ourselves so that being spiritually healthy and bringing no wood to fuel the fire of Gehenna, we might not be condemned with the world but eternally rule with Christ, to whom belong glory, honor and worship, together with the Father and the Holy Spirit forever. Amen.

BOOK NINE

Chapter 25

Concerning the fourth angel and the darkening of the lights

[8:12] ***The fourth angel blew his trumpet, and a third of the sun was struck, and a third of the moon, and a third of the stars, so that a third of them was darkened, and a third of the day did not shine, and likewise the night.***

We think that this is similar to what Joel said concerning the sun and moon[1] and which according to dominical decree is already determined for the consummation. We repeat that the "third part of the lights and the stars" indicates a third part of the day and of the night. For we understand that at that time God will not bring the disaster totally but will allow those who are smitten to suffer one third at a time. He secretly exhorts those who make up the greater part. For who can endure the cup of divine wrath unmixed?

[8:13] ***Then I looked, and I heard an angel crying with a loud voice, as it flew in midheaven, "Woe, woe, woe to those who dwell on the earth, at the blasts of the other trumpets that the three angels are about to blow."***

This passage shows the sympathy and goodness of the holy angels, who, like God, are merciful toward the transgressors who are being chastised, and especially toward those who do not recognize that their suffering is for the purpose of their conversion. For these especially the woe is fitting, since they live on the earth, think earthly thoughts and exhale dust rather than the perfume that has been

[9]Andrew is referring to Oecumenius. [10]Is 14:12. [11]Mt 24:29. [12]1 Cor 11:31-32. **Book Nine** [1]Joel 3:4.

poured out for us. For those whose citizenship is in heaven,[2] the sufferings become the cause of unfading crowns and rewards.

Chapter 26

Concerning the fifth angel and the spiritual locusts and their various forms

[9:1-5] ***And the fifth angel blew his trumpet, and I saw a star fallen from heaven to earth, and he was given the key of the shaft of the bottomless pit; he opened the shaft of the bottomless pit, and from the shaft rose smoke like the smoke of a great furnace, and the sun and the air were darkened with the smoke from the shaft. Then from the smoke came locusts on the earth, and they were given power like the power of scorpions on the earth; they were told not to harm the grass of the earth or any green growth or any tree, but only those of humankind who have not the seal on their foreheads; they were allowed to torture them for five months but not to kill them, and their torture was like the torture of a scorpion when it stings a person.***

Some claim that the star fallen to the earth, that is, to the Valley of Josaphat, which has been set aside for judgment,[3] is a divine angel come for punishment. The "shaft of the bottomless pit" is Gehenna, out of which comes smoke that darkens the sun and the air for those who are to be punished. The locusts are those worms of which the prophet spoke: "Their worm shall not die."[4] These worms will torment only human persons, not the earth or any plant, because these are to be set free from that corruption to which they at the present time are subjected because of us.[5] They are tormented for five months; that is, for a certain determined period of time they are tormented with great intensity, but afterward less intensely, nonetheless eternally.[6] I am also of the opinion that the star is a divine angel who with God's permission leads up from the pit the evil demons who have been condemned to the pit, namely, those whom Christ bound at his incarnation. He leads them up so that they might do their work before the consummation but then attain to never-ending torment.

The smoke symbolizes the darkness that precedes the evil deeds done at the demons' instigation, and when such works are shown, authority to torment human beings is given to them. The darkening of the sun and of the air reveals the spiritual blindness of those who benefit from their light. It may also indicate the disposition that comes on the hateful, for in difficulties darkness can be regarded as light. That these spiritual locusts sting people after the manner of scorpions shows the baneful death of the soul that lies hidden at the end of evil deeds. Those are subjected to such a death who have not signed their forehead with the divine seal and with the enlightenment of the life-giving cross through the Holy Spirit, so that, as the Lord says, "they may let their light shine before people for the glory of the divine name."[7] We think that the five months of their torment signifies either the shortness of time—"For had those days not been shortened, no flesh would have been saved,"[8] as the Lord says—or a certain five-day period representing the five senses through which sin enters into people, or a determined period that is known to God alone.

[9:6] ***And in those days people will seek death and will not find it; they will long to die, and death will flee from them.***

Through these words the magnitude of the evils is revealed. For it is common among those in severe troubles to call on death. But it is

[2]Phil 3:20. [3]Joel 3:12, 14. [4]Is 66:24. [5]Rom 8:21. [6]To this point Andrew has summarized the interpretations of Oecumenius. [7]Mt 5:16. [8]Mt 25:22.

from the judgments of God that death does not come to those in the midst of trouble who seek it. For he considers it beneficial to use the bitterness of the tribulations that come to make hateful that sin that was the mother and patron of their torments.

[9:7-9] ***In appearance the locusts were like horses arrayed for battle; on their heads were what looked like crowns of gold; their faces were like human faces, their hair like women's hair, and their teeth like lions' teeth; they had scales like iron breastplates.***

Some have interpreted these words and those that come afterward to indicate that the locusts are angels who administer the divine punishment and who are metaphorically described through each of the various images. These images would then describe either their fearsomeness and the panic they arouse or their swiftness or the destruction that comes on those worthy of condemnation in Gehenna.[9] However, I think that the image of these locusts depicts rather evil demons who are prepared for war against us and who wear on their heads crowns as of gold in expectation of victory against us. Whenever we submit to these demons and win an evil victory through pleasure, we believe ourselves also to be crowned with such crowns. That their hair is like that of women reveals their love of luxury and their arousal to fornication. The teeth like those of a lion signify their murderous and poisonous character, and their iron breastplates show the hardness of their hearts.

[9:9-12] ***And the noise of their wings was like the noise of many chariots with horses rushing into battle. They have tails like scorpions, and stings in their tails. And they have power to hurt people for five months. They have as king over them the angel of the bottomless pit; his name in Hebrew is Abaddon, and in the Greek he is called Apollyon. The first woe has passed; behold, two woes are still to come.***

We think that the sound of the wings of these spiritual locusts is said to resemble the sound of war chariots because of their speed in the air. For, as the blessed David says, "They make war on us from on high."[10] And their tails, which are like those of scorpions, symbolize the result of sins, the producing of spiritual death. For "sin when it is perfected brings forth death."[11] The five-month trial that comes on humankind refers either to the five senses or to a period of time, short when compared with the coming age yet not understood by us. It follows that the devil is to be regarded as their king, for he certainly destroys those who obey him. In order that we might wage an unremitting war against him, the passage threatens us with the two woes that are yet to come.

Chapter 27
Concerning the sixth angel and the angels loosed at the Euphrates

[9:13-16] ***The sixth angel blew his trumpet, and I heard a voice from the four corners of the golden altar before God, saying to the sixth angel who had the trumpet, "Release the four angels who are bound at the great river Euphrates." So the four angels were released, who had been held ready for the hour, the day, the month and the year, to kill a third of humankind. The number of the troops of cavalry was twice ten thousand times ten thousand. I heard their number.***

Some say that these four angels are Michael, Gabriel, Uriel and Raphael. Although bound to the joy of the divine vision, on the day of judgment they will be loosed with innumerable angels for the condemnation of the wicked,

[9]Andrew has summarized the interpretation of Oecumenius. [10]Ps 56:2 (55:2 lxx). [11]Jas 1:15.

and through them one third of humankind will disappear.[12] However, I think that these angels are the most evil of the demons who were bound at the coming of Christ and who, according to a divine command that comes from the heavenly altar (whose image was the ancient tabernacle), will be loosed by a divine angel so that they might trouble the nations. They will fight not only against the Christians but also against each other, so that while some, like ripe wheat, might be made manifest as approved and faithful and worthy of the best rewards and of the highest mansions and dwellings, others, like chaff, namely the wicked and the gross sinners and those unrepentant, might at that time be justly punished but receive at the judgment an even harsher condemnation.

It is not strange that they are bound at the Euphrates.[13] For according to the ordinance of God, some demons were condemned for a time to the abyss,[14] others to the swine[15] and others to other places, so that after the conclusion of their war against humankind they might receive eternal punishment. And perhaps the mention of Euphrates indicates that the antichrist will come from those regions. And we have no reason to doubt concerning the multitude of demons, for all the saints say that the air is replete with them. Why it is revealed that a third are to be killed, we have already said.[16]

[9:17-19] ***And this was how I saw the horses in my vision: the riders who sat on them wore breastplates as of fire and of sapphire and of sulfur, and the heads of the horses were like lions' heads, and fire and smoke and sulfur issued from their mouths. By these three plagues a third of humankind was killed, by the fire and smoke and sulfur issuing from their mouths. For the power of the horses is in their mouths; their tails are like serpents, with heads, and by means of them they wound.***

I think that these horses are either men who, like beasts, lust after women, or they are those who are submitted to demons and are ruled by them. For those who sit on others are those who govern them. It is common for these to use not only each other as servants but also to use evil people as instruments for plotting against people of similar kind. We interpret "the breastplates of fire and of smoke and of sulfur" to signify the aerial nature of the evil demons and of their destructive work, and the heads of lions show their murderous and beastly nature. "The fire that proceeds with smoke and sulfur from their mouths," through which one third of humankind is killed, signifies those sins that consume the fruits of the heart by means of the poisonous assaults and instigations of the demons. Or the fire signifies the devastation of cities by fire and by the shedding of blood, which God allows to be done through the hands of the barbarians. It aptly says that their tails are like serpents with heads, for that which demons sow has poisonous sin and spiritual death as its end result.

[9:20-21] ***The rest of humankind, who were not killed by these plagues, did not repent of the works of their hands or give up worshiping demons and idols of gold and silver and bronze and stone and wood, which cannot either see or hear or walk; nor did they repent of their murders or their sorceries or their immorality or their thefts.***

This is dependent on the foregoing. For just above it said "by these three plagues a third of humankind was killed," but in the middle some things are interjected and introduced. But the rest of humankind, who were spared and did not suffer these things, yet remained

[12]Andrew has summarized the interpretation of Oecumenius. [13]Andrew is probably responding to Oecumenius. [14]Lk 8:31. [15]Mt 8:31-32; Lk 8:32-33. [16]See Andrew's comments on Rev 8:7, 10-11.

unrepentant. They will suffer these same things, since they did not keep themselves from idolatries and murders and fornications and thefts and works of magic. It is clear that the universal wrath comes from such things as these.[17] These various deceits effect a frenzy in those nations that do not acknowledge the truth[18] and that worship idols and the creature rather than the creator.[19] And this is certainly so among those who confess to know God but deny him by their works[20] and who wrap themselves up in the form of piety but deny the power of it.[21] Paul labeled the service of mammon "idolatry" saying, "and greed which is idolatry."[22] May it be that we display the purity and authenticity of our faith in Christ by deeds so that we never hear those terrible words, "Truly, truly I say to you, I do not know you.[23] Depart from me, you workers of iniquity."[24] Rather, may we hear this blessed invitation, "Come, you blessed of my Father, inherit the kingdom prepared for you from the foundation of the world."[25] For by grace and mercy Christ, our God, willingly endured the cross for us, with whom be glory to the Father together with the Holy Spirit now and always and forever and ever. Amen.

BOOK TEN

Chapter 28

Concerning the angel wrapped in a cloud and a rainbow foretelling the consummation

[10:1] ***Then I saw another mighty angel coming down from heaven, wrapped in a cloud, with a rainbow over his head, and his face was like the sun and his legs like pillars of fire.***

The cloud, the rainbow and the light like the sun show how we are to understand this holy angel. For through these symbols the manifold character of its virtues and the brightness of its angelic nature and understanding is revealed. The pillars of fire signify the fearsomeness of his vengeance against those who have done evil, whether it is those who have robbed on the land or those who have been pirates at sea. That he might symbolize the judgment coming to these two groups of transgressors, the angel placed his right foot on the one and his left foot on the other.

[10:2-3] ***He had a little scroll open in his hand. And he set his right foot on the sea and his left foot on the land. And he called out with a loud voice, like a lion roaring; when he called out, the seven thunders sounded.***

Since it is small and is mentioned in the diminutive,[1] I think the little scroll contains the names and deeds of the most grievous sinners, such as those who have robbed or done other works of wickedness on the land and those who have robbed on the sea. To indicate the punishment of such persons, the angel places his fiery feet on the land and on the sea. The voice of the angel is likened to the roaring of a lion and symbolizes its fearsomeness and the irresistibility of its threats. Daniel is witness that he was able to see an angel who was unpleasant, not to say threatening.[2]

In our opinion the seven thunders are either seven voices spoken from one angel or seven other holy angels who proclaim what is to come. In this latter case they are shown to be second to the former angel and receive from him occasion to prophesy, according to the angelic order determined by the blessed Dionysius.[3]

[10:4] ***And when the seven thunders had***

[17]See Rom 1:18. [18]See 1 Tim 4:3. [19]Rom 1:25. [20]Tit 1:16. [21]2 Tim 3:5. [22]Col 3:5. [23]Mt 25:12. [24]Mt 7:23; Lk 13:27. [25]Mt 25:34.
Book Ten [1]The Greek word is βιβλιδάριον. [2]See Dan 10:5-11. [3]Dionysius the Areopagite *The Heavenly Hierarchies* 7.1-4 (PG 3:205-12); 9:1-4 (PG 3:357-61).

sounded, I was about to write. But I heard a voice from heaven saying, "Seal up what the seven thunders have said, and after these things write."

This shows that what is now undisclosed is to be explained through experience and the course of the events themselves. And from the heavenly voice the Evangelist learned that the voices are to be imprinted on the mind but that the final understanding and the clear interpretation of them is reserved for the last times. Also Daniel learned that such words are to be sealed and locked away.[4]

[10:5-6] ***And the angel whom I saw standing on sea and land lifted up his right hand to heaven and swore by him who lives forever and ever, who created heaven and what is in it, the earth and what is in it, and the sea and what is in it, that there is no longer time.***

God swears by himself, since "he has no one greater by whom to swear."[5] But the angels, being creatures, swear by the Creator, for due to our untrustworthiness, they are the guarantors of what is said by them. They swear that there is no longer any time. They are speaking either of the coming age in which time is not measured by the sun, since eternal life is transcendent to temporal measure, or they are swearing that there is not much time after the six voices of the angel before the prophecies are fulfilled. And therefore he continues:

[10:7] ***But in the days of the voice of the seventh angel, when he is about to blow his trumpet, the mystery of God, as he announced to his servants the prophets, should be fulfilled.***

This signifies, I think, that after the course of the six ages, in the days of the seventh age indicated by the seventh trumpet, that which the holy prophets proclaimed shall happen before the consummation receives it completion. It is good news that the fulfillment of these things is for the sake of the rest prepared for the saints.

Chapter 29

That the Evangelist received the little scroll from the angel

[10:8] ***Then the voice that I had heard from heaven spoke to me again, saying, "Go, take the scroll that is open in the hand of the angel who is standing on the sea and on the land."***

Here a certain other, more eminent angelic power appears to command the Evangelist to receive through the book the knowledge of what has been prophesied.

[10:9] ***And I went to the angel and said to him, "Give me the little scroll." And he said to me, "Take it and eat; it will be bitter to your stomach but sweet as honey in your mouth."***

He says that although the knowledge of future things will be sweet to you, at the same time it will be bitter to your stomach, that is, to your heart, which is the dwelling place of spiritual foods. For you will have compassion on those who receive punishments given according to God's judgment. There is another possible interpretation. Since the Evangelist was holy and had not tasted the experience of evil works, through the eating of the book that contains the deeds of evildoers, he is taught that although at the beginning sin is sweet, after the deed is done, sin becomes bitter because of its consequences.

[10:10] ***And I took the little scroll from the hand of the angel and ate it; it was sweet as honey in my mouth, but when I had eaten it,***

[4]Dan 8:26; 9:24; 12:4, 9. [5]Heb 6:13.

my stomach was made bitter.

At the beginning the book is sweet because of its joyous content. However, at the conclusion it is bitter because of the plagues. It is similar with sin. It is sweet in the tasting, but in the digesting it is bitter, as we said. However, the saints are sympathetic, for "they rejoice with those who rejoice and they weep with those who weep."[6]

[10:11] ***And he said to me, "You must again prophesy about many peoples and nations and tongues and kings."***

This passage indicates either that after the vision of the divine Revelation, that which was seen will not immediately receive its fulfillment but that the saint must prophesy to those who read his Gospel and his Revelation until the consummation. Or the passage indicates that John would not yet taste death, but that at the end he would come to hinder the acceptance of the deceit of the antichrist.[7]

[11:1-2] ***Then I was given a measuring rod like a staff saying, "Rise and measure the temple of God and the altar and those who worship there, but do not measure the court outside the temple; leave that out, for it is given over to the nations, and they will trample over the holy city for forty-two months."***

Through the measuring rod it is revealed that everything that appears in heaven and that is inanimate among us are intellectual, including the altar and the throne and the other things. How else did the measuring rod given to him say, "Rise and measure the temple of God"? We learn through this that he measures the temple of God by an angelic understanding. And should someone say that it was the same angel who gave to him the rod that heard, "Rise and measure this temple," we say that the measuring rod shows the measure of knowledge appropriate to the one who receives it. Those who are known by God and by the divine angels are regarded as worthy of such knowledge, for the divine word says, "The Lord knows those who are his."[8]

We should know that some understand the temple of God to represent the old covenant and the court outside the new covenant, since the multitude of those being redeemed in it makes it unmeasurable. Moreover, they interpret the forty-two months to symbolize the brevity of time for attaining the mysteries of the new covenant[9] before the second coming of Christ.[10] But we think that the church is called the "temple of the living God," for in it we offer spiritual sacrifices to God. And I think that the court outside is the assembly of the unbelieving Gentiles and Jews, and so by virtue of their impiety they are unworthy to be measured by the angel. "For the Lord knows those who are his," as it says, but he who knows all things is said not to know the transgressors.[11]

That the holy city, whether that is the new Jerusalem or the catholic church, will be trampled by the nations for forty-two months signifies, I believe, that at the appearance of the antichrist those who are faithful and trustworthy will be trampled and persecuted for three and a half years.

Chapter 30
Concerning Enoch and Elijah

[11:3-4] ***"And I will grant my two witnesses power to prophesy for one thousand two hundred and sixty days, clothed in sackcloth." These are the two olive trees and the two lamp-***

[6]See Rom 12:15. [7]See Jn 21:23; also Rev 11:3. The tradition that John would return at the end to fight the antichrist appears first in the fourth century. Augustine reports the tradition that John was buried alive at Ephesus and that the ground above his grave heaves at his breathing (*Tract. Ev. Jo.* 124.2). [8]2 Tim 2:19. [9]These "mysteries" would be at least baptism and the Lord's Supper. [10]Andrew is summarizing the views of Oecumenius. [11]Mt 7:23.

stands that stand before the God of the earth.

Many teachers have thought that these witnesses are Enoch and Elijah who at the consummation will receive from God opportunity to prophesy for three and a half years (which are reckoned from 360 days).[12] They will show their sadness and grief for those deceived by the wearing of sackcloth and at that time will guide those away from the deception of the antichrist. These are the same whom Zechariah saw imaged in the form of two olive trees and lampstands,[13] that they might supply the food of the light of knowledge by the oil of God-pleasing works.

[11:5-6] ***And if anyone would harm them, fire pours from their mouth and consumes their foes; and if anyone would harm them, thus he must be killed. They have power to shut the sky, that no rain may fall during the days of their prophesying, and they have power over the waters to turn them into blood and to smite the earth with every plague, as often as they desire.***

How deep is the divine goodness! For he brings a healing that is commensurate with the wound. For since he has received the full operation of the devil, the antichrist will come with every false sign and wonder and will be more wondrous than every sorcery and enchantment. And so in the power of true signs and wonders, God will equip these saints for the promotion of truth and light, and they will expose the lies and darkness [of the antichrist], and to those who have been deceived they will give correction through the word of their teaching and through chastising scourges (drought, fire, changes in the elements and the like), and they will make an example of the deceiver, while until the completion of their prophesying they will remain uninfluenced either by him or by someone other.

[11:7-8] ***And when they have finished their testimony, the beast that ascends from the bottomless pit will make war on them and conquer them, and their dead bodies will lie in the street of the great city that is spiritually called Sodom and Egypt, where their Lord was crucified.***

After the two witnesses have witnessed and urged escape from this deceit, the beast, that is, the antichrist, comes forth from the dark and deep recesses of the earth to which the devil had been condemned. And, with God's allowance, he will kill them and leave their unburied bodies in Jerusalem, no doubt the ancient one that is now in ruins and in which also the Lord suffered. As it seems, he will establish his kingdom in Jerusalem in imitation of David, whose son is Christ, our true God, who is come in the flesh. In this way the antichrist intends to prove that he is the Christ who is fulfilling the prophetic word that says, "I will raise up the booth of David that is fallen and rebuild its ruins."[14] And having been deceived at his coming, the Jews will accept this.

[11:9-10] ***For three days and a half men from the peoples and tribes and tongues and nations gaze at their dead bodies and refuse to let them be placed in a tomb, and those who dwell on the earth will rejoice over them and make merry and exchange presents, because these two prophets had been a torment to those who dwell on the earth.***

Those Jews and Gentiles who once were overpowered by the false wonders of the antichrist and who had indelibly engrafted that abomi-

[12]This interpretation of the two witnesses was the common opinion of the ancient commentators from the time of Irenaeus (*Haer.* 5.5.1).
[13]Zech 4:3, 11-14. [14]Amos 9:11.

nable name on their hearts prohibited the holy bodies from being buried, and they rejoiced because they were free from the torments that the prophets gave for their correction. For they did not acknowledge that "the Lord reproves him whom he loves"[15] and that "he scourges every son whom he receives" and "by muzzle and bridle he will pull and tug at those who are not near to him."[16] And God works in this way so that they might turn from necessity into the straight way from which they turned aside when they were deceived.

But we must make petition of the Lord and pray, "It is good for me that you have afflicted me, that I might learn your statutes,"[17] and "Turn us, O God of our salvation, that you do not enter into judgment with your servant."[18] "When we are judged by you, our beneficent master, we are chastened so that we may not be condemned along with the world"[19] but may rather through a few torments escape an eternal punishment.

BOOK ELEVEN

Chapter 31

How those killed by the antichrist will rise again

[11:11-12] ***And after the three and a half days a breath of life from God entered them, and they stood up on their feet, and great fear fell on those who saw them. And I heard a loud voice from heaven saying to them, "Come up here!" And they went up to heaven on a cloud.***

Being dead for as many days as there were years of their prophecy, it says, they will rise up and ascend into heaven on a cloud, that dominical chariot. And fear and perplexity will seize those who see it.

[11:13] ***And their foes saw them. And at that hour there was a great earthquake, and a tenth of the city fell; and seven thousand people were killed in the earthquake.***

It is possible that these things will happen at that time in a physical way. But we think that the earthquake gives a mental symbol[1] for the transposition of those things that are shaking and tottering to something more firm and secure. That a tenth of the city falls refers to the corpse of impiety that did not act wisely in the seizing of those prophets or in the seizing of any others of those who are going to be saved. The seven thousand who are killed signify those who remained attached to the seven days of the present life but did not wait for the eighth day of the resurrection and who must also be killed with the second death in Gehenna, namely, eternal punishment. Or, perhaps the seven thousand will be those Jews who were persuaded by the antichrist.

[11:13-14] ***And the rest were terrified and gave glory to the God of heaven. The second woe has passed; behold, the third woe is soon to come.***

It says that as the unbelieving are being punished and these witnesses of Christ are being glorified, those who are worthy of salvation give praise to God. After the first two woes, it says, the third woe comes, namely, that one that comes through the seventh trumpet.

Chapter 32

Concerning the seventh trumpet and the saints who praise God for the coming judgment

[11:15-18] ***Then the seventh angel blew his trumpet, and there were loud voices in heaven,***

[15]Prov 3:12. [16]See Ps 32:9 (31:9 LXX). [17]Ps 119:71 (118:71 LXX). [18]Ps 85:4; 143:2 (84:4; 142:2 LXX). [19]1 Cor 11:32. **Book Eleven**
[1]Andrew distinguishes between that which happens physically (αἰσθητῶς) and that which happens mentally (νοητῶς).

saying, "The kingdom of the world has become the kingdom of our Lord and of his Christ, and he shall reign forever and ever." And the twenty-four elders who sit on their thrones before God fell on their faces and worshiped God, saying, "We give thanks to you, O Lord God Almighty, who is and who was, for you have taken your great power and begun to reign. The nations raged, but your wrath came and the time of the dead."

Here again he says that the holy angels and those who live as do the angels send a hymn of thanksgiving to God, because for our sake he has become worthy to receive as man that kingdom that as God he possessed from the beginning. And having been patient with the unbelieving nations who were enraged at this as though it were a new and strange teaching, at the end he brings judgment on them. Therefore, it says:

[11:18] ***"But your wrath came, and the time for the dead to be judged, for rewarding your servants, the prophets and saints, and those who fear your name, both small and great, and for destroying the destroyers of the earth."***

The time of the dead is the time of the resurrection of the dead, at which time recompense will be given to each, one after the other. In the prophets and saints and those who fear God we are perhaps to recognize the three orders of those who produce fruit a hundredfold, sixtyfold and thirtyfold.[2] However, certainly the apostles will receive the first place and sit on the twelve thrones.[3] We think that the small and great are either the lesser saints and those who are rather more preeminent than they, or the small are the sinners who are subjects of contempt and the great are the righteous.

Chapter 33
Concerning the persecutions of the church, both those formerly and those under the antichrist

[11:19] ***And the temple of God in heaven was opened, and the ark of his covenant was seen within his temple; and there were flashes of lightning, voices, peals of thunder, and earthquake and heavy hail.***

By the opening of the heaven and the vision of the ark is shown the revelation of those blessings that have been prepared for the saints. According to the apostle, these blessings are hidden in Christ in whom the fullness of deity dwells bodily.[4] And these things will be revealed when the punishments of Gehenna rain down on the lawless and impious like terrifying voices and lightnings and thunder and hail. The earthquake signifies the transposition of present things.

[12:1] ***And a great sign appeared in heaven, a woman clothed with the sun, with the moon under her feet, and on her head a crown of twelve stars.***

Some believe that the woman refers generally to the mother of God who suffered that which was soon to happen before her bearing of God was known.[5] However, the great Methodius understands her to be the holy church, believing that what is narrated concerning her is unsuited of the divine birth since the Lord had been born already a long time previously. It is well to recall these words of the blessed Methodius who in his Symposium says in the person of the virgin Procles: "The woman clothed with the sun is the church. Instead of such clothing as we have, she has light. She uses stars as we do gold and brilliant stones; however, her stars are better and brighter than

[2]Mt 13:23. [3]Mt 19:28. [4]Col 2:9; also Col 2:3; 3:3. [5]Andrew is referring to Oecumenius.

those on earth." And afterward Methodius continues: "She stands on the moon. I think that the moon symbolically refers to the faith of those who have been purified from corruption by the laver, for every moist substance is dependent on the moon. Laboring and giving birth to natural persons as spiritual persons, the church forms them according to the likeness and the form of Christ." And later he says, "It is not necessary to think that it is Christ who is the one born. For long before the Apocalypse, the mystery of the incarnation of the Word was fulfilled. But John speaks concerning things present and things to come." And a little later he writes, "So it is necessary to confess that the church is she who labors and gives birth to those who are baptized. As the Spirit says in Isaiah: 'Before she who travails brought forth; she fled and brought forth a male child.'[6] From whom did she flee? Surely from the dragon, that the spiritual Zion might give birth to a masculine people." And a little later: "So that in each one Christ is born spiritually. And for this reason the church swells and labors until Christ who is born be formed in us, so that each one, partaking of Christ, might become Christ."[7] Therefore, the church is clothed with the sun of righteousness.[8] She holds under her feet both the light of the Law, which, as does the moon, gives light at night and the life of the world which, as the moon, is changing. On her head she wears the crown of the apostolic teachings and of the virtues. The author teaches that just as moist substances are dependent on the moon, so the figure of the moon signifies baptism. Here baptism is figuratively called the sea, which is salvation to those who have been born anew but is destruction to the demons.

[12:2] ***And she was with child, and she cried out in her pangs of birth, in anguish for delivery.***

We say that the church is in birth pangs for each one of those who are being born anew through water and the Spirit, "until Christ is formed in them," as the apostle says.[9] Those who have fallen from the true light of Christ are regarded as miscarriages and experience death at the end of their life because of unfaithfulness.

[12:3] ***And another sign appeared in the heaven. And, behold, a great red dragon, with seven heads and seven horns and seven diadems on his head.***

Here we think that heaven signifies the air and that the red dragon is that creature that was deceived and mocked by the angels of God, as it is written in Job.[10] He is red either because of his murderous and bloodthirsty character or because of the fiery nature of his angelic essence, since he did fall from the angels. The seven heads that he has are seven powers more wicked than himself and that are opposed to the [seven] powers of the Spirit. Or perhaps they correspond to the seven spirits of whom Christ spoke in the Gospels and that established themselves in the man who had a heart swept clean and emptied of good thoughts and deeds.[11] Or perhaps they are the seven evils that Solomon says are in the heart of the evil one, who with a great voice deceitfully seeks followers for himself.[12] The horns either signify those sins that are in opposition to the Ten Commandments of the Law, or they signify the divisions of the kingdom that bring renown to him who rejoices in seditions. And there are "seven diadems on his heads," since those who conquer the demonical powers receive again the crowns of victory, since they have gained victory with toils and sweat. Concerning these matters Methodius speaks as follows: "The great red

[6]Is 66:7. [7]Methodius *Symp.* 8.5-8 (ACW 27:110-13). In his commentary on Rev 12 Andrew closely follows Methodius and quotes him extensively. [8]Mal 4:2. [9]Gal 4:19. [10]Job 40:14; 41:24 (LXX). [11]Mt 12:43-45. [12]Prov 26:25.

dragon with seven heads that drags down the third of the stars, and lies in wait to devour the child of the woman in labor, is the devil." And a little later he continues: "But he misses and loses his prey, for the reborn are snatched up on high." And after a few other comments, he continues: "They are called a third part of the stars who have gone astray with respect to one of the numbers of the Trinity."[13] Then: "The desert into which the church comes and is nourished is a wilderness truly bare of evil and barren of corruption." "The thousand, consisting of one hundred times ten, contains the full and perfect number."[14] And a little later he writes concerning his crowns: "She who first overcomes the devil and destroys his seven heads wins seven diadems of virtue."[15]

[12:4] ***And his tail swept down a third of the stars of heaven and cast them to the earth.***

It is our opinion that this passage refers either to the former fall of the devil from heaven that through a final movement of envy—for elevation was first—brought down with him the apostate angels, or to that movement of his tail that, after the crushing of his head,[16] drags down those who have moved from their heavenly minds. They are figuratively called stars because of the brightness of their baptism. David prophesied in a similar way concerning Antiochus, since he was a type of the coming of the antichrist.[17]

[12:4] ***And the dragon stood before the woman who was about to bear a child, that he might devour the child when she brought it forth.***

The apostate always arms himself against the church, desiring to make those food for himself who are being born anew from her. Rather, through the church he persecutes Christ himself, since he is the church's head, and he makes his own what belongs to the faithful. And therefore Christ said to Saul, "Why are you persecuting me?"[18]

[12:5] ***She brought forth a male child, one who is to rule all the nations with a rod of iron.***

Through those who are baptized the church is always giving birth to Christ, since in them he is being formed to the fullness of spiritual maturity, as the apostle says.[19] The male child is the people of the church who are not effeminate in their desires, through whom Christ, our God, as though an iron rod has already ruled the nations by the mighty hands of the powerful Romans.[20] However, also after the resurrection of the dead he will establish those strong in the faith as judges and will rule as with iron the nations that are crumbling and weak vessels. For by their unfaithfulness they did not possess the mystical new wine.

[12:5] ***But her child was caught up to God and his throne.***

The saints are caught up in the midst of temptations, lest they be subdued by difficulties beyond their powers. And "they will be caught up in the clouds to meet the Lord in the air,"[21] and they will be with God and his throne, that is, with the most excellent of the angelic powers.

[12:6] ***And the woman fled into the wilderness, where she has a place prepared by God, in which to be nourished for one thousand two hundred and sixty days.***

[13]Methodius *Symp.* 10 (ACW 27:115). [14]Methodius *Symp.* 11 (ACW 27:116). [15]Methodius *Symp.* 13 (ACW 27:119). [16]See Gen 3:15-16. [17]Dan 8:10. Hippolytus also sees in Antiochus Epiphanes a foreshadowing of the antichrist (*Antichr.* 49 [ANF 5:214]). [18]Acts 9:4. [19]Eph 4:13. [20]Andrew apparently refers to the rule of Rome and Byzantium after the empire's conversion to Christianity. [21]1 Thess 4:17.

When the devil through the antichrist in whom he works arrays himself for battle against the church, those in the church who are elect and preeminent will spit on the tumults of life and the desires of the world and flee into that desert devoid of every evil, that life that bears every virtue, as Methodius says,[22] and there escape the assaults of people and demons who war against them. It is likely that the physical desert will also save those who flee from the plot of the apostate to the mountains and caves and holes in the earth, as was recently the case with the martyrs, for in the three and a half years are reckoned the 1,260 days during which the apostasy will rage. During this time the great judge will not think to tempt us beyond what we are able to bear, but freeing us will present to us a strong mind free from any weakness against the onslaughts on it, so that fighting against the principalities and power of the darkness,[23] we may be decorated with the crown of righteousness and receive the rewards of victory. For to him who through those who are weak puts to flight the mighty principalities of the air, it is proper to ascribe victory and might, together with the Father and the life-giving Spirit forever and ever. Amen.

BOOK TWELVE

Chapter 34

Concerning the war between the angels and the demons and the casting out of Satan

[12:7-8] ***Now war arose in heaven. Michael and his angels fought with the dragon; and the dragon and his angels fought, but they were defeated, and there was no longer any place for them in heaven.***

These words can refer to the first fall of the devil from his angelic rank because of his pride and envy, or it can refer to his destruction through the cross of the Lord, when, as the Lord says, "the ruler of this world is judged," cast out of his ancient tyranny.[1] It is probable that the holy angels, together with their chief leader, Michael, could not tolerate the pride of the devil and previously threw him out of any association they had with him, since they found in him a lack of righteousness. As Ezekiel says, he was cast out by the cherubim "from the midst of the stones of fire,"[2] that is, as I think, from the angelic ranks. When Christ came, they served him after the temptation,[3] since the slave, although dishonored, was once more being loathsome. We should note that, as the Fathers thought, after the creation of the physical world, the devil was thrown down because of his arrogance and envy, although he had at first been entrusted as the prince of the air, as the apostle says.[4] Papias also speaks of this passage: "To some of them, clearly the holy angels of that time, he gave dominion over the arrangement of the earth, and he commissioned them to exercise their dominion well." And then he says, "But it happened that their arrangement came to nothing."[5]

[12:9] ***And the great dragon was thrown down, that ancient serpent, who is called the devil and Satan, the deceiver of the whole world—he was thrown down to the earth, and his angels were thrown down.***

This is most proper. For heaven has nothing to do with a base, earthly mind, since the darkness has nothing in common with the light. If the term "the Satan" occurs here with the definite article, it does not suggest that he is someone other than the devil—for it occurs by way of transposition, as if it were indicat-

[22]Methodius *Symp.* 8.11 (ACW 27:116). [23]See Eph 6:12. **Book Twelve** [1]See Jn 16:11; 12:31. [2]Ezek 28:16. [3]Mt 4:11. [4]See Eph 2:2. [5]Papias, from an unknown work.

ing "the devil, that is, the Satan"—but as one named with two names. He is called "devil" because he accuses and slanders the virtues and those who love them, and he has even slandered God to people, as he did when he suggested to Adam that God was envious.[6] He is called Satan because he opposes himself against the Master and his servants.

It is therefore to be noted that the downfall of the devil did not only occur after the cross, as though he was inactive in former times. Rather, as he confessed to Anthony, the saying of the psalm is fulfilled in him, "The swords of the enemy have come to their end."[7] Therefore, his banishment is the abolition of all his evil enterprises along with his total exclusion from heaven and from his rank, as we said. The blessed Justin Martyr noted that after the coming of Christ and after the devil's sentence to Gehenna, the devil especially became a blasphemer, while in former times he did not blaspheme God so brazenly.[8] And so it is accurately said about him, "His heart is hard as stone,"[9] since he is unyielding in his evil. And if the expectation of punishment makes him even more evil, how would punishing either him or his followers in Gehenna through fire wash out the filth of sin? And not attaining to this, how would there be a cessation of punishment against those who think vain thoughts?[10]

[12:10] ***And I heard a loud voice in heaven, saying, "Now the salvation and the power and the kingdom of our God and the authority of his Christ have come, for the accuser of our brethren has been thrown down, who accuses them day and night before our God."***

Because of his accusations and calumny against people, he has been called "accuser," which he is, as we said. The angels rejoice at his downfall, for faith has nothing to do with faithlessness.[11]

[12:11-12] ***"And they conquered him by the blood of the Lamb and by the word of their testimony, for they loved not their lives even to death. Rejoice, then, O heavens and you that dwell therein! But woe to you, O earth and sea, for the devil has come down to you in great wrath, because he knows that his time is short."***

And although the saints have been accused and slandered by him, as was also Job,[12] yet by their sufferings for the sake of Christ they have conquered him as well as all who trusted in him. In imitation of God, it follows that the powers above rejoice at his downfall but grieve over those who by his plot cling to earthly things. But woe to those who dwell on the earth, that is, clearly to those who have no citizenship in heaven but only on earth.[13] For many on the earth do defeat the enemy and will continue to do so, although because of the nearness of his punishment he now is especially enraged against those who fight him. And so it is necessary to think that those are unhappy who have an earthly mind and are buffeted about by the sea of life.

Chapter 35

That the dragon never ceases persecuting the church

[12:13-14] ***And when the dragon saw that he had been thrown down to the earth, he pursued the woman who had borne the male child. But the woman was given the two wings of the great eagle that she might fly from the serpent into the wilderness, to the place where she is to be nourished for a time, and times, and half a time.***

[6]See Gen 3:5. [7]Ps 9:6 (LXX). See Athanasius *Vit. Ant.* 41 (NPNF 2 4:207). [8]See Irenaeus *Haer.* 5.26.2; Eusebius *Hist. eccl.* 4.18.9. The work of Justin quoted by Irenaeus and Eusebius is lost. [9]Job 41:24. [10]These comments most likely are against the Origenist doctrine of the restoration of all things, which was condemned at the Fifth Ecumenical Council (553). [11]See 2 Cor 6:15. [12]Job 1:9-11; 2:4-5. [13]See Phil 3:20.

When the devil wrestled with Christ after his baptism, he was overcome.[14] Then arming himself against the holy apostles, he was again shamed when he saw that they found life through death,[15] while as a snake he had been condemned to crawl on the ground and to eat dirt,[16] that is, earthly thoughts. He then began again to persecute the church, for she has borne and continues to bear the manly people of God who are not distracted by effeminate desire. And from the beginning love for God and the neighbor and a mind receptive of him who was crucified for us was given to the church, as were the two Testaments. All of these things are symbolized by the wings of the eagle, and they were given to the church so that taking flight by them into the desert, that is, into a citizenship devoid of every desire, she might be nourished. To be sure, this occurs always, but it will especially be so at the coming of the antichrist, who will rule everywhere, it is written, for the designated time of three and a half years. It may be that during that time even those who have hid themselves in the mountains and caves of the literal, physical desert will flee him [the devil].

[12:15-16] ***The serpent poured water like a river out of his mouth after the woman, to sweep her away with the flood. But the earth came to the help of the woman, and the earth opened its mouth and swallowed the river that the dragon had poured from its mouth.***

When the church fled to inaccessible places where the deceiver makes his approach, out of his mouth, that is, clearly by his command, came water like a river after her. That is, he sent out against her a host of godless people and evil demons and all kinds of temptations that he might enslave her. But the earth, it says, came to the church's aid. This may refer to the very great distances of travel in the desert and the aridity and dryness of those places and in this way the river of temptations were swallowed up, halting the attacks of these evils.[17] Or [the demons and their temptations were overcome] by the humility of the saints who say with utter sincerity, "I am earth and dust," and so bring to naught all the snares of the devil, even as the angel said to the holy Anthony.[18]

[12:17] ***And the dragon was angry with the woman and went off to make war on the rest of her offspring, on those who keep the commandments of God and bear testimony of Jesus.***

Since the orthodox teachers of the church and those who disdain the world retreat to the rigor of the desert, the antichrist does not neglect them but wages war, it says, against those who struggle in the world for Christ. Just as one can make the smoothness of olive oil course by allowing dust in it, so the antichrist wishes to turn those whom he can through the cares and obligations of life. However, many of these shall overcome him through the genuine love that they have for Christ.

Chapter 36

Concerning the beast with the ten horns and seven heads

[13:1] ***And I stood on the sand of the sea. And I saw a beast rising out of the sea, with ten horns and seven heads, with ten diadems on its horns and a blasphemous name on its heads.***

Some have interpreted this beast to be a certain power, a leader of the other demons, who is second to Satan, and that after this beast the antichrist arises from the earth.[19] However, according to holy Methodius and holy Hippolytus

[14]Mt 4:1-11. [15]See Mt 10:38-39. [16]Gen 3:14. [17]The very remoteness of the hermits shielded them from outside temptations. [18]This scene is not found in *Vita Antonii*. [19]Andrew is referring to Oecumenius.

and others, this beast is to be interpreted as the antichrist who comes from the tumultuous and rough sea of this life.[20] The ten horns with the diadems and the seven heads signify the unity that the devil has with him—for these characteristics were interpreted above as also belonging to him.[21] The ten horns and seven heads also signify the division of the earthly government at the end of time into ten, and the earthly government corresponds to this world, which is calculated as consisting of seven days and is divided into seven successive kingdoms, as will be discussed below. For this reason, Satan, who operates in him, is called "the ruler of this age."[22] "A blasphemous name is on its heads" clearly refers to his supporters. For from the beginning these never ceased from blaspheming Christ until the accession of the great Constantine. But after him, the emperors Julian and Valens again slandered against Christ.[23]

[13:2] ***And the beast that I saw was like a leopard, and its feet were like a bear's, and its mouth was like a lion's mouth.***

The kingdom of the Greeks is signified by the leopard; the Persians are signified by the bear; the Babylonians are signified by the lion. The antichrist, who will come as a king of the Romans, will rule over them and destroy their empires, when he beholds the clay toes of their feet, by which is indicated the destruction of a weak and brittle kingdom into ten kingdoms.[24]

[13:2] ***And to it the dragon gave his power and his throne and great authority.***

Satan, that spiritual dragon, will give all of his authority to the antichrist who through false signs and wonders will work for the ruination of those who are weak and unstable.

[13:3] ***One of its heads seemed to have a mortal wound, but its mortal wound was healed.***

That he had a head that was wounded indicates that one of his lieutenants, having been put to death, deceptively seems to be raised again by him through his sorcery, in a way similar to Simon the magician, who, in light of his magic tricks, was unmasked by the chief of the apostles.[25] Or the phrase could indicate that the Roman Empire, having suffered a kind of wound through division, seems to be healed by a unified rule, as occurred at the time of Augustus Caesar.[26]

[13:3-4] ***And the beast was followed with wonder in the whole world. And they worshiped the dragon, for he had given authority to the beast, saying, "Who is like the beast, and who can fight against it?"***

The wonder directed at the antichrist will be transferred to the devil, who is working through him. For through him the dragon will be worshiped, and through him he will seem, to those blinded in the eyes of the mind, to raise the dead and perform signs.

[13:5-6] ***And the beast was given a mouth uttering haughty words and blasphemy, and it was allowed to exercise authority for forty-two months; it opened its mouth to utter blasphemies against God, blaspheming his name and his dwelling and those who dwell in heaven.***

With the allowance of God, it says, he will

[20]This view cannot be found in the literary remains of Methodius. Hippolytus consistently interprets this beast to be the Roman Empire and the beast from the earth as antichrist (see *Antichr.* 49). Andrew follows the interpretation of Irenaeus (*Haer.* 5.28.2). [21]See the comments on Rev 12:3. [22]Jn 12:31. [23]From 324 to 337 Constantine ruled as the first Christian emperor. Julian the Apostate (361–363) attempted to reestablish pagan worship, and Valens (d. 378) made laws against the Christians that favored the Arian cause. [24]See Irenaeus *Haer.* 5.26.1 (ANF 1:555). [25]See *Acts of Peter* 25–26. [26]In 27 B.C. Augustus defeated Mark Antony and Cleopatra, effectively ending years of civil war and inaugurating the peaceful times of his principiate. The interpretation of Andrew echoes that of Hippolytus *Antichr.* 49 (ANF 5:214).

have authority for three and a half years to blaspheme against God and to harm the saints. The dwelling of God is the dwelling of the Word in the flesh, that is, his incarnation, as well as his repose among the saints, against whom, as also against the holy angels, he will fully direct his blasphemy.

[13:7-8] ***And authority was given it over every tribe and tongue and nation, and all who dwell on the earth will worship it, everyone whose name has not been written before the foundation of the world in the book of life of the Lamb that was slain.***

It says that he will exercise an evil authority against every tribe and tongue and that he will rule over those whose names are not written in the book of life.

[13:9-10] ***If anyone has an ear, let him hear: If anyone is to be taken captive, to captivity he goes; if anyone slays with the sword, with the sword he must he be slain. Here is a call for the endurance and faith of the saints.***

Everyone will receive a recompense worthy of his deeds. Those who are willing to harm their neighbor will be captured by the devil and will undergo the death of his soul by the satanic sword. For, as the great James says, they are made slaves of that one by whom they have been conquered through their works.[27] But those who have a pure faith and unshakeable endurance in trials will be indelibly written in the book of life. With such may the all-merciful God also find us partakers who consider "that the sufferings of this present time are not worth comparing with the glory that is to be revealed" to the saints,[28] and who walk valiantly the narrow way, so that, finding at the end of it glory in the coming age and rest and paradise, we might reign with Christ, with whom to the Father be all thanksgiving and worship with the Holy Spirit forever. Amen.

BOOK THIRTEEN

Chapter 37
Concerning the false prophet

[13:11] ***Then I saw another beast that rose out of the earth; it had two horns like a lamb, and it spoke like a dragon.***

Some say that this beast is the antichrist, while to others its two horns signify the antichrist and the false prophet.[1] But since also the false prophet is thought to come in his own person, it is proper to think that the dragon is to be interpreted as Satan, the beast that arises from the sea as the antichrist, and this beast that comes up from the earth as the false prophet, which is the opinion of the blessed Irenaeus. That he comes up from the earth symbolizes that he arises from an earthly and groveling manner of life. That he has two horns like a lamb indicates that in the skin of a lamb he cloaks the murderousness of the wolf hiding within him[2] and that at the beginning he will have the form of piety. Of him Irenaeus says, "Concerning his armor-bearer, whom he also calls the false prophet, he says, 'he spoke like a dragon.'"[3]

The authority of signs and wonders was given to him, so that going before the antichrist, he might prepare the way of destruction for him. We say that the healing of the wound of the beast is either the apparent, short-lived unity of the divided empire, or the temporary restoration by the antichrist of the tyranny of Satan that had been destroyed or the fraudulent resurrection of one of his associates who had died. It says that he speaks like a dragon,

[27]See Jas 3:3-4. [28]Rom 8:18. **Book Thirteen** [1]Hippolytus *Antichr.* 49 (ANF 5:214). [2]See Mt 7:15. [3]Irenaeus *Haer.* 5.28.2 (ANF 1:557).

because he will do and say the things of the devil, who is the author of evil.

[13:12-13] ***It exercises all the authority of the first beast in its presence and makes the earth and its inhabitants worship the first beast, whose mortal wound was healed. It works great signs, even making fire come down from heaven to earth in the sight of people.***

The forerunner of the apostate false christ will do all things through sorcery for the deception of humankind, so that the antichrist will be regarded as God. And since the antichrist receives the witness of the worker of such marvels, he receives undisputed honor, in imitation of the Baptist, who led those who believed to the Savior.[4] For falsehood is zealous to imitate the truth for the deception of humankind. Therefore, it is not remarkable that to the eyes of those deceived, fire is seen coming down from heaven. For somewhere in the story of Job we are taught that, with the permission of God and by the activity of Satan, fire came down and consumed his flock.[5]

[13:14] ***And by the signs that it is allowed to work in the presence of the beast, it deceives those who dwell on earth.***

The beast deceives those who continually dwell on the earth in their hearts. For those who possess their citizenship in heaven are not deceived by false appearances, since they have been sufficiently fortified by the prediction of his coming.

[13:14-17] ***Bidding them make an image for the beast that was wounded by the sword and yet lived; and it was allowed to give breath to the image of the beast so that the image of the beast should even speak, and to cause those who would not worship the image of the beast to be slain. Also it causes all, both small and great, both rich and poor, both free and slave, to be marked on the right hand or the forehead, so that no one can buy or sell unless he has the mark, that is, the name of the beast or the number of its name.***

It is reported that demons often speak by sorcery through images and statues and trees and streams, also through Apollonius[6] and others, and I think, even through dead bodies. For example, in the presence of Peter, Simon the magician showed the Romans a dead body that he was moving. However, the apostle unmasked his deception by showing through those whom he raised how the dead were raised by Simon.[7] And so there is nothing strange in the fact that working through demons, this standard-bearer of the antichrist should make an image for the beast and contrive to show it speaking and see to it that those who did not worship it were killed. And he will eagerly strive to place the mark of the ruinous name of the apostate on everyone. He will make the mark on their right hands to bring to an end the doing of good works and on their foreheads in order to teach those deceived to be bold in their deception and darkness. But those who have had their faces sealed with the divine light will not receive the mark. He will undertake to spread the mark of the beast everywhere through buying and selling, so that a violent death might come to all who have not received it from the lack of necessities.

Chapter 38

Concerning the name of the antichrist

[13:18] ***This calls for wisdom: let him who has understanding reckon the number of the beast, for it is a number of a man. And its number is six hundred and sixty-six.***

[4]See Jn 1:29-34. [5]Job 1:16. [6]See Eusebius *Hier.* 31 (PG 22:840-41). Hierocles was a governor of Bithynia who had written a treatise claiming that Apollonius of Tyana was superior to Jesus. [7]See *Acts of Pilate* 28.

For the sober-minded, time and experience will reveal the actual significance of the number and the truth of whatever has been written about it. For, were it necessary, as some of the teachers say, that such a name be clearly known, the seer would have revealed it.[8] But the divine grace did not consent that the name of the destroyer be noted in the divine book. However, as though by way of a verbal exercise, many names, both proper names and titles, that correspond to this number have been found by the blessed Hippolytus and others.[9] Among the proper names are such as Λαμπέτις, Τειτάν with the diphthong coming from τενῶ, according to Hippolytus, likewise Λατεῖνος, Βενέδικτος which means "being blessed" or "blessed," perhaps by way of imitation of Christ, our God, who was truly blessed. Among the titles are such as κακὸς ὁδηγός, ἀληθὴς βλαβερός, πάλαι βάσκανος, ἀμνὸς ἄδικος.[10] He will be given such names by those who oppose his deception, for he places "his own glory in his shame."[11]

Chapter 39
Concerning the Lamb and the 144,000

[14:1] ***And I looked, and lo, on Mount Zion stood a Lamb, and with him a hundred and forty-four thousand who had his name and his Father's name written on their foreheads.***

Without any doubt whatsoever, the Lamb is Christ. He is standing on Mount Zion, not the ancient city, but the new city of the living God. These thousands indicate either the full harvest of the apostolic seed, the grace in each being completed twelve times a thousand, the perfect fruit of the faith of those being saved, or they signify those from the New Testament who are chaste in both the inner and the outer person. For among the ancients the virtue of virginity was rare, found only in a very few, and from this fact one must suppose that these are different from those mentioned earlier who were introduced with the names of the tribes of Israel,[12] to whom he did not attribute virginity. The foreheads of all of these are sealed with the light of the divine countenance, by which they are revealed as holy to the avenging angels.

[14:2-3] ***And I heard a voice from heaven like the sound of many waters and like the sound of loud thunder; and I heard the sound of harpers playing on their harps, and they sing a new song before the throne and before the four living creatures and before the elders.***

The voice of many waters and of thunder and of the harpers indicates the penetrating clarity of the singing of the saints and of the harmonious and melodious euphony of their song, which resounds throughout "the assembly and festal gathering of the firstborn who are enrolled in heaven"[13] and which, just as in the harmony of strings, sounds forth with the united breath of the saints and is accomplished by the dying of the desires of the body. No one else, its says, can learn this song except these, for the knowledge [of the song] is coextensive to the measure of their behavior, just as the servants of people are allowed to know their master's secrets in proportion to their good will.

[14:3-5] ***No one could learn that song except the hundred and forty-four thousand who had been redeemed from the earth. It is these who have not been defiled with women, for they are chaste; it is these who follow the Lamb wherever he goes; these have been redeemed from humankind as first fruits for God and the Lamb, and in their mouth no lie was found, for they are spotless.***

[8]See Irenaeus *Haer.* 5.30.3 (ANF 1:559). [9]See Hippolytus *Antichr.* 50 (ANF 5:214-15) and the comments of Oecumenius. [10]These titles mean "evil guide," "truly harmful," "ancient slanderer," "unjust lamb." [11]See Phil 3:19. [12]Rev 7:4-8. [13]Heb 12:23.

We think that, after the twenty-four elders, these are leaders of the rest who because of their chastity and purity in word and deed have, after the sojourn of Christ, come to possess the brightness of the virtues. Taught by the virtues, they sing the new song, which remains unknown to most, not only in this life but also in that to come. For although when "the perfection of knowledge will come, then the imperfect will cease," as the apostle says,[14] the appearance of the divine mysteries will be proportionate to the life of the saints here. For "in my Father's house are many rooms,"[15] and "star differs from star in glory,"[16] just as also there is a difference of torments. Redeeming us from these, may the Lord of all count us among those who are being saved through his own goodness, not regarding the multitude of our sins but his own mercies, on account of which he came to the earth and shed his precious blood for us, that washing away our stains and spots, he might bring us to the Father, with whom glory, power and honor are due to him, the Leader of our salvation,[17] together with the all-holy Spirit, now and forever and ever. Amen.

BOOK FOURTEEN

Chapter 40

Concerning the angel who foretells the nearness of the coming judgment

[14:6-7] ***Then I saw an angel flying in mid-heaven, with an eternal gospel to proclaim to those who dwell on earth, to every nation and tribe and tongue and people; and he said with a loud voice, "Fear God and give him glory, for the hour of his judgment has come; and worship him who made heaven and earth, the sea and the fountains of water."***

The phrase "in mid-heaven" indicates that the angel that here appears is exceedingly lofty and heavenly. It has been sent from above to people who come from the ground, so that through this middle position it might be a mediator and lead them, in imitation of God, to heaven. And so the body of the church will be united to Christ, our head. The eternal gospel, which from eternity was foreordained by God, says, "Fear God, but have no fear of the antichrist who cannot kill the soul with the body;[1] rather, fervently stand opposed to him who has power but for a short time, for the time of his judgment and the reward for what he has done is near."

Chapter 41

Concerning the angel who proclaims the fall of Babylon

[14:8] ***Another angel, a second, followed, saying, "Fallen, fallen is Babylon the great, she who made all nations drink the wine of the wrath of her fornication."***

He speaks of Babylon, which refers to the confusion of the world and the troubled disorder of this life, which in no way have abated. By "the wine of the wrath of her fornication" he means not only the frenzy that attends to idol-worship and the ecstasy of their minds but also to the drunkenness and derangement that attends all sin, by which everyone who whores against God is wholly destroyed, as the saying of the psalm goes.[2] As it were, pulled up by its roots, such a Babylon falls completely at the appearance of the Jerusalem that is above, for those who have been workers of iniquity are sent to the everlasting fire.

Chapter 42

Concerning the angel who encourages the faithful not to accept the antichrist

[14] 1 Cor 13:10. [15] Jn 14:2. [16] 1 Cor 15:41. [17] See Heb 2:10. **Book Fourteen** [1] See Mt 10:28. [2] Ps 73:27 (72:27 LXX).

[14:9-10] ***And another angel, a third, followed them, saying with a loud voice, "If anyone worships the beast and its image and receives a mark on his forehead or on his hand, he also shall drink the wine of God's wrath, poured unmixed into the cup of his anger, and he shall be tormented with fire and sulfur in the presence of the holy angels and in the presence of the Lamb."***

It says that should anyone bow down to the beastlike antichrist and pursue an ungodly life like his, should anyone proclaim him to be God in word or deed—for the mark given on the forehead and on the hand would show this—that person will share with the antichrist in the drinking of the revenge-filled cup, which is unmixed and devoid of any divine mercy because of the justice of the judgment. And this cup is of wine poured from different punishments because of the diversity and variety of evils that were freely chosen. He aptly calls this torment the "wine of wrath," since it follows on the wine of godlessness, which inebriates those who drink of it, for "in that way by which one sins, shall one also be punished."[3]

[14:11] ***"And the smoke of their torment goes up forever and ever."***

We must understand this smoke to be either the sighing of those being tormented, which arises from below along with their lamentation, or the smoke that comes from the fire that torments the fallen. It says that it "goes up forever and ever," and by this we learn that even as the bliss of the righteous is everlasting, so also is the torment of the sinners.

[14:11] ***"And they have no rest, day or night, these worshipers of the beast and its image, and whoever receives the mark of its name."***

He says "day and night," not as though the condition of the future age in which the ungodly will have no rest will be measured by the sun, but he rather accommodates himself to the custom in the present time, which is reckoned in nights and days. Or it might be that the day is to be regarded as the life of the saints and the night as the torment of the impure, which those who do the works of the devil and blaspheme against Christ in the manner of the apostate beast will attain. For through the doing of these things they make an image [of the beast] and engrave his name on their hearts as though it were precious.

[14:12] ***Here is the endurance of the saints; here are those who keep the commandments of God and the faith of Jesus Christ.***

While the impious will be tormented eternally in the coming age, the saints here show their patient endurance, keeping inviolate the commandments of God and their faith in Christ during the present time, which is quickly passing away.

[14:13] ***And I heard a voice from heaven saying to me, "Write this: Blessed are the dead who die in the Lord henceforth." "Yes indeed," says the Spirit, "that they might rest from their labors, for their deeds follow them."***

The voice from heaven does not bless all the dead, but only those who die in the Lord, who have died to the world and "carry about the dying of Jesus in the body"[4] and suffer with Christ. For these persons the departure from the body is truly a rest from their labor. Moreover, the obedience of their works is the reason for their unfading crowns and the rewards of glory that are the prizes given in great measure to those who prevail in the contests that the contestants of Christ, our God, endure to the

[3]Wis 11:16. [4]2 Cor 4:10.

end against invisible powers. "For the sufferings of the present time are not worth comparing with the glory that is to be revealed" to those who please God, as the apostle says.[5] It is necessary also that we who yearn for such glory should pray unceasingly to God, saying, "Incline our hearts, O Lord, to your testimonies, and turn our eyes from every vanity,"[6] and "enter not into judgment with your servants, for no living creature will be righteous before you."[7] Rather, visit us with your bountiful mercies, for the might and the kingdom and the power and the glory are yours, namely, of the Father and of the Son and of the Holy Spirit, now and forever and unto the ages of ages. Amen.

BOOK FIFTEEN

Chapter 43

How the one who sits on a cloud will reap the harvest from the earth with a sickle

[14:14] ***Then I looked, and lo, a white cloud, and seated on the cloud one like a son of man, with a golden crown on his head and a sharp sickle in his hand.***

We think that this cloud is either the visible cloud that took our Lord Jesus Christ from the eyes of the apostles[1] or that it is a certain angelic power [here called a cloud] because of its purity and sublimity, for the psalmist says, "He rode on a cherub and flew."[2] For this reason, we believe that the one seen on the cloud similar to a son of man is Christ, and that the crown on his head signifies his governance over both the visible and invisible powers. The crown is gold because of the value of this substance among us. The sickle indicates the consummation, for indeed the Lord called the end of the world a "harvest."[3]

[14:15-16] ***And another angel came out from heaven, calling with a loud voice to him who sat on the cloud, "Put in your sickle, and reap, for your hour to reap has come, for the harvest of the earth is fully ripe." So he who sat upon the cloud swung his sickle on the earth, and the earth was reaped.***

The cry of the angel symbolically represents the supplications of all the heavenly powers who desire to see both the honoring of the saints and the separation of the transgression of the sinners. At that time, that which is changeable and transient will cease to exist and that which is immoveable and enduring will be manifested. That the harvest is ripe indicates that the time of the consummation has come when the seed of piety, having matured as ripe wheat, will be regarded as ready for the heavenly granaries and will yield for the husbandman thirtyfold, sixtyfold and a hundredfold.

Chapter 44

Concerning the angel who gathers the vintage of bitterness

[14:17] ***And another angel came out of the temple in heaven, and he too had a sharp sickle.***

Although Christ is called the "angel of great counsel"[4] of the Father, nonetheless from the following words the present angel is shown to be one of the ministering angels, for he comes out of the heavenly temple with a sharp sickle in order to accomplish the cutting off of those who are most impious.

[14:18] ***Then another angel came out from the altar, having authority over fire, and he called with a loud cry to him who had the sharp sickle, "Put in your sharp sickle, and gather***

[5]Rom 8:18. [6]Ps 119:36-37 (118:36-37 LXX). [7]Ps 143:2 (142:2 LXX). **Book Fifteen** [1]Acts 1:9. [2]Ps 18:10 (17:10 LXX). [3]Mt 13:30. [4]Is 9:6 (LXX).

the clusters of the vine of the earth, for its grapes are ripe."

From this passage we learn that angelic powers have been placed over the creatures, one is over water, another is over fire, and another over some other part of creation. We learn of the fearsomeness of this particular angel because he is placed over fire. It says that he is of the highest angels, for with a cry he commands the one having a sickle to gather grapes of the vine of the earth. The grapes indicate the impious and the transgressors who have filled the cup of the wrath of the Lord and who receive as harvest the wrath of demons and of asps[5] instead of the wine of gladness from the good husbandman.

[14:19] ***So the angel swung his sickle on the earth and gathered the vintage of the earth and threw it into the great wine press of the wrath of God.***

The wine press of God is the place of torment prepared for the devil and his angels. Because of the multitude of those who are to be punished, it is great. For the "way of destruction is wide" and spacious.[6]

[14:20] And the wine press was trodden outside the city, and blood flowed from the wine press, as high as a horse's bridle, for one thousand six hundred stadia.

To be sure, the place of the punishment for those deserving of it is outside the city of the heavenly Jerusalem. Their blood reaches to the bridles of horses for 1,600 stadia. This indicates perhaps that the punishment is through the avenging angels from afar, for the holy Scriptures sometimes figuratively call the avenging angels "horses,"[7] and that the wailing of those torments extends to their bridles. The holy powers have as bridles the divine commandment by which they guide according to what is demanded. As Habakkuk says, "You will ride on your horses,"[8] and the Song of Songs, "I have compared you to a mare of Pharaoh's chariot."[9]

However, it is possible to understand this another way. For since those who transgressed by giving themselves over to pleasure have become horses full of lust, they will be overtaken by tortures unto their bridles, for they knew no bridle in their pleasures. By the 1,600 stadia we learn of the great chasm that separates the righteous from the sinners. For these were perfect in evil and did that which is abominable, and therefore ten times one hundred signifies the complete magnitude of their evil, while the six hundred suggests their eager engagement in sin through the misuse of the creation, which was created in six days, and also in the six hundredth year of Noah all land was inundated by water.[10]

[The wine press will be trodden outside the city of the righteous. For "the rod of sinners will never come near the lot of the righteous," as the prophetic saying goes.[11] The abode of the righteous will be unmixed, as the manner of their life had been. By the blood that flows from those who are being trampled he means the righteous and impartial judgment of God. For wine is the blood of the grape. The cup is filled with the unmixed wine of the divine wrath. This cup signifies that torment that will overtake those worthy of it. This torment will extend to their bridles, as though they were horses made mad by women, for they knew no bridle to their lusts and to their unlawful actions. The torment will go for 1,600 stadia because of the completeness of their evil. For one thousand is the most perfect of all numbers. And we know that in the sixth

[5]See Deut 32:33. [6]See Mt 7:13. [7]Andrew is referring to the comments of Oecumenius. [8]Hab 3:8. [9]Song 1:9. [10]Gen 7:11. [11]Ps 125:3 (124:3 LXX).

hundredth year of Noah sin was inundated by water. And it speaks of six because by the evil deeds of their lives they insulted the creation, which occurred in six days. The number of the six days, in which the world was established, is symbolic of the active life.][12]

Chapter 45

Concerning the seven angels who bring plagues on humankind before the end of all things, and concerning the sea of glass

[15:1] ***Then I saw another portent in heaven, great and wonderful, seven angels with seven plagues, which are the last, for with them the wrath of God is ended.***

Everywhere he uses the number seven, signifying that the injustices done brazenly during the seven days of the present age will be held back by the seven plagues and the seven angels. After these, the future life of the saints, symbolized by the glass sea, will commence.

[15:2] ***And I saw what appeared to be a sea of glass mingled with fire, and those who had conquered the beast and its image and its character and the number of its name, standing beside the sea of glass with harps of God.***

We think that the sea of glass signifies the multitude of those who are being saved, the purity of the coming reward and the brightness that the saints will radiate by the sparkling of their virtue. The fire that is mixed with it may be understood from what was written by the apostle, "Fire will test the work of each, whatever it is."[13] Although this fire does not harm the pure and the undefiled, it is divided without mixture into two energies, according to the word of the psalmist.[14] As the great Basil understood it, such a fire gives a burning punishment to the sinners but gives illumination to the righteous.[15] It is possible that the fire indicates both the divine knowledge and the grace of the life-giving Spirit. For God appeared to Moses in fire,[16] and the Holy Spirit descended on the apostles in the form of tongues of fire.[17] The harps suggest the dying of members and the harmonious life in the symphony of virtues, plucked with the plectrum of the divine Spirit.

[15:3-4] ***And they sing the song of Moses, the servant of God, and the song of the Lamb, saying, "Great and wonderful are your works, O Lord God the Almighty! Just and true are your ways, O King of the nations! Who shall not fear and glorify your name, O Lord? For you alone are holy. All nations shall come and worship you, for your judgments have been revealed."***

From the song of Moses we learn the hymn sent up to God by those who were justified by the Law before grace. From the song of the Lamb we learn the unending thanksgiving of those who lived in holiness after the coming of the Christ. This thanksgiving is for those benefactions and gifts from him that have come to our race, since through the holy apostles he has called all nations to the knowledge of him.

[15:5-6] ***After this I looked, and the temple of the tent of witness in heaven was opened, and out of the temple came the seven angels with the seven plagues, robed in pure bright linen, and their breasts girded with golden girdles.***

The seer says that a tent was in heaven, and it

[12]Some manuscripts include this section as authentic to Andrew. Schmid places the section in brackets, suggesting it is secondary. [13]1 Cor 3:13. [14]Ps 29:7 (28:7 LXX). [15]See Basil of Caesarea *Homilies on the Six Days* 6.3 (PG 29:121); *Homilies on the Psalms* 28.6 (PG 29:297-80). [16]Ex 3:1-6. [17]Acts 2:3.

was according to the likeness of this tent that God commanded Moses to build the tabernacle below.[18] He says that from this temple angels proceeded out, dressed in "pure linen" or, as some copies have it, in a "pure stone." Their dress indicates the purity of their natures and the proximity that they have to Christ, the cornerstone, and the brightness of their virtue. The phrase "girded with golden girdles" refers to the power and the purity and the honor of their nature and to the freedom they have in their works of service.

[15:7] ***And one of the four living creatures gave the seven angels seven golden bowls full of the wrath of God who lives forever and ever.***

The angels take the golden bowls filled with the wrath of the Lord from the four living creatures, as it says also in Ezekiel.[19] This shows that eternally in heaven the knowledge of God's plans is shared by those who are preeminent to those who are of second rank, even as the great Dionysius says.[20]

[15:8] ***And the temple was filled with smoke from the glory of God and from his power.***

From the smoke we learn of the frightful, terrible and tormenting character of the wrath of God. We are taught that the temple is filled with this wrath, which comes at the time of judgment against those who are worthy of it, and especially against those who obey the antichrist and do the works of apostasy. This is shown by what follows, for it says:

[15:8-16:1] ***And no one could enter the temple until the seven plagues of the seven angels were ended. Then I heard a loud voice from the temple, saying to the seven angels, "Go, pour out on the earth the bowls of wrath."***

From this we are led to think that until the divine vexation with the wicked distinguishes who the righteous are, the saints in no wise obtain the lot of the Jerusalem above or the priesthood in the temple of God or the final rest. "It is necessary," it says, "that the plagues be completed." By way of the plagues the wages of sin are brought to light for those who are worthy of them, and these obtain the judicial sentence that has been determined for them. Then the habitation in the metropolis above will be awarded to the saints. I think that no one who considers each of the plagues in relation to those persons who are found at the consummation shall make an error concerning what is fitting and right. For being beneficent to humankind, God will determine that the unending torments in the coming age be lessened but that in the present life the avenging scourges be brought on those who deserve them, either through the prophets, Enoch and Elijah, or through the change of the elements or through the sufferings that occur from wars. Through such scourges there will be a moderation in the payment for sins. However, let us pray that we be chastised in a fatherly manner and not be scourged with harsh treatment by the wrath that comes from the Lord—"for there is no health in our flesh because of his anger"[21] —so that having cleansed through the tears of repentance our robes that have been stained by sins, and being dressed as for a wedding, we might enter into the bridal chamber of Christ, our God, to whom belong all glory, honor and worship together with the Father and the Holy Spirit forever and ever. Amen.

BOOK SIXTEEN

Chapter 46
How sores came against the wicked when the first bowl was poured out

[18]See Ex 25-27. [19]Ezek 9:8; 14:19; 20:8, 13, 21, *passim*. [20]See Pseudo-Dionysius *Celestial Hierarchy* 8.2; 13.2 (PG 3:240-41, 300). [21]Ps 38:3 (37:3 LXX). Andrew represents a slight variant reading to accommodate the purpose of this exhortation to prayer.

[16:2] ***So the first angel went and poured his bowl on the earth, and a foul and evil sore came on the people who bore the mark of the beast and worshiped its image.***

The bowl here, just as the cup, is to be interpreted as tormenting activity that, when poured out by the angel, produces an evil sore, which here is symbolic of grief that throbs in the heart even as puss oozes from a sore. This grief occurs in the hearts of apostates, for since they are punished by plagues sent from God, they receive no healing from the antichrist whom they have made their god. Perhaps also their bodies are physically wounded as a reproach to their souls, which have been wounded by the arrows of that deceitful rogue, the devil.

Chapter 47

The second plague against every living thing in the sea

[16:3] ***The second angel poured his bowl into the sea, and it became blood as of a dead person, and every living thing died that was in the sea.***

It is not surprising that to expose the weakness of the false christ and the light-mindedness of the deceived, the divine power would through the holy prophets, Enoch and Elijah, change the sea into "blood as of a dead person," that is, as of one who had been slain, and would effect the corruption of all in it, just as long ago in Egypt God worked through Moses to expose the hardheartedness of Pharaoh and to demonstrate his own power.[1] And therefore, those who were of secure faith were strengthened and the unstable were made fearful, seeing the creation arrayed against those who fought for the honor of the destroyer. It is also possible that through these words the slaughters that will happen in wars at the coming [of the antichrist] are indicated. For when Gog and Magog will move against each other in the four parts of the world and, in addition, the kings who had not obeyed him will be annihilated with their whole armies and there will be slaughter in every place, then the sea will be defiled by sea-battles, and the rivers will be mingled with the blood of those who were killed there.

Chapter 48

How the third bowl caused the rivers to be mixed with blood

[16:4-6] ***The third angel poured his bowl into the rivers and the fountains of water, and they became blood. And I heard the angel of the waters say, "Just are you in these your judgments, who is and was, the Holy One. For they have shed the blood of saints and prophets, and you have given them blood to drink. It is their due!"***

As it was said above, here also it is shown that angels are placed over the elements. One of these, who is over the waters, it says, sings a hymn to God for the just condemnation that has come on the transgressors. For since they soiled their hands in the blood of the saints, God has given them blood to drink. By means of these words, it is shown either that at that time many are accounted worthy of the prophetic grace because of their standing steadfast in faith, those, namely, who are killed by the henchmen of the devil, or that those who turn from the preaching of the prophets of God and justify their murder at the hands of the hard-hearted Jews become purposefully participants in their slaughter, as the Lord said to the Jews: "For although you build the tombs of the prophets, you consent in their murder."[2]

Book Sixteen [1]See Ex 7:14-25; 9:16. [2]Lk 11:47-48.

[16:7] ***And I heard the altar say, "Yea, Lord God the Almighty, true and just are your judgments!"***

Sometimes the altar signifies Christ, for in him and through him are brought to the Father our spiritual offerings and living sacrifices, which the apostle has taught us to render.[3] At other times the altar signifies the angelic powers who, we read, "are sent forth to serve for the sake of those who are to obtain salvation,"[4] and so they carry upward our intercessions and spiritual sacrifices. From this ministering altar, it says, a voice proceeded, commending as just all the judgments of God that surpass both thought and expression.

We have learned from the Gospels that the intellectual powers are glad and rejoice over the salvation of those who turn through repentance but grieve over those who leave the straight way and yet give thanks to God for the punishment of those who transgress the divine commandments.[5] So let us hasten to bestow on them joy and gladness for our repentance, recognizing that a divine angel attends each one of us and by a certain unutterable word implants in us what must be done, in as much as his mind imperceptibly converses with our mind and he intends to rejoice over that which is heeded, but like God to grieve over that which is disregarded. And so from this converse that profits the soul we should understand that the angel, sad and from afar, follows a person who has been darkened by many sins and enters into the church. But if this person has been made contrite and confesses from the heart to him who delights[6] in mercy that he has rejected his former life and has converted to a better one, when he departs [from the church], the angel leads the way cheerfully and joyfully, while the wicked demon, having been shamed, follows behind at a distance. May it be, then, that our holy manner of life gives cause for dejection to the demons but cause for joy to the angels, so that together with them, rejoicing with a shout of gladness and the sound of confession,[7] we might give thanks to Christ, our God, for his victory over the evil powers, with whom glory is due to the Father together with the Holy Spirit, now and always and forever and ever. Amen.

BOOK SEVENTEEN

Chapter 49

How humankind is scorched through the fourth plague

[16:8-9] ***The fourth angel poured his bowl on the sun, and it was allowed to scorch people with fire; people were scorched by the fierce heat, and they cursed the name of God who had power over these plagues, and they did not repent and give him glory.***

Perhaps humankind will literally be burned by the fierce heat of the sun. While God in his goodness "curbs them with bit and bridle who do not draw near to him,"[1] so that they might look toward repentance, some have fallen to such depths of evil that by the depravity of their minds they will not turn to conversion but turn rather to blasphemy.

Perhaps, however, the image of the sun signifies the course of the day that always burns those worthy of scourging by the heat of temptations, so that by the experience of sufferings they might learn to hate the mother of these things, namely, sin. However, those who are mindless concerning any knowledge of their own faults will "sharpen their tongue"[2] against God, just as even now we see many who are distressed by the unspeakable horrors that encompass us at the hands of the barbar-

[3]Rom 12:1. [4]Heb 1:14. [5]See Lk 15:7, 10. [6]Mic 7:18. [7]Ps 42:4 (41:4 LXX). **Book Seventeen** [1]See Ps 32:9 (31:9 LXX). [2]See Ps 64:3 (63:3 LXX).

ians and who blame the goodness of God, since he has held such evils for our own generation.

Chapter 50

How the kingdom of the beast is darkened through the fifth plague

[16:10-11] ***The fifth angel poured his bowl on the throne of the beast, and its kingdom was in darkness; people gnawed their tongues in anguish and cursed the God of heaven for their pain and sores and did not repent of their deeds.***

Pouring the bowl on the throne of the beast signifies the pouring out of a great wrath on the kingdom of the antichrist. This kingdom is shown to be in darkness, that is, it is bereft of the light of "the sun of righteousness." The gnawing of tongues reveals the intensity of the pain that those who have been deceived by him will have when they are struck by these plagues sent from God. These things will occur so that they might recognize that he whom they have worshiped as God is a fraud and so might cease from this deception. However, they will not turn from this to repentance. Rather, they will turn to further blasphemy.

Since these persons turn to blasphemy at the coming of torments and those who later are smitten by hail as heavy as a hundredweight are persuaded to the same course, as we with God's help will make clear when we come to the passage,[3] and since even the evil demons, when they are tormented by the saints, do not abstain from blaspheming their own tormentors through the human bodies which they use as instruments, the question arises how we are to think about the impious who are punished by the gehenna of fire. Are we to think that in this way they perfectly cease from their innate evil even to the very thought of it, or only that they are refrained from effecting their evil intentions, in a way similar to evildoers who are thrown into prison and by constraint, not by their own design, are kept from carrying out their plans against others?

When I hear of eternal torment, I am not able to distrust him who speaks of it. Knowing that God is most disposed toward mercy and goodness, I wonder whether he would ever threaten or exact endless condemnation on those who deserve it, were he to know that those who had been condemned had repented or hated the evil that they had done willingly. For it was not by necessity that they were being tormented, but because of the evil that they freely did. For if he would let Pharaoh go, who had relented in the midst of torments but then again grew hard of heart after relief from them came, even encouraging him by Moses to be spared of the deserved torments, how much more these, if he really knew that they were putting off their filth by fire, as some interpret who use the image of gold as an analogy for this viewpoint.[4] However, filth accrues to gold, namely, to that which is soulless by nature, but it attaches itself to those who have reason by their intention and will, rather indeed it arises out of them. Therefore, those who believe that the goodness of God and his foreknowledge and his power serve as a hindrance to eternal punishment should also add to these the divine justice. They will see that the divine justice apportions to each according to that which is deserved and never serves to overthrow the divine verdict. And if this is not to their liking, then let them also accuse the rulers of the earth so that they might at least be consistent. Those who enter the lists of a wrestling match, or of a boxing match, or of a foot race or of a horse race know beforehand that not everyone will be victorious. Rather, although the stadium opens its doors for all to compete, only

[3]See the comments on Rev 16:21. [4]Andrew apparently has in mind the view of Origen, who believed the fire of Gehenna was only corrective and purifying.

one of the contestants will be crowned. Just as the stadium is opened to those who are going to compete, the entrance into this life gives to everyone this opportunity. To be born or not to be born is not within our power. However, to struggle and to defeat the evil demons and to acquire to eternal rewards is within our power. It is necessary that those who are themselves defeated by the demonic powers should regret this and lament this in vain and be punished eternally. For as the psalm says, "in hades there is no one to give praise,"[5] since there is no longer the assistance of the Spirit for the condemned, as there is now. "They shall be cut in pieces," as the Lord says,[6] separated from the living-giving Spirit who had been abused by them. We think that this understanding of the matter is also suggested by this saying of the psalm, "The Lord will not allow the rod of sinners to be upon the lot of the righteous, lest the righteous put forth their hands to iniquity."[7] Their life is unmixed, not only because of the purity and constancy of the life that each conducted but also because they were solidly rooted in the good. Their will was never enticed to the admixture of that which is base and leads toward sin, nor did the weakness of the flesh or the fear of change detract from their joy. They now inherit in God what is firm and unchangeable.

That which has been interpreted until now will influence the remaining details of the text, as was promised. Therefore, we follow closely what comes next.

Chapter 51

How the sixth bowl opens the path through the Euphrates for the kings of the east

[16:12] ***The sixth angel poured his bowl on the great river Euphrates, and its water was dried up, to prepare the way for the kings from the east.***

Perhaps by divine providence the Euphrates River will diminish in size and provide passage to the kings of the nations for their wars of destruction against each other and the rest of humankind. According to what is adduced in subsequent portions of Revelation, we think that the mention of Gog and Magog suggests that these kings will arise out of the region of the Scythians. But it is also possible that the antichrist, coming out of the eastern regions of Persia, where the Hebrew tribe of Dan resides, will cross the Euphrates with other kings or with strong men who have received a royal name and will inflict on humankind either bodily death to some on account of their faith and perseverance or spiritual death to others because of their cowardice and faintheartedness.

[16:13] ***And I saw, issuing from the mouth of the dragon and from the mouth of the beast and from the mouth of the false prophet, three foul spirits like frogs.***

This passage mentions individually the devil as a dragon, the antichrist as a beast and the false prophet as another figure distinct from the other two. It says that spirits similar to frogs come out from these, for they are characterized by a poisonous and filthy nature, and these evil powers love the mud and creep toward foul and moist pleasures. By the commands of the devil and of the antichrist and of the false prophet, they will use their mouths to show false signs and wonders to humankind, as we learn in what follows.

[16:14] ***For they are demonic spirits, performing signs, who go abroad to the kings of the whole world, to assemble them for battle on the great day of God the Almighty.***

The false signs produced by the demons will

[5]Ps 6:5 (6:6 LXX). [6]Mt 24:51. [7]Ps 125:3 (124:3 LXX).

cause those who follow them to make war on the "great and terrible day of God, the judge of the living and the dead."[8] On that day, those who fight against God will be utterly defeated and, although they lament over their former deception, they will weep in vain.

[16:15-16] ***"Lo, I am coming like a thief! Blessed is he who is awake, keeping his garments that he may not go naked and be seen exposed!" And they assembled them at the place that is called in Hebrew Armageddon.***

"To be awake and to keep one's garments" means to remain vigilant and always concerned with good works. For good works are the garments of the saints, and were one to be without these, one would necessarily be made ashamed as one naked and full of shamefulness. "Armageddon" is translated as "cutting" or "being thoroughly cut up." And therefore we are led to think that the nations that the devil gathers and leads to battle there will be slaughtered, since the devil rejoices in human blood.

We are taught in this passage that it is a terrible thing to be naked of the garments of virtue, and we have learned from the Gospel parable that he who is without this is thrown out of the bridal chamber,[9] and we have learned from the apostolic saying that speaks of incorruptibility, "that putting this on, we shall not be found naked,"[10] clearly referring to good works. Therefore let us earnestly beseech the Lord that he wash the robes of our souls, so that, as the word of the psalm says, "they may be made whiter than snow,"[11] lest we hear, "Friend, how did you get in here without a wedding garment?" and "having our hands and feet bound, be cast into outer darkness."[12] Rather, as the wise Solomon says, let us "always have our garments white"[13] and wear robes bright and white from a virtuous life, decorated with sympathy. And so let us enter into the bridal chamber with the pure and blameless Bridegroom of holy souls, Christ our God, with whom glory, might and honor is due to the Father, together with the Holy Spirit, now and always, and forever and ever. Amen.

BOOK EIGHTEEN

Chapter 52

How the seventh bowl brings hail and an earthquake against humankind

[16:17-18] ***The seventh angel poured his bowl into the air, and a voice came out of heaven, from the throne, saying, "It is done!" And there were flashes of lightning, voices, peals of thunder and a great earthquake such as had never been since people were on the earth, so great was that earthquake.***

The angelic voice from heaven said, "It is done!" That is, the commandment of God has been accomplished. The flashes of lightning and the voices and the thunders are symbolic of the terrifying nature of these occurrences and of the future coming of Christ, just as long ago they announced the descent of God on Mount Sinai.[1] The earthquake signifies the transformation of that which exists, as the apostle explained, "Yet once more I will shake not only the earth but also the heaven."[2]

[16:19] ***The great city was split into three parts, and the cities of the nations fell.***

We understand Jerusalem to be this great city, not because of the number and size of its buildings but as that which is the most ancient and greatest in regard to godliness, in as much as it was made great by the sufferings of Christ and is to be distinguished from the

[8]Joel 2:11; Mal 4:5 (3:2 LXX). [9]Mt 22:11-13. [10]2 Cor 5:3. [11]Ps 51:7 (50:7 LXX). [12]Mt 22:12-13. [13]Eccl 9:8. **Book Eighteen** [1]See Ex 19:16-19. [2]Heb 12:26.

cities of the nations. We think that the division of this city into three parts suggests the division between the Christians and the Jews and the Samaritans who live in it. Or, the division is of those who are steadfast in faith and those who have defiled their baptism with filthy works and the Jews who have in no way received the proclamation. This reveals the unhindered and utterly free fulfillment of their own desires and the sending of them to those regions appropriately allotted to each. For at the present time the Jews and Samaritans hide their real intentions out of fear of our pious rulers, and they seem to be associated with us, not daring to separate themselves with their own people. It is similar to the fact that those who are truly Christians are intermingled with those who possess the name of Christian alone. But when the cleansing fire of temptations will unmask them, then there will occur the division of these people into the three groups of the impious, the pious and the sinners, and these will gather together with those of like habits and be associated with their own kind. The falling of the cities of the nations indicates either their destruction or the cessation of the pagan manner of life at the coming of the kingdom of God, which, according to Daniel, the saints will possess.[3]

[16:19] ***And God remembered great Babylon, to make her drain the cup of the wine of the fury of his wrath.***

The thronging multitude, confounded by the meaningless distractions of life and made great by the wealth of their injustices, will drink the cup of the wrath of God. It is as though they went from a merciful forgetfulness to a remembrance and now faced the retribution for their trampling of the righteous One and for the impiety of their words and deeds.

[16:20] ***And every island fled away, and no mountains were to be found.***

The holy Scriptures have taught us that islands refer to the churches and mountains refer to those who are leaders in them. That they flee at the time of the arrival of the aforementioned occurrences, we have heard from the Lord, who said, "Then they will flee from the east to the west and from the west to the east. For there will be a great tribulation, such as has not been from the foundation of the world, nor will ever be."[4] At that time some will be tormented for their sins, and others will endure misfortunes for the testing of their virtue. Such misfortunes will not only be those from the antichrist that they suffer for the sake of Christ, but also their flights and their sufferings among the mountains and caves. For they will prefer the mountains and caves to living in the cities for the sake of preserving their piety.

[16:21] ***And great hailstones, heavy as a hundredweight, dropped on people from heaven; and people cursed God for the plague of the hail, so fearful was that plague.***

We think that the hail that comes down from heaven is the wrath from God, which also comes from above. That this hail weighs a hundredweight indicates its completeness [of its fearful torment] on account of the extremity and seriousness of the sins, which the image of the talent suggests and as Zechariah saw.[5] That those who are struck by this hail are moved to blasphemy rather than to repentance reveals the unyielding hardness of their hearts. And so they will be like Pharaoh,[6] or rather they will be even more intransigent than he was. For he at least to some extent was softened by the plagues sent from God and confessed his own ungodliness, but these persons will blaspheme even in the midst of being tormented.

[3]Dan 7:18, 22, 27. [4]See Mt 24:21. The first part of this quotation is not in the Gospel text. [5]Zech 5:7-8. [6]See Ex 4:21; 7:3; 9:12.

Chapter 53

Concerning one of the seven angels who shows the destruction of the harlot city to the blessed John, and concerning the seven heads and the ten horns

[17:1-3] ***Then one of the seven angels who had the seven bowls came and spoke with me, saying to me, "Come, I will show you the judgment of the great harlot who is seated on many waters, with whom the kings of the earth have committed fornication, and with the wine of whose fornication the dwellers on earth have become drunk." And he carried me away in the spirit into a wilderness, and I saw a woman sitting on a scarlet beast that was full of blasphemous names, and it had seven heads and seven horns.***

Some consider this harlot to be old Rome, since she sits on seven hills, and the seven heads of the beast that carries the harlot to be the more ungodly kings from Domitian to Diocletian who persecuted the church.[7] However, we are guided as much as possible by the sequence of events and think that she is either the earthly kingdom generally, depicted as in one body, or that city that is ruled until the arrival of the antichrist. For old Rome lost the power of dominion a long time ago, and we do not suppose that the ancient status will again return to it. But should we grant this, the power that governs today will have been destroyed beforehand. For Revelation says, "The woman that you saw is the great city that has dominion over the kings of the earth."[8] But concerning this we will discuss more thoroughly in the following, should God supply the need.

But it is necessary to say what we think concerning the wilderness into which he says he was led in the spirit. We think that in spiritual matters every city or populated place is a wilderness that is blameworthy because of a drunkenness of soul and fornication from God and of other such affronts. It is also to be noted that in the vision that the spirit gives, the apostle sees the devastation of the harlot, whom he saw as a woman because she was softened for sin and unmanly. She was seated on a scarlet beast because through evil deeds she reposed on the devil, who is murderous and delights in blood. Through such evil deeds she becomes a coworker with the apostate in his blasphemies against God. The beast with its scarlet appearance is an indication of its cruelty and savagery and murderous intention.

Concerning the seven heads and the ten horns we will be instructed, with God's help, by the holy angel in what follows.

[17:4] ***The woman was arrayed in purple and scarlet and bedecked with gold and a precious stone and pearls.***

She is clothed in scarlet and purple, for these are symbols of her dominion and rule over all. Therefore, she is decorated with a precious stone and pearls.

[17:4] ***Holding in her hand a golden cup full of abominations and the impurities of her fornication.***

The cup indicates the sweetness of evil deeds before they are tasted, and it is gold because such deeds seem precious, as someone said of Job, "who drinks scoffing like water."[9] The cup moreover demonstrates that she is not sated by her evil but pursues further evil with a thirst for her own destruction. Therefore, she multiplies abominations for herself, that is, she demands practices that are abominable to God, and she makes the multitude who love the martyrs to drink of it. In this way she draws, as though it were a sweet drink, the

[7]Andrew is referring to the opinion of Oecumenius. [8]Rev 17:18. [9]Job 34:7.

abominable stupor of sin and the pollution of fornication from God.

[17:5] ***And on her forehead was written a name of mystery, "Babylon the great, mother of harlots and of earth's abominations."***

The writing on the forehead indicates the shamelessness of the fullness of sins and of the confusion of the heart. She is mother because for those cities ruled by her she is the teacher of their spiritual fornication, giving birth to transgressions that are loathsome to God.

Chapter 54
How the angel explained the mystery that he had seen

[17:6-7] ***And I saw the woman, drunk with the blood of the saints and the blood of the martyrs of Jesus. And when I saw her I marveled greatly. But the angel said to me, "Why marvel? I will tell you the mystery of the woman, and of the beast with seven heads and ten horns that carries her."***

From many examples we learn that descriptive names can be ascribed to cities because of their reputations. Ancient Babylon is named in this way and is called a "pleasant harlot, skilled in sorcery,"[10] and ancient Jerusalem is named "you had a whore's face,"[11] and in the letter of Peter the older Rome is called "Babylon."[12] More recently, she who held power among the Persians is called "Babylon" and a "harlot," as well as any other city that rejoices in murder and blood. And so, when the Evangelist saw one of these cities polluted with the blood of the saints, he was perplexed and learned about it from the angel, namely, that she who bears the power of the earthly kingdom at the end of time must suffer for her trespasses. And this is so whether one believes it to be the power of the Persians, or old Rome or new Rome, or whether the kingdom is taken generically as in one body. For we know that in each of these there are different sins and the shedding of innocent blood, sometimes more, sometimes less. Indeed, who could reckon the blood of the martyrs shed until Diocletian or the torments of these at the hands of the Persians? Moreover, for those who read them, the histories relate the perfidies done secretly under Julian and those done in new Rome against the orthodox during the time of the Arians.[13]

[17:8] ***"The beast that you saw was, and is not, and is to ascend from the bottomless pit and go to perdition."***

The beast is the devil who is always seeking someone to devour.[14] He was killed by the cross of Christ, but, it is said, he will live again at the end, effecting the denial of salvation through the deceit of the antichrist in signs and wonders. In this way he "was" and was powerful before the cross, but he "no longer is" after the salvific sufferings, for he has become powerless and is deprived of his authority that he had over the nations on account of idolatry. And at the end he will come, in the way we have indicated, arising from the abyss or from wherever he was condemned and where the demons, thrown out by Christ, begged him not to send them, but rather into the swine.[15] Or he will come out of the present life, which is figuratively called "abyss" because of the depth of sin that lives in it and because it is blown about and agitated by the winds of passion. From this place the antichrist, having Satan in himself, will come for the destruction of people, going himself to perdition in the age to come.

[17:8] ***"And the dwellers on earth whose names have not been written in the book of life from***

[10]Nahum 3:4. [11]Jer 3:3. [12]1 Pet 5:13. [13]See Sozomen *Ecclesiastical History* 2.9.14 (NPNF 2 2:264-68). [14]See 1 Pet 5:8. [15]Lk 8:30-33.

the foundation of the world, will marvel to behold the beast, because it was and is not and is to come."

On account of the false miracles, those whose names are not written in the book of those who live forever and who have not been sufficiently taught in the prophecies of Christ concerning him will be astonished at his coming and wonder how he had regained his ancient power.

[17:9] ***"This calls for a mind with wisdom."***

Since what is to be interpreted is spiritual, there is need, it says, for a spiritual wisdom, not a worldly wisdom to understand what is being said.

[17:9] ***"The seven heads are seven mountains on which the woman is seated."***

We believe that the seven heads and the seven mountains are to be interpreted as seven places that excel the rest in excellence and worldly power. In these places we recognize that at various times the kingdom of the world is established, such as at first the rule of the Assyrians in Nineveh. Second, in Ecbatana there was the power of the Medians who from the time of Arbakes seized power from the Assyrians whose king, Sardanapal, Arbakes is said to have destroyed. After these there was the power of the Chaldeans in Babylon, whose king was Nebuchanezzar. Then after their fall the rule of the Persians in Susa was initiated by Cyrus. And after the destruction of this kingdom by Alexander, there was the rule of the Macedonians. After these there was in old Rome the power of the Romans that was sovereign under Augustus Caesar and its recent emperors and consuls and was possessed by wicked men until Constantine. After the fall of these, the royal powers of emperors favorable to Christ were transferred to new Rome.[16]

We think that the seven kings display the same idea [as the seven mountains], for the change of peoples in no way damages the identity of the notion, even though there the seven heads are shown in the form of a woman and the seven mountains in a neutral way. Here he showed seven kings. For often in the Scripture male names indifferently are given in the place of female names, and vice versa. For example, "Ephraim is a heifer made mad,"[17] or again, "Ephraim is a dove having no heart."[18] According to the theologian, "There are three who witness to Christ, the blood and the water and the Spirit,"[19] and according to Solomon, "There are three, the goat and the rooster and a king who is speaking publicly."[20] Therefore, through the seven heads he shows the cities after the manner of a woman, and through the seven mountains he depicts in neutral form seven majestic powers that at various times rise up over the rest of the earth, not by any geographical placement among the nations but because of their position of glory. And, as we said, we have interpreted the kings to be either those places made glorious by their royal prominence or those kings who have ruled first in each of the aforementioned kingdoms, by periphrasis each standing for the entire kingdom—so, Nines for Assyria, Arbakes for Media, Nebuchanezzar for Babylon, Cyrus for Persia, Alexander for Macedonia, Romulus for old Rome and Constantine for new Rome.

[17:10] ***They are also seven kings, five of whom have fallen, one is, the other has not yet come, and when he comes he must remain only a little while."***

The blessed Hippolytus interprets these to be ages, of which five have already passed, the sixth, in which the apostle had his vision, is still remaining, and the seventh, which is after

[16]New Rome refers to the city of Constantinople. [17]Hos 10:11; 4:16. [18]Hos 7:11. [19]1 Jn 5:8. [20]Prov 30:29, 31.

the six thousand years, has not yet come.[21] But when it comes, it will "remain only a little while." And these things are so. But if, as Irenaeus says, just as seven days have been created, so also there are seven heavens and seven preeminent angels,[22] it seems reasonable when we say that there are also seven kingdoms that have been prominent from the beginning until the present time. Of these seven, five have already fallen. The sixth kingdom is that of old Rome, during whose rule the revelation was seen. The seventh kingdom that has not yet come would be the new Rome. The passage concerning the universal Babylon would well find its completion in that city that rules until the antichrist. It would exercise power for a short period of time, even as those did that ruled previously. For some of them governed for more than five hundred years, and others ruled for more than a thousand years. To be sure, every temporal period is short in comparison with the future kingdom of the saints that is without end.

[17:11] ***"And the beast that was and is not, it is an eighth, but it belongs to the seven, and it goes to perdition."***

The beast is the antichrist. He is the eighth because he arises after the seven kingdoms for the deception and devastation of the earth. He is from the seven because he arises from one of these. For he will not come forth from a nation other than those mentioned before, but as a king of the Romans for the defeat and destruction of those who believed in him. And after this he will go into the destruction of Gehenna.

[17:12] ***"And the ten horns that you saw are ten kings who have not yet received royal power, but they are to receive authority as kings for one hour, together with the beast."***

Daniel also saw these ten horns that precede the antichrist.[23] After rooting out three of them, the accursed one will subdue the others. The "one hour" indicates either the brevity of time or the one hour of the year, or by way of figure of speech, clearly meaning a three-month period, after which they will submit themselves to the antichrist as to their leader.

[17:13-14] ***"These are of one mind and give over their power and authority to the beast; they will make war on the Lamb, and the Lamb will conquer them, for he is Lord of lords and King of kings, and those with him are called and chosen and faithful."***

Indeed! For "no one can serve two masters."[24] And so those who conspire together with an evil agreement and ally themselves with the antichrist will oppose themselves to Christ. However, the Lamb of God who was slain for us will conquer them. For he was not deprived of his kingdom and lordship over all things when he became man, so that he might acquire even his elect as participants in his own rule.

[17:15-18] ***And he said to me, "The waters that you saw, where the harlot is seated, are peoples and multitudes and nations and tongues. And the ten horns that you saw, they and the beast will hate the harlot; they will make her desolate and devour her flesh and burn her up with fire, for God has put it into their hearts to carry out his purpose by being of one mind and giving over their royal power to the beast, until the words of God shall be fulfilled. And the woman that you saw is the great city that has dominion over the kings of the earth."***

Since the angel explained these things clearly, a more detailed explanation of them is superfluous. It is remarkable to me how the devil

[21]Hippolytus *Comm. Dan.* 4.23 (GCS 1:242-44; ANF 5:179). [22]Irenaeus *Haer.* 1.5.2 (ANF 1:322). [23]Dan 7:7-12. [24]Mt 6:24.

is both enemy and avenger. For he will work through the ten horns, who are guided by him, to oppose that lover of good and virtue, Christ our God, and to lay waste that populous city that has abandoned the divine laws and become servant to his pleasures, and like a bloodthirsty beast they will glut themselves on its blood. He will regard its conflagration as an occasion for rejoicing and the mutilation of human flesh as proper food, and he who always rejoices in duplicity will grant harmony to those ten apostate horns. That which continues makes very clear that the woman who was seen is the great city that exercises power over the kings of the earth, and he clearly prophesies the sufferings of that power that is ruling during those times. From these trials the beneficent God will redeem us and enlist us in the heavenly city, namely, in the Jerusalem above. In this city "he will be everything to everyone," as the apostle says,[25] "when he shall destroy every rule," clearly every apostate rule, "and every authority and power."[26] In addition, he will recline with and serve those who have served him here faithfully and wisely, that is, he will give them the enjoyment of the eternal blessings that have been "prepared from the foundation of the world."[27] Of this bliss may also we be found worthy in Christ, the savior and redeemer of our souls, with whom be glory and power to the Father, together with the Holy Spirit forever and ever. Amen.

BOOK NINETEEN

Chapter 55

Concerning another angel who shows the fall of Babylon and the voice from heaven that commands flight from the city, and concerning the loss of pleasures that the city formerly had

[18:1] ***After this I saw another angel coming down from heaven, having great authority; and the earth was made bright with his splendor.***

This passage reveals the brilliance and brightness of the holy powers that greatly surpasses the light of the stars and the heavenly bodies.

[18:2-3] ***And he called out with a great and mighty voice, saying, "Fallen, fallen is Babylon the great! It has become a dwelling place of demons, a haunt of every foul and hated spirit, for all nations have drunk the wrath of the wine of her fornication."***

Something similar to this was foretold in Isaiah about the Chaldean capital city of Babylon when it was captured by Cyrus and the Persians, namely, that it would be filled with beasts and impure spirits on account of its utter desolation.[1] For it is the habit of beasts and of evil demons to stalk in arid places. This is due both to the divine economy, which frees people from their harm, and to their own dislike of humankind. And how did the present Babylon cause the nations to drink the wine of its fornication? By becoming in every way their leader in every transgression and by sending gifts to obedient cities making their rulers enemies of truth and righteousness.

[18:3] ***"And the kings of the earth have committed fornication with her, and the merchants of the earth have grown rich with the wealth of her wantonness."***

It says that because of the abundance of the riches of its injustice, it gave the merchants of the earth opportunities for profit because it consumed well beyond its needs and was wanton toward those in need.

[18:4-5] ***Then I heard another voice from***

[25]1 Cor 15:28. [26]1 Cor 15:24. [27]See Mt 25:34. **Book Nineteen** [1]See Is 13:21-22.

heaven, saying, "Come out of her, my people, lest you take part in her sins, lest you receive her plagues, for her sins are heaped high as heaven, and God has remembered her iniquities."

What once was said to Lot, "Flee, save your life,"[2] and was spoken in Isaiah, "Depart from her, go out thence, do not touch an unclean thing,"[3] is now also spoken here. For cohabitation with those who provoke God is to be avoided.

[18:6-7] ***"Render to her as she herself has rendered to you, and repay her double for her deeds; mix a double draught for her in the cup she mixed. As she glorified herself and played the wanton, so give her a like measure of torment and mourning."***

These words may refer to those who, although innocent in Babylon, yet suffered the most terrible things at the hands of those who ruled it and through their endurance of these agonies were the reason for the punishment of their tormentors. Or these words may refer to a change of persons and circumstances, from those who were tormented to certain holy powers that have acquired the power of punishment and through love of God exercise those torments that had been done by it against their fellow servants. He speaks of the cup as double, either because sinners and transgressors are punished both here and in the age to come, or because both the soul and the body are punished for their common deeds or because of the depth of divine benevolence that is reckoned as double that is lacking of pure justice on account of sin, and punishment is often endured in the conscience.

[18:7] "In her heart she says, 'A queen I sit, I am no widow, mourning I will never see.'"

If there is no fear of God in them, it is the habit of those in prosperity to say, "I shall never be moved."[4] This is what the city has spoken to herself.

[18:8] ***"So shall her plagues come in a single day, death and mourning and famine, and she will be burned with fire, for mighty is the Lord God who judges her."***

By a single day he means either the suddenness and shortness of the time in which mourning will come to her either from the sword or from famine, and she will be wasted from pestilence and will be consumed by fire. Or it refers to the course of the day itself in which the city will experience these things that are prophesied. For after the enemies gain control of the city, only one day will suffice to bring every evil and every form of death on those who have been defeated. For God is strong both to save those who please him and to punish those who are unrepentant sinners.

[18:9-10] ***And the kings of the earth, who committed fornication and were wanton with her, will weep and wail over her when they see the smoke of her burning; they will stand far off, in fear of her torment, and say, "Alas! Alas! Thou great city, Babylon, the mighty city! In one hour has your judgment come."***

We think that in this passage the "kings" refer to the rulers, as the psalmist said concerning Jerusalem, "Behold, her kings have assembled."[5] It says that those who committed fornication in her against the divine commandments will weep, since they see or hear of her burning and desolation, and they are thoroughly terrified at the sudden change that had taken place in such a short time.

[18:11-12] ***And the merchants of the earth***

[2]Gen 19:17. [3]Is 52:11. [4]Ps 30:6 (29:6 LXX). [5]Ps 48:4 (47:5 LXX).

weep and mourn for themselves, since no one buys their cargo any more, cargo of gold, silver, jewels and pearls, fine linen, purple, silk and scarlet.

The buying and the consumption of those who are being corrupted by power and indulgence is extraordinary.

[18:12-13] ***All kinds of scented wood, all articles of ivory, all articles of costly wood, bronze, iron and marble, cinnamon, spice, incense, myrrh, frankincense, wine, oil, fine flour and wheat, cattle and sheep.***

We should understand through these words that no one is buying. We should consider which city is in the habit of purchasing such items and what people so desire the possession of such excess for the purpose of dissolute indulgence.

[18:13] ***And horses and chariots, and slaves.***

The use of these things, it says, is extraordinary. Through the word rhedōn[6] perhaps chariots are meant. For rhedioum[7] [= radium] is Latin for chariot. And the general plural of this is rhedioroum[8] [= radiorum], which he has shortened to rhedōn.[9]

[18:13-14] ***That is, human souls. "The fruit for which your soul longed has gone from you, and all your dainties and your splendor are gone from you, never to be found again!"***

You will never again traffic in human lives, it says, or enslave the free. Nor will you enjoy your former wealth and magnificence.

[18:15-17] ***The merchants of these wares, who gained wealth from her, will stand far off, in fear of her torment, weeping and mourning aloud, "Alas, alas, for the great city that was clothed in fine linen, in purple and scarlet, bedecked with gold, with jewels, and with pearls! In one hour all this wealth has been laid waste."***

He leads before our eyes the sufferings of this Babylon and through the laments made over her he depicts the greatness of her misfortune that she, who formerly boasted of her royal majesty, will suffer.

[18:17-19] ***And all shipmasters and seafaring men, sailors and all whose trade is on the sea, stood afar off and cried out as they saw the smoke of her burning, saying, "What city was like the great city?" And they threw dust on their heads, as they wept and mourned, crying out, "Alas, alas, for the great city where all who had ships at sea grew rich by her wealth! In one hour she has been laid waste."***

He speaks figuratively of the present life as a sea, since it is heaving with waves. Those who make commerce on the sea swim in the turbulence of this life as though they were fishes. However, perhaps that city that suffers these things lies beside a physical sea and receives these misfortunes from those who sail on it, giving them an opportunity to loot her of her own wealth. But it is necessary to add that the merchants of this universal Babylon, that is, Confusion, will suffer the same thing at the conclusion of the visible world and will sob inconsolably, since they are unwillingly deprived of the pleasures of this life and are reproached by their conscience because of their deeds.

[18:20] ***"Rejoice over her, O heaven, O holy apostles and prophets, for God has given judgment for you against her!"***

By heaven he means either the angels or the

[6] ῥεδῶν. [7] ῥεδιούμ. [8] ῥεδιόρουμ. [9] ῥεδῶν.

saints who make their dwelling in heaven. The apostles and the prophets are urged to rejoice with these, and so to avenge those who were maltreated by the city. Their rejoicing would also avenge those who were often dishonored through transgressions of the divine laws while they vainly entreated the inhabitants of that city, or those who were forcibly scattered throughout the earth and were slaughtered for the sake of God and because they were servants of his words. In this way, the prophets were killed by the Jews, and the apostles by the Gentiles, to whom they especially preached the word. They rejoice for the coming of these chastisements, not because they rejoice in hardships but because they ardently desire a cessation to sin. And perhaps those who have been slaves to sin might obtain a milder punishment in the age to come because they were tormented to some extent here.

[18:21-24] ***Then a mighty angel took a stone like a great millstone and threw it into the sea, saying, "So shall Babylon the great city be thrown down with violence and shall be found no more; and the sound of harpers and minstrels, of flute players and trumpeters shall be heard in thee no more; and a craftsman of any craft shall be found in thee no more; and the sound of the millstone shall be heard in thee no more; and the light of a lamp shall shine in thee no more; and the voice of the bridegroom and bride shall be heard in thee no more; for thy merchants were the great men of the earth, and all nations were deceived by thy sorcery. And in her was found the blood of prophets and of saints, and of all who have been slain on earth."***

Just as a millstone sinks with force into the sea, so also the destruction of this Babylon will be sudden, so that afterward no trace of it will be found. The absence of harpers, minstrels and the rest is an indication of this. And he gives the reason for this. Babylon deceived all nations with its sorcery and was the recipient of the blood of prophets and the other saints. It is possible that this passage depicts the impious Babylon among the Persians, for at various times until now it has received the blood of many saints and continually rejoices in sorceries and deceptions. And this gives us an occasion for prayer, that it receive the rewards prophesied for arrogance against Christ and his servants.

But against this opinion is that of the ancient teachers of the church, which supposes that these things are prophesied against the Babylon of the Romans. They refer to the vision in which the ten horns are on the fourth beast, that is, on the Roman rule, and from it another one comes that roots out three of the ten and subdues the others.[10] And when this king of the Romans comes in the pretence of assisting and helping their rule, he in fact comes to effect their complete ruin. Therefore, as we said, whoever interprets this kingdom as though it were one body that from the beginning until now exercised power and that truly has shed the blood of apostles, prophets and martyrs, such a one would not be mistaken concerning the present passage. For even as it is said that there is one chorus and one army and one city, although those who populate each of these might change, so also there is one kingdom, although it is divided into many times and places.

Chapter 56

Concerning the song of the saints and the threefold hallelujah that they sing at the destruction of Babylon

[19:1-4] ***After this I heard a voice of a great multitude in heaven, saying, "Hallelujah! Salvation and glory and power belong of our***

[10]See Dan 7:8, 19-20.

God, for his judgments are true and just; he has judged the great harlot who corrupted the earth with her fornication, and he has avenged the blood of his servants from her hand." Once more they cried, "Hallelujah! The smoke from her goes up forever and ever." And the twenty-four elders and the four living creatures fell down and worshiped God who is seated on the throne, saying: "Amen. Hallelujah!"

"Hallelujah" signifies divine praise, while "Amen" means "truly" or "let it be so." This praise is common both from the angelic powers as well as from humankind, which is similar to the angels, and this praise is sent up to God three times on account of the tri-hypostatic deity of Father and of Son and of Holy Spirit, one God.[11] The praise is that God has "avenged the blood of his servants from the hand" of Babylon and has benefited its inhabitants by accomplishing the cessation of sin through its punishment. The words that the smoke from the city goes up forever and ever show either the unforgettable nature of the punishments that have come on the city or that although it meted out punishments in part and to some extent, it will, nevertheless, be punished eternally in the coming age.

[19:5] ***And from the throne came a voice, "Praise our God, all you his servants, you who fear him, small and great."***

The throne of God is the cherubim and the seraphim. Whether these are great or small in their accomplishments, all are urged to praise God according to their abilities. However, I think that also those who are small in age and children who are not yet grown shall be great when they sing to God who has done such great things.

[19:6-7] ***Then I heard what seemed to be the voice of a great multitude, like the sound of many waters and like the sound of mighty thunder peals, crying, "Hallelujah! For our God the Almighty reigns. Let us rejoice and exult and give him the glory, for the marriage of the Lamb has come."***

"The voice of a great multitude and of many waters and thunder peals" signifies the piercing clarity of the hymn, for all the angelic and heavenly powers are without number, although some have interpreted these to be the waters above the heavens.[12] With these heavenly powers the whole body of the righteous give glory to the Creator. Indeed, Christ rules as king. By nature he governs all those of whom he is creator, but he rules these also by virtue of his incarnation, either according to his free and purposeful fellowship with them or according to the authority that is proper to him as king and judge.

The marriage of the Lamb is the union of the church with Christ. The holy apostles governed the church, and through them she was given "the guarantee of the Spirit,"[13] since then [at the consummation] she will receive that perfect union that is face to face.

Chapter 57
Concerning the mystical marriage and the supper of the Lamb

[19:7-9] ***"And his bride has made herself ready; it was granted her to be clothed with fine linen, pure and bright."—for the fine linen is the righteous deeds of the saints. And the angel said to me, "Write this. Blessed are those who are invited to the supper of the Lamb." And he said to me, "These are true words of God."***

The church is clothed in fine linen because of the brightness of her virtues, the excellency of

[11]Andrew has in mind the threefold hallelujah of Rev 19:1, 3, 6. [12]It is not certain to whom Andrew refers. [13]2 Cor 1:22; 5:5.

her understanding, and the exalted character of her contemplation. For the judgments of God find their completion in these things.

The marriage supper of Christ is the feast of those who are being saved and the joy that accompanies it. The blessed will come into these things when they enter into the eternal bridal chamber with the holy Bridegroom of their purified souls. For he who has promised this is faithful. Since there are many blessings in the coming age, which surpass every understanding, the participation in them is indicated through various terms. Sometimes they are called the kingdom of heaven on account of their glory and honor; sometimes they are called paradise on account of the everlasting banquet of good things, sometimes they are called the bosom of Abraham on account of the rest of those who repose there, or the bridal chamber and marriage because of the endless joy and the perfect and inexpressible union of God with his servants. This union surpasses every carnal and bodily union as much as light is separated from darkness or a perfume from a foul odor.

[19:10] ***Then I fell down at his feet and worshiped him, but he said to me, "You must not do that! I am a fellow servant with you and your brethren who hold the testimony of Jesus. Worship God." For the testimony of Jesus is the spirit of prophecy.***

"Do not worship me as the one who is foretelling the future," the holy angel says. For the confession of Christ, that is, the testimony, is the gift of the prophetic Spirit. And you should note also this. The prophecy is given for this reason, so that the testimony of Christ may be made strong and the faith be given witness by the saints. Therefore, do not pay homage to me, as fellow servant, but to him who possesses power over all things. From this passage we also learn of the humble disposition of the holy angels, for they do not claim for themselves divine glory as do the evil demons but ascribe this glory to the Lord. May it be that we "outdo one another" with a humble mind,[14] thus fulfilling the saying of the Lord, "Learn from me, for I am gentle and lowly in heart, and you will find rest for your souls."[15] And may we receive rest in the coming age, where "sorrow and pain and groaning have fled"[16] and where the dwelling is of all who rejoice and gaze on the light of the face of Christ our God,[17] to whom every song of praise, honor and worship be given, together with the Father and the life-giving Spirit forever and ever. Amen.

BOOK TWENTY

Chapter 58

How the Evangelist saw Christ on a horse with the hosts of heaven

[19:11-12] ***Then I saw heaven opened, and behold, a white horse! He who sat on it is faithful and true, and in righteousness he judges and makes war. His eyes are like a flame of fire, and on his head are many diadems.***

The open heaven reveals that the coming of the judge who was seen was about to happen, as though it were the drawing back of curtains of the judges of the earth for the judgment and sentencing of those responsible.

The white horse signifies the future brilliance of the saints, on whom is seated the one who will judge the nations. He sends forth flames of fire from his eyes, that is, from his all-seeing power. For those who are righteous, this fire does not harm but illumines and makes bright. However, for the sinners the fire burns but does not make bright.

The multiple diadems symbolize either his

[14]See Rom 12:10. [15]Mt 11:29. [16]See Is 35:10. [17]See Ps 87:7 (86:7 LXX); 2 Cor 4:6.

kingdom, which is over all things in heaven and on earth—as many as there are ranks of angels and kingdoms on the earth and assemblies among holy people—or they signify the victory against the sinners that was won for us by all of his acts of mercy, as a certain holy person said: "And you will gain victory when you are judged."[1]

[19:12] ***And he has a name inscribed that no one knows but himself.***

That his name is unknown signifies the incomprehensibility of his essence. By virtue of his works he is known by many names, such as Good, Shepherd, Sun, Light, Life, Righteousness, Holiness, Redemption.[2] Similarly, he is called by terms of negation, such as Incorruptible, Invisible, Immortal, Unchangeable.[3] However, according to his essence he is without name and unapproachable, being known by himself alone with the Father and the Spirit.[4]

[19:13] ***He is clad in a robe dipped in blood, and the name by which he is called is the Word of God.***

[The robe of the Word of God here is his all-holy and incorruptible flesh, which he dipped in his own blood at his voluntary passion.[5]] Through these words, those things just expounded are confirmed. But how is it that he who is without name and is unknown to all is here named "Word"? This is either to demonstrate his filial personhood and his impassible generation from the Father, just as our speech comes from our minds [impassibly], or his name suggests that he bears within himself the causes of all things that exist or that he is the interpreter of the wisdom and power of the Father.

[19:14] ***And the armies of heaven followed him, many horsemen, arrayed in fine linen, white and pure.***

The heavenly armies signify the heavenly orders that are resplendent with the excellence of their nature, with the sublimity of their thoughts and with the brightness of their virtues and their intimate union with God.

[19:15] ***From his mouth issues a sharp sword with which to smite the nations, and he will rule them with a rod of iron; he will tread the wine press of the wine of the fury of the wrath of God the Almighty.***

This sword reveals the punishment that will come on the wicked and the sinful according to the righteous judgment and command that issues from the mouth of God. Through this they will be governed by the unbreakable rod of never-ending torments and be subject to various forms of evil. The saints will be free of this, "for the Lord will not allow the rod of sinners to be on them," according to the psalm.[6] "He walks the wine press of wrath," because "the Father judges no one but has given to him as a man that judgment"[7] that as the Son he possessed by nature from the beginning.

[19:16] ***On his robe and on his thigh he has a name inscribed, King of kings and Lord of lords.***

This name reveals the unity of the divine incarnation. For in this unity he who is God suffered in the flesh, and although man, he

Book Twenty [1]See Ps 51:4 (50:6 LXX). [2]For these names, see Lk 18:19; Jn 10:11; Heb 13:20; Jn 1:9; 8:12; 14:6; 1 Cor 1:30. [3]For these terms, see 1 Tim 1:17; Col 1:15; Mal 3:6; Heb 1:10-12. [4]According to his essence (οὐσία), God is unknowable. However, according to his economy (οἰκονομία), he is knowable. See Gregory of Nazianzus *Or.* 29.17 (NPNF 2 7:307); *Or.* 30.20, 21 (NPNF 2 7:316-17). [5]The manuscript evidence here is uncertain and complex. These words appear in some manuscripts. [6]Ps 125:3 (124:3 LXX). [7]See Jn 5:22.

is King of kings and Lord of lords. Those who have ruled the passions and in cooperation with Christ have possessed authority and power over sin shall also rule with him in the coming age.

Chapter 59

Concerning the antichrist and those who with him are thrown into Gehenna

[19:17] ***Then I saw an angel standing in the sun, and he called with a loud voice to all the birds that fly in mid-heaven.***

We think that this angel is one of the highest of the angels and exhorts the others to rejoice over the punishment of the sinners and the cessation of sin. He has called the angels birds due to the exalted and sublime nature that they have in comparison with ours. In imitation of Christ, their food is the fulfilling of the divine will.[8] They are in mid-heaven so that they might share their ascent and joy, just mentioned, with those persons who are similar to the angels. For through their mediation there is a way up from the things below, and through them the saints "are caught up to meet the Lord."[9]

[19:17-18] ***"Come to the supper of the great God, to eat the flesh of kings, the flesh of captains, the flesh of mighty men, the flesh of horses and their riders, and the flesh of all people both free and slave, both small and great."***

That will of God is to be regarded as foremost that is called both his good pleasure and the supper most desired by him, namely, that "people be saved and come to the knowledge of the truth" and that they turn and live.[10] But second, it is his will that those who have trusted in themselves suffer punishment. Therefore, Christ said that his food was the will of the Father.[11] In this passage he calls this the supper of God, since each of those who are present desired through their works either the supper of the kingdom or the supper of torment. Through the eating of flesh it indicates the destruction of everything fleshly and the end of kings and rulers on the earth. It mentions horses, not because they will rise again, but through them it signifies either the excessive desire for women or those who have submitted to evil, or perhaps both. The riders symbolize those who are especially wicked. And a little further on it clarifies, saying, "both free and slave, both great and small." By the free and great it refers to those who sinned freely and willingly, and by the slave and small it indicates those who transgressed in a lesser manner, either because of their intent or because of their age or because of weakness.

[19:19] ***And I saw the beast and the kings of the earth with their armies gathered to make war against him who sits on the horse and against his army.***

It speaks of the armies allied with the devil in the plural, because of the many forms of their sin and their divisions and various opinions. By contrast, it speaks of the angelic powers and of those persons like the angels who follow Christ in the singular as an army, because of the unity of their mind and their will that is well-pleasing to the divine Word.

[19:20] ***And the beast was captured, and with it the false prophet who in its presence had worked the signs by which he deceived those who had received the mark of the beast and those who worshiped its image.***

Although these, together with the kings and rulers who trusted them, arrayed themselves

[8]See Jn 4:34. [9]1 Thess 4:17. [10]See 1 Tim 2:4; 2 Tim 2:25. [11]Jn 4:34.

against Christ the Savior, both the antichrist and the false prophet, who by signs and wonders made the rogue acceptable, are bested and overcome by the divine wrath.

[19:20] ***These two shall be thrown alive into the lake of fire that burns with sulfur.***

Perhaps these will not die that death that is common to all, but in the twinkling of an eye they will be made immortal by being condemned to the second death of the lake of fire, just as the apostle spoke of others who "will not sleep but will be changed, in a moment, in the twinkling of an eye."[12] These [mentioned by Paul] will probably go to judgment. But the two mentioned in this passage, being wicked and against God, will not go to judgment but to condemnation. And although some do not hold this opinion, we base ourselves (1) on the saying of the apostle that the antichrist will be destroyed by the Spirit on the command of God[13] and (2) on one of our teachers who said that some will be found living after the destruction of the antichrist.[14] We affirm that those living are those blessed by Daniel,[15] but that after the destruction of their power these two will be handed over with their incorruptible bodies to the fire Gehenna. This will be their death and destruction by the divine command of Christ.

[19:21] ***And the rest were slain by the sword of him who sits on the horse, the sword that issues from his mouth; and all the birds were gorged with their flesh.***

There are two deaths, the first that of the separation of the soul and body, and the second that of being sent to Gehenna. Concerning those who ally themselves with the antichrist, there is reason to think that they will suffer the first death, that of the flesh, by the sword of God, that is, by his command, and that then the second death will follow. However, should this not be the case, then they will share with those who deceived them the second death, that of eternal torment. That the birds are gorged on their flesh is to be understood as previously narrated and now interpreted. To this we might add, that just as God spoke to some through Isaiah, "You have become loathsome to me,"[16] so every fleshly deed is tiresome, grievous and loathsome to the saints.

Chapter 60

How Satan is bound from the time of the crucifixion of Christ until the time of the consummation, and concerning the thousand years

[20:1-3] ***Then I saw an angel coming down from heaven, holding in his hand the key of the bottomless pit and a great chain. And he seized the dragon, that ancient serpent, who is the devil and Satan, and bound him for a thousand years, and threw him into the pit and bound him and sealed it over him, that he should deceive the nations no more, till the thousand years were ended. After that he must be loosed for a little while.***

This passage expresses the destruction of the devil that occurred through the passion of our Lord. For through his passion, the one who is stronger than the devil, namely, Christ our God, bound him who seemed to be strong and freed us, who were his spoils,[17] from his hands and condemned him by throwing him into the pit. This is shown by those demons who pleaded that he not send them into the pit.[18] The demonstration that the devil is bound is the disappearance of idol worship, the destruction of pagan temples, the abandonment of the defilement of altars and the knowledge of the will of God

[12]1 Cor 15:51-52. [13]See 2 Thess 2:8. [14]It is unknown to whom Andrew is referring. [15]See Dan 12:2-3. [16]Is 1:14. [17]See Mt 12:29. [18]See Lk 8:31.

throughout the world. Also the great Justin says that at the coming of Christ the devil will first learn that he is condemned to the abyss, that is, to the Gehenna of fire.[19] It is, therefore, possible also to understand the sentence of Christ against the devil in the words just spoken. The seer says that the angel administers this sentence, thereby revealing that the devil is weaker in power than the ministering powers and to show the vanity of one who insolently opposes him who has rule over all things. For our understanding, he speaks of a chain, meaning the work of restraining the devil's evil.

It is in no way good to understand the thousand years as referring to a thousand years as such. For when David says "of the word that he commanded for a thousand generations,"[20] we ought not to understand this to mean a hundred years times ten. Rather, David means many generations taken as a whole. So also in this case, we regard the number "thousand" to signify either many or that which is complete. If we take it to mean "many," then it refers to the preaching of the gospel into all the world and the sowing of the seeds of piety in the world. Should it mean "complete," then it signifies that during this time, having been released from the life learned from the Law, we have been called to the "perfect man," to the measure of the maturity of the fullness of Christ.[21] Therefore, the thousand years are the time from the incarnation of the Lord until the arrival of the antichrist.[22] Whether the matter is as we have interpreted it, or the thousand years are one hundred times ten, as some believe, or the thousand years are less than this, this is known to God alone, who knows how long his patience is beneficial to us, and he determines the continuance of the present life.

After this, the antichrist will put the whole world into confusion, bearing in himself the activity of the evil one and pouring out on humankind the wine of his venomous wickedness, since he knows that his torment is without end. Redeeming us from his works, the all-merciful God will save us from the punishment that has been "prepared for him and his angels,"[23] and he will manifest those who partake of the eternal blessings that are being made ready for those who opposed him [antichrist] even to the shedding of blood. For it is proper to ascribe to him mercy for those who trusted him, and he is worthy of thanksgiving and worship from every holy power, together with the Father and the life-giving Spirit forever and ever. Amen.

BOOK TWENTY-ONE

Chapter 61

Concerning the thrones prepared for those who preserved their confession of Christ without denial

[20:4] ***Then I saw thrones, and seated on them were those to whom judgment was committed. Also I saw the souls of those who had been beheaded for their testimony to Jesus and for the word of God and who had not worshiped the beast or its image and had not received its mark on their foreheads or their hands. They came to life and reigned with Christ a thousand years.***

Indeed, the teaching thrones had already been given to the holy apostles through whom the nations have been enlightened. However, thrones will also be given according to the purpose of God in the age to come for the condemnation of those who rejected the preaching of the gospel. As David said, "For there the tribes went up, the tribes of the Lord, as a

[19]Although this text of Justin is lost, this view of Justin is quoted by Irenaeus *Haer.* 5.26.2 (ANF 1:555). [20]Ps 105:8 (104:8 LXX). [21]See Eph 4:13. [22]Although this view had been represented in the West since the fourth century by Tyconius and Augustine, among the Greek interpreters, Andrew is the first to interpret the thousand years in this way. [23]See Mt 25:41.

testimony for Israel," and again, "For there are set thrones for judgment."[1] Judgment, that is, the authority to judge, was given to the rest of the saints, namely, to the martyrs who suffered for Christ and did not receive the mark of that spiritual beast, the devil, that is, the image of his apostasy. And as we can see, even to the present time they judge the demons by this authority, for they are glorified with Christ until the consummation of the present age and are honored by pious kings and faithful rulers and demonstrate their God-given power against every bodily weakness and demonic activity.

It is clear that the devil, the antichrist and the false prophet share with one another both their deeds and their names, since each of them is called "beast," and the dragon, clearly Satan, is shown with seven heads and ten horns with as many diadems. Moreover, the beast that comes up out of the sea, clearly the antichrist, appears in a similar form and testifies to the same will and activity for the destruction of those who have been deceived. Those who have been freed from this will reign with Christ in the manner just mentioned until his second coming, and after that they will enjoy more abundantly the promises of God.

Chapter 62
What the first resurrection is, and what the second death is

[20:5-6] ***The rest of the dead did not come to life until the thousand years were ended. This is the first resurrection. Blessed and holy is he who shares in the first resurrection. Over such the second death has no power, but they shall be priests of God and of Christ, and they shall reign with him a thousand years.***

From the holy Scriptures we are taught that there are two lives and two types of dying, or deaths. The first life, which is after the transgression of the commandment, is temporary and fleshly. The second life is eternal and is promised to the saints after their obedience to the divine commandments of Christ. Likewise, there are two deaths. The first is that of the flesh and is temporary. The other is eternal and is the reward for sins. This occurs in the age to come and is the Gehenna of fire. We also know a distinction among the dead. There are the accused, of whom Isaiah wrote, "The dead shall not see life."[2] These are those persons who by their deeds bring on themselves both stench and death. There are, by contrast, the praiseworthy, who in Christ put to death the deeds of the body[3] and crucified themselves with Christ and died to the world. The dead who are rejected, who were not buried with Christ and did not rise with him through baptism[4] but who remained in that death that comes through sins, they shall not live with him until the completion of the thousand years, that is, that perfect number that extends from his first appearance until his second, glorious appearance, as was noted above. But having been born only from the earth and not from the Spirit, these return to the earth.[5] Their death becomes the beginning of the punishment coming to them. However, those who have a portion in the first resurrection, that is, in the rising from thoughts that bring death and from dead works, these are blessed, for the second death, that is, the unending torment, shall have no power over them. These rather serve as priests and reign with Christ, as we see, for the thousand years as they are interpreted by us, until Satan is loosed and deceives the nations. Not that these will then be deprived of the kingdom. Rather, they will possess it more certainly and more manifestly with the passing of temporal reality and the arrival of things eternal. For the time between the loosing of the devil and the verdict against him and his punishment in Gehenna is short.

Book Twenty-one [1]Ps 122:4-5 (121:4-5 LXX). [2]Is 26:14. [3]See Rom 8:13. [4]See Rom 6:4. [5]See Jn 3:31.

So, that "they shall be priests of God and of Christ" ought to be regarded as the restoration of former things. For that which now is seen through trial and the passage of events will then be honors and wonders of the saints, namely, at the time they were seen by the Evangelist, as we noted.[6] Therefore, since there are two deaths, it is necessary also to accept two resurrections. There is the first, physical death, given as a wage for human disobedience. The second death is eternal punishment. The first resurrection is the giving of life[7] from dead works. The second resurrection is the transformation from the corruption of our bodies into incorruptibility.

Chapter 63
Concerning Gog and Magog

[20:7-8] ***And when the thousand years are ended, Satan will be loosed from his prison and will come out to deceive the nations that are at the four corners of the earth, that is, Gog and Magog, to gather them for battle; their number is like the sand of the sea.***

Some interpret the period of a thousand years to be the three and a half years from the baptism of Christ to his ascension into heaven, and they believe that after this the devil is to be loosed.[8] Others say that after the completion of six thousand years the first resurrection of the dead will occur for the saints alone, so that on this very earth on which they endured suffering, they might enjoy temporal largess and glory for a thousand years, and that after this the general resurrection will occur, which will be not only of the righteous but also of sinners.[9] It is unnecessary to say that the church receives nothing of this.

Rather, we listen to the Lord when he says to the Sadducees that the righteous will be "as the angels in heaven."[10] We listen also to the apostle who says, "The kingdom of God is not food and drink."[11] And so we interpret the thousand-year period to be that of the preaching of the gospel. As we previously noted,[12] it is not necessary to think of these thousand years in terms of a number. When it is said in the Song of Songs "everyone was to bring for its fruit a thousand pieces of silver," and again, "Solomon shall have a thousand and they who keep its fruit two hundred,"[13] the precise number is not indicated, but the full and complete harvest. So also here, the harvest of faith in its entirety is meant, after which "the son of perdition, the man of lawlessness" will come "so that all may be condemned who did not believe the truth but had pleasure in unrighteousness," as the apostle says.[14] And the Lord said, "I have come in my Father's name, and you do not receive me; another will come in his own name, him you will receive."[15]

Then, as we have noted, Satan will be loosed from his prison and will deceive all nations and will rouse Gog and Magog to war for the devastation of the world. Some believe that these two are the remote northern people of the Scythians,[16] whom we call the Huns,[17] and, as we see, are the most populous and warlike

[6]The reigning with Christ is now experienced in faith and hope, in the realities of trials and temptations. The seer, however, sees this royalty as the open, revealed reality of the consummation. [7]The Greek word ζωοποίησις suggests the work of the Holy Spirit in baptism. [8]No known interpreter represents this opinion. Schmid surmises that Andrew is referring to Oecumenius, although inexactly (MTS 1:221). According to Oecumenius, the thousand years represent the entire earthly life of Christ. [9]See Irenaeus *Haer.* 5.32.1; 5.35.1-2 (ANF 1:561, 565-66). [10]Mt 22:30. [11]Rom 14:17. [12]See Andrew's comments on Rev 20:3. [13]Song 8:11-12. [14]2 Thess 2:3, 12. [15]Jn 5:43. Irenaeus also referred this passage to the coming of the antichrist (*Haer.* 5.25.4; ANF 1:554). [16]A view already advanced by Josephus, who writes that Magog founded the Magogites whom the Greeks call Scythians (*Ant.* 1.6.1). [17]Theodoret identifies Gog and Magog (= Scythians) with the Huns under Rugila (*Hist. eccl.* 5.37.4; GCS 19:340). Although Andrew speaks of the Huns as though they are a present reality ("as we see"), the Huns under Attila are in the historical past. Like other Byzantine writers, Andrew called Huns any northern barbarian people who, like the Huns, threatened the Byzantine Empire. See Franz Diekamp, "Das Zeitalter des Erzbischofs Andreas von Caesarea," *Historisches Jahrbuch* 18 (1897): 17-18.

of any kingdom on earth, and we keep them from seizing the whole earth until the loosing of the devil by the hand of God alone. Some interpret on the basis of the Hebrew language and render Gog as "one who gathers" or "that which is gathered" and Magog as "one who is exalted." In this way, these names signify either the gathering of the nations or their exaltation. We should note that Ezekiel prophesied that these nations would come on the earth with great power at the end of time, that Israel would fall and for a period of seven years would burn by their arms as though through a great fire.[18] Some interpreters refer this to the fall of the Assyrians under Sennacherib at the time of Hezekiah, which happened a long time prior to the prophecy of Ezekiel.[19] Others refer this to the destruction of the nations that attacked those coming to rebuild Jerusalem after the conquest by the Babylonians, when first Cyrus the Persian and then Darius ordered the governors of Syria to do this.[20] Yet others refer to the forces of Antiochus that were defeated by the Maccabees.

However, it is clear that the arrival of these nations best suits the final times. First, it is nowhere written that the nation of the Scythians waged war against the Jews at that time, but only those nations round about them that envied their prosperity. Second, concerning Gog it is written, "He will be prepared from the days of old and will come at the end of time."[21] Third, in the present revelation, which foretells future events, it is written that Gog and Magog will come toward the end of this age.

[20:9-10] ***And they marched up over the broad earth and surrounded the camp of the saints and the beloved city; but fire came down from God, out of heaven, and consumed them, and the devil who had deceived them was thrown into the lake of fire and sulfur where the beast and the false prophet were, and they will be tormented day and night forever and ever.***

Just as fierce animals come out of their caves, so, it says, those led by the devil and the demons with him will come from their various locations and spread themselves out over the earth to ravage the camp of the saints, clearly meaning the church, which is established throughout the four corners of the world. But they do not know that it is not only a single angel but many angels who encamp round about them who fear God, as the psalm says.[22] Moreover, they will come to subdue the new Jerusalem, the beloved city, from which the divine law has gone into all the world through the apostles. Then, they say, the antichrist will seat himself in the temple of God. This refers either to the ancient temple of God among the Jews that was destroyed because of their audacity against Christ and which the Jews who hate God still expect to be rebuilt by him,[23] or it refers to the true temple of God, namely, the catholic church.[24] The antichrist will usurp for himself what does not belong to him and "proclaim himself to be God," as the holy apostle says.[25] Not long afterward, it says, fire comes down from heaven. This will be either a physical fire such as that which burned the two groups of fifty at the time of Elijah,[26] or the passage refers to the glorious coming of Christ, who will slay them "by the breath of his mouth"[27] and consume the aforementioned nations and their leader, the devil. And Christ will hand them, along with the antichrist and the false prophet, over to the lake of fire, where they will be tormented forever and ever.

[18]See Ezek 38–39. [19]See 2 Chron 32:1-23. It is unknown to which interpreters Andrew is referring. [20]See Theodoret *Commentary on Ezekiel* 38.7-8 (PG 81:1201). [21]Ezek 38:8. [22]See Ps 34:7 (33:8 LXX). At the time of Hezekiah, God saved Jerusalem with but a single angel (2 Chron 32:21); at the end there will be many angels protecting the saints. How certain, then, the outcome! [23]See Irenaeus *Haer.* 5.25.4 (ANF 1:544). [24]Chrysostom *On 2 Thessalonians*, Homily 3.2 (PG 62:482). [25]2 Thess 2:4. [26]2 Kings 1:9-12 (4 Kings 1:9-12 LXX). [27]2 Thess 2:8.

But Christ the Savior has taught us to pray that we enter not into temptation,[28] and so, recognizing our weakness, let us do that earnestly, that we be saved from the trials of that which is prophesied. Let us pray that we not see the coming of the false prophet or the gathering of the nations that brings danger and death, lest we be moved to fall from our saving faith. Rather, preserving intact "the testimony of our conscience,"[29] as we are able and manifesting through good works the ardent love that we have toward Christ who redeemed us by his precious blood, let us hope for the enjoyment of the eternal blessings, being strengthened toward this end by the rich mercies of God. May we attain to these things in Christ, who is our savior and redeemer, with whom to the Father together with the Holy Spirit be glory, power and honor now and forever and ever. Amen.

BOOK TWENTY-TWO

Chapter 64

Concerning him who sits on the throne and the universal resurrection and judgment

[20:11] ***Then I saw a great white throne and him who sat on it, from whose face the earth and the sky fled away, and no place was found for them.***

The image of the white throne signifies the divine rest that God will establish among the saints, who are resplendent with virtues and among whom God will be enthroned. The flight of the sky and of the earth signifies their transformation and renewal from what they were into something better. And there will be found no longer any place for change. For if the creation was subjected to corruption because of us, as the apostle says, it will also be transformed with us "into the freedom of the glory of the children of God,"[1] being made new into that which is more brilliant.[2] The creation will not be subjected to complete annihilation, as we learn from Irenaeus, Antipater[3] and other saints. For the blessed Irenaeus writes, "For neither is the substance nor the essence of the creation annihilated (for faithful and true is he who has established it), but the fashion of the world passes away, that is, those things among which transgression has occurred, since humankind has grown old in them. And therefore this fashion has been formed temporary, God foreknowing all things."[4] Similarly, Methodius comments as follows in *On the Resurrection:* "It is not satisfactory to say that the universe will be utterly destroyed, and sea and air and sky will be no longer. For the whole world will be deluged with fire from heaven and burned for the purpose of purification and renewal; it will not, however, come to complete ruin and corruption." And a little later he says, "And Paul clearly testifies to this, saying, 'For the creation waits with eager longing for the manifestation of the sons of God; for the creation was subjected to futility, not willingly but through him who subjected it in hope. Therefore, the creation itself will be set free from its bondage to decay' " and so on.[5] But before these saints the holy David sang to the Lord, saying, "You sent forth your Spirit, and they are created; and you renew the face of the ground."[6] And Isaiah says, "There will be a new heaven and a new earth, and the former

[28]Mt 6:13. [29]2 Cor 1:12. **Book Twenty-two** [1]Rom 8:20-21. [2]Andrew is arguing against Origen, who argues that "the end is like the beginning" so that rational creatures will return to a previous, primordial position (*Princ.* 1.6.2; 2.1.1-2). [3]Antipater of Bostra in John of Damascus *Sacra Parallela* (PG 96:497). Antipater argues, against Origen, that the saints will become more glorious in the resurrection and uses the story of Christ's transfiguration to illustrate his point. [4]Irenaeus *Haer.* 5.36.1. Irenaeus does not quote Rev 20:11 in connection with "the fashion of the world" passing away. Rather, he quotes Rev 21:1-4 (*Haer.* 5.35.2 [ANF 1:566]). [5]Rom 8:19-21. Methodius *Res.* 1.8 (ANF 6:365). Methodius does not quote Rev 20:11 in this context. He was also arguing against Origen. [6]Ps 104:30 (103:30 LXX).

things will not be remembered or come into mind; but they will find gladness and rejoicing in it."[7] To be sure! In the superabundance of joy and in the greatness of their rewards they will forget the struggles and pains that they endured. In another place Isaiah says, "For as the new heavens and the new earth that I will make shall remain before me, so shall your descendants and your name remain."[8] It follows, therefore, that the creation, which was made for our sake, receives with us a change for the better, not going into nonexistence, just as we do not go into nonexistence after our death.

[20:12] *And I saw the dead, great and small, standing before the throne, and books were opened. Also another book was opened, which is the book of life. And the dead were judged by what was written in the books, by what they had done.*

By the dead he means either all persons, since they experience the death of the body, or those who have died through their transgressions.[9] The great and small are either those who are older or younger, or more likely those who have done the works of death and will appropriately be punished for these acts. Or the great are the righteous and the small are those sinners who are worthless because of the baseness of their soul.

The books that are opened symbolize the deeds and the conscience of each person. There is but one book of life in which the names of the saints are written.

[20:13] *And the sea gave up the dead in it, Death and Hades gave up the dead in them, and all were judged by what they had done.*

It says that each body is returned to those elements from which it was constituted and given up, whether it had been given over to the earth or to the sea. Death and hades are not ensouled living creatures, as some have written.[10] Rather, death is the separation of the soul and the body, and hades is that place that is to us formless and unseen and that receives the souls that travel there. Those souls are dead that carry death-bearing deeds. As a wise man said, "The souls of the righteous are in the hand of God, and no torment shall touch them."[11]

[20:14-15] *Then Death and Hades were thrown into the lake of fire; and if anyone was not found written in the book of life, he was thrown into the lake of fire.*

Death and Hades are thrown into the lake of fire. This shows either that "the last enemy to be destroyed is death,"[12] or that the evil powers who are the patrons of the death caused by sin and who have their abode in hades and escort their followers there will be condemned to this fire. For just as the term "city" encompasses all the inhabitants in it, so also those worthy of death and hades are included in the terms "death" and "hades." However, that fire has no destructive power over those who have been born of God and are exceptionally good. It is written, "God did not make death."[13] For this reason, this passage signifies that death and corruption shall be no more but that incorruptibility and immortality will reign. And it should not amaze if all who are not written in the book of life will be thrown into the lake of fire. For just as with the Father there are many mansions for those being saved, so also there are distinctions among the places and manners of punishment. Some punishments will be more harsh, some more endurable, which those not worthy to be in the book of life will suffer.

Chapter 65
Concerning the new heaven and earth and the heavenly Jerusalem

[7]Is 65:17-18. [8]Is 66:22. [9]See Eph 2:1, 5. [10]The source is unknown. [11]Wis 3:1. [12]1 Cor 15:26. [13]Wis 1:13.

[21:1] ***Then I saw a new heaven and a new earth; for the first heaven and the first earth had passed away, and the sea was no more.***

This passage does not speak of the obliteration of creation but of its renewal into something better.[14] For as the apostle says, "This creation will be freed from the bondage of corruption into the freedom of the glory of the children of God."[15] Also the holy psalmist says, "You change them like a raiment, and they pass away."[16] The renewal of that which has grown old does not involve the annihilation of its substance but rather indicates the smoothing out of its agedness and its wrinkles. It is a custom among us to say concerning persons who have in some way become better or have become worse, "someone has become someone else." And so it is indicated concerning the heaven and the earth that they have "passed away" instead of have "changed." And this is also the same with us who have received death; we will change from a former condition to a better lot. Concerning the sea, it says that "the sea was no more." For what use is there of a sea when people no longer need to sail it or to acquire by means of it the goods grown in regions lying far away? Moreover the sea is symbolic of the turbulence and unsettledness of life, and so there will then be no need of it when there remains no trouble or fear among the saints.

[21:2] ***And I saw the holy city, new Jerusalem, coming down from God out of heaven, prepared as a bride adorned for her husband.***

This passage shows the renewal and transformation to a more brilliant appearance that the Jerusalem above will acquire when it comes down from the incorporeal powers above to humankind, since Christ, our God, has become the common head of both. This city is constructed of the saints concerning whom it is written, "Holy stones are rolled on the land,"[17] and it has Christ as its cornerstone.[18] It is called a city, since it is the dwelling-place of the kingly Trinity—for the Trinity dwells in it and walks in it, as he promised—and it is called bride, since it is joined to the Lord and is united with him in the highest, inseparable conjunction. It is adorned, since within, as the psalm says, it has glory and youth in its manifold virtues.[19]

[21:3-4] ***And I heard a loud voice from heaven saying, "Behold, the dwelling of God is with people. He will dwell with them, and they shall be his people, and God himself will be with them and be their God; he will wipe away every tear from their eyes."***

The saint is instructed from heaven that this is the true dwelling whose type was indicated by Moses,[20] or rather the prefiguration of the type, since the type exists in the church of the present day.[21] In this tent made without hands there is no weeping or any tears, for he who supplies the joy of the eternal temple will give to all the saints the vision of inexpressible gladness.

[21:4] ***"And death shall be no more, neither shall there be mourning nor crying nor pain any more, for the first things have passed away."***

That is, it is written, "pain and sorrow and sighing have passed away."[22] That "the first things have passed away" signifies that the suffering of the saints and the arrogance of the wicked have ceased, for an exchange of circumstances will occur for each of these groups.

[14]Against the views of Origen. See Rev 20:11. [15]See Rom 8:21. [16]Ps 102:26 (101:27 LXX). [17]Zech 9:16. [18]See Eph 2:20. [19]Ps 45:14 (44:14 LXX). [20]See Ex 25:1-40. [21]The heavenly Jerusalem is the reality (ἀλήθεια) of which the church is type (τύπος). The church was prefigured in the ark that Moses was commanded to build (προτύπωσις τύπου). [22]Is 51:11.

Chapter 66

Concerning what was said by him who sits on the throne

[21:5-6] ***And he who sat upon the throne said, "Behold, I make all things new." And he said to me, "Write, for these words are true and trustworthy." And he said to me, "It is done! I am the Alpha and the Omega, the Beginning and the End."***

These words are true, for they issue from the Truth himself[23] and are expressed no longer by way of symbols. Rather, they are known through the realities themselves. Christ is "the beginning and the end," since he is "beginning" because of his divinity and "end" because of his humanity. Moreover, his providence extends from the first creation of the incorporeal creatures to the last human beings.

[21:6] ***"To the thirsty I will give from the fountain of the water of life without payment."***

To the one who thirsts after righteousness he promises to grant the gift of the life-giving Spirit that he supplied in the Gospels to those who believed in him.[24] It is "without payment" either because "the sufferings of this present time are not worth comparing with the glory that is to be revealed to the saints"[25] or because it is not possessed except by the good works and the goodness of him who gives it.

[21:7] ***"He who conquers shall inherit these things, and I will be their God and they will be my sons."***

He who conquers in the war against the invisible demons will receive these good things, becoming a son of God and reveling in the good gifts of the Father.

[21:8] ***"But as for the cowardly, the faithless, the polluted, as for murderers, fornicators, sorcerers, idolater, and all liars, their lot will be in the lake that burns with fire and sulfur, which is the second death."***

The God who thirsts after our salvation urges us in every way, both through kindness and through anger, toward the inheritance of his blessings. He brings now before our eyes the brightness of the heavenly Jerusalem and the dark, painful wrathfulness of the fiery Gehenna, so that whether through a desire for eternal bliss or through fear of unending torment, we might, as there is opportunity, acquire that which is good together with the rest of those in need. He indicates that those who were cowards and deserters in the battle against the devil will be condemned to the second death.

May we propitiate him who desires mercy and does not will the death of sinners but their conversion, and so obtain his gifts by good deeds. To these gifts he exhorts us, not only through the enticement of words but also through the enticement of works and sufferings. For it suffices him to encourage toward the good and to discourage from evil, and afterward either to punish or to honor those worthy of glory or punishment. He did not disdain to suffer for us lest by his own power or by his appearance he might harm or disregard anything that pertains to our healing and restoration. Therefore, let us not receive the grace of God in vain, but let us render his beneficence effective by conversion and the demonstration of good works, so that we might attain to the promised blessings in Christ, our God, with whom be glory to the Father, together with the Holy Spirit forever and ever. Amen.

[23]See Jn 14:6. [24]See Lk 24:49; Jn 14:16-17; 20:22. [25]Rom 8:18.

BOOK TWENTY-THREE

Chapter 67

Concerning the angel who shows the city of the saints and who measures its walls with the gates

[21:9] ***Then came one of the seven angels who had the seven bowls full of the seven last plagues, and spoke to me, saying, "Come, I will show you the bride of the Lamb, his wife."***[1]

Through this passage it is shown that the angels not only induce the worst plagues but also act as physicians, at one time cutting and at another time applying healing medications. For he who once brought on a plague to those who deserved it now shows to the saint the beatitude of the church. And fittingly does he call the bride of the Lamb his wife. For when Christ was slaughtered as a lamb, he at that time betrothed the church with his own blood. For just as when Adam was sleeping, the woman was formed through the taking of the rib, so also the church, formed through the shedding of blood from the side of Christ as he was sleeping voluntarily on the cross through death,[2] was united with him who suffered for us.[3]

[21:10-11] ***And in the Spirit he carried me away to a great, high mountain and showed me the great and holy city Jerusalem coming down out of heaven from God, having the glory of God.***

That he was "carried away in the Spirit" indicates that through the Spirit he was elevated in his mind from earthly things to the contemplation of heavenly realities. The image of the great mountain indicates the sublime and transcendent life of the saints, in which the wife of the Lamb, the Jerusalem above, will be made beautiful and glorified by God.

[21:11] ***Its radiance is like a most valuable jewel, like a jasper, clear as crystal.***

The radiance of the church is Christ, who here is depicted as a jasper and clear as crystal to indicate that he is unfading and life-giving and pure. He is also depicted by means of other images. For the manifold diversity of his generosity for us cannot be described merely through the illustration of one form.

[21:12] ***It had a great, high wall, with twelve gates, and at the gates twelve angels, and on the gates the names of the twelve tribes of Israel were inscribed.***

Christ is the great and high wall of the church that protects those in the holy city. In the wall are twelve gates, which are his holy apostles through whom we have acquired access and entry to the Father.[4] And these are assisted by twelve angels who are preeminent and especially close to God in their holiness. For if we believe that a protecting angel follows each one of the faithful, how much more does it follow that those ranked first among the angels accompany those who are the foundations of the church and are sowers of the evangelical word and serve as assistants in the preaching of the gospel? The names of the tribes of the spiritual Israel are written over the gates of the apostles, even as they were written on the shoulder strap of the physical high priest long ago.[5] The writing of these names now testifies to the solicitude of the apostles for the faithful, just as Paul said that he had "anxiety for all the churches"[6] and that "his heart is wide"[7]

Book Twenty-three [1]The text of Andrew reads τὴν νύμφην τοῦ ἀρνίου τὴν γυναῖκα. [2]See Jn 19:34. [3]This understanding of the piercing of Christ's side was widely spread in the ancient church. It appears already in Tertullian *On the Soul* 43 (ANF 3:222). See also Chrysostom *Homilies on John* 85 (FC 41:435); Augustine *Tract. Ev. Jo.* 120 (FC 92:50-51). [4]See Eph 2:18; 3:12, where this access is through Christ. [5]Ex 28:17-21; 39:8-14. [6]2 Cor 11:28. [7]2 Cor 6:11.

and that he comes to all "those whom he begot through the gospel."[8]

[21:13] ***On the east three gates, on the north three gates, on the south three gates, and on the west three gates.***

The four-sided form of the gates and their threefold entries signify the understanding of the one who worships the Trinity. This understanding is throughout the four-cornered universe, and we have received it through the life-giving cross. For the cruciform shape of the position of the gates is according to the form of the twelve oxen that bore the Sea erected by Solomon.[9] These oxen signify the threefold grouping of the apostles by fours, the herald of the holy Trinity and the extension of the four Gospels into the four corners of the earth. Through this is symbolized the spiritual sea of baptism that cleanses the world from its sins and that was instituted by the spiritual Solomon.

[21:14] ***And the wall of the city had twelve foundations, and on them the twelve names of the twelve apostles of the Lamb.***

The foundations of the wall are the blessed apostles, on whom the church of Christ has been established. Their names have been inscribed on them, as on a public placard, for the easy instruction of those who read them.

[21:15] ***And he who talked with me had a measuring rod of gold to measure the city and its gates and wall.***

The golden measuring rod indicates the excellence of the angel who measures, whom he saw in the form of a man. It indicates as well the excellence of the city that is being measured, whose wall we have interpreted to be Christ. The city is measured not by people but by an angel because of the purity and wisdom of its transcendent nature, to whom, as is probable, the greatness or the comely dignity of the city above is known. However, in this passage we think that the wall is suggestive of the divine covering and shelter by which the saints will be protected.

[21:16] ***The city lies foursquare, its length the same as its breadth; and he measured the city with his rod, twelve thousand stadia; its length and breadth and height are equal.***

The city is foursquare because of its stability and solidity. That which is of equal length in its depth and breadth and height is called by some a cube, and it suggests stability.

The twelve thousand stadia that the city measures perhaps signify the size of the city, for, as David says, its inhabitants "shall be multiplied beyond the sand."[10] Or perhaps they are mentioned because of the number of the apostles through whom the city was established.

The number seven, which is mystical, presents a solution through a certain line of reasoning. The thousands of stadia, which are mentioned, are equivalent to 1,714 miles, the thousand representing the perfection of eternal life, the seven hundred indicating the perfection of the rest, and the fourteen indicating the twofold sabbath of the soul and the body. For seven times two is fourteen.

[21:17] ***And he measured its wall, a hundred and forty-four cubits, the measure of a man, that is, of an angel.***

The height of the wall is 144 cubits. When multiplied twelve times, the number twelve, which signifies the apostolic teaching, produces this number.

[8]1 Cor 4:15. [9]See 1 Kings 7:23-25. [10]Ps 139:18 (138:18 LXX).

[21:18] ***The wall was built of jasper, while the city was pure gold, similar to pure glass.***

The structure of the wall was of jasper to show the ever green and unfading life of the saints, as has often been noted. The city is of "pure gold as though of glass" because of the clarity and brightness of its inhabitants.

[21:19] ***The foundations of the wall of the city were adorned with every precious jewel.***

The twelve foundations were twelve precious stones,[11] eight of which were worn in ancient times on the breastplate of the high priest,[12] and four have been added to show the agreement of the new covenant with the old covenant and the superiority of the things brought to light in it. And so, the apostles are decorated with every virtue, which is made clear through the precious stones.

[21:19] ***The first foundation was jasper.***[13]

It is likely that through the jasper, which has the color green like the emerald, the chief apostle Peter is indicated. For he bore the death of Christ in the body[14] and in his love for Christ made known that which is everlasting and always new, guiding us to green pastures through the warmth of his faith.

[21:19] ***The second is sapphire.***

I think that this stone, which is like the heavenly body, from which also the color azure comes, symbolizes the blessed Paul. For he was caught up into the third heaven[15] and drew there those who were persuaded by him, and there in the heavens he has his citizenship.[16]

[21:19] ***The third is chalcedony.***[17]

This stone was not borne on the breastplate of the high-priest, but rather anthracite, which does not appear here. We are then of the opinion that at that time the saint called anthracite by another name. But anthracite indicates the blessed apostle Andrew, who like coal was ignited by the Spirit.

[21:19] ***The fourth is emerald.***[18]

The emerald is green in color, and when rubbed with oil it receives a brilliant shine and beauty. We believe that this stone indicates the proclamation of the Evangelist John, which by divine oil makes bright the sorrow that has come to us through sins and by the most precious gift of theology grants to faith that which is everlasting.

[21:20] ***The fifth is sardonyx.***[19]

This stone, which has the color of a shining human fingernail, perhaps symbolizes the person of James. For before the others he received the bodily death of martyrdom for the sake of Christ,[20] which the nail characterizes, for when cut it experiences no feelings.

[21:20] ***The sixth is sardion.***[21]

Sardion has a shiny red color and possesses therapeutic powers for swellings and wounds from iron. For this reason I believe that this stone represents the beauty of the virtue of Philip. For by the fire of the divine Spirit this makes bright and heals the spiritual wounds of those who are deceived, which they received from the attacks of the devil.

[11]For the twelve jewels, compare the discussion of Epiphanius *On the Twelve Gems* (PG 43:293-304. [12]Ex 28:17-21; 39:8-14. [13]See Epiphanius *On the Twelve Gems* 6 (PG 43:297). [14]See 2 Cor 4:10. [15]2 Cor 12:2. [16]Phil 3:20. [17]See Epiphanius *On the Twelve Gems* 4 (PG 43:295-97). [18]See Epiphanius *On the Twelve Gems* 3 (PG 43:295). [19]See Epiphanius *On the Twelve Gems* 12 (PG 43:301). [20]See Acts 12:2. [21]See Epiphanius *On the Twelve Gems* 1 (PG 43:293-96).

[21:20] ***The seventh is chrysolite.***

Chrysolite glitters like gold and perhaps symbolizes Bartholomew, for he was made glorious by his precious virtues and by his divine preaching.

[21:20] ***The eighth is beryl.***

This stone has the color of the sea and of the air and is close to that of the hyacinth. Beryl very likely represents Thomas, for he was sent on journeys far beyond the sea, even to India, for their salvation.

[21:20] ***The ninth is topaz.***[22]

By means of the topaz, which is deep red and like charcoal, and which, as they say, sends forth a milk-like juice that relieves the pain of those suffering from eye disease, it is possible that the person of Matthew is indicated. For he was enflamed by divine zeal and was adorned by the pouring out of his own blood for the sake of Christ. Through the gospel he also healed those who were blind in their hearts and gave milk to drink to those newly born in the faith.

[21:20] ***The tenth is chrysoprase.***

Chrysoprase is deeper in color than gold itself, and through it I think that Thaddeus is indicated. For to Abgar, king of Edessa, he proclaimed the kingdom of Christ, which is signified by gold, and his death, which is indicated by ashes.[23]

[21:20] ***The eleventh is hyacinth.***

It seems likely that the hyacinth, which is deep blue, that is, like the sky, symbolizes Simon. For he was a zealot[24] for the gifts of Christ and possessed a heavenly wisdom.

[21:20] ***The twelfth is amethyst.***

It seems to me that through the amethyst, which is somewhat like fire in appearance, Matthias is indicated. He was accounted worthy of the divine fire at the distribution of the tongues, and he filled the place of him who had fallen away, for by a fiery desire he wished to please him who elected him.[25]

We have inserted these things from that which was said concerning gems by the holy Epiphanius and moreover from those jewels associated with the high priests of Israel. This serves as an exercise for those who ponder the enigmas and concern themselves with the truth that is known accurately only by him who revealed them. For in reality the apostles are both foundations and precious jewels, each the one and the other, and in an manner common to all each preserves that which is personal and specific to himself among the virtues. Therefore, I urge you not to accuse the ideas that were offered as though they were merely forced. For we did not destroy their fellowship and solidarity by apportioning to each of the apostles a virtue characteristic of himself. Rather, we were eager to demonstrate their complete harmony by means of their individual differences. For they relate to one another in a way similar to a chain.

[21:21] ***And the twelve gates were twelve pearls, each of the gates made of a single pearl.***

The twelve gates are manifestly the twelve disciples of Christ, through whom we have come to know the door and the way.[26] They are also the twelve pearls that have received their splendor from the one, most precious pearl, namely, Christ.

[22]See Epiphanius *On the Twelve Gems* 2 (PG 43:296). [23]See Eusebius *Hist. eccl.* 1.13.11-22. [24]See Lk 6:15; Acts 1:13. [25]See Acts 1:23-24. [26]Jn 10:7, 9; 14:6.

[21:21] ***And the street of the city was pure gold, transparent as glass.***

It is not possible to present in one image an exact description of the good things of the heavenly city. Therefore, the seer perceived the street of the city as gold on account of its costliness and its beautiful color, and as crystal, that is, as transparent glass on account of it purity. We are not able to bring both of these things together in one symbol. But the saint perceived all of these things as he was able. However, an unsullied understanding of the city above surpasses our hearing and sight and mind.

[21:22] ***And I saw no temple in the city, for its temple is the Lord God the Almighty and the Lamb.***

For what need of a physical temple is there for one who will have God as protection and shelter, in whom "we live and move and have our being"?[27] For he himself is both temple and indweller of the saints, dwelling in them and walking among them, as he promised. The Lamb is the Lamb of God who was slain for us, to whom manifestly the coessential and life-giving Spirit is conjoined, who is mentioned a little later through the image of the river.[28]

[21:23] ***And the city has no need of sun or moon to shine on it, for the glory of God enlightens it, and its lamp is the Lamb.***

Where there is the intellectual Sun of righteousness,[29] there is no need of perceptible luminaries. For he is both the glory and the lamp of the city, and the nations of those who are being saved will walk in its light, concerning whom he says:

[21:24-25] ***By its light shall the nations walk; and the kings of the earth shall bring their glory into it, and its gates shall never be shut by day, for there will be no night there.***

The nations that are being saved, as it was said, shall walk in its light,[30] and those who on earth ruled their passions shall carry into it the glory and honor of their good deeds. That "the gates will not be shut" reveals either the security and immutability of the city's inhabitants or that there the divine gates of the apostolic teaching will be opened to all for instruction in the more perfect things. And there will be day there, but no night. For night will be allotted to the sinners.

[21:26-27] ***They shall bring into it the glory and honor of the nations. But nothing unclean shall enter it, nor anything that practices abomination or falsehood, but only those who are written in the book of the life of the Lamb.***

The brightness and the glory of the nations, that is, those who among these have pleased Christ, shall bear fruit and bring offerings into that city. But anything common and unclean will not enter there. "For what communion does light have with darkness?"[31]

Chapter 68

Concerning the pure and bright river that flows from the throne

[22:1] ***And he showed me a pure river of the water of life, bright as crystal, flowing from the throne of God and of the Lamb in the middle of its street.***

The river that flows from the church in the present life indicates the baptism of regeneration that is made effective through the Spirit and makes those who are washed more clean than snow and crystal. But the river of God,

[27]Acts 17:28. [28]See Rev 22:1. [29]Mal 4:2. [30]Is 60:3. [31]2 Cor 6:14.

filled up with waters, namely, the life-giving Spirit, flows through the Jerusalem above, flowing from God the Father and through the Lamb. And this river flows in the midst of the most excellent powers, which are named here the "throne of God," making full the streets of the holy city, that is, the multitude of its inhabitants who are, according to the psalmist, "more in number than the sand."[32]

[22:2] ***On either side of the river, the tree of life producing twelve fruits, yielding its fruit each month.***

This river, it says, waters the saints who are planted alongside it. They are here figuratively called the "tree of life" by virtue of their participation and imitation of him who is the Tree of Life. Moreover, they give forth "twelve fruits," that is, they unceasingly yield the production of fruit. For there will there be no winter of sin that causes the trees of life to shed their leaves, such as we see now. Rather, the time of the production of fruit by the saints will be complete and uninterrupted, and this time is here said to be twelve months. It speaks in these terms equally because of the customary year among us, as well as because of the proclamation of the twelve apostles. This present passage may also be interpreted in another way. As we have said, the river might signify the gifts of the life-giving Spirit, which flow down from the throne of the Father and of the Son, that is, from the ranks of the cherubim, among whom God is enthroned. This river flows into the streets of the city, that is, to the full citizenry of the saints, as coming from the first ranks into the second that are made to share in the well-ordered arrangement of the heavenly hierarchy. The tree of life signifies Christ, whom we know by the Holy Spirit and through the Spirit. For in him is the Spirit, and he is worshiped in Spirit, and he is the supplier of the Spirit, and through him the twelve fruits of the apostolic chorus give to us the inexhaustible fruit of the knowledge of God, through whom "the acceptable year of the Lord and the day of recompense," foretold by the prophet[33] is proclaimed to us.

[22:2] ***And the leaves of the tree were for the healing of the nations.***

The leaves of the tree, namely, of Christ, are the more exalted understandings of the divine judgments, even as its fruits are the more perfect knowledge that is to be revealed in the age to come. The leaves will be for healing, that is, for the cleansing of the ignorance of those who have been deficient in the exercise of the virtues, for "there is one glory of the sun, and another glory of the moon, and another glory of the stars."[34] Moreover, "in my Father's home there are many rooms,"[35] so that one is accounted worthy of less and another of more brightness according to the measure of the works of each. This present passage may also be interpreted otherwise. The tree of life produces twelve fruits, namely, the apostolic chorus that shares in him who is truly the Tree of Life, who through his participation in the flesh has given us to share in his deity. Their fruits are those who yield fruit a hundredfold. The leaves are those who yield sixtyfold. These carry to those who come later the illumination of the divine light that they had received from those who had yielded a hundredfold, and they bring healing to those from the nations who yield thirtyfold.[36] For at that time there will be a difference between those who are saved as great as there is a difference between fruit and leaves. Some will be glorified to a lesser extent, some to a greater extent, as it is written. It writes of a tree in the singular rather than trees in the plural to indicate the unity and harmony of the life that the saints have

[32]Ps 139:18 (138:18 LXX). [33]Is 61:2. [34]1 Cor 15:41. [35]Jn 14:2. [36]See Mt 13:23.

together. It is often the custom of the Scriptures to speak of a tree in the singular instead of trees in the plural,[37] [and of a horse] instead of horses[38] and other singular names instead of plurals.

[22:3] ***There shall be nothing accursed there.***

Anathema can be interpreted in a twofold manner. It either refers to that which is holy for many but is dedicated to God alone, or it refers to that which is sacred to the whole of creation and to the holy powers but is attributed to the devil because of his utter alienation and separation from that which is good. We think that here *katathema* is used in an emphatic sense. For such a thing is not dedicated to anyone, but it is put aside for the devil, being subordinated to him and condemned along with him. Such a thing will not exist within that city.

[22:3-4] ***But the throne of God and of the Lamb shall be in it, and his servants shall worship him; they shall see his face, and his name shall be on their foreheads.***

Those who become the throne of God because of the rest of the Lord among them will be the inhabitants of that city. They will see him no longer in shadows but face to face, even as the holy apostles saw him on the holy mount,[39] as the great Dionysius says.[40] And instead of the golden breastplate worn in ancient times by the high priest, they will have the divine name imprinted not only on their foreheads but also within their hearts, and this shows their firm, bold and immoveable love toward him. For the writing on the forehead symbolizes the ornamentation of boldness.

[22:5] ***And there will be there no night, and they will have no need of lamp or the light of the sun, for the Lord God will be their light, and they will reign forever and ever.***

If, as the Lord says, "the righteous will shine as the sun,"[41] how will there be any necessity for the light of a lamp or of the sun for those who have the Lord of glory as their illumination and king? And they will be ruled by him forever, or rather they will reign with him, as the holy apostle says.[42]

Chapter 69
That Christ is God of the prophets and the ruler of the angels

[22:6] ***And he said to me, "These words are trustworthy and true."***

They are "trustworthy and true" because they come from the Truth. Until now he has presented the vision of the angel and the explanation of what he had seen. Next he speaks from his own person.

[22:6] ***And the Lord, the God of the holy prophets, has sent his angel to show his servants what soon must take place.***

Since Christ is "the God of the prophets, who sent his angel" by means of the blessed John who saw this vision, "to show his servants what is to take place," it is clear that he gave the revelation for the sake of the flesh according to the condescension of the economy of the Son, as it said at the beginning.[43] For he who is the God of the prophets and who sent his angels as ministering spirits for the revelation of coming things would not be ignorant of the hour or of the day of the consummation, so that he who has all "the hidden treasures of wisdom and knowledge"[44] would learn these

[37]For example, Gen 1:11, 12; 3:8; 1 Chron 16:32; Joel 2:22. [38]For example, Gen 14:11, 16, 21; Ex 14:7, 9, 23; Deut 11:4. [39]See Mt 17:1-8; 2 Pet 1:18. [40]Pseudo-Dionysius *On Divine Names* 1.4 (PG 3:592). [41]Mt 13:43. [42]2 Tim 2:12. [43]See Rev 1:1. [44]Col 2:3.

things only now from the Father. To his person the Evangelist now turns, saying:

[22:7] ***"Behold, I am coming soon. Blessed is he who keeps the words of the prophecy of this book."***

It is often customary for the prophets to speak divine words as though it were from their own person. The words "I am coming soon" indicate either the shortness of the present time in comparison with the future age or the sudden swiftness of the death of each person. For his departure from here is the end of every person. Therefore, since "we do not know at what hour the thief will come,"[45] we are commanded "to watch and to gird ourselves and to keep our lamps burning,"[46] letting our godly behavior shine even for our neighbor.[47] Therefore, let us not cease to beseech God with a contrite heart to "save us from all our pursuers," lest our souls, having been defeated by them, be snatched away unprepared "with no one to rescue or to save."[48] Let us also pray God lest any soul, bound by the chains of earthly affairs and not able to free itself from them, should vainly turn again to them and then, when constrained to leave them by the authority of the angels and the command of God, will lament in vain for the lost opportunities of a life now passed. Rather, singing without ceasing the song of David, "I prepared myself and was not fearful to keep your commandments,"[49] let us receive as a reward for keeping [his commandments] the praise of God, who will say, "Well done, good and faithful servant; you have been faithful over a little, I will set you over much; enter into the joy of your master."[50] Together with him glory, honor and power is fittingly given to the Father and also to the Holy Spirit now and always and forever and ever. Amen.

BOOK TWENTY-FOUR

Chapter 70

Concerning the trustworthiness of what was seen by the apostle

[22:8-9] ***I John am he who saw and heard these things. And when I heard and saw them, I fell down to worship at the feet of the angel who showed them to me; but he said to me, "You must not do that! I am a fellow servant with you and your brethren the prophets, who keep the words of this book. Worship God!"***

[To witness by eye and ear] is characteristic of one who is an apostle. Just as he said in the Gospel, "He who has seen bears witness, and his testimony is true,"[1] so also in this passage John confesses that he is an eyewitness and earwitness of what has been foretold and so makes himself to be a guarantee of what has been seen. He shows as well the piety of the angel who has described and interpreted the vision, indicating that the angel would not allow himself to be worshiped by a fellow servant. Rather, with a good conscience we are to give homage to our common Lord.

Chapter 71

How he was commanded not to seal the revelation but to proclaim it

[22:10] ***And he said to me, "Do not seal up the words of the prophecy of this book, for the time is near."***

Until now he has presented the words of the angel, but here he changes to the person of the Lord Christ, saying, "Do not seal up the words of the prophecy." Indeed, the book is worthy to be read by the faithful. In view of the punishment prepared for the sinners and of the rest

[45]Lk 12:39; Mt 24:43. [46]Lk 12:35. [47]See Mt 5:16. [48]Ps 7:1-2 (7:2-3 LXX). [49]Ps 119:60 (118:60 LXX). [50]Mt 25:21, 23. **Book Twenty-four** [1]Jn 21:24.

promised to the saints, it guides those who read it to the true life.

[22:11-12] *"Let the evildoer still do evil, and the filthy still be filthy, and the righteous still do right, and the holy still be holy. Behold, I am coming soon, bringing my recompense, to repay every one for what he has done."*

He does not say these things as though he were exhorting to unrighteousness and filthiness. By no means! Rather, preserving the freedom of the will, it is as though he said, "Let each one do what is pleasing to him. I do not force any choice." Moreover, he shows that for every undertaking there is an appropriate end, namely, as he says, when "I am coming to repay to every one" the reward of their deeds.

[22:13] *"I am the Alpha and the Omega, the Beginning and the End, the First and the Last."*

There is no God before me, nor is there any God after me. For there is nothing more ancient than the beginning, and there is no end to the kingdom and power of God. In previous passages Christ has often been called first because of his deity and last because of his humanity.

[22:14] *Blessed are those who do his commandments, that they may have the right to the tree of life and that they may enter the city by the gates.*

Those [who keep the commandments] are truly worthy of blessedness. For in life eternal they shall possess authority to find rest in the tree of life, namely, Christ our God, and to delight in the vision of him without any evil power becoming a hindrance. And they shall enter into that city above by the apostolic gates, that is, by the apostles' teachings, through the true door. Nor shall they, as though shepherds for hire, sneak in by some other way, but they will be guided in by the gatekeeper of life.[2]

[22:15] *Outside are the dogs and sorcerers and fornicators and murderers and idolaters, and everyone who loves and practices falsehood.*

The dogs are not only the shameless and the unfaithful and those evildoers in the circumcision, for whom the apostle wept,[3] but also those who, after their baptism, "returned to their own vomit."[4] Therefore, with the fornicators and the murderers and the idolaters, they are foreigners to the heavenly city.

Chapter 72

How the church and the Spirit in her summon the glorious appearance of Christ, and concerning the curse on all those who falsify this book

[22:16] *"I Jesus have sent my angel to you with this testimony for the churches."*

Also here the lordship and dignity of him who sent the angel is demonstrated. He uses "to testify" instead of "to admonish."

[22:16] *"I am the root and the offspring of David."*

As God, Christ is the root of David. He is the offspring of David as the one who sprouted from him according to the flesh.

[22:16] *"The bright morning star."*

He is the morning star, since he rose for us early in the morning after the three days. Moreover, after the night of the present life he

[2]Jn 10:7-15. [3]Phil 3:2. [4]2 Pet 2:22.

will manifest himself to the saints in the early morning of the common resurrection and bring to pass the unending day.

[22:17] ***The Spirit and the bride say, "Come." And let him who hears say, "Come."***

Crying out in our hearts "Abba, Father,"[5] the church and the Spirit in her call for the coming of the only-begotten Son of God. Indeed, every faithful person who hears prays to God the Father as he has been taught, "Your kingdom come!"[6]

[22:17] ***And let him who is thirsty come, let him who desires take the water of life without price.***

To make secure the possession of that which is received, it is necessary to thirst for the drinking of life. This is especially so since such a gift is offered not to those who are hardly wearied at all but to those who bring nothing worthy of the magnificence of the gift, such as gold or silver or bodily labors, but bring only a genuine and ardent mind.

[22:18-19] ***I testify to every one who hears the words of the prophecy of this book: if anyone adds to them, God will add to him the seven plagues described in this book, and if anyone takes away from the words of the book of this prophecy, God will take away his share in the tree of life and in the holy city, which are described in this book.***

The curse against those who falsify the divine Scriptures is terrible, since the daring insolence of such self-willed persons can deprive them of the blessings of the coming age. In order that we might not suffer that lot, he testifies to us who listen neither to add nor to subtract anything. Rather, we should regard the characteristics of the Scriptures as more trustworthy and venerable than Attic compositions and dialectical arguments. For even among those should anyone find anything that is contrary to the rules, he is referred to the trustworthiness of their poets and authors. How great the difference is between those who have a great reputation among them and those who are of repute among us is impossible to conceive. I would judge that it is greater than the difference between light and darkness.

[22:20-21] ***He who testifies to these things says, "Surely I am coming soon." Amen. Come, Lord Jesus Christ! The grace of the Lord Jesus Christ be with all the saints.***

Also I who am speaking these things say to you, who are the Life, "I am coming." And you yourself also come, O Lord. Or perhaps he is saying this in the person of Christ, "I who witness to these things," clearly the one who is testifying, "I am coming." Then what follows is said in the person of the apostle, "Come, Lord Jesus Christ." For the coming of Christ is much desired by the saints, since he will recompense those who have labored with a manifold reward. Therefore, this present book is holy and inspired by God and leads those who read it to their blessed end and inheritance.

To bring everything together, let me make a helpful summary of the contents of this book. Through the letters to the seven churches we are taught endurance in temptations, eagerness in the doing of good works and various other forms of virtue. We are to desire above all earthy things to see with the pure eye of the soul the glory of God in heaven, to be sure, not his essence itself but the appearance of God in the forms it assumes, whether that is the abundance of precious stone or the multicolored form of the rainbow or other such shapes of the divine economies. We learn of the holy,

[5]Rom 8:15; Gal 4:6. [6]Mt 6:10.

incorporeal powers that are near God's glory and of those who in the body have pleased the Lord and of the thunder and lightning that announce the coming of God. Furthermore, we are taught that the interpretation of the book of the divine judgments, which is sealed with seven seals of the Spirit, is incomprehensible, but that through the Lamb of God the book is opened, revealing that which has happened and will happen from his coming until the consummation.

We are taught about the stout courage of the martyrs and of the double torment of the unfaithful and about the harvest of the seed of the gospel and the exclusion of those of little faith and the cowardly. In this way the saints are to expect the second coming of Christ and the arrival of evils before the antichrist and the arrogant affronts against Christians by him. In addition to these things we learn that although the saints are precious to God, he defers the punishment of the impious until they are made known to the avenging angels through the seal of the antichrist. From this book we learn of the seven plagues that will come on those on the earth in the last times so that by the magnitude of them we might look toward conversion and beseech God that we not be tempted by them. We learn of the kindness of the angels who uphold the gospel and proclaim it to those who are on the earth, and of the strong and manly courage of the saints who at the consummation will come to convict the antichrist.+ We see as well the destruction of Jerusalem, the disappearance of the cities of the nations and the thanksgiving of the powers above for the coming of these things. The book displays the persecution against the church, the downfall of the devil, the coming of the antichrist and the deceit of the false prophet, but also of the great number of those who are being saved. Moreover, we see the fall of Babylon, the reaping of the threshing floor of the world, the vintage of the grapes of bitterness, the perfect purity of the inheritance of the saints that is like a sea of glass.

The revelation portrays the pouring out of the seven bowls of the divine wrath that because of the evil of the human race will bring torments on all the earth and in the sea and on the rivers and all other elements. It will also darken the throne of the beast and open a way and passage through the Euphrates for the assistants of the devil, but it will also expose their weakness. We learn of the final and complete earthquake that will come on the world and effect the transformation of present reality, namely, when that harlot city that is like a beast and is supported by the devil shall receive its much-deserved destruction. After this occurs, the powers above sing hymns to God, and the church, the Jerusalem above, is joined with Christ in a most intimate union. We further are told of the treading of the winepress of wrath and that when all things earthly are gone and the antichrist and his associate have been given over to Gehenna, then the angels and humankind that is like the angels will partake of the spiritual supper.

We learn from this book that the devil will be bound and then for a short time will be let loose and then sent to his destruction. We learn of the blessedness of the holy martyrs who reign with Christ before the coming of the antichrist and that after this, when the devil has been released for a short time and has aroused Gog and Magog to battle, he shall then be punished along with them. We learn that at this time the books containing the works of each person and the book of life will be opened and that some will receive the second death but others will be found worthy to receive the heavenly Jerusalem and the marriage with Christ. From this divine book we are taught by the angel, to the extent we are able, of the breadth of the city above and of its walls and gates and foundations. We learn of the river of God the Spirit that flows from there and that no description can portray the beauty of the realities above or their unfading glory. To this the seer[7] encourages us and bids us to say, "Come," that is, that he who has prepared these things for the saints would supply them.

May it be that we who desire to see and to enjoy these things might by an eager longing for obedience to the divine commandments receive them by longsuffering, meekness, humility and purity of heart. From such a heart is engendered an unwavering and confident prayer that presents to God, who sees all that is hidden, a mind free from every earthly thought and uncorrupted by the deceits and seductions of the demons. For during the prayers of the heart that is fixed toward God, the hostile seducer attempts an adulterous relationship with it, sowing seeds of corruption and attempting to dislodge the heart from its union with God, so that a fire will not be kindled in the heart by such practice that consumes all his treacheries. For, to be sure, our God is a "consuming fire,"[8] and the soul that converses with God in purity and with confidence, he will make eager and fruitful by the working of a burning fire, even though the soul might have become cold because of sins. As the sun brightly shines on a glass vessel full of water, and from the water warmth proceeds by way of certain reflection and diffusion, in such a manner we will present to the "sun of righteousness"[9] the temple of the Spirit pure as glass, and not a temple made of clay or earth and unable to receive the divine rays. He "wishes that all be saved and come to the knowledge of the truth,"[10] and so he enlightens all with the unhindered grace of his own radiance. However, each person partakes of this light according to the measure of the purity of their spiritual eyes. May he who is all-merciful, Christ our God, who suffered for us in the flesh, deem us worthy to receive this grace pure and undefiled. To him we owe all praise, honor and worship, together with the Father and the life-giving Spirit, forever and ever. Amen.

[7]Some manuscripts here call the seer "the divine theologian." [8]Deut 4:24; 9:3. [9]Mal 4:2. [10]1 Tim 2:4.

Scripture Index